Complex Ethnic
Households in America

Complex Ethnic Households in America

Edited by
Laurel Schwede
Rae Lesser Blumberg
Anna Y. Chan

ROWMAN & LITTLEFIELD PUBLISHERS, INC.
Lanham • Boulder • New York • Toronto • Oxford

ROWMAN & LITTLEFIELD PUBLISHERS, INC.

Published in the United States of America
by Rowman & Littlefield Publishers, Inc.
A wholly owned subsidiary of The Rowman & Littlefield Publishing Group, Inc.
4501 Forbes Boulevard, Suite 200, Lanham, Maryland 20706
www.rowmanlittlefield.com

PO Box 317
Oxford
OX2 9RU, UK

British Library Cataloguing in Publication Information Available

Library of Congress Cataloging-in-Publication Data

Complex ethnic households in America / edited by Laurel Schwede, Rae Lesser
Blumberg, and Anna Y. Chan.
 p.   cm.
Includes bibliographical references.
ISBN 0-7425-4636-5 (cloth : alk. paper)—ISBN 0-7425-4637-3 (pbk. : alk. paper)
 1. Minorities—United States—Social conditions—Case studies.   2. Ethnology—
United States—Case studies.   3. Households—United States—Case studies.
4. Family—United States—Case studies.   5. United States—Social conditions—
1980—Case studies.   6. United States—Ethnic relations—Case studies.
7. Household surveys—United States.   8. United States—Census.   I. Title: Complex
ethnic households in America.   II. Schwede, Laurel.   III. Blumberg, Rae Lesser.
IV. Chan, Anna Y.

E184.A1W425 2006
305.8′00973—dc22   2005018139

Printed in the United States of America

∞ ™ The paper used in this publication meets the minimum requirements of American
National Standard for Information Sciences—Permanence of Paper for Printed Library
Materials, ANSI/NISO Z39.48-1992.

Contents

Tables and Figures

Acknowledgments

 $\mathcal{F}$ irst and foremost, we thank our contributors for providing such a fascinating and compelling view of the diverse and changing structure of U.S. households today; their efforts have yielded new, sometimes surprising information that will serve as an invaluable complement to the "hard" data of Census 2000. We also thank them for their patience and forbearance as we worked our way through the long editing process that produced the final manuscript. Just as importantly, we extend heartfelt thanks to all of the gracious people who welcomed the ethnographers into their homes, answering their many questions, and sharing rich, and often very personal, information and illuminating insights on their living situations.

The success of this project is due in substantial measure to the steady support of individuals who gave us time to devote to research, writing, and editing. We are deeply grateful for the support and efforts of our colleagues within the Methodology and Standards Directorate of the U.S. Census Bureau and the Department of Sociology at the University of Virginia. At the Census Bureau, we express deep appreciation to Tommy Wright, chief of the Statistical Research Division, for securing funding for this project as part of the overall research program, "Ethnography for the New Millennium," as well as for his continued support and his careful review of the manuscript. We also thank Ruth Ann Killion, chief of the Planning, Research and Evaluation Division, for funding the project and Cynthia Clark, former Associate Director of the Methodology and Standards Directorate, for approving the original complex households research and reviewing the final project report, as well as approving and supporting the preparation of this book before she left the Census Bureau. Additionally, we thank Manuel de la Puente, Eleanor Gerber, and Jeffrey Moore for their continued support, encouragement, and feedback and their reviews of the evolving manuscript. At the University of Virginia, we want to commend the patience and administrative support of two successive Sociology Department chairs, James Hunter and Paul Kingston.

We also give special thanks to our colleagues in the Fertility and Family Statistics Branch of the Census Bureau's Population Division, Martin O'Connell, Tavia Simmons, Rose Kreider, as well as to Jason Fields for providing helpful advice and answers to our many questions over the long course of the complex households project for reviewing previous reports and papers, and for their reviews of this manuscript.

In addition, we are grateful to Claudette Bennett, Nicholas Jones, Art Cresce, Jr., Stella Ogunwole, Philip Harris, Terrance Reeves, Jesse McKinnon, Karen Humes and Renee Spraggins on Jorge del Pinal's staff for careful and thorough reviews of the manuscript, and Juanita Tamayo Lott for her comments on theory. We also thank Patricia Goerman, Jennifer Hunter Childs, and Nancy Tongue for their very helpful manuscript reviews, and all of the ethnographers for reviewing their own chapters. For assistance in the preparation of this volume, we thank Tina Arbogast and Juanita Rasmann of the Census Bureau.

We are publishing this book to inform interested people of ongoing research and to encourage discussion. The views expressed are those of the authors and not necessarily those of the U.S. Census Bureau. To maintain our pledge of confidentiality to those we interviewed, we use pseudonyms or case numbers, not real names, when referring to respondents in the text, and include no photographs of them.

We are indebted to Mitch Allen, formerly of AltaMira Press, who with boundless patience and wise guidance, shaped this book in many ways before he left Rowman & Littlefield to fulfill his dream of starting his own publishing company, Left Coast Press, Inc. We count ourselves extremely fortunate to have had his guidance throughout the process of writing the manuscript and wish him the best. We very much thank Alan McClare, Alex Masulis, Stephen Driver, and Terry Fischer of Rowman & Littlefield for their support and their efforts in transforming this manuscript into a book, as well as Jan Kelland, for her very careful copy editing, and Allison St. Cyr for marketing. We have been fortunate, indeed, to have developed a close, collaborative, and enthusiastic relationship with our Rowman & Littlefield team.

Finally, we are in debt to our spouses and significant others, Martin Wulfe, John Gundersen, and Paul Jackson, for their understanding and never-ending support while we immersed ourselves in this long and rewarding project.

The Way We Live: Complex Ethnic Households in America

Anna Y. Chan

INTRODUCTION

$\mathscr{T}$his is a book about how people of six different ethnic groups[1] in the United States form and feel about their households. It is based on qualitative research conducted in 2000 and 2002 among Navajos of the reservation in Arizona; Iñupiat of frigid Alaska; Korean migrants in cramped living quarters in Queens, New York; Latino migrants in the lush, green heart of central Virginia; urban African Americans in coastal Virginia; and rural whites in the upstate New York snowbelt. Chapters on each group chronicle both great diversity and some common themes. The overall impression is that the living arrangements and relationships among the members of some households are more complex and ambiguous than those of others and, as we shall see, are not always well reflected in the response categories of the U.S. Census Bureau for key decennial census questions: (1) Who lives or stays here? and (2) How is this person related to the householder?[2] Consider the living arrangements in two study households.

Karen, a divorced mother, lives in her own house in rural upstate New York with her fiancé, Jim, two adopted daughters from a previous marriage, and Janet, an "adopted" grandmother. Janet takes care of the girls when Karen goes to work. She has been living with Karen since Karen and her ex-husband adopted Janet's foster daughter. Janet is unrelated to Karen by blood, marriage, or formal adoption. The girls call Janet "grandma." Neither "adopted grandmother" nor "fiancé" is an official response category on the census form. Hence, when Karen filled out the mock census form during her ethnographic

1

interview, she selected the category "other relative" for Janet and "other non-relative" for her fiancé.

On the other side of the country, Ella lives on the vast Navajo reservation in Arizona with her husband and their five children. The household also includes the live-in boyfriend of one of their daughters and the child of that boyfriend and daughter. On the interview day, Ella's mother was also at her house. Her mother suffers from diabetes, and when she gets very ill, she goes to live with Ella's sister, who is a nurse. Ella's mother also maintains a house of her own some miles from the interview house. When the researcher asked if her mother lived with them, Ella answered "yes," her husband replied "no," and the children said "sometimes." Ella's mother actually sleeps and eats with them "unless she's at her own place or living with her other daughter, which is about half of the time." She adds that her mother sleeps in Ella's house during the day but leaves at night: "We take her home around midnight each night and then she usually stays up weaving or doing her work and then we go and pick her up around 7:00 a.m. and bring her over here for breakfast. Then, she spends the day with us, mostly sleeping."

While Karen's household may be unusually complex for what we might conceive to be the norm for middle-class whites, Ella's household reflects the generally more fluid and complex household arrangements common among the Navajo. But both vignettes illustrate that for some Americans, it is not easy to portray their household relationships and living arrangements fully using the classification system of the U.S. Census Bureau. Karen and Ella, however, are not the only people with problems answering questions about who lives or stays in their household or how each household member is related to them. In fact, it was to throw further light on this issue that we undertook our study.

THE STORY OF OUR STUDY

The Problem

All research starts with a problem. The growing diversity of household and family forms accompanying an ever more ethnically diverse U.S. population has led to puzzles and problems for the Census Bureau. Minority groups have been disproportionately undercounted for at least 50 years in decennial censuses (Robinson et al. 1993); this is perhaps the thorniest problem the Census Bureau faces in trying to make sure that everyone is counted once, and only once, and in the correct location. Prior ethnographic research shows that ethnic minority households with complex living arrangements are particularly difficult to count and portray accurately (de la Puente 1995), and ethnic minority households are growing at a faster rate than those of non-Hispanic whites. In

2004, 67% of the U.S. population was estimated to be non-Hispanic white (U.S. Census Bureau 2005), but by 2050, it is estimated that non-Hispanic whites will make up only about 50% of the U.S. population (U.S. Census Bureau 2003). As ethnic populations are growing at a faster rate than non-Hispanic whites, it is important to study such households. Let's take a closer look at how households and families are changing and some of the reasons why this is happening.

CHANGING HOUSEHOLDS AND FAMILY IN AMERICA

Trends in Households and Families

Traditionally, a large majority of U.S. households has been classified as "family" households.[3] In the 1950s and early 1960s, the dominant ideal of a family was a "traditional nuclear family" where the parents marry for life and have children within marriage (Casper and Bianchi 2002). In this traditional nuclear family, children live with full siblings and two married biological parents. But the proportion of such households has fallen. From 1960 to 2000, households of any family type declined from 85% to 69% (Casper and Bianchi 2002; Fields and Casper 2001). The proportion of households classified as "married couple with children" (under age 18) shrank more dramatically: from 44% in 1960 (the modal household then) to 24% in 2000 (Casper and Bianchi 2002). During this same time period, the number and proportion of one-person households have also undergone large increases (from 13.1% in 1960 to 25.7% in 1998) (Casper and Bianchi 2002).[4]

Causes of Change

In large part, decisions people make about their lives and other demographic forces ultimately determine household composition. Trends in marriage, cohabitation, divorce, fertility, and mortality have certainly influenced family and household composition. In the last 40 years, the divorce rate skyrocketed before stabilizing at a high level around 1980; age at first marriage rose markedly. Concomitantly, there have been steady increases in nonmarital cohabitation and childbearing (Coltrane and Collins 2001). Remarriage and blended families have become more common, while households and families have become increasingly diverse and often more complex (Coltrane and Collins 2001; Casper and Bianchi 2002). Not only changing norms and values, but also the economy, culture, traditions, settlement patterns, and social organization, may affect people's decisions about how they arrange their living situations.

Ethnic Diversity

As American household and family forms have shifted away from the traditional nuclear family, they also have become ethnically more diverse. From 1960 to 2004, the proportion of the U.S. population in minority ethnic groups (i.e., those other than non-Hispanic whites) increased from 11.4% to 32.6% (Gibson and Jung 2002; Schmidley 2001; U.S. Census Bureau 2005). The fastest growing ethnic group is the Hispanics (Latinos).[5] In 1970, there were 9 million Latinos in the United States, just 4.5% of the total (Gibson and Jung 2002). By 2004, Latinos had become the largest minority group: there were an estimated 41.3 million Hispanics (of any race): 14.1% of the total population (U.S. Census Bureau 2005). Ethnic minority households may be more diverse and are more likely to be multigenerational, include nonrelatives, or both. As the proportion of ethnic minority households continues to rise, we would expect family forms in America to shift further away from the traditional nuclear family.

The change in ethnic composition results in part from the fact that recent immigrants to the United States now come predominantly from Latin America and Asia, rather than from Europe (Gibson and Lennon 1999).[6] Until 1970, over 90% of the U.S. foreign-born population came from Europe (Gibson and Lennon 1999). By 2000, only a quarter of the foreign-born population were non-Hispanic whites, compared to about half from Latin America and a quarter from Asia (Schmidley 2001, table 9). The number of foreign-born in the United States has tripled since 1970. By 2002, the foreign born numbered 32.5 million, or 11.5% of the U.S. population (Schmidley 2003).

Variations of Household Types by Ethnicity

Some of the most significant differences between various minority ethnic groups and non-Hispanic whites involve variations in household and family structures (Casper and Bianchi 2002; Fields 2001). For instance, family households predominate to a greater extent among Hispanics (81.1%) and Asians (73.2%) than among whites (67.9) or blacks (66.4%) (U.S. Census Bureau 2002b). Perhaps the most dramatic difference, however, involves the proportion of family households with children under age 18 headed by two parents. Here we turn to data from the Survey of Income and Program Participation (SIPP), which, unlike the census, allows us not only to identify both parents in married as well as unmarried households, but also whether each is a biological, step, or adoptive parent (so these proportions of family structure from SIPP will differ somewhat from those derived from the census and other surveys). According to SIPP data, family households in which children under age 18 live with two married or unmarried parents are more common in some ethnic groups than others: a much higher proportion of Asian and Pacific Islander children (83%), non-Hispanic white children (78%), and Hispanic children (69%) lived with two parents–biological, step, adoptive, or some combination of these–compared with American Indian and Alaska Native children (57%) and black children (40%) (Kreider and Fields 2005).

Recognizing that household structure is changing and that it varies among different ethnic groups, the Census Bureau funded exploratory ethnographic research in the spring of 2000. The overall goals of the study were to learn more about complex households—which include people other than those in the "traditional" nuclear family (biological parents and children)—and to identify ways we might improve enumerating them. The research project, "Complex Households and Relationships in the Decennial Census and in Ethnographic Studies of Six Race/Ethnic Groups," was funded as part of the Census 2000 Testing and Experimentation Program (Schwede 2003).[7]

As you will read in this book, the ethnographic studies provide an often fascinating portrait of the many diverse ways in which people live with loved ones, cope with adversity, and consider themselves a unit. Before we examine these, let us give a little orientation to existing census operations and definitions.

First, let's consider the primary purpose of the U.S. decennial census, which is to count everyone in the country once, and only once, in his or her "usual residence," so that congressional representation can be allocated properly. The requirement that each person should be counted in only one household or place seems reasonable until we encounter complex households such as Ella's.

The decennial census counts people in their dwelling; it uses a "structure-based" method to enumerate the U.S. population. Though the ultimate goal is to count individuals, enumeration begins at the physical structure, the *household* or *housing unit*, where everyone living or staying at that housing unit is supposed to be counted.[8] One of this book's major goals is to explore the various cultural definitions of households and how they may be at odds with the official census definition of "household," leading to possible miscounts. Undercounts can have important, often negative, consequences for the groups affected.

Second, let us consider the various household types defined in Census Bureau publications and reports. They are constructed from the "relationship question," such as the one used on the Census 2000 form: "How is this person related to Person 1?" (shown in figure 1.1). In turn, Person 1 is the individual, or one of the people, who owns or rents the residence; this person is often referred to as the *householder*. The Census Bureau distinguishes two general types of households: family households and nonfamily households. *Family households*[9] consist of two or more people living together, at least one of whom is related to the householder by birth, marriage, or adoption. *Nonfamily households*[10] are of two types: one-person households and households with two or

How is this person related to Person 1? *Mark one.*

____ Husband/wife   If NOT RELATED to Person 1.

____ Natural-born son/daughter   ____ Roomer, boarder

____ Adopted son/daughter   ____ Housemate, roommate

____ Stepson/stepdaughter   ____ Unmarried partner

____ Brother/sister   ____ Foster child

____ Father/mother   ____ Other nonrelative

____ Grandchild

____ Parent-in-law

____ Son-in-law/daughter-in-law

____ Other relative—*Print exact relationship* _____

Figure 1.1   Relationship question and response categories (Census 2000 form)

more people, all of whom are unrelated to the householder (though some of them may be related to each other, which can lead to underestimation of the number of family households). Five basic household types are most often used in Census Bureau data and reports. Three classify family households—*married couple family; female householder, no husband present family*; and *male householder, no wife present family*—and two categorize nonfamily households: *female householder nonfamily* and *male householder nonfamily* households. Depending on the purpose of the publication, added breakdowns may be made on factors like the presence or absence of children, subfamilies, and nonrelatives or the size of household, and so forth.

As mentioned, figure 1.1 shows the relationship categories listed on the Census 2000 form. As we will show in this book, these categories are insufficient to describe fully all of the complex and diverse household relationships in our country. Moreover, depending on who was listed as the householder, the household types may be classified differently, especially in households where nonrelatives are present. In such cases, households consisting of family groups could be classified as nonfamily households if the nonrelative was listed as the householder. For example, cohabitation of unmarried partners is becoming increasingly common. The National Survey of Family Growth estimated that by 1995, half of all American women between the ages of 25 and 40 had cohabited (U.S. Census Bureau 1999a). Yet, there is no agreed–upon term for one's cohabiting partner, and calling a man "other nonrelative" in a household where the woman is the householder, as Karen was, does not tell the whole story.

Consider the following: If Karen is listed as the householder, her household is classified as a *female householder, no husband present, family household*. Karen's fiancé, Jim, may be the loving, supportive father figure of the children in that household, but his social role as father is invisible as a result of the household's being classified as a *female householder, no husband present, family household*. But if Jim had been listed as the householder, Karen and her children, as well as Janet, the "adopted grandmother," all would have been recorded as "non-relatives." The same household would then have been classified as a *male householder nonfamily household*. The likelihood of recording the same household as either family or nonfamily, female householder versus male householder, depending on who is listed first on a census form, may skew the relative proportions of household types, perhaps affecting policies and programs. In short, asking only about the relationship to Person 1 sometimes masks household types.[11]

Moreover, as we considered these issues, we suspected that much of the rich complexity of ethnic households could not be reflected in those categories either, that some important types of relationships were being masked by the method of reckoning relationships only to the householder, so we formulated a qualitative ethnographic study to address the problem.

Ethnographic Study

In late 1999, the Census Bureau issued a call for research proposals for small-scale ethnographic studies of complex households in different ethnic groups. Six ethnic groups were selected. Earlier, we mentioned only their names and locations. We'll now provide a bit more detail on each of these groups.

The first selected study group is the Navajo, the second largest Indian tribe in the United States. They have matrilineal kinship, which means that they reckon descent and pass inheritance primarily through the maternal line; they also tend to live near their maternal kin, especially the maternal grandmother. They still maintain many aspects of their traditional herding and weaving subsistence pursuits on the "Rez" in Arizona, New Mexico, and Utah (the largest in the United States). As the vignette about Ella's household shows, Navajo households are frequently complex and fluid, exemplifying the difficulty of applying census residence rules in determining where people live. Their elaborate kinship terms are not well captured by the census relationship categories, which are better at measuring nuclear family relationships in households.[12]

The second group is the Iñupiat of northern Alaska. They have a similar kind of kinship system as most Americans—bilateral (kin from both the mother's and father's side are equally important). But the Iñupiat also maintain many aspects of their traditional hunting, fishing, and gathering subsistence lifestyle.

This leads to high mobility and often complex and ambiguous household forms.

The third group comprises Korean immigrants who mostly reside in cramped apartments in Queens, New York. They come from a country that has been transformed by a half-century of economic growth and urbanization, where extended patriarchal, patrilineal, patrilocal households have given way to mostly nuclear households. Low income and the lack of affordable housing have prompted many of these immigrant Korean households in Queens to share a residence with relatives other than nuclear family members, to take in friends and other nonrelatives, or to do both.

The fourth group consists of Latino migrants living in the healthy central Virginia economy. They hail mostly from Mexico, have bilateral kinship, and generally lived in nuclear, noncomplex households in their home countries. Here in the United States, they share housing with a variety of kin and nonkin, mostly of the same generation. They put up with the inconveniences to save money to help them get ahead in the United States, to send money home to family members, or to save to return home one day with a tidy nest egg.

The fifth group comprises African Americans in urban, coastal Virginia. A defining feature of these households is their traditional interdependence, involving extended kin networks and diverse family forms. African Americans at varying levels of social class frequently prefer to share resources and living quarters with kin when this is beneficial or urgently necessary. Many of these complex households revolve around a female householder, and a number of the respondents stressed that this family form has been misinterpreted and maligned by white mainstream America.

Lastly, the sixth group represented in the study consists of rural whites from the upstate New York snowbelt, where agriculture and industry have been declining. These people live in an area from which many young people seem to be migrating away, leaving a population that may be tilted toward older age groups. In fact, many of these households in our study group were classified as complex as a result of families providing care for their elderly. Others were complex due to the presence of unmarried partners or people whose relationships with other household members were difficult to describe (as in Karen's household).

THE METHODS AND SPECIAL
DIFFICULTIES OF OUR STUDY

The Methodology

We chose to use qualitative ethnographic methods in our exploratory study of complex households. The key strength of qualitative research is the comprehensive perspective it gives researchers concerning the social phenomenon under study. Going directly to the complex ethnic households, observing the residents and their living environment, and asking open-ended and unscripted follow-up questions permits us to develop a deeper and fuller understanding of these households. In fact, qualitative research methods enable us to reveal the underlying reasons why some ethnic households are difficult to enumerate accurately. For example, Nancy Tongue's study of the Navajo identifies two reasons why it is so difficult to record responses from Navajo Indians. First, their traditional subsistence patterns are nomadic, involving frequent mobility, while the census is based on the concept of usual residence in fixed structures. Second, even the very terms they use for kinship differ from the U.S. mainstream; since they have matrilineal kinship, they use different terms for matrilineally related and patrilineally related kin. If they say "grandmother," they are surely referring to the maternal grandmother.

Qualitative research also can help us discover reasons for anomalous quantitative findings. For example, Census 2000 data show disproportionately more foster children in Latino households. Ethnographic research (see chapter 7) was able to solve the puzzle: it turned out to be, in part, a translation problem involving the Spanish version of the Census 2000 form. As a result, the Latinos' common practice of informal, often temporary, child fostering was counted as formal foster care.

While small-scale, local, qualitative ethnographic studies such as ours provide rich, in-depth information on household structure, the results are specific to each study and cannot be generalized to the larger population. To provide reliable estimates for the population as a whole and for ethnic or geographical subpopulations, we need to turn to quantitative data collected from large-scale censuses and surveys based on representative sampling methods. These have strengths and weaknesses. Their main strength is that these data may accurately describe overall trends in household and family change. But their main weakness is that they provide little context to understand why and how households and families are changing. Another weakness is that surveys to date have not been able to provide complete, reliable statistics on very small ethnic populations, such as American Indians/Alaska Natives and Asians. Even monthly surveys (e.g., the Current Population Survey with a sample size of 60,000 households) are not large enough to provide reliable estimates on such very small ethnic populations. The decennial census is large enough to provide reliable estimates for small ethnic or geographical areas, but it is only conducted once every ten years, and the data become outdated.[13]

In this book, we present both qualitative data from our small-scale ethnographic studies and quantitative data from Census 2000 to provide a richer examination of household structure by ethnicity than either source of data could provide alone. We chose to use data from Census 2000 because it is the only data collection large enough to yield reliable statistics on household structure for all six of our ethnic groups, some of which make up less than 4% of our nation's population. We present Census 2000 data at two geographic levels for each ethnic group: the nation as a whole and specific, local geographical areas surrounding our six ethnographic research sites that we custom-designed.

The Interview, Research Protocol, and Mock Census Forms   We developed a semistructured core protocol for this study of complex households in six ethnic groups. All the ethnographers used this core protocol, and they also addressed special topics deemed relevant for their group.

We also provided guidelines on how the interviews were to be conducted and audiotaped. Before each interview began, the ethnographer asked the household respondent to complete a "mock" Census 2000 form as if he or she were filling it out alone in a real census; the ethnographer observed passively and did not assist or answer questions unless absolutely necessary. (Korean and Latino respondents filled out mock census forms in their own languages; Tongue's Navajo liaison helped translate the English version for the Navajo respondents.) The purpose of this exercise was to find out whom the respondent independently identified on the census form as living or staying in the household. After the form was completed, the ethnographer probed (in English, Korean, or Spanish) to identify any other people with various ties to the household. The ethnographer then asked how each of the people identified either on the form or during follow-up questions was related to every other person in the household, writing answers on a relationship matrix. Ethnographers also subjectively classified the households' standard of living vis-à-vis other households in the same community into one of five categories: low low, low, lower middle, middle, or upper middle. They asked open-ended questions and probed at will about peoples' living situations and mobility patterns and about the social and economic functioning of the household.[14]

It was this flexibility that enabled the ethnographers to get such interesting results: they illuminated not only how these people fit into census categories but also how they fit into their families and households, as well as how their households and families fit into their needs to make a living while caring about, and for, each other. The ethnographic chapters tell distinct stories despite the common framework.

SAMPLE

Each of the six ethnographic studies was based on a sample of 25 complex households, chosen purposively. The selection of the 25 households was based on the ethnographers' expert knowledge of the range of variation and prevalence of different household types in their research sites. All of the interviews were conducted from May through July 2000, coincident with the last phase of Census 2000 data collection (except for the African American study reported here, done in 2002).[15] In 2002, for the purposes of this book, the ethnographers returned to their research sites to conduct follow-up and new interviews to collect more information on cultural conceptions of households and other topics.

In many ways, this research project breaks rarely tilled (if not virgin) ground. For one thing, it explores how the diverse household structures encountered among the various ethnic groups relate to the culture and ethnicity of the residents. For another, it is one of the few U.S. cross-cultural or cross-ethnic studies to examine the validity of important cultural concepts (such as household and family) often used as the unit of analysis in social science. Our study does this by observing multiple ethnic groups during the same time period, using a standardized instrument to allow comparability. Such comparability of research objectives, methods, instruments, and timing across groups is very unusual in qualitative studies.

Special Difficulties

The ethnographers participating in this project had to overcome many difficulties and obstacles to complete their research. Nancy Tongue, the ethnographer for the Navajo study, had to drive for days over almost impassable dirt tracks for some interviews, and she ran into enough problems to make an adventure movie for college social science classes about the perils of conducting ethnographic fieldwork. Her experiences are recounted in some detail in her chapter because few books provide students with the sights, smells, and tastes of conducting field research. She also includes some of her Navajo respondents' observations and perceptions about white people's household arrangements and level of attachments to relatives. These observations give a different take on patterns that some Americans may take for granted.

Amy Craver, the expert on Alaskan Natives, had to prepare for her field research as if she were going to a survival boot camp. Craver had to bring her own food and appropriate clothing to deal with the extreme cold. Conducting interviews successfully required careful planning to avoid competition with favorite TV shows in the winter, as well as enormous patience during the brief summer, when people had to lay in their provisions for the long winter and had almost no time to talk with her.

Fear and mistrust of government proved to be so important to some Korean respondents that the Korean researcher in this project, Tai Kang, was chased out of one flat with a broom by one respondent! Also, shame and saving face were important enough to the Korean respondents that Kang had major problems eliciting certain kinds of information from them. In particular, they were reluctant to reveal the kinds of work they did (especially if it was low-status) or, in one case, whether the opposite gender "roommate" was actually an unmarried partner. Some respondents were uncomfortable admitting that more people lived in the apartment than the lease allowed. After several unsuccessful attempts to record his interviews led to early interview terminations, Kang had to abandon tape recording his interviews.

The Latinos in central Virginia echoed the Koreans' fears about government. Specifically, some had deep concerns that the study could somehow be connected with *la migra*, the immigration service; this was especially true for those who were undocumented immigrants. Even so, most of the interviews were conducted in a friendly environment, which meant that anyone in the house at the time might decide to listen in. As a result, many seemed guarded in their discussions of negative aspects of complex household living. Patricia Goerman also had to contend with an irate husband who (falsely) accused her of sheltering his abused wife, who had, in fact, been staying at a shelter for abused women.

Among the urban African Americans in coastal Virginia, there was a different problem. Many felt they have been so frequently criticized for their family system (which tends to be based less on nuclear households than on extended family units that provide considerable mutual support and frequently have women householders) that they were initially very sensitive or defensive, even with Bernadette Holmes, the principal project researcher, who is herself African American. The importance of extended family networks proved a common theme regardless of social class: indeed, more affluent respondents espoused a philosophy of "lift as you climb." This same sense of mutual support and caring extended to frequent informal fostering and adoptions by grandparents when a parent (usually the mother) was unable to care for a child due to personal problems. Both the African Americans and the Iñupiat had relatively high proportions of skip-generation households where grandparents took care of grandchildren whose mothers were absent. This finding was consistent with national estimates from the Survey of Income and Program Participation showing that almost 10% of black children and 7% of American Indian and Alaska Native children lived with neither parent in 2001 (as compared to less than 3% of non-Hispanic white children). The majority of these children lived with their grandparents, with other relatives, or with both (Kreider and Fields 2005).

The rural whites in upstate New York had a milder version of the Koreans' shame, a sort of embarrassment that they were not living in the nuclear family households that popular culture continues to hold up as an ideal. Some did not like to admit they cohabited either. Many of the 25 households were chosen because they had elderly members; how to deal with them in a rural area where many young people had left proved to be a key issue. The rural milieu also caused some initial problems: even though ethnographer Sharon Hewner was white, the first time she entered the local restaurant, she drew stares and stopped conversation—her clothing and demeanor gave away that she was an outsider.

THE MAIN ISSUES

Purpose of this Book

This book is an extension of the original ethnographic project.[16] We aim to explore the diversity and variation of household types in each ethnic group in this study and to examine the interaction between ethnicity and household structure and how it plays out in each culture. To do this, we use qualitative information from the ethnographic studies and quantitative data from Census 2000 for the local areas surrounding our ethnographic research sites. Using the "etic/emic" approach, we compare and contrast cultural conceptions of households among the ethnic groups and with the "ideal" in the overall society.

Etic and Emic Constructs: Household and Family

Two overriding and related concepts—household and family—are the main conceptual focus of this study. Many social scientists use concepts from censuses and surveys in their analyses as if they were objective, etic categories. *Etic* constructs are "accounts, descriptions, and analyses expressed in terms of the conceptual schemes and categories regarded as meaningful and appropriate by the community of the scientific observer" (the "outsider" view) (Lett 1996, 323). In this study, we start with the assumption that concepts used on the census form are etic constructs—meaningful to outsiders such as social scientists, Census Bureau staff, members of Congress, and minority organizations. *Emic* constructs are "accounts, descriptions, and analyses expressed in terms of the conceptual schemes and categories that are regarded as meaningful and appropriate by the members of the culture under study" (the "insider" view) (Lett 1996, 322).

In this book, ethnographers compare and contrast the emic concepts of household and family held by the respondents in the six ethnic groups with those of our dominant Western culture, where the traditional nuclear family household still appears to be held as an ideal.

There are two major consequences of this gap between census concepts and the different cultural (emic) assumptions among the six ethnic groups about (1) what constitutes a household or a family, (2) what each ethnic group considers to be the ideal household structure and composition, and (3) what criteria are used to determine membership in a household, in a family, or in both. First, misreporting of household membership is possible. Second, these varying cultural assumptions also may lead to differential miscounting of minority ethnic groups in the census. Therefore, findings from the ethnographic research presented in this book that suggest differing cultural meanings of key Census Bureau concepts may ultimately lead to improved questionnaire design, as well as better interviewer selection and training. They may also lead to modified procedures and special programs[17] intended for populations with potential enumeration error. In short, the findings of this research may have wider policy implications.

Complex Households as Survival Strategy among the Six Ethnic Groups

Though unintended, the majority of households in four of our six study groups were from lower socioeconomic strata. It should be noted that the rural white and urban African American purposive samples had a higher proportion of middle-class respondents than the other groups. Economic struggle is one of the main reasons for household complexity among those in this study. A complex household may not be the cultural ideal in the four non–Native American groups, but in all six samples, it proved to be a survival strategy for some, and for many, it reflects the social reality confronting these households.

Economic factors influenced household complexity most obviously among our two immigrant groups. During the initial stages of migration, economic resources are often sparse. Faced with low income and a lack of affordable housing, some Latinos and Koreans went against their preference for living in nuclear or independent households and put up with more complex living arrangements. Some of the family households were, in fact, financially capable of establishing their own nuclear households. But many felt it was their obligation to help newly arrived family members and friends, which required them to forgo the simpler household structure that they may have preferred.

The Navajo and Iñupiat are similar in that their complex living arrangements are closely related to their traditional subsistence adaptation strategies. But they differ in that complex living arrangements are seen as positive, not negative (as among many of the Koreans and Hispanics): their traditional lifestyles, in fact, require both mobility and residential fluidity.

For African American and rural white households in this study, however, complex living arrangements most frequently seemed to arise from a combination of economic necessity and the provision of caring services. For rural whites, complex living situations often arose from the need to aid the elderly with daily activities and chores or to overcome illnesses. For blacks, caring for grandchildren, nieces, and nephews when the mother was unable to do so was often a factor in forming a complex household.

RANGE OF VARIATION OF HOUSEHOLD TYPES ENCOUNTERED: SOME EXAMPLES

Skip-Generation Households among the Iñupiat and African Americans

Though each ethnic group in this study differs from the others in many ways, we encountered some cross-group similarities in household types. For instance, the prevalence of skip-generation households among both Iñupiat and African American households in our study reveals the important role of grandparents in raising children. It supports V. L. Bengston's (2001) theory of the increasing importance of multigenerational bonds in America. For the Iñupiat, it is primarily for economic reasons that women (whose traditional role in village subsistence is less valued than that of men) often leave their children with their parents and move to other areas where jobs are available.

Prevalence of Informal Adoption/Fostering among Latinos, Blacks, and the Indigenous Groups

Another unexpected similarity is the prevalence of informal adoption (mostly involving grandchildren) among African Americans and both indigenous groups, as well as the informal foster care that Latino households frequently provided to nieces and nephews and children of friends and other kin. In fact, only the Korean group had almost no such arrangements, as lingering patrilineal traditions made it unlikely that any child who was not a lineal male descendent would be taken in. Similar to what emerged among the blacks, the other four ethnic groups frequently nurtured and cared for needy children they felt close to, even some entrusted to them by distant relatives or friends.

The Decline of the American Family?

Some people interpret the decline in the number of "married couple with children" families to be evidence of the deterioration of the American family. Others see this "decline" merely as diversification of family forms that remain functional and caring. In this study, we did not find much evidence for the deterioration of the family hypothesis; rather, we found diversity of complex family forms in which caring, more often than not, was coupled with coping. As you read the stories of our Navajo, Iñupiat, Korean, Latino, African American, and rural white respondents, you are less likely to come away with a picture of the "decline and fall of the American family" than with a perception of how these groups have found varied, but often effective, ways to live together and help each other in a time of rapid change, often under difficult economic circumstances.

In this book, we set out to examine family households that, though consisting of nonnuclear families, are mostly intact family households—albeit in a variety of forms—as well as nonfamily households. The pitfall of the declining-family hypothesis is its too-narrow definition of family; that is, the nuclear family is often seen as the only true embodiment of "the family." When viewed with such a narrow definition of family, the proponents of this view see the American family as no doubt declining. But this volume illustrates quite clearly the strong sense of family and the importance of caring and coping that we found among these nonnuclear ethnic households. It is time to revise the narrow view of the "declining family in America" and to extend the definition of family beyond the nuclear family.

ORGANIZATION OF THE
REMAINDER OF THIS BOOK

The remainder of this book is divided into two major parts. The first part consists of six ethnographic chapters arranged in three sections: (1) the first section, "The First Arrivals," contains two ethnographic chapters that describe the Navajo and Iñupiat groups' complex households, kinship systems, and fluid living arrangements, (2) the second section, "The Recent Arrivals," contains two chapters on our immigrant groups that discuss the Latino and Korean immigrants' complex living situations as their survival strategies, and (3) the third section, "The African Americans and Whites," contains the last two ethnographic chapters, which examine the adaptation of African American and rural New York white households to stressful social and economic demands. Each of these three sections has an introductory chapter that provides descriptive and statistical data from Census 2000 on each group as a whole, including the size of the ethnic group, its growth rate, and a brief description of where they live in our country. The section introductions also compare and contrast household structure patterns for each ethnic group with the overall population, first at the national level, then in the local geographical area in which each ethnographic study was conducted.

The second part of the book comprises two conceptual and overview chapters written by two of our editors for this volume. First, Rae Lesser Blumberg, who also worked on the Latino study, carefully analyzes the role of gender in the households of each of our ethnic study groups. Her chapter views the six ethnic groups through the lens of her general theory of gender stratification. She looks at the relative economic power of men and women in each group as the most important key to the group's level of gender equality. But she also looks at other factors from her theory, including the organization of the kinship system and the prevailing gender ideology. All in all, Blumberg's theory helps illuminate and explain the big gender differences and emerging trends toward greater male-female equality that she identifies in the six groups. Finally, in our concluding chapter, Laurel Schwede pulls together information from all six ethnographic chapters to tease out links among household structure, ethnicity, kinship systems, residence patterns, economic adaptations, gender, and conceptions of household and family, and how they play out in each culture. She identifies factors influencing the formation, maintenance, and dissolution of complex households in this comparative qualitative study and also summarizes factors identified by demographers and sociologists for the country as a whole. She discusses factors involved in people's decisions about who is and is not a household member. Finally, Schwede discusses the implications of these findings.

In conclusion, the book presents an eclectic mix of rarely published details on how field research is actually conducted, studies of six ethnic groups that revolve around a common core so that comparisons and contrasts shine through clearly, and two interpretive conclusion chapters that link the research to some big picture issues. And although we are biased, we find it fun to read. Enjoy!

NOTES

1. Throughout this book, we use the terms *ethnic groups* and *ethnicity* rather than the standard federal government terms: *race* and *ethnic groups*. Our usage focuses on the cultural dimension and does not distinguish race and ethnicity. The federal government designates five "race" groups: white, African American/black, Asian, American Indian/Alaska Native, and Native Hawaiian/Other Pacific Islander. It considers "Hispanic" to be an "ethnicity"; Hispanics can be of any "race."

2. The *householder* is defined as the person or one of the people in whose name the home is owned, being bought, or rented. On the Census 2000 short form, the first person listed is called "Person 1" and is considered to be the householder. "A 'household' includes all of the people who occupy a housing unit. A *housing unit* is a house, an apartment, a mobile home, a group of rooms, or a single room occupied (or if vacant, intended for occupancy) as separate living quarters. *Separate living quarters* are those in which the occupants live separately from any other people in the building and that have direct access from the outside of the building or through a common hall. The occupants may be a single family,

one person living alone, two or more families living together, or any group of related or unrelated people who share living quarters" (U.S. Census Bureau 2002a, B-9, definition of "household").

3. A household is defined as a family household by the Census Bureau when there are two or more people in the household, and at least one of them is related to the householder by blood, marriage, or adoption.

4. For more information on changes in households during the twentieth century, see F. Hobbs and N. Stoops (2002).

5. According to Office of Management and Budget definitions, which govern federal data collections, "Hispanic" is an ethnicity; a person of Hispanic descent can be of any race.

6. The major difference between immigrants from 1850 to 1970, as compared to present immigrants, is that in the past, over 90% (at times close to 100%) of immigrants were white.

7. The main objectives of the original "Complex Households and Relationships in the Decennial Census and in Ethnographic Studies of Six Race/Ethnic Groups" were (1) to explore the range and functioning of complex households within different ethnic groups, and (2) to assess how well census methods, questions, relationship categories, and household-composition typologies capture and describe the emerging diversity of household types (Schwede 2003).

8. People are also enumerated at group quarters (e.g., nursing homes, military bases, group homes).

9. Family households are divided into three categories, based on answers to the relationship question and sex: married couple family, female householder family with no husband present, and male householder family with no wife present. Other people related or unrelated to the householder may also be part of the family household, but their presence or absence does not change the household's classification.

10. Nonfamily households are often subdivided into two categories based on the sex of Person 1: female householder nonfamily household and male householder nonfamily household.

11. Other Census Bureau surveys, such as Survey of Income and Program Participation (SIPP), ask detailed questions about the interrelationships of all household members and give a better overall picture of household types. Due to the relatively small sample size (e.g., less than 50,000 households for SIPP) and the survey sampling techniques, however, it is impossible to get representative estimates for some small minority groups.

12. In 1990, new relationship categories such as adopted child, stepchild, foster child, and grandchild were added to the census form. In 2000, parent-in-law and son- and daughter-in-law were added, reflecting the growing complexity of American households, which the Census Bureau sought to measure (Schwede 2003).

13. The American Community Survey sample rose to 3 million households per year in 2005 and will provide timely, reliable estimates on more small populations and small areas than other current surveys.

14. For details on the methodology, protocol, and other interview instruments, see Schwede (2003).

15. Due to methodological issues with the African American study in 2000, a new study was done in 2002.

16. For the details on the original project, as well as the findings from it, see Schwede (2003).

17. It is important to note that special efforts were made by the Census Bureau in Census 2000 (and in previous censuses as well) to improve coverage for populations, in particular, minority populations, prone to enumeration errors. Some of the programs offered in conjunction with Census 2000 included

1. The Census 2000 language program provided census information and assistance in languages other than English. Census 2000 forms were printed in six languages—English, Vietnamese, Tagalog, Spanish, Chinese, and Korean—and telephone assistance was also provided in these languages. Also, about 15 million language-assistance guides were printed in 49 languages (U.S. Census Bureau 1999b) and made available to enumerators to aid in translation; bilingual enumerators also were used.

2. The American Indian and Alaska Native (AIAN) Program worked to integrate AIAN issues into Census 2000 operations and strove to hire indigenous people as enumerators (U.S. Census Bureau 2000b). Alaska special teams visited remote living areas starting in January 2000 before the spring thaw, when these areas become inaccessible, and people leave their homes for seasonal fishing and hunting (U.S. Census Bureau 2000c).

3. A paid advertising campaign targeted historically undercounted groups.

REFERENCES

Bengston, V. L. 2001. "Beyond the nuclear family: the increasing importance of multigenerational bonds." *Journal of Marriage and the Family* 63 (1): 1–16.

Casper, L. M., and S. M. Bianchi. 2002. *Continuity and Change in the American Family*. Newbury Park, CA: Sage.

Coltrane, S., and R. Collins. 2001. *Sociology of Marriage and the Family: Gender, Love, and Property*. 5th ed. Belmont, CA: Warwoth.

de la Puente, M. 1995. "Using ethnography to explain why people are missed or erroneously included by the census: evidence from sall area ethnographic studies." In *Proceedings of the section survey research methods*. Alexandria, VA: American Statistical Association.

Fields, J. 2001. "Living arrangements of children." Current Population Reports P70-74. Washington, DC: U.S. Census Bureau, issued in April.

Fields, J., and L. M. Casper. 2001. "America's families and living arrangements." Current Population Reports P20-537. Washington, DC: U.S. Census Bureau, issued in June.

Gibson, C., and K. Jung. 2002. "Historical census statistics on population totals by race, 1790 to 1990, and by Hispanic origin, 1970 to 1990, for the United States, regions, divisions, and states." Population Division Working Paper Series No. 56. Washington, DC: U.S. Census Bureau.

Gibson, C., and E. Lennon. 1999. "Historical census statistics on the foreign-born population of the United States: 1850–1990." Population Division Working Paper No. 29. Washington, DC: U.S. Bureau of the Census.

Grieco, E. M., and R. C. Cassidy. 2001. "Overview of race and Hispanic origin." Census 2000 Brief C2KBR/01-1. Washington, DC: U.S. Census Bureau.

Hobbs, F., and N. Stoops. 2002. "Demographic trends in the 20th century." Census 2000 Special Reports CENSR-4, issued November 2002. Washington, DC: U.S. Census Bureau.

Kreider, R., and J. Fields. 2005. "Living arrangements of children: 2001." *Current Population Reports*. P70-104. Washington, DC: U.S. Census Bureau, issued in July.

Lett, J. 1996. "Emic/etic distinctions." In *Encyclopedia of Cultural Anthropology*, ed. David Levinson and Melvin Ember, 382–83. New York: Henry Holt and Company.

Robinson, J. G., B. Ahmed, P. D. Gupta, and K. A. Woodrow. 1993. "Estimation of population coverage in the 1990 United States Census based on demographic analysis." *Journal of the American Statistical Association* 88 (423).

Schmidley, D. 2001. "Profile of the foreign-born in the United States: 2000." Current Population Reports. Special Studies P23-206, Table 9-1, 24. Washington, DC: U.S. Census Bureau, issued in December.

———. 2003. "The foreign-born population in the United States. March 2002." Current Population Reports P20–539. Washington, DC: U.S. Census Bureau, issued in February.

Schwede, L. 2003. "Complex households and relationships in the decennial census and in ethnographic studies of six race/ethnic groups." Final Report. Washington, DC: U.S. Census Bureau, at www.census.gov/srd/www/byname.html (accessed December 24, 2005).

U.S. Census Bureau. 1999a. "Marriage and cohabitation experience of women 15 to 44 years of age, by selected characteristics: 1995." *Statistical Abstract of United States: 1999*. Section 1. Population, P59, Table No. 66.

———. 1999b. "Process used to select languages for Census 2000 language assistance guides." Census 2000 Informational Memorandum No. 18. June 21, 1999. Decennial Management Division.

———. 2000a. "Our diverse population: race and Hispanic origin, 2000." In *The Population Profile of the United States: 2000*, chapter 16, at www.census.gov/population/pop-profile/2000/chap16.pdf (accessed April 15, 2004).

———. 2000b. "Remote Alaska program master plan." Internal Census Bureau document. February 28, 2000.

———. 2000c. "Census 2000 American Indian/Alaska Native program master plan." Internal Census Bureau document.

———. 2002a. "Summary file 2: census of population and housing technical documentation, appendix B: definitions of subject characteristics." SF2/04 (RV), at www.census.gov/prod/cen2000/doc/sf2.pdf.

———. 2002b. "Current Population Survey, March 2002, Table H1," at www.census.gov/population/www/socdemo/hh-fam/cps2002.html (accessed April 15, 2004).

———. 2003. "Resident population by race and Hispanic origin status—projections: 2005 to 2050." *Statistical Abstract of the United States: 2003*. Section 1. Population, P18, Table No. 15, at www.census.gov/prod/2004pubs/03statab/pop.pdf (accessed April 15, 2004).

———. 2005. "U.S. Census Bureau News CB05-77. Table 1." June 9. Washington, DC: U.S. Department of Commerce, at www.census.gov/press-release/www/releases/archives/natracepop2004_tb1.pdf (accessed August 9, 2005).

2

The First Arrivals:
Navajo and Iñupiaq Eskimos

Laurel Schwede and Rae Lesser Blumberg

INTRODUCTION

$\mathcal{W}$e present two data tracks akin to parallel universes in this book. One of these is represented by the six ethnographic chapters, which are small scale and qualitative. The other is represented by this and two later section introductions, which are large scale and primarily statistical.

The story told by the three section introductions provides the background and context of our ethnic groups and complex households for the three pairs of ethnographic chapters: (1) American Indians and Alaska Natives, (2) Korean and Latino immigrants, and (3) African Americans and whites. These descriptive and statistical section introductions tell an important story in their own right because the Census Bureau is continuously making special efforts to improve the accuracy and completeness of counts in censuses of subpopulations that are differentially miscounted. Among these are ethnic minorities (U.S. Census Bureau 2003, table 1; National Research Council 2004), nonrelatives in households, and complex households (de la Puente 1993). Our section introductions cover these three differentially miscounted subpopulations. As these section introductions document, the proportion of households consisting of minorities is increasing, so more special efforts are needed to improve census coverage of them.

We also provide some preliminary, first-ever counts of complex households containing nonrelatives. This is an initial step in counting complex households. We document that all the ethnic minority groups we studied have higher proportions of complex households containing nonrelatives than do non-Hispanic whites, the group that is still the majority in the United States. We also document that non-Hispanic whites have been, and are projected to continue, shrinking as a proportion of the overall U.S. population, while the minority groups are growing at the same or, in some cases, far higher rates.

The two parallel universes intersect because they tell a complementary story, told in terms of both statistical and qualitative data to answer the question asked in our concluding chapter, Who lives here? It is unusual to provide complementary qualitative and quantitative data in this way. We believe it provides an excellent framework for the story.

From the statistical universe—Census 2000—we provide, in these section introductions, descriptive and statistical data on household-structure patterns. Coming from the largest and most complete data collection in the United States, these data provide reliable, comparative measures of "who lives here."

From the other universe—small-scale, qualitative, ethnographic data from localized research sites—our ethnographers literally and figuratively take us inside the houses and into living rooms to talk in a more personal and open-ended manner with a small number of respondents from each of the six ethnic groups. With this qualitative method, through our respondents' own words, we can learn how they themselves see and construct their living arrangements, and why these may change over time. Together, the statistical and qualitative data from our parallel universes provide a more complete portrait of complex households than either one alone could provide.

We begin each overview with a definition of who is included in each race or ethnic group, along with a brief description of where they live in our country. Using Census 2000 data, we tell you what proportion of the total population each group represents and provide data on the growth rate of that group before and after Census 2000. Again, using Census 2000 data, we compare and contrast each ethnic group's living arrangements with the overall population at two levels of geography: nationwide and at the local study-area level. We start at the national level, comparing and contrasting each ethnic group with the total U.S. population in terms of (1) household size, (2) relative proportions of family versus nonfamily households, (3) relative proportions of the three types of family households—those classified as "married couple households," "male householder with no wife present," and "female householder with no husband present," as well as (4) the proportions of nonfamily households.

Our book focuses on complex households. These, as Anna Chan's introductory chapter discusses, are households that include people other than, or in addition to, nuclear family kin (i.e., parents and one or more of their own biological children). In the qualitative chapters, our ethnographers will take you inside complex households from each group so that you can learn about them directly from our ethnic respondents. Since this is our focus, it would be very nice to use Census 2000 data to tell you what proportion of households in each ethnic group are complex. So, in these section introductions, we use Census 2000 data tables to identify the minimum proportion of complex households for each ethnic group at the national, as well as local study-area, levels.

Why, you may ask, are we just identifying the minimum proportion of complex households rather than as many as we can? Unfortunately for us, the authors, the Census Bureau does not tally the number of complex households in the data tables it provides. To find clear evidence of complex households, we must peruse the census tables very carefully.

Our problem is that there are many kinds of residents whose presence make a household complex, but the Census 2000 data tables on the website that we use for statistics in this book identify only one type of complex household, and that not in detail. Let us explain the specifics.

Households can be complex by including, for example (1) *lineal* relatives, such as grandparents or grandchildren, (2) *lateral* relatives, such as adult siblings, nephews, or cousins, (3) *blended* family relatives, such as stepchildren, (4) in-laws, (5) more than one coresident family, or (6) nonrelatives. Our difficulty is that only the last type is clearly identifiable from Census 2000 data tables on the website. Nonrelatives can include such folks as an unmarried partner, a boarder, a roommate, or a foster child. But the Census 2000 data tables we used do not break down all of these types of nonrelatives by household.

Hence, with just one unambiguous, general type of complex household identifiable from Census 2000 website tables, we can only present here the minimum proportion of complex households for each group and for the overall population. (There is one consolation: we can disaggregate the households containing nonrelatives into family and nonfamily types, and, as it turns out, there is interesting variation among our six ethnic groups vis-à-vis the two types.) Of course, it would be possible to identify more types of complex households by writing special programs to run with the actual Census 2000 database, but that is beyond the scope of this primarily qualitative book. Regardless, we decided that we could not just drop the quantitative component completely. Accordingly, in these three sections, we also present indirect clues to other types of complex households. We do this by using person-level relationship data at the national level, even though, as we explain below, we cannot convert person-level data into household-level data from prepared data tables.

Following these comparisons and contrasts at the national level, we then provide the same comparisons for the specific groups in our study: Navajos, Iñupiaq Eskimos, Korean immigrants, Latino immigrants, African Americans, and rural, non-Hispanic whites. Here, we compare each group to the overall population at their respective local research sites. For each of our ethnic research sites, we wanted to determine the appropriate size of the geographical comparison areas so that, on the one hand, they would be small enough to provide meaningful data on the local conditions and communities where our respondents live. On the other hand, the local geographical comparison areas also had to be large enough, with a sufficient population size, to (1) provide a clear picture of the statistical differences between our ethnic groups and the overall population in their local areas, and (2) protect our respondents' confidentiality. After spending a very interesting weekend immersed in the electronic system that can be accessed from the Census Bureau's public website, we were able to "right-size" local geographical comparison areas for each of our six groups, using Census 2000 SF-2 data on the Census Bureau's website. It was both relatively easy and fun. (Okay, so we're data junkies, or nerds, take your pick.)

If you are a student reading this book for a course and the course requires a paper, or if you are a planner or a business person who wishes to know more about a particular community, you can access the website and do your own research. It is (fairly) easy to define and carry out your own small study, based on a geographical area and a group of your choice. We suggest you try it out yourself![1]

Our overview for the American Indians and Alaska Natives (AIANs) starts at the national level. Then, we look at our two specific groups: the Navajos in Arizona and the Iñupiaq Eskimos in Alaska.

AMERICAN INDIANS AND ALASKA NATIVES

American Indians and Alaska Natives are considered to be the original inhabitants of the Americas, here for thousands of years before the first Scandinavian or other European explorers came from across the Atlantic Ocean. The AIAN category includes people "having origins in any of the original peoples of North and South America (including Central America) and who maintain tribal affiliation or community attachment" (U.S. Office of Management and Budget 1997, 17).

Cowboy-and-Indian TV shows and movies may have left many of us with the stereotype that most American Indians live in the West. American Indian and Alaska Natives are pretty concentrated, but perhaps not as you would expect. The largest proportion of Indians does live in the West, but they are only 43% of the total U.S. AIAN population. American Indians and Alaska Natives are found, to a greater or lesser extent, in all four regions of our coun-

In Census 2000, 43% of American Indian and Alaska Natives lived in the West, 31% in the South, 17% in the Midwest, and 9% in the Northeast. States with the highest numbers of American Indians and Alaska Natives, in order, were California, Oklahoma, Arizona, Texas, New Mexico, New York, Washington, North Carolina, Michigan, and Alaska (Ogunwole 2002).

try. According to Census 2000, more than half of all American Indians and lived in just 10 states, including California (which has the most AIANs), as well as Arizona and Alaska (Ogunwole 2002), where our ethnographic studies were done.

In the 1990 U.S. Census, when just one race could be recorded for each individual, nearly 2 million people were classified as AIAN (Ogunwole 2002). In Census 2000, the procedure was changed so that each person could check more than one race category.[2] In 2000, 4.1 million people were categorized as AIAN, either alone or in combination with other races. In fact, a very large proportion (about 4 in 10) of American Indian and Alaska Natives did mark more than one race in Census 2000. Since we do not know how many people would have recorded themselves as part AIAN in the 1990 Census had they been allowed to mark more than one race, the population numbers from the 1990 and 2000 censuses are not directly comparable.

This change between censuses in the way we collect and tabulate race means that we cannot calculate an exact rate of increase: we can only say that the AIAN population increased over that decade by a minimum of 26% to a maximum of 110%. This means that if you count only those who marked AIAN alone in 2000, the group's population rose by a minimum of 26% from 1990 to 2000. But if you include everyone who marked AIAN either alone or in combination with one or more other races, the AIAN population rose a maximum of 110% (Ogunwole 2002).[3]

There are many more American Indians than Alaska Natives. Of the total AIAN population in Census 2000, 71% were specified as American Indians and 3% as part of an Alaska Native tribe. The remaining 26% did not specify an American Indian and Alaska Native tribal grouping (Ogunwole 2002).

From Census Day (April 1, 2000) to July 2004, the AIAN population of those reporting one or more races is estimated to have grown at a slightly higher rate than the overall population (4.4% to 4.3%) to 4.4 million people (U.S. Census Bureau 2005).

Household and Family Types at the National Level

What does Census 2000 tell us about American Indian and Alaska Natives and how they differ from our overall population? As compared to the overall U.S. population,

- American Indian households and Alaska Native households in the nation are larger on average: there are 2.9 people per household for American Indians and 2.88 for Alaska Natives alone or in any combination, as compared to 2.59 for the overall U.S. population.[4]
- While AIAN households taken as a whole differ little from those of the overall population in the proportion consisting of families,[5] their average family sizes are considerably larger.[6]
- American Indian and Alaska Native households are much more likely to include "own" (biological, step, or adopted) children than all U.S. households.[7]

Minimum Proportion of Complex Households at the National Level

American Indian and Alaska Natives have much higher proportions of households with nonrelatives than the overall population of our country. For the nation as a whole, 10.6% of households include nonrelatives. For American Indian households, the proportion is 15.5%; it is 16.2% for Alaska Natives (see table 2.1). To reiterate, since "household with nonrelative" is the only type of complex household that we can identify unambiguously from Census 2000

Table 2.1   Minimum Proportion of Complex Households for American Indians, Alaska Natives, and the Overall Population at the National Level (Family and Nonfamily Households with Any Nonrelatives)

National Population Group	Percentage of Households with Nonrelatives in Family Households[1]	Percentage of Households with Nonrelatives in Nonfamily Households[2]	Minimum Proportion of Complex Households (Households with Any Nonrelatives)[3]
Overall U.S. population	4.5	6.1	**10.6**
American Indian population	8.6	6.9	**15.5**
Alaska Native population	8.9	7.3	**16.2**

1. Calculated by subtracting percentage of nonfamily households with nonrelatives from all households with nonrelatives (PCT 16 − PCT 9).
2. Calculated from Census 2000 SF-2, PCT 9 data.
3. Calculated from Census 2000 SF-2, PCT 16 data.

website tables, these figures provide us with the minimum proportion of complex households for the overall population, as well as for each ethnic group.[8]

When we break these households with nonrelatives into family and nonfamily types, we find different patterns for American Indian and Alaska Natives, on the one hand, and the total U.S. population, on the other. Among the American Indians, households with nonrelatives are more commonly of the family than the nonfamily type (8.6% to 6.9%),[9] and the same pattern is evident for the Alaska Natives (8.9% to 7.3%). The reverse is true for the whole United States: households with nonrelatives are less commonly of the family than the nonfamily type (4.5% to 6.1%). (Note: 4.5% + 6.1% = 10.6%; that is, the nonfamily and family types add up to the minimum proportion of complex households for each group.)

Indirect Clues to Complex Households with Nonnuclear Relatives at the National Level

Our search for additional clues about the prevalence of complex households takes us to the person-level data. We have found data tables that provide us with counts of some types of people who are living in the homes of householders who are not their nuclear family relatives. We can examine these to see if there are differences among our ethnic groups at the person level. For example, a recent report using Census 2000 person-level data (Lugaila and Overturf 2004) focuses on one special case: children who are related to the householder in their household as other than "own" children. In census terms, the "own" children category includes biological, step, and adopted children, who, in Census 2000, made up 92.3%, 5.2%, and 2.5% of children, respectively (Kreider 2003). Focusing on "other than own children" allows us to identify children who are grandchildren or more distant relatives of their householders.

Let's look at what T. Lugaila and J. Overturf's person-level study reveals about ethnic differences in the proportions of children who are related to their householders as other than biological, step, or adopted ("own") children. American Indian and Alaska Native children are much more likely to be in this category. Children reported as American Indian or Alaska Native alone[10] made up 1.1% of all children under 18 included in Census 2000, but 2.1% of all grandchildren, and 1.9% of other relatives, such as nieces, nephews, cousins, and others in the entire country (Lugaila and Overturf 2004, table 3). While the difference between 1.1% and 2.1% does not, at first glance, seem to be much, note that 2.1% is nearly double 1.1%.

These clues from the person-level statistics tell us that there might be disproportionate numbers of AIAN households that are complex because they include children or other people who are not nuclear family relatives of the householder. There is no one-to-one correspondence between children and households in Lugaila and Overturf's paper, so, sad to say, we cannot automatically convert the number of people (children, in this case) living with a householder who is a relative but not their parent into the number of complex households. This is because, while some households have just one child living with a related householder who is not their parent, other households may have two or more.

Since the Lugaila and Overturf data allow us to identify unambiguously a particular set of relationships that make up a complex household type—those with at least one nonnuclear family relative—we will be presenting comparable statistics from Lugaila and Overturf on children living with householders who are not their own parents in the introductions to the other ethnic groups as well. However, we need to identify and keep in mind some caveats with the statistics we cite from their report. The statistics show the relationships of children to the householder alone (Person 1 on the census form). We do not know from these particular data whether one or both of the children's parents also live in these households: they may or may not. The converse is also true—we do not learn from these data whether children living with a householder who is an "own" parent also have a grandparent or other distant relative living with them. These caveats mean that with the Lugaila and Overturf data we cite, we can identify some, but not all, of the children living with nonnuclear kin.

So, we leave you, our readers, with these tantalizing clues from person-level data such as these to the potential existence of ethnic differences in the proportions of complex households of the type with one or more nonnuclear relatives. We invite those of you who are quantitatively oriented to do the requisite programming with the Census 2000 database and generate the proportions of these types of complex households for ethnic subpopulations in our country.

Next, let's find out more about the Navajo and the Iñupiat.

THE NAVAJO INDIANS AND THE IÑUPIAQ ESKIMO[11]

The two specific AIAN ethnic groups included in this study are the Navajo living primarily on their reservation in Arizona and the Iñupiaq Eskimo living in northern Alaskan villages. The Navajo are the second largest American Indian group in the United States. Nearly 300,000 people identified themselves as Navajo alone or in combination with another race or tribal grouping in the Census 2000 race question (Ogunwole 2002).

The Eskimo, which include the Iñupiat and the Yup'ik, are the largest of four Alaska Native groups, with just under 55,000 people reporting themselves to be Eskimo alone or in combination with other races or tribal groupings (Ogunwole 2002). Interestingly, the Navajos and Eskimos have the lowest rates among the largest tribal groupings of recording more than one race in their respective umbrella groups, American Indians and Alaska Natives: 9.7% for the Navajo and 16% for the Eskimos (Ogunwole 2002). This suggests that many of them may still be living in fairly homogeneous groups. Indeed, Nancy Tongue's research focused primarily on the Navajo reservation, where 93% identified as Navajo alone or in combination with other races or tribes. Likewise, Amy Craver selected villages in Alaska Native Regional Corporation (ANRC) areas where Eskimos constituted more than half of the population.

Both study areas are also similar in that (1) they are rural, with most of the populations spread sparsely over vast expanses of land; (2) their climates are harsh—hot and dry in Arizona (cold at night) and very frigid in Alaska; and (3) they are relatively underdeveloped economically, so many residents need to leave for other areas, either temporarily or permanently, to supplement household incomes back home.

In terms of kinship structure, however, the Navajos are very different from not only the Iñupiaq Eskimos but also from our overall society. Both Eskimos and the overall U.S. population have *bilateral kinship:* maternal and paternal relatives are considered equally important, have the same sets of obligations and rights, and are called by the same terms (e.g., the word "aunt" is used for both one's mother's sister and one's father's sister). Additionally, inheritance is generally the same through the maternal and paternal lines. In contrast, the Navajo kinship system is *matrilineal,* meaning that the maternal kin are considered primary for many purposes. Maternal and paternal relatives have different sets of obligations, responsibilities, and rights and are called by different names (e.g., the word for an aunt is different for one's mother's sister and one's father's sister). And inheritance passes down among relatives on the mother's side. Tongue provides us with fascinating glimpses of how aspects of the matrilineal system affect household structure and how the Navajo people live (see also chapter 11 by Rae Lesser Blumberg). Be prepared: sometimes Tongue turns the mirror around and tells us how Navajo people view the living arrangements of whites in our wider society. You may be taken aback at how living arrangements that many of us take for granted are viewed by someone from another culture!

To set the context for this section's ethnographic studies of the Navajo and Iñupiat, let's zoom down from the national level to the geographic areas where each study was conducted and compare the characteristics of both groups' households with the overall population in (1) northern Arizona for the Navajo, and (2) northern Alaska for the Iñupiat.

NAVAJOS IN NORTHERN ARIZONA

Fully 93% of the people living on the huge Navajo reservation are Navajos, so we had to expand our focus to an even larger area to find an appropriate comparison zone with more ethnic variation. To include all parts of the Arizona Navajo reservation in our analysis, we combined data from three counties spread across northern Arizona: Apache, Navajo, and Coconino.[12] In this three-county area, according to Census 2000, "white alone" made up 46.5% of the population, while "American Indian alone" constituted 47%, and the remainder was split among other groups. Most of the American Indians were Navajos.[13]

Household and Family Types in the Local Study Area

As compared to all households in this three-county area of northern Arizona,

* Navajo households are larger: 3.87 people per household, compared to 3.06 overall.[14]

Navajo households also are much more likely to be family households[15] that are

* Very much more likely to be of the "female householder, no husband present" type (over one-fourth of Navajo households, compared to just under one-sixth in the three-county area). To a lesser extent, they also are more likely to be of the "male householder, no wife present" type, but there are fewer married couple households.[16]
* Very much more likely to include children. An astonishing half of all Navajo households in this area have one or more "own" (biological, step, or adopted) children under age 18, compared to less than 4 in 10 of all households in these three Arizona counties (the overall national average is 32.8%). This is true for all types of family households: married couple, male householder without wife present, and female householder without husband present.[17]

Minimum Proportion of Complex Households in the Local Study Area

As table 2.2 shows, in our three-county area, Navajo households were less likely to include nonrelatives than the overall population (9.3% to 12.3%).[18] This contrasts with the pattern at the national level for all American Indians,

Table 2.2   Minimum Proportion of Complex Households for Navajos and the Overall Population in Northern Arizona[1] (Family and Nonfamily Households with Any Nonrelatives)

Northern Arizona Population Groups	Percentage of Households with Nonrelatives in Family Households[3]	Percentage of Households with Nonrelatives in Nonfamily Households[4]	Minimum Proportion of Complex Households (Households with Any Nonrelatives)[5]
Overall population	5.6	6.7	**12.3**
Navajo population[2]	7.2	2.1	**9.3**

1. Three northern Arizona counties encompassing the Navajo reservation and the Navajo ethnographic research site.
2. Navajo alone or in combination with other races.
3. Calculated by subtracting the percentage of nonfamily households with nonrelatives from all households with nonrelatives (column 3 minus column 2) (PCT 16 − PCT 9).
4. Calculated from Census 2000 SF-2, PCT 9 data.
5. Calculated from Census 2000 SF-2, PCT 16 data.

whose households were more likely than all U.S. households to have nonrelatives (15.5% to 10.6%), as mentioned earlier.

Similar to the pattern at the national level for all American Indian and Alaska Natives, Navajo households with nonrelatives in this three-county area were more likely to be of the family- than the *non*-family-type households (7.2% to 2.1%), while the overall three-county area had the reverse pattern (5.6% family to 6.7% nonfamily). Note here that Navajos had a much lower proportion of nonfamily households; their households were less than one-third as likely as all area households to be living in complex nonfamily households with two or more people (2.1% to 6.7%). We attribute the very low proportion of Navajo nonfamily households with nonrelatives, as well as the lower incidence of all households with nonrelatives, to the fact that most of the Navajo in this local area are living with family on the very ethnically homogeneous Navajo reservation.

Summary of Navajo Household Types in Northern Arizona

The distinctive features of Navajo household structure in northern Arizona, then, are the high prevalence of family households that are (1) considerably more likely than all area households to consist of female householder families, (2) more likely to consist of male householder families, and (3) somewhat less likely to consist of married couples, but (4) very much more likely to include children under 18 in all family types. Also, they are much less likely to be nonfamily households. Finally, a minimum of 9.3% of Navajo households in northern Arizona can be classified as complex households because they include one or more nonrelatives, and these were more likely to be family than nonfamily households.

IÑUPIAQ ESKIMOS IN NORTHERN ALASKA

The Iñupiaq Eskimos live in rural northern Alaska where the temperature can drop to −40°. As Craver shows, the Iñupiat support their family households through a combination of hunting and gathering and—when they can get it— wage-labor work. They have the strong ethos of sharing resources that is very common to hunters and gatherers (see chapter 11). Since there are few jobs in these areas, many adults leave their children with their parent(s) in the village and go elsewhere in search of work to supplement the village household income, sometimes cycling back and forth between home and other places. Households are generally fluid in composition. Often they consist of one or more grandparents who care for children and grandchildren who move in and out. Adoption of children is very common among the Iñupiat and in Alaska as a whole: Alaska had the highest proportion of all states of adopted children to all children: 3.9% compared to the national average of 2.5% (Kreider 2003).

For our ethnic-group comparison to the wider surrounding population, we had to make several adjustments for the unique case of the Iñupiaq Eskimo. First, Census 2000 Summary File 2 data tables do not include household-type breakdowns for the Iñupiaq Eskimo specifically, but they do permit breakdowns for the entire Eskimo category (which includes the Yup'ik). According to ethnographer Craver, providing information for the Eskimo as a whole gives a fairly representative statistical portrait of the Iñupiat. For the geographical comparison area, we pooled census data from five ANRC areas in northern and western Alaska, where most residents are Eskimo and where residence is overwhelmingly rural, matching the conditions in Craver's sites.

In this wider geographical area encompassing Craver's villages, a total of 54,713 residents were counted in Census 2000; 63% in this area were recorded as Eskimos alone or in combination.[19]

Household and Family Types in the Local Study Area

Compared with all households in these five ANRC areas,

- Eskimo households are larger (4.11 people per household, compared to 3.59 for this region).[20]

- More than four-fifths of Eskimo households are family households, compared to just under three-quarters in the overall population.
- A greater proportion of Eskimo households are categorized as female householders without spouses and male householders without spouses, but the very same proportion is classified as married couple households,[21] and Eskimo family households are larger (4.60 to 4.24 people).[22]
- A stunning 56.7% of all Eskimo households are family households that include one or more "own" (biological, step, or adopted) children under 18, exceeding a still very high 49.9% of all households in this area (recall that the overall U.S. average is only 32.0%). All three types of Eskimo family households (married couple, female householder with no spouse present, and male householder with no spouse present) are more likely to include children under 18 than all households in this geographical area.[23]
- Eskimo households are less likely to consist of one person living alone.[24]

Minimum Proportion of Complex Households in the Local Study Area

For the Iñupiat living in the five ANRC areas, we calculate that 16% of the households are complex because they include nonrelatives, virtually the same as the 16.1% found in the overall area population (see table 2.3). In terms of the family/nonfamily breakdown, however, we see that the Iñupiaq households with nonrelatives are dramatically more likely to be of the family than the nonfamily type (13.1% to 2.9%), a pattern similar to that of the Navajo but

Table 2.3   **Minimum Proportion of Complex Households for Eskimos and the Overall Population in Northern Alaska[1] (Family and Nonfamily Households with Any Nonrelatives)**

Northern Alaska Population Groups	Percentage of Households with Nonrelatives in Family Households[3]	Percentage of Households with Nonrelatives in Nonfamily Households[4]	Minimum Proportion of Complex Households (Households with Any Nonrelatives)[5]
Overall population	11.0	5.1	**16.1**
Eskimo population[2]	13.1	2.9	**16.0**

1. Five Alaska Native Regional Corporation areas encompassing the area where the Iñupiat ethnographic research was conducted.
2. Eskimo alone or in combination with other races (Iñupiat are included in this category).
3. Calculated by subtracting the percentage of nonfamily households with nonrelatives from all households with nonrelatives (column 3 minus column 2) (PCT 16 − PCT 9).
4. Calculated from Census 2000 SF-2, PCT 9 data.
5. Calculated from Census 2000 SF-2, PCT 16 data.

much more pronounced. This is also the pattern for the overall population of the area, although not as strongly so (11% to 5.1%).[25]

Summary of Iñupiaq Household Types in Northern Alaska

From these results, we see that the Iñupiaq Eskimo have some household-structure patterns that are very similar, but not identical, to those of the Navajo. Like the Navajos in northern Arizona, the Iñupiat are more likely than the overall population in the five ANRC areas to be living in family households, with a higher prevalence of female- and male-householder families. In contrast to the Navajos, however, the prevalence of married couple households is the same as that in the overall population. Iñupiaq households are even more likely than Navajo households to include young children, at more than twice the overall national rate of 32.8%. Finally, the minimum proportion of Iñupiaq complex households in the northern Alaska geographical comparison area is 16%, compared to 9.3% for the Navajo, and these are very much more likely to be of the family type.

Now for the ethnographies: Let's first hop into the back seat of Nancy Tongue's old car as she drives across the hot and sandy Arizona desert to find one-room circular hogans that face east toward the rising sun, as well as more conventional houses that remain somewhat foreign to more traditional Navajos. Tongue vividly evokes the sights, smells, and tastes of Navajo life. Then, we fly to the frigid Alaska country with Amy Craver, hoping the weather will permit us to land. Perhaps these trips will change your conceptions of what a household really is.

NOTES

1. To do your own customized research for a topic of interest to you for a specific geographical area or ethnic group, here are guidelines, based on our own experience. Go to www.census.gov, and click on "Your Gateway to Census 2000." On the next screen, in the right-hand column headed "Census 2000 Data Releases," click on the data file you want to use. We used "Summary File 2," which gives data on age, sex, households, families, and occupied housing units for the whole U.S. population for 249 detailed population groups based on geography, race, and ethnicity. Then, click on "Data: Access to all tables and maps in American FactFinder." In the next screen, click on "Census 2000 Summary File 2 (SF 2) 100% data." Then, on the right side, select "Custom Table." From then on, the software will guide you through a series of selections: (1) general geographical area (e.g., for the nation, counties, American Indian Area/Alaska Native Area/Hawaiian Homeland), then specific subregions; (2) data elements (such as "Table 9: Household Size, Household Type and Presence of Own Children"); (3) filters; and, finally, (4) population groups. In the

population group section, scroll through the list. You can select general race, such as AIAN either alone or in combination with other races, or you can become more specific, looking for American Indian without Alaska Natives or Navajo alone or in combination. For most of these levels, you can include or exclude Latinos, who, in the federal system, are of any race. Once you have a table, click on "Options" to get a rural or urban breakdown. For example, if you select the "Urbanized Area of Virginia Beach, Virginia" as your geographical area, you could duplicate our findings for African Americans alone or in combination.

2. The change from collecting and tabulating just one race in the 1990 U.S. Census to allowing more than one race to be marked in Census 2000 was made by the Office of Management and Budget for collecting race data in federal data collections (U.S. Office of Management and Budget 1997). This was implemented in Census 2000 and in other federal data collections by 2003. This policy change does not necessarily apply to nonfederal data collections.

3. Because race tabulations can now be presented in different ways—"one race" or "race in combination with other races"—it is important for analysts to pick one way of reporting race data and stick to it throughout a research project—and to be aware that other reports might differ in the inclusion of people marking more than one race. This is especially true when the percentages of all people in the population are compared by race: here, we must use "one race" so that each person is counted just once, and percentages sum to 100. In this book (unless otherwise specified), we use population counts for each group alone or in combination to show the maximum count of people wholly or partially identifying with that race.

4. All statistics in this section come from Census 2000 Summary File 2. Average household-size data come from table DP-1: Profile of General Demographic Characteristics: 2000, for the total population, for American Indians alone or in any combination, and for Alaska Native alone or in any combination.

5. Of all U.S. households, 68.1% are "family households" (defined as a household with two or more residents, with at least one related to the householder by blood, marriage, or adoption). For American Indian and Alaska Natives, the proportions of family households are 69.7% and 67.1% (Census 2000 Summary File 2, table PCT 9).

6. The average family-household size for the overall U.S. population is 3.14, for American Indians, it is 3.44, and for Alaska Natives, it is 3.47 (tables DP-1 and PCT 26).

7. At the national level, 39% of American Indian households and 38.1% of Alaska Native households were family households with "own" (biological, step, or adopted) children under age 18, which was considerably higher than the 32.8% for all U.S. households (PCT 27).

8. We considered adding another type of complex household that we could derive from Census 2000 data tables to our minimum proportion of complex households. After looking at households that include "own" children (see statistics in note 8 above), we took a wider view and looked at households that included both "own" children and the more general, overall category of "related" children (including both "own" children as well as grandchildren, nieces, great-nephews, and so forth) in Summary File 2, PCT 28. We found that 44.2% of American Indian and 42.8% of Alaska Native households include children who are any type of relative of the householder, as compared to 35.5% for all U.S. households.

Laurel Schwede then reasoned that subtracting the proportion of households with "own" children from the proportion of households with "related" children would allow us to derive the number of households for each ethnic group that have only children who are nonnuclear relatives of the householder. To illustrate, we subtracted the proportion of Navajo households with "own" children in table 27 (39%) from the proportion of Navajo households with any "related" children in table 28 (44.2%). The remainder—5.2% of American Indian households with children under 18 (44.2% to 39%)—includes only children who are nonnuclear family relatives of the householder, such as grandchildren, nieces, and grandnephews. These meet our definition of complex households because they include nonnuclear relatives! Schwede brought this up to the other editors, and we considered whether we could just add the proportion of these complex households with nonnuclear family relatives under age 18 to the proportion of our complex households with nonrelatives from PCT 16, to come up with a somewhat more complete proportion of the different types of complex households to present in this book. We quickly realized, however, that there were problems with this. Some unknown proportion of households would meet both criteria for complex households—having children who are all nonnuclear relatives of the householder, as well as having one or more nonrelatives—and these households would be double counted if we simply added the proportions of the two complex household types from different data tables. Unless we could find a way to identify these duplicated households and remove one of them so that each household would be counted just once, we would get an erroneously high proportion of complex households. We could not identify these duplicated households with our data source—the Census 2000 website tables—and writing and running programs on the actual Census 2000 database was beyond the scope of this primarily qualitative book. We tried to overcome this limitation by drafting text providing "minimum-range guesstimates" (along the lines of confidence intervals that statisticians use) for the total of our two types of complex households, with the minimum proportion assuming full duplication between the two complex household types, and the maximum assuming no duplication. In the end, we abandoned attempts to produce minimum-range guesstimates. These two types of complex households did not give a representative picture of all complex households (e.g., they did not allow us to identify complex households that had both "own" children and "other relatives," which may be more common than households with only "other" relatives, and we were not identifying households where adults were nonnuclear relatives). By presenting ranges for just the two types, we would produce an incomplete, and perhaps very misleading, picture of differences between ethnic groups in their proportions and types of complex households. So, we decided not to present our minimum-range guesstimates. We want to clarify, not obfuscate, differences in ethnic household types. We provide the proportions of these complex households with children who are nonnuclear in footnotes for interested readers, but we do not add them to our minimum proportions of complex households and advise readers not to do this either.

9. Proportions of households with nonrelatives were calculated from PCT 16. Proportions of nonfamily households with two or more people were calculated from PCT 9. We derived proportions of family households with nonrelatives by subtracting the latter from the former.

10. Note that we report here statistics for just AIAN alone because we are presenting

percentages of the total U.S. population, so each person can only be counted once in one race category. Were we to tabulate people in two or more race categories, we would get a total for the number of race categories marked that would exceed 100% of the population count.

11. In Canada and Greenland, the word "Inuit" has been replacing "Eskimo." In Alaska, "Eskimo" is still used to distinguish the Iñupiat and Yup'ik from other Alaska Native groups, such as Aleuts (Craver, personal communication). We decided to stick with Eskimo here because it is still used in Alaska and because it is the designation for this group in the Census 2000 electronic files we are using.

12. We wanted the geographical comparison area to include the whole Navajo reservation in Arizona, which sprawls across three northern counties: Apache, Navajo, and Coconino counties. The first two counties are mostly rural with a few small towns, similar to the Navajo reservation. Coconino County has rural areas but also two quite different towns. Flagstaff has more than 50,000 people, and some Navajo work there, so we did not reject this city outright. Sedona is a wealthy town of under 10,000 people and a tourist magnet, with variation in household structure from the rest of the county. To choose the right comparison area, we examined the statistics with and without the towns. Including them did not alter the direction of differences between the Navajos and the overall population in any major household types but just accentuated the magnitude of those differences. Thus, we included them in the comparison area.

13. The proportions were calculated from Census 2000 SF-1, table QT-P6 data for the three counties as a whole, for whites alone, and for American Indians alone, so each person is counted only once.

14. Average household size was calculated from Census 2000 Summary File 2 data by developing custom table PCTs 6 and 7 versions for the three Arizona counties. (To get the average household size for this new region, we summed the overall population-in-household counts for the three counties in PCT 7, then divided by the sum of the three overall total household counts in PCT 6 to obtain the overall average household size.) We ran the same tables for the Navajo alone or in combination. We used this method whenever we included two or more census geographical units in our local comparison areas.

15. In these northern Arizona counties, 80.8% of Navajo households are family households, compared to 72.2% for all households (PCT 9).

16. In our northern Arizona area, far larger proportions of Navajo households are classed as female family householder without husband present (26.3% to 15.6%) or male family householder without wife present (6.8% to 5.0%). Fewer Navajo households are married couple households (47.8% to 51.5%) (PCT 9).

17. Of all Navajo households in this northern Arizona area, 50.1% included "own" (biological, step, or adopted) children, compared to 38.7% for all area households (PCT 27). An additional 10.9% of all Navajo households were family households that included children, all of whom were related to the householder, but not as "own" children, compared to 5.5% for the overall area (PCT 28 – PCT 27). On the one hand, it is not appropriate to add these complex households to the number of households that are complex because they include nonrelatives (see note 9 for the reason). On the other hand, it is appropriate to note that 61% of all Navajo households included children under 18 who were related to the householder as "own" child or as "other relative," compared to 44% of all area households (table 28).

18. See note 10 for the method of calculation.

19. Calculated from Census 2000 SF-2, PCTs 6 and 7 for the five ANRC areas.

20. See note 15 on how we calculated statistics for more than one geographical area.

21. In the five ANRC areas, Eskimos differed from the overall population in the proportion of households classified as family households (81.1% to 74.1%), female householder families with no husband present (21.2% to 16.2%), and male householder families with no wife present (12.7% to 10.6%). They did not differ in terms of the proportion of married couple households: 47.2% (PCT 9).

22. Calculated from PCTs 24 and 25.

23. In these five ANRC areas, 56.7% of Eskimo households are family households with "own" (biological, step, or adopted) children under 18, compared to 49.9% for the area overall (PCT 27). An added 9.3% of all Eskimo households include related children under 18, all of whom are more distant relatives, bringing the total of Eskimo households with any type of related child to a huge 66%! For all area households, an added 6.5% are households with related children, all of whom are other than "own" children, yielding a total of 56.4% of all area households with any type of related child (PCT 28).

24. Eskimo households were less likely than all households in this five ANRC area to be of the nonfamily type with a person living alone (15.9% to 20.8%) (PCT 9).

25. See note 10.

REFERENCES

de la Puente, M. 1993. "Why are people missed or erroneously included by the census: a summary of findings from ethnographic reports." In *Proceedings of the 1993 Research Conference on Undercounted Ethnic Populations*, 29–66. Suitland, MD: U.S. Census Bureau.

Kreider, R. 2003. "Adopted children and stepchildren: 2000." Census 2000 special reports CENSR-6, issued August 2003.

Lugaila, T., and J. Overturf. 2004. "Children and the households they live in: 2000." Census 2000 special reports CENSR-14, issued February 2004.

National Research Council. 2004. *The 2000 Census: counting under adversity. Panel to review the 2000 Census*, ed. D. F. Citro, D. L. Cork, and J. L. Norwood. Sponsored by Committee on National Statistics, Division of Behavioral and Social Sciences and Education. Washington, DC: National Academies Press.

Ogunwole, S. 2002. "The American Indian and Alaska Native population: 2000." Census 2000 brief C2KBR/01-15, issued February 2002.

U.S. Census Bureau. 2003. *Technical assessment of A.C.E. revision II*. Washington, DC: U.S. Census Bureau, issued March 12.

———. 2005. "Table 3: Annual estimates of the population by sex, race, and Hispanic or Latino origin for the United States: April 1, 2000, to April 1, 2004" (NC-EST2004-03), at www.census.gov/popest/national/asrh/NC-EST2004-srh.html (accessed September 1, 2005).

U.S. Office of Management and Budget. 1997. "Revisions to the standards for the classification of federal data on race and ethnicity: notices." *Federal Register* 62 (210): 58781–59790. Also available at www.whitehouse.gov/omb/fedreg/1997standards.html.

3

I Live Here and I Stay There: Navajo Perceptions of Households on the Reservation

Nancy E. Tongue

DEDICATION

𝒯he work that follows could not have been undertaken without the advice, dedication, perseverance, and thoughtfulness of a Navajo man who served as the cultural specialist and translator on much of this project. His name is Leo. Such people always deserve more credit than they are given. Leo is a member of the Navajo tribe, or the *Diné*,[1] and his first language is Navajo. It is also the primary language spoken in his home. In the Navajo tradition, one introduces oneself and is introduced to others by identifying one's clans or ancestry. Members of clans are considered to be descendants of common ancestors, although it is not always scientifically possible to establish actual genealogical links between all the members (Kelley 1986). Clan identification is important to Navajo people as it helps "place" them within the cultural and the physical regions of the tribe. One respondent expressed it better than I am able:

> All people have traditions and origins—the Irish, the Scandinavians and so forth. But as Navajos, we're so few in number compared to the whole of other peoples who have sort of lost their placement and meaning because of their numbers. We are still connected to our roots. . . . We need this sense of identity to hold everyone together.

To do justice to the Navajo way of introduction, I therefore present to you Leo Tsinnijinnie, born to the Red House clan (maternal lineage), born for[2] the Salt clan (paternal lineage), part of the Bitter Water clan (maternal grandparent's lineage), as well as of the Mexican clan (paternal grandparent's lineage). Leo is in his early forties and lives with his wife. He was selected to reside with her through a traditional arranged marriage. The primary language spoken in their home is Navajo, and English, consequently, is Leo's second language. They and their four children reside in a small wooden home beside a separate building used for cooking and eating, which sits on land that has been passed down matrilineally through his wife's family. His wife's mother and her spouse reside next door in a traditional home from which she herds sheep. They all share one outhouse. Leo's wife's single brother lives behind the hill next to them, and his wife's sister's family lives part time down the dirt road.

Leo has his own extensive network of clan and biological relatives in the more general area. They heat with a wood stove, have no electricity or running water, and live at the foot of a pristine mesa at an elevation of 6,000 feet, accessed only by a dirt road. This region is on the western side of the vast Navajo reservation. Because Leo is well respected, soft-spoken, discrete, and trusted, his presence allowed me to gain the trust of the respondents much more quickly than I could have on my own.

It took work and courage for Leo to look at local communities and lifestyles from both emic and etic[3] points of view. Neither Leo nor I pose the findings we came up with as the "truth" but rather as part of a glimpse into ways of living in a certain part of the United States at a static point in time through our eyes as ultimately conveyed by me, an outsider. Were Leo to have written this, the story might be different. The wording and the perspective surely would not be the same. That is the nature of oral history; the goal is to maintain the stories and information, although the descriptions may vary. As social scientists, we are responsible for packaging valuable knowledge and for conveying that information across cultural bridges. Sometimes we misinterpret. Sometimes we lose pieces along the way.

The many Navajo people who participated in this project deserve a great deal of thanks. Their patience with what to many surely seemed senseless questions and their willingness to sit through numerous hours of interviews deserves more than the honorarium paid to them. Navajos have been "studied" for years and understandably often feel that things and knowledge are being taken from them and that little is given back. I hope that some of this material can contribute to the Navajo people, as they have contributed to this research and to me. Many did not agree to be interviewed at all, but of those who did, the majority seemed to view the interview as an opportunity to state feelings and to be heard. I sense that, in some cases, true sharing occurred and many expressed to me that they even enjoyed and learned from the interview process. In some instances, it provoked discussion between elders and youth as we attempted to determine terminology, and they tried to explain their life-styles. Traditional beliefs are critical to the older generation in particular, and some used our interviews as a way of reiterating these values and creating a forum of discussion with family members of other generations.

Protection of privacy was not a problem for most of these Navajo people who volunteered so much information about their families. On the contrary, many wanted me to photograph them and their homes and land "so that Washington can know how it really is out here." And so, on behalf of these people who are part of an incredibly complex culture and history, I hope to give the reader a feeling for their lives and a partial sense of "how it is." This chapter is dedicated to them.

Figure 3.1   Leo Tsinnijinnie in front of traditional hogan on his wife's mother's land in Arizona. His mother-in-law is Linda Begay and his wife is Irene Begay.

INTRODUCTION

The Navajo Nation encompasses an area larger than Massachusetts, New Hampshire, and Vermont combined, or 24,000 square miles (Redoly 1995). The Navajo population is the second largest of all Indian groups in the United States. In 2000, the total number of people who reported themselves as being Navajo alone or with other races or tribal groupings was 167,539 for those living on the Navajo Nation Reservation or on off-reservation trust land in Arizona, New Mexico, and Utah; for the country as a whole, the number was 298,197 (U.S. Census Bureau 2001a, 2001b). In 1990, when only one race could be marked, the Navajo population was numbered at 225,298 (Shapiro 1998). In 1987, 125,000 Navajos on the reservation spoke fluent Navajo (Vecoli 1995).

Navajos have always depended heavily on their livestock, which consists of sheep, goats, cattle, and often a few horses. Traditionally, many people spent their days herding their animals back and forth from their homes to grazing land and moved seasonally to areas with better grasslands, living in temporary shelters in each place. Despite the fact that today the majority of Navajos no longer have summer and winter camps and do not spend their year moving from one sheep camp to another, it is my impression that the households and lifestyles have remained fluid; at heart, the Navajo are still a nomadic people.

Fluctuating and low rainfall causes annual crops to be unpredictable as most of the farming done is dry farming; irrigation is not generally used (Aberle 1981a, 1981b). As the tribe expands and the reservation land remains limited and contained, land-use areas are becoming more crowded, and erosion is a constant problem and concern for residents. People are less and less able to

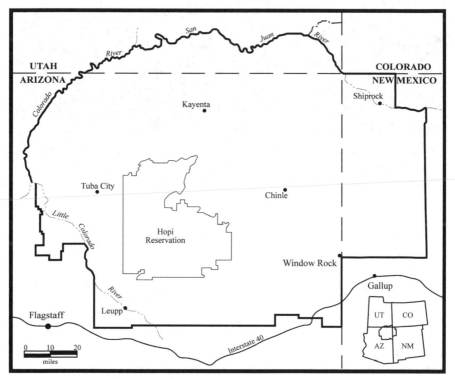

Figure 3.2   Map of the Navajo reservation

maintain their herds or grow corn and are being forced closer to each other's dwellings, making it more difficult for extended families to remain in nearby dwellings.

The Navajo people obviously have a unique way of living. Traditionally, they resided in a structure known as a *hogan*, which is a one-room, round or octagonal dwelling, shown in figure 3.1. Originally, it had earthen floors and was mudded on the outside. Today, most hogans still have only one, central room, are made of wood and roofed with shingles, and have a concrete floor, central woodstove, and no running water. The only entrance is a door that faces east. These were built on land passed down matrilineally from generation to generation. Therefore, Navajos traditionally had no mortgages and paid no rent or fee for using the land. In fact, reservation land is still typically held in trust, either by the U.S. or tribal governments, and reservation residents have been prohibited by law from actually owning land, making it difficult, if not impossible, to secure mortgages.

As my "Politics and Policies" section will better describe, much of this changed in the 1930s due to livestock-reduction programs and again in the 1960s due to Navajo Housing Authority (NHA) programs to develop more housing for people, causing breaks in tradition that did not always please those whom they were supposed to benefit. The NHA houses are square, do not necessarily face east, and are very unsettling, especially to the older generation who must wake to the rising sun and are most comfortable living in a circular environment. Historically, Navajo people have not lived in multiroomed homes placed next to unfamiliar, unrelated neighbors. And yet, current economics and politics have forced many to break with tradition, affecting and altering former household constructs.

The Navajo kinship system is very different from that of mainstream America in that (1) it is matrilineal, meaning that the most important kinship ties are among the mother's (not the father's) relatives; (2) it is matrilocal, meaning that traditionally the bride and groom go to live near (or with) the bride's parents and maternal kin; (3) inheritance traditionally goes through the female line; and (4) maternal kin are also emphasized in patterns of intimacy. Although matrifocused kinship is very different from the average American household, as discussed by Rae Lesser Blumberg (chapter 11), it is actually the most common pattern found in the 10 largest Indian tribes in the United States.

The Navajo people and lifestyle defy categorization because their fundamental cognitive organization of life differs from that of the Western model. They do not live linearly. Their worldview is better represented by a circle or a spiral, just as their traditional hogans (homes) are round. To force a description of Navajo people in categorical terms would be to dislodge them from their round hogans into square government homes or to attempt to place a round peg into a square hole. In sum, Navajos are a challenge to enumerate, and their household constructs are difficult to understand from an Anglo-American viewpoint because, in many ways, they maintain a migratory lifestyle in which their structural dwellings are not necessarily representative of what they call home. They "live" and "stay" in a variety of places; their addresses do not adequately reflect this. Their historical and cultural foundations are profound and necessarily influence their way of life. They do not fit nicely into a graph.

We have this tendency to look for, or to impose, order and pattern, but the categories of peoples that we create and the types of experience that we assign to these categories remove what matters from people and their lives (Farella 1993, ix).

Stories provide a template for some sort of order. They describe the features of parts of the world that matter to people. As life takes detours, so do stories (Farella 1993). Explanations in Navajo are rarely simple, and point *A* does not always lead to point *B*. For example, one respondent stated that he is Catholic. I asked him what church he attended, and he described a Protestant church in the region. He also seeks the advice of medicine men and, on occasion, attends the Full Gospel church and its Sunday meals. I asked this man again if he was Catholic. He said he was. I asked him if he was Protestant and he agreed. I asked him if he saw himself as a traditional Navajo. He said yes. Multiple-choice answers do not usually work in the Navajo culture. Rather than answer "all of the above," however, a Navajo might say, "Some of the above, sometimes." Just because someone is Navajo does not mean that generalizations can be made any more than they can with someone of any culture. Therefore, this is an imperfect presentation of a piece of a culture and warrants further examination and consideration. Rather than impose my own meanings, I will convey many points to the reader through the voices of the people themselves.

THE FIELDWORK

It is important to state that fieldwork is a challenge, and mine proved to be an extreme challenge! The bulk of reservation work was carried out in the spring and summer of 2000. At that time, all but two of my 25 home interviews took place in northern Arizona on the Navajo reservation. This Indian reservation, known to Navajos as the "Rez," is divided into eastern and western halves. Part of the region in which I worked reaches to the Utah border, and some of the areas are remote enough that they have been officially mapped by the U.S.

Geological Survey only in the last two decades. Most of the original 25 respondents live on unmarked and unnamed roads and have no physical mailbox at their homes. They have post office box numbers for addresses, and the actual boxes are usually miles away from their homes at local trading posts or general stores, making their household construct a challenge to understand, as I will demonstrate.

I initially encountered various barriers to collecting information from this population, such as contacting people. It was stated that in 2000 only 22.5% of Navajo households on the reservation had telephone service (Perine 2000). My suspicion is that this estimate was high; only a few respondents had phones at the time of my research, and all but two lived along rugged dirt roads. On a return visit in 2002, however, I learned that a local phone company was issuing some free cell phones to people over 65 who live in rural areas. To reach people during my primary research, I had to find them physically and connect with them. My sample was shaped by whom I could reach and who was home.

My car often got stuck in deep sand ruts, preventing me from interviewing certain families because I could not get to them. Over the course of the project, I accrued four flat tires from barbed wire and miscellaneous nails in the roads. Daytime summer temperatures could reach 100° with nights dipping into the forties. Connecting with Leo on given days or meeting at someone's house involved, for example, driving an approximate number of miles, heading toward a natural rock arch to the northeast of a given mesa, turning left at a stand of cottonwood trees, and then taking a right by the large flock of sheep. Some of the rendezvous appointments were obviously hit or miss.

I conducted preliminary fieldwork in the spring of 2000, a month prior to when the fieldwork actually began. This allowed me to make initial contacts with people and to explain the project. Navajo people tend not to want to participate in research as they rarely "get anything from it." It was a challenge to convince many that this was a worthwhile project, especially since I am not Navajo. Because I was white and affiliated with the U.S. government, a few did not want to participate at all for fear that I was there to take away more of their land or to get rid of their sheep. But those who finally understood the project embraced it fully and expressed gratitude that someone was interested in the Navajo perspective.

Our strategy was for Leo to drive his own vehicle (when it ran) to various trading posts and to homes to explain the project and our goals. I followed up on my own on some days or joined him at times. Our meeting spot was about two hours from my home. Many Navajos seem to spend much of their time going back and forth between places such as the sheep corrals, the homes of other relatives, the Laundromat, and the general stores. Because distances between places are so great, few are home much of the time. We found many respondents when we went to local trading posts for sodas. Because Leo knows many vehicles in his region, he could determine who was shopping or doing laundry. Then, we would renegotiate to meet them later that day or wait so we could follow them home.

I sent out letters to those who expressed interest in participating and further described the intent of the project, including the fact that participants would be paid $35 for their time and knowledge. During this preliminary research, Leo would consult with me from a payphone at a trading post by calling me collect and having me call him back. The seemingly simple task of connecting by phone with Leo often took days. Many who expressed interest to Leo were distrustful of me, and Leo would gently have to tell me that certain people had to meet and know me first. I sometimes drove for half a day only to find that the particular family with whom I was to have a preliminary meeting was not home.

Despite our extensive efforts to accrue a list of 25 rural families who were willing to be interviewed, when the fieldwork season finally began, only a few on my original list actually participated. The rest were busy with sheep shearing and other important tasks around the house, had either forgotten the date and were not at home, or were possibly shopping in Flagstaff or simply out visiting. Others were now distrustful of the project. Navajos adhere to daylight savings time, while the rest of Arizona and the Hopi reservation do not. Many Navajos do not wear watches and live their lives according to the sun and the resulting daily activities anyway. Leo's watch never even kept correct time, but it did keep us laughing. Making appointments according to time was generally a pointless endeavor. Much of my preliminary work was wasted, and I could have accomplished the same ends with less financial and physical expense had I not bothered to connect with people ahead of time.

In the Navajo culture, as in many cultures, it is inappropriate to walk up to someone or to knock on a door and begin an interview. First, Navajos rarely knock at someone's door. They sit in the driveway and wait for someone to come to their vehicle. After some time, if no one approaches, then it is appropriate to honk the horn. Patience is critical. Second, one makes general greetings while standing beside the car after someone has approached. On our visits, if we were invited in, Leo would then introduce me, or even if I had been to the house on a prior visit to explain the project, we still had to be introduced to one another in the Navajo way with Leo stating his clan relations and explaining where I was from, something about my background, and our purpose in being there. Then, we would chat about some local issues, the sheep, or even the weather. Usually, additional family members would wander in during the greetings, and we would have to begin again, often translating back and forth in Navajo and English.

It was not enough for one person to consent to the interview; frequently everyone, even those who were going out to do chores or were leaving the area, had to be in accord. It is not an exaggeration to say that this process of setting up the interview could take anywhere from 30 minutes to several hours. At times, the family might agree to an interview, but the person they had appointed to answer the questions would not be at home. This necessitated our waiting hours for her or him and being told, "She'll be home in just a few more minutes." On some occasions, we waited all day and part of the evening before the person came home, only to learn that the person had decided that the whole family was going out visiting elsewhere. It would be suggested that we return the next day!

Even Leo and I had some communication problems. For instance, he had arranged an interview with a family whom we were en route to visit. He was a passenger in my old car and led us farther and farther up a mesa on a sandy, unpaved road, which seemed nearly to disappear ahead of us. It took me a while to become accustomed to staying on the road while simultaneously looking at Leo when there was a fork in the road so as not to miss the directional signal he gave me in the Navajo manner of pursing his lips in the direction we were to take—a subtle gesture to be sure. At times, I really could not distinguish left from right from straight ahead, either on the actual road or in Leo's unfamiliar nod. The wind had been fierce and significant dunes had built up over the dirt road. I hesitated at one point and Leo told me to "floor it." The Mazda "sunk like the Titanic" (to use Leo's words, which had an unusual ring for someone land-locked in a desert environment), right down to its headlights! After laughter and then the realization on my part that we were in the middle of what felt like nowhere with insufficient spare water, we proceeded to peel off juniper bush branches and lay them in the sand, digging to place them beneath the wheels as one would put a board under a wheel spinning on ice. We extended the "juniper road" ahead of us, hoping to be able to drive on top of the sand. The car spun in place and did not budge. We waited. We ate our lunch and waited some more. Eventually, a pickup headed toward us. Leo said that the occupants might have four-wheel drive or at least a tow chain. They had the latter. They were a couple about Leo's age, and they all chatted in Navajo about our dilemma, surely laughing at my out-of-place vehicle, which should have been a pickup truck. Their conversation lasted a seemingly long time. Finally, they tried to tow us, but the effort failed. We dug the tires out again and retried. Then, they all sat on the tailgate of the pickup and drank water. The piercing, dry sun was scalding. Since we seemed to be making no progress from my "time equals money" perspective, I asked Leo to ask them if we could conduct an interview on the tailgate. Much discussion in Navajo ensued. I waited patiently. Then, the towing began again. Eventually, I quietly asked Leo what they had said, and he simply replied that they had said no.

This time the towing was successful, and Leo and I were off again, crossing the sand-dune region with Leo guiding us in a new, circuitous route to bypass the deepest sand. He asked where we should go, and I said that I thought we were going to the family with whom he had arranged the interview. He looked puzzled but continued to direct me for about another hour. When we finally pulled into the driveway, I recognized the white truck that had pulled us out of the sand and commented that it was strange that they were visiting this house. He calmly stated that the people who had towed us were the residents of this house and the people we were initially headed to interview. Now I looked puzzled. He said that since they had said no out in the dune, it was odd that I wanted to go to their house anyway, especially given the circumstances of the road and their change of mind. I said I had no idea that they were the people with whom we had an "appointment" and that I was relying on his guidance. He gingerly reminded me that I was running the project and that he was trying to go along with my decisions.

Dusk was falling. We laughed at the absurdity of it all, but I was discouraged. We had not conducted a single interview, and I had left my house about 10 hours earlier. We ate some snacks from my hot trunk, while Leo commented that he thought we were having a pretty good day. I felt that we had done nothing but fail. This was an endeavor in which I, the researcher, was being paid by the project, not by the hour, and I explained that to Leo. He felt that since we were working with Navajo people, it was a shame that the project had been set up the "white way" and not the "Navajo way," which always paid by the hour! I had, however, agreed to pay him by the hour, a fact that hardly compensated for our long days and nights on the road. It was not unusual to be interviewing until midnight.

People living in remote parts of the reservation, despite their profound sense of strength and independence, seem to exist with a type of vulnerability caused by their isolation and dependence on external needs that are not always reliable. A respondent confirmed this feeling by relaying a story about how much she wished she could get a phone and how she believed that to be more important than having running water or electricity. She explained that her sister's home burned to the ground in recent months. She had to drive 17 miles on a rutted dirt road to get to the nearest payphone to call the fire department, which was about 20 miles away from the phone by highway. As there are no water lines in this part of the reservation, the trucks had to pump themselves full of water in the city. Despite the fact that she explained in great detail where the burning house was located, the fire trucks remained lost and most people in the region could see them driving around the distant mesas in the wrong location. The house had long since burned to the ground, so the trucks were unable to find the house by its flames. Eventually, the fire department arrived to no avail. Similar situations occur when an ambulance is needed.

Thus, the people whom we ultimately interviewed were often people we found in the process of looking for other respondents. Although most of the respondents could understand basic English, and the majority moved back and forth between English and Navajo, it was critical to have Leo with me because his presence helped to quell the logical distrust that so many Navajos have of white people, especially white people working for the U.S. government. He also was able to help me decipher Navajo terminology and taught me a tremendous amount about Navajo lifestyles and kinship. I also suspect that Leo's presence helped other men or male household members participate more than they otherwise would have, thus enriching the interviews with male perspectives.

It is important to realize that all relationships create a certain "filter" through which dialog and understanding occur. In this sense, it is sometimes easier to play the "ignorant ethnographer" when alone as it is possible to probe more deeply and get away with cultural faux pas. I conducted one of my early interviews alone in English with a family of three women. I wondered aloud if maybe it was easier for me to ask a lot of questions because I'm not so knowledgeable about the culture, whereas a Navajo would be expected to know certain things and would be embarrassed if she or he did not. One of the women said,

> That's exactly right, and if a Navajo asked the things you asked, they wouldn't write it down . . . so it wouldn't really get accurately recorded. If you were a Navajo, they wouldn't give you the true facts. They'd sort of hold back themselves, too. It's better that you're white because we can give you more information than we could with our own people.

Clearly, the fact that I am a white woman and Leo is a Navajo man influenced answers in ways that can never truly be evaluated. Some interviews were conducted primarily in Navajo, and others primarily in English, and the effect that each had in the calculation of the final data can also never be objectively measured. At times, Leo's presence made me more comfortable, and at others, I purposely probed and reasked questions in different ways to get at deeper levels of meaning. This sometimes confused Leo as well as the informants. Leo, trying to conceal what he thought was my ignorance (which it sometimes was!), would attempt to move us along, when in reality, I felt that we were just getting started on an important point. In this sense, it is easier to play the ignorant ethnographer when alone.

METHODOLOGICAL APPROACHES AND
DESCRIPTION OF THE PEOPLE SAMPLED

My fieldwork was conducted in two phases. In the first phase in 2000, I conducted semistructured ethnographic interviews with 25 Navajo respondents in their homes. The aim of this phase was to examine the range and functioning of complex[4] Navajo households and to better understand how well the U.S. Census Bureau's relationship questions captured the diversity of Navajo living arrangements. In this first phase, I used the same standard interview protocol and methodology used for all of the other ethnic groups in this comparative research project. I describe the details of this process below.

The members of the 25 households in which I conducted my original interviews in 2000 had the following characteristics: All were U.S. citizens, and being Native American, they were born in this country. All were in family households. The breakdown into the census's basic household types is as follows: 14 married couple households, 9 female-householder households, and 2 male-householder households.[5] Of the 25 households, 14 had 7 or more occupants and the smallest had two. Among the largest households, five had 10 occupants, and one had 11. The rest fell in-between.

Of the 25 primary householders, 18 were 50 years old or older, with an average age of 47. It is important to mention that of all of the householders, 10 had never attended any school at all, including primary school, although a few had younger members who were then in school. I found it astonishing that so many people had not received even an elementary school education, which demonstrates how isolated some of these communities are. In 11 households, either the householder or spouse had completed high school. Only one householder had attended school beyond high school, although several houses had residents and family members who had taken a year or two of college or skilled-labor training past high school.

The majority of my respondents were either self-employed and working at home tending sheep, doing beadwork, making pottery, or weaving, or they were retired, unemployed, or on disability. Most households had at least one person, usually a male, trained in a trade skill. That person would generally leave intermittently to work at construction or labor jobs or at power plants or similar places. A few, usually female, worked in local schools, local health clinics, or regional service jobs.

All said that they had enough clothes to keep warm in the winter, and nearly all felt they had enough to eat. However, many said they felt anxiety at the end of each month before their paychecks or government-assistance checks arrived, when the food stamp money had run out, or when the canned "commodity" food (dispersed to low-income families by the government) had been consumed. The end of the month is generally a lean time for many Navajos on the reservation. Most people's homes are minimally insulated and heated by wood stoves. By national U.S. standards, these people are impoverished. After visiting one subsistence homestead, which appeared very "poor," Leo asked me if I thought it was the poorest house we had yet visited. He felt that since its occupants lived on a subsistence basis with essentially no cash flow, they would be considered poor from an Anglo-American perspective. But, he added, since they had a sizeable flock of healthy sheep, good wool to shear, an apricot and peach orchard, a cornfield, and natural springs, as well as healthy children whom they were raising, they actually were pretty wealthy. Then, he asked me if his own family would be considered poor. It all began to seem relative. From an outside perspective, it was impossible to know who had invisible debt, who lived for free, or how much family responsibility people had. None had house payments, and the majority had vehicles I envied. But a new or reliable vehicle is as much a necessity to Navajos as food.

The second phase of my fieldwork occurred in the spring of 2002 when I returned to clarify what the terms *family*, *household*, *home*, and *address* mean to Navajo people. After I had analyzed my original data, I also sensed that some families were including members in their households who were actually living in other places. I began to wonder if the members who had "left" to find wage work in other places claimed their new residences as home, or if, as their relatives on the reservation were doing, the off-reservation people were calling the reservation home. Since all the households in my first-phase study had as their listed post office boxes addresses that seemed to have only minimal correlation with where they physically resided, I was curious about how one's address was determined and wished to learn how Navajos perceive their sense of belonging in relationship to place.

Therefore, in the spring of 2002, I returned with a specific set of my own questions for the 10 follow-up interviews. This time, I decided to focus 7 of my 10 individual and small focus-group interviews on a new set of respondents: those living in "border towns."[6] Because my goals for this fieldwork were different, specific, descriptive, demographic and relationship data were unavailable.

Methodology and Protocol

In the first-phase interviews in 2000, each respondent completed a predetermined section of a mock census form so that I could determine ease of completion and accuracy. Through participant observation, I was able to assess which parts were difficult for respondents to understand. Out of 25 respondents, 11 could not complete their own forms due to language or literacy problems.[7] In the ethnographic phase of the interviews, some questions were brief and others were open-ended probes used to gather more in-depth, culturally rich data that I could not have obtained through brief questionnaires. I audiotaped the interviews (which included Leo's simultaneous translation where necessary), listened to all twice, and then created lengthy summaries, often transcribing verbatim.

Cultural sensitivity is critical in conducting home-visit interviews. One must respect other ways of life and work around sometimes frustrating differences in perception. Despite the fact that I told people I'd be paying them in cash, all were surprised to open the envelope I gave them at the close of the interview and find "cash money." One said, "We thought you'd let us down in the end given our history with white people and all." Others presumed I had intended to give "cash vouchers," which are all but useless in the rural regions as they are difficult to cash and people expend as much in gasoline as the vouchers are worth just getting to a cashing location. One woman, upon seeing the cash said, "I liked you and thought that I could trust you, but you never know. Thank you for being honest." My first respondent had told me that I should give people the cash in increments of $5 bills. This way the money could be shared, as resources within a household often are. On some occasions, more than one person in the family would contribute to the interview, and with small bills, they could divide the money easily. After interviewing three female relatives in a follow-up focus group, I gave each an envelope of bills. Two turned to the third saying, "Here, this is to pay the medicine man for your healing ceremony." This theme of extended families sharing resources would be repeated in many interviews.

Small common courtesies such as these help restore peoples' trust and make future reentry into the field easier. One man said, "$35.00 is so much for just talking." I told him he was teaching others and me, and that his knowledge was invaluable. He nodded and thanked me for respecting what he had to say. Among a population for whom trust of the white world does not come easily, such gestures are significant.

In the second phase of fieldwork in 2002, I devised a general questionnaire containing open-ended probes, with ample room for deviation and discussion, to see what respondents could offer me regarding use of post office boxes, addresses, and sense of family and identity. I also found the use of vignettes,[8] which I had based on composites of actual families, to be extremely useful. I would tell a brief story about three generations of family members, one of whom had a live-in partner with a child, for example. I would then suggest various scenarios in which people moved to certain places, asking the respondent to then describe who actually lived where and who was part of which household, and so forth. This was a useful tool in eliciting information that would not have arisen during general questioning. Most would reply that the scenario was just like theirs except for a few details, and they would proceed to explain, "But it actually goes like this . . ."

Additionally, in all 10 of my follow-up interviews, as well as in many of my first 25 interviews, I used drawing as a tool in determining household composition. For instance, people would talk about certain relatives who lived with them but apparently slept in separate edifices. So that I could gain a clearer understanding of the locations they were discussing, I made stick figure drawings of edifices and people as they were speaking. Then, I would ask if I sort of had the right idea. The family members would join in and correct my drawings, indicating exactly who slept where, how certain people were related, how far away one hogan was from another, and so forth. I found this a superb tool.

Problems with the Methodology

Navajos have traditionally relied on oral and visual traditions for relaying information. The language was not even written until relatively recent times. The mock census form and the "relationship matrix" (the form that we used to ask how each household member was related to the householder or, in most cases, the interviewee) were cumbersome and confusing to people. Most respondents seemed to think in terms of how the householder was related to a given household member, not vice versa. It was as if the questionnaire were backward to them, and this caused confusion. In other words, when asking a woman in her fifties how a niece was related to her she would usually answer "aunt" and not "niece."

I soon realized that beginning the interview with a quick drawing of a family tree allowed me to see errors quickly when they occurred. It also helped me keep family members and relationships straight in a manner that was congruent with my own way of thinking. The visual diagram also allowed all of us to point to certain people and clearly define whom we were discussing. Everyone seemed familiar with a general family-tree diagram, and I combined these with the charts and data in my field notes. It also kept Leo and me in alignment when we got into some tricky territory, such as when someone referred, for example, to a relative as "little uncle" in Navajo. I could ask the name of the person to whom they were referring, locate that person on the tree, and then determine that the child was a maternal nephew.

Ethical Considerations

I have strong personal feelings against being perceived as one who takes away without giving. Clearly, I was the researcher, and the people I interviewed were respondents, and on some level, we all concurred with this arrangement when people agreed to be interviewed. Any long conversation involving personal data that occurs in someone's private space and lasts for a long time is an intimate interface. It should be an appropriately respected, valued, and dually shared adventure, when at all possible. After certain sections of the interview were completed, I would pause, giving people a chance to think, at which time they would usually ask me how I live or how my family works or what my family tree looks like. I felt it important to share in such dialogs.

One elderly woman, in speaking to me through Leo, asked me if I had a clan. I wondered how I was going to answer this. I already lacked a category in which she could place me because I have no children—something she found disheartening. She was perplexed and saddened to hear that no relatives had given me a child to raise. She also was distraught over the fact that I had no sheep. When her husband offered me a lamb, I only saddened her more by telling her that I lived in town and had no place to keep it. She seemed to think my life quite tragic. When I was able to tell her that my name derived from a Scottish clan named (as my family story goes) for the tongue-shaped land of my ancestors, she was at least able to know that I was somehow connected somewhere to something. She expressed great relief by saying, "Oh, sort of like our Edgewater clan then!" Naturally, the idea that I also emanated from a clan appealed to her. Then, we were able to proceed with the interview. In other words, sharing on a human level is a necessary part of gaining trust on both sides.

HISTORICAL AND ENVIRONMENTAL CONTEXT

A historical overview is critical in describing current and past Navajo household constructs, as politics have affected the lifestyles of the Navajo people for generations. If one is not somewhat cognizant of land-reform issues, relocation programs, and livestock-reduction initiatives, then one misses a tremendous piece of the picture as to how households are externally created and how they are changing.

Traditional Economic Base

Navajos throughout history have had a profound connection to the land, and this connection continues to affect much of their navigation in the world. Although few Navajos today completely subsist off the land,

> Inherited lands, nevertheless, still offer most families havens from which even poverty and unemployment cannot dislodge them. Many Navajos today conse-

quently fear that if they leave their lands they will lose the last shreds of security.
. . . The bonds between Navajo families and their lands constitute a central, but
often neglected, aspect of Navajo society. (Kelley 1986, 1)

It is the Navajo belief that they were given land to use by the Holy People and
that anyone can and should live where she or he wishes. In other words, land
need not be owned but rather is used or borrowed from the earth while one is
alive. The Anglo concept of landownership does not exist in the Navajo tradition. Typically, one's grandmother's family settled and lived within a general
region and built hogans and sheds and fences for the sheep within that region.
A broad area could be considered as grazing land, and within that area, the
family would migrate seasonally to find the appropriate land for themselves and
their sheep. That land region was then transferred matrilineally to the female
of the next generation to use and care for. Men would move to their spouse's
region's land to live. Navajos lived in matrilineal, matrilocal household clusters
consisting of one or more hogans, whose doors faced east. These matrilocal
household clusters included grandparents, the daughters' families, and perhaps
additional kin. Each lived near or beside one another, with individual nuclear
families typically living under separate roofs. The combined groups made up a
family or, perhaps, a household.

When I asked Leo how he would describe the people he resides with, he
initially paused, then suggested the Navajo word *k'é*,[9] which he defined as

> The people I live with who are part of my family and are my people. They are
> the ones I shake hands with, and the ones I feel good with above, in front and
> behind. They are the ones that I have peace with. K'é means family group. It
> also is our word for peace.

I feel quite certain that this definition has changed little through time. He also
stated that he could not recall a literal Navajo word for household.

According to G. Witherspoon (1983), the fundamental unit of Navajo
social organization is the residence group. This might be what Leo described
as *k'é*. This group was traditionally created around a mother who served as its
head, a herd of sheep, and a common land-use area. Since residence groups
often pooled their sheep herds, the work of caring for the sheep was shared.
At the residence-group level, social groups corresponded to the grouping of
commonly held sheep.

> When the distance between houses does not clearly indicate which households
> form distinct residence groups, the matter can be clarified by ascertaining who
> puts their sheep in which herd. (Witherspoon 1983, 528)

In other words, divisions between households or families were not delineated by number of dwellings, roofs, or even entrances to homes, as they often are in more urban, mainstream American neighborhoods, but rather by family groupings and by sheep.

Traditional Relationship Constructs

Navajos are connected to one another through clan obligations as well as through kinship threads. Clan obligations function to help create a horizontal redistribution of income (Francisconi 1998). *Clan*, which is the largest structural unit in Navajo society and based on kinship, can be defined as a "consanguineal kin-group whose members acknowledge a traditional bond of common descent in the maternal or paternal line" but are not always able to "trace the actual genealogical relations between individuals" (Bellah 1952, 139). Historically, Navajo clans were matrilineal, owned no property, were ascribed at birth, and served to regulate marriage and provide a widespread network for social interaction. Even in contemporary times, one is always welcome in the home of a clan relation. Although Navajos take their mother's clan as their primary affiliation, they also speak of being "born for" their father's clan; this acknowledges both patrilineal and matrilineal relationships (Young and Morgan 1994).

Traditionally, marriage has always been prohibited within one's own clan, into one's father's clan, or with a person whose father's clan is the same as one's own father's clan. In other words, marriage is forbidden between cousins on both sides of the family. Failure to abide by these rules was believed to result in an illness called *iich'aa* or "moth madness" (Shepardson and Hammond 1970). Today, although many young people cannot state exactly why they marry within clan rules, most still abide by these laws, and the majority of people, young and old, continue to respect and know their clans.

Mothers and daughters traditionally lived within a compound of hogans or edifices that were nearby or adjacent. Even today, if a mother and daughter live separately for economic or other reasons, many still see each other at least once a week; more commonly, they see each other daily. A maternal uncle and his nieces and nephews are generally emotionally close. However, the closest relationship of any kin outside of the biological parent–child relationship is with one's mother's sisters, or maternal aunts. The mother's sister is called "little mother" by her sister's children. She addresses her sister's children by the same term she uses for her own children, making the distinction between first cousins and siblings quite confusing to an outsider, as the following interview excerpt demonstrates. I asked two sisters if they had children.

Sister 1: I have two children, 13 and 11.
Sister 2: I have an 11 year old [also]. They all call each other sisters.
Sister 1: We call each other's kids, our kids. We are considered their parents [not aunts],

In other words, all three children call each other "sister," even though they have different mothers, and both adult women call all three children "daughter."

Traditionally, the father is not expected to support his children if the nuclear family breaks up (Shepardson and Hammond 1970). Illegitimate children are absorbed into the extended family. Childless couples often adopt the child of a close relative. Likewise, it is not unusual for a family enduring hardship to "give" a child to a relative to raise. Sometimes this child is merely "loaned out" during the time of hardship, then given back to the biological parents. If a grandmother is widowed, a granddaughter or daughter often goes to live with her, care for her, and provide companionship.

Politics and Policies

The nineteenth-century history of Native Americans is widely known. For the Navajos, political decisions had, and continue to have, an effect on Navajo lifestyle, housing location, and household composition. The year 1923 brought about the formation of the Tribal Council, originally created for the purpose of signing oil leases. It has since become the central government of the Navajo Nation and oversees 100 local chapters, which are organized into 18 districts (Witherspoon 1983, 533).

By 1928, the Bureau of Indian Affairs determined that overgrazing had become a critical environmental problem. The 1930s saw the devastating livestock-reduction program imposed on the Navajo Nation by Secretary of the Interior Harold Ickes and Commissioner of Indian Affairs John Collier. This program damaged smallholders and was essentially ineffective from a conservation perspective (Aberle 1983, 642). In the process, many local people lost their primary source of income as their subsistence base was destroyed. They therefore became more dependent on trading posts, and many relocated from their migratory homes, hogans, or shelters to permanent homes in order to be closer to commercial centers that subsequently reduced dependence on farming (Kelley 1986). A 1936 study estimated that Navajos produced 53% of the food they consumed, whereas by 1940 that figure was reduced to 35% (U.S. Soil Conservation Service 1938, table 24). With sheep herds and farmland reduced, not just the poor, but nearly every family, had to find wage work (Bailey and Bailey 1986).

The 1960s brought about more change in lifestyles on the reservation. The Tribal Council created new tribal agencies to fill voids in federal services. The Navajo Tribal Utility Authority was formed to bring electric power to certain regions. The NHA was founded in 1964 through the Department of Housing and Urban Development (Bailey and Bailey 1986) and soon created its first low-rent housing project. Chapter houses and chapter regions became the loci for voting and for discussions of important regional issues. In other words, people who traditionally resided in locations according to matrilineal and matrilocal clan and kinship patterns began relocating based on politics and geography determined by public-service availability. When NHA housing expanded, many were encouraged to move from their rural, isolated hogans to areas where they could have amenities such as running water, gas, and electricity. Due to bureaucratic red tape, limited resources, and the dispersed population in some areas, which makes them ineligible for services due to low density, many are still awaiting what was promised.

The NHA homes are typically two- or three-bedroom rectangular homes in a tract housing layout with units close to one another. As previously discussed, people who were not related did not traditionally live in the same family compounds. According to Robert Johnson (personal communication 2000), living in non-kinship-determined housing units within close proximity to one another is believed to have raised the rate of crime and youth-gang activity. It has, in other words, placed people who would not customarily have chosen to reside beside each other next to one another. Many are still emotionally or psychologically uncomfortable living in NHA houses. One elderly woman put it thus:

> I had to have my granddaughter move in with me because I get scared living all alone in a rectangular house with separate rooms where I can't see everything at once. The house faces the wrong way, and I can't look out [east] and see the sun rise.

Contemporary demographics of parts of the western reservation have also been affected by what is referred to as the Bennett Freeze. In 1882, a portion of land in the midst of the Navajo reservation was awarded to the Hopi tribe, although primarily Navajos lived on it and have continued to do so for over a century. Nearly 6,000 Navajos faced relocation during the Navajo-Hopi land dispute, which has lasted from the 1960s through the present time. In 1966, Indian Affairs Commissioner Robert Bennett instituted a land "freeze," whereupon thousands of Navajos in certain disputed regions of land were prevented from moving in or out of houses as well as from building or otherwise altering their homes. It was ostensibly illegal for people to even repair their roofs, to say nothing of building outhouses, kitchens, or extensions on their homes. People were prohibited from receiving utilities and water, as well. Navajos who became frustrated with waiting finally moved to locations they might not otherwise have chosen, while others remained in hopeful expectation. More than 25 years later, some are still awaiting these conveniences.

In 1974, Congress passed the Navajo-Hopi Land Settlement Act providing for division of a certain area of land called the Joint Use Area between the Navajo and the Hopi tribes (Benedek 1993). This act stipulated that 10,000 Navajos and 100 Hopis who lived in the "wrong" areas be compulsorily moved. Not until years later were boundaries even finalized. As of 1989, only two-thirds (or 1,696) of Navajo households and about two-thirds of the Hopi tribes' affected members had been relocated (Tamir 1991, 173).

Several of my respondents were affected by this act. One respondent's grandparents used to live on a mesa, but because of the Navajo-Hopi land dispute, they were relocated to land below the mesa to a trailer that had been built for them. They lost their grazing land in the process. The respondent currently lives below the mesa with her siblings, her own children, and her parents in a "doublewide" trailer that clearly cannot accommodate this extended family. She has applied for her own homesite lease.[10] If it is granted, she will be able to put her own trailer beside that of her parents, thereby providing them all with more indoor living space but not restoring the grazing land.

According to D. F. Aberle (1981a, 169), "Although Navajos recognize that the U.S. government has the power to draw lines on a map and relocate them, they do not accept that they have the right to do so." To Navajos, land is not a salable commodity. It possesses a value beyond what can be measured in purely economic terms. Tending sheep was traditionally used as a way of teaching youths responsibility, nurturing, and business management. Livestock has been a large part of families' psychological and economic security. The idea of relocation is alien, disorienting, and disturbing, particularly for the women whose land it is. And, in all likelihood, this is why women have been especially devastated by relocation because they then have no land or place of livelihood to pass on to their children (Aberle 1981a, 1981b).

Traditional Land Use versus Current Homesite Leases and Residence Issues

Today, some Navajo families still share herds of sheep, although few can actually subsist on income from them. Many, however, do have reciprocal economic arrangements with one another. For instance, family members often share vehicles and other commodities. Additionally, a niece or grandchild might attend to a grandparent or sister of a grandparent (great aunt) living alone, bringing food to her house or going to her home and cooking for her. Such groups are clearly interconnected and interdependent. I was told,

> It is traditional [for us] to live in small families next to one another, helping each other out. It is only after land-reform issues and relocation and with people not being able to get land that we are moving in with relatives and sleeping in the same houses with each other. Traditionally, we would not have lived that way. Each nuclear family would have lived in its own house, and the elders would still have lived alone but would have been taken care of by the daughters living next door with their families.

There was not a single one among my 25 original interviews or my 10 follow-up interviews in which a respondent did not raise the issue of land use. Relocation and land-use problems predate the days of Fort Sumner and the destructive Long Walk instigated by Kit Carson in 1868, forcing Navajos off their land into confinement (Roessel 1983), and they continue into the present as many Navajos continue to be caught in land-regulation laws. Politics have affected how, when, and where Navajos can live and build, causing them to present a very different profile from that of non-reservation-living home-owners.

Not one of my respondents has a mortgage, and only a few pay rent; the rest either built their own houses, the government gave them their houses for reasons previously outlined, or other maternal family members passed the houses down to them. Therefore, the expenditures and responsibilities of people in this culture vary from what one would expect in mainstream white society. In the absences of mortgages and with minimal rent for some, the primary expenses for those on the reservation take the form of vehicle payments, utility bills for those who do have electricity, and gas for vehicles used to collect water and wood, shop, or get to work. Vehicles are liberally used to drive relatives back and forth from one another's houses or between off-reservation dwellings and on-reservation hogans. The distances are vast, and gasoline is not cheap in remote areas. There are also expenses for propane for cooking, fencing to contain livestock, and clothing and other personal necessities. Yet, tradition influences the perception and use of land. Today, Navajo people must balance all of these factors—both contemporary and traditional—which affect subsistence, income, and household structure in daily life.

One of the most important tribal requirements today to continue to live on the reservation is the homesite lease. Without one, the tribe will not install utilities or water, approve building additions, or allow the transfer of land or dwellings, even for those who do not live in otherwise restricted regions. Regulations like these contribute to the vocabulary Navajos use to explain the term *household*. In fact, homesite may be a more accurate translation of "household":

Person 1: Homesite is where you have your home, where you stay. You have
to apply for a lease. You would pick a place and then there is a committee
that has to approve it from the Chapter House, and then, once it's
approved there, it goes to the Navajo Nation. It's been a long time that
they've required leases. You can't build your house just any where on the
reservation.

Person 2: People still live mostly on the mother's land, and they can build on
that land even today, but once the parents pass away, then the children will
have to apply for a homesite lease for themselves. It has to be on paper, but
it still goes down on the mother's side.

Another woman lives on land that had been her grandmother's and then
her maternal aunt's. Now, she needs a homesite lease to continue living there
and is working through the chapter officials to get a consent form so that it can
be legally transferred into her name. She explains this process:

The land is in my mom's name, and eventually they will ask my mother if it is
okay to pass it on to me. For a while, it was an empty lot, and we were going
to lose it, so we brought the trailer in, but we don't own the trailer because we
are still paying for it. I think we have to pay about a dollar each year to use the
lot. They say it isn't anybody's land. We just lease it.

She further explains that in order for an additional trailer to receive electricity and water, the Navajo utility company must bring in more lines. But she
adds that there would be just one electric pole for everyone on the site from
which an extension line would run to each trailer. Therefore, each edifice
would share one bill. I wondered in this instance whether all would be considered one household. The answer given me was, "No, they'd be separate
households sharing the bills as one family." In this respondent's view, "household" and "family" are not equivalent.

A respondent explained that although she is currently residing off the reservation for work purposes, the family homesite-lease land on the reservation
is where she feels she lives. Her grandmother is the holder of the homesite
lease, and the respondent added:

They [the chapter houses] say you have to have one [homesite lease] to build
another house or to improve yours. The utility company won't come in and
put more electricity in unless you can show that you're the owner of that lease.
You have to have archaeological clearance to put up another trailer.

The following respondent "lives" off the reservation and although she,
personally, does not have sheep, maintaining a connection with the family's
land is critical to her. By securing a grazing permit adjacent to her grandmoth-

er's land, she is able to help her family accrue a wider grazing strip for the family's sheep herd, which economically benefits everyone.

> The grazing permit is in my name but . . . I don't have enough animals to use it, but the whole family's livestock is using it, and I think it's like a lot of things where certain things belong to the clan, to the family for use according to cultural values. The permit in my name issues a certain amount of land and the same with my [parents], and so, we have a strip that we use as a family. . . . [S]o, it's not as if it's all mine exclusively. That's not what we do.

As the Navajo population increases, land with adequate water and grazing becomes harder to find. It is a widely held belief that water is the most valuable commodity on the reservation.

In sum, due to the aforementioned political issues, Navajos feel that they have lost some of their land and have been forced into living situations that are contrary to their traditional values. Others may feel comfortable where they are living but are prevented from expanding their houses, from building other dwellings near their homes and hogans to accommodate expanding families, and from receiving water and electricity because of freezes. Because they cannot expand their dwellings, some caught in these situations, who would not traditionally have chosen to live together in one edifice, have moved in with relatives with more space. Others are simply still waiting to receive homesite leases from local chapters, a process that can take years due to bureaucratic complexities and lack of resources. As a result, many people move back and forth between family members' homes to best use the amenities that each has. To some, water may be more important than electricity; members of a family may spend more time eating and sleeping at a relative's house that has water. A teenager in high school may feel that electricity is more important for blow-drying hair and for staying up to complete homework assignments and so forth.

Concerning land-use and residency issues, as with everything else, Navajo society has been extremely adaptive, while remaining strongly rooted in tradition. The maintenance of tradition has perhaps been easier for Navajo people than for some other tribes because a sense of tribal identity and geographical isolation continue to separate them from the surrounding culture and from Anglo influence. Their reservation was established in the general area of their traditional homeland. Few North American Indian tribes have maintained such cultural continuity during the past century (Bailey and Bailey 1986). Unlike many other Indian populations, the Navajo were never completely dominated for a long period of time by other societies, so their cultural autonomy has never been seriously challenged (Spicer 1954, 675). For example, as recently as the end of World War II, each of the 36,000 Navajo veterans who served in that war underwent a cleansing ceremony referred to as the *Enemyway* upon their return (Vecoli 1995).

> Navajo culture proved to be extraordinarily flexible and adaptive as it absorbed a major infusion of new cultural items, incorporating ideas, beliefs, and technology while limiting cultural loss through displacement. . . . As a result, far from destroying Navajo culture, these changes expanded the cultural inventory. (Bailey and Bailey 1986, 287)

As one local resident said, "We just play basketball with whoever is winning! We pick out what we like from each culture and use what works best."

The data from both fieldwork phases exemplify the struggles and successes Navajo people have had in maintaining their cultural identity while straddling two worlds, Anglo culture and traditional Navajo society. The following section portrays the specifics of these challenges.

My fieldwork demonstrated to me that many people who have migrated to off-reservation towns for work still maintain trailers, hogans, or homesites on reservation land usually associated with the maternal grandmother's homesite. Grandparents have often remained at the old homesteads. When one spouse dies, although the younger generation is less available to take care of the single elders due to off-reservation work and longer traveling time, many older people are still cared for by relatives traveling back and forth between border towns and the reservation. Sometimes a grandchild is still expected to live with an elder or at least to care for one. Often that elder will keep his or her hogan and move back and forth between the traditional home and the younger person's home. This movement is common and makes it hard, from the etic point of view, to determine exactly which people live in which house, as I will explain. In such cases, people often "live" and "stay" in multiple dwellings and have multiple addresses.

As people on the reservation become consolidated into regions with less surrounding land for crops and sheep, many retain rural secondary and even tertiary hogans determined by, and to determine, grazing permits, and they reside near matrilineal relatives. In other words, regardless of where someone might be currently living, most still possess strong ties to the homeland.

In contemporary times, lifestyles are evolving, but not without tremendous emotional, physical, and financial cost. In order to maintain traditional ties to the "Rez" and all that it signifies, the middle generation, in particular, pays dearly, for they want to give their children "better" opportunities than they had in terms of schooling and employment, while also wanting their children to retain their Navajo language and participate in their culture, including ceremonies and ranch life. They strive to ensure that their youngsters can spend as much time at the grandmothers' hogans as possible, partaking in all that life entails. Frequently, one spouse spends a good deal of time away working, requiring the upkeep of a separate dwelling. Ensuring that grandparents or children are never left alone requires unending shuttling across vast expanses of land. As one respondent stated, "There are obligations, and sometimes trying to fit into both cultures is just exhausting." Another added, "You try to live a life on the reservation, and you try to live a life in town. It's very hard, very hard."

In current Navajo family structure, the maintenance of numerous dwellings results in a multitude of post office box numbers, addresses, and movement patterns, ultimately causing the formation of unusual household constructs and unique definitions and determinations of "home," "address," and "household." Through this, one witnesses the complexities of managing the layers of pressures from the strong bureaucracies and social organization of both Navajo and Anglo cultures.

What follows below are the specifics of how these complicated issues are juggled by Navajo people. The multifaceted balancing act results in households that cannot adequately be classified by the terminology commonly used by the majority culture, including the census forms, which are modeled primarily to reflect mainstream America's basic "married couple with children" household. Some households cannot even be truly understood without viewing life from an entirely Navajo perspective.

WHAT'S YOUR ADDRESS?

After I had completed my 2000 fieldwork, I examined people's addresses in greater detail. I also learned from the initial Census 2000 findings that many of my respondents had not been located easily or at all, despite having completed census interviews or forms. I pondered who determined peoples' addresses and where peoples' mail was directed. I wondered why some Navajo respondents who seemed to live near one trading post actually received mail at another, often many miles from what seemed the more convenient one. Also, I questioned if there were correlations between where people physically lived and where their mailboxes were. I began my 2002 interviews asking, Where do you live?

The Post Office Box Dilemma

This seemingly simple query prompted such unexpected responses as "Are you asking as a Navajo person or as yourself, a *bilaga'ana*?"[11] "Do you want to know our physical address or our box number?" "Are you asking us during tax season or during a 'regular' time of year?" "Do you want to know our address here [off-reservation town] or over there [on-reservation]?" Obviously, I had opened a can of worms. The reasons for having more than one box or for keeping addresses in multiple locations are complex and the explanations complicated.

> Woman 1: I keep my [off-reservation] address because my two kids go to school here, and we use [town] resources and so we should support [this town], and I vote here in the city and county elections because that's the right thing to do. But I still keep my reservation P.O. box that is the same as my sister's so that I can vote in the tribal elections and so that I can use tribal resources when I need to for benefits and things like that. You need to sort of work both worlds.
>
> Woman 2: When it counts, I use my reservation address. Like on vehicle registrations, we get a huge discount if we use the reservation address. When I know there are savings that I can use, then I use my reservation address, my sister's address.

A young woman who currently resides with her husband and children in a well-furnished apartment in town for school and work reasons and who plans to be there for a few years states that she has a mailing address in that town but "it's not permanent at all."

> We get the important mail at my [mother-in-law's] place on the reservation— like our income tax papers, insurance. Our bills like lights, electric and gas would come here [to this town address] but other mail goes there.

When I asked for her address, expecting her to write her town address, she gave me her reservation address up north at the end of a 40-mile dirt road. This seems to signify that she perceives the reservation as her "home" or that my "release form" should contain the address of where her "important" mail goes.

Actually, I learned that anyone can obtain a box if he or she pays for it, and often, every adult does get one! The box number is assigned to the client at the post office or the trading post. A woman explains,

> The neighbors over here have 2 or 3 boxes too. . . . We all get our own forms, or whatever, in our own boxes. It works. It's like having separate cars, really.

But it is not quite as simple as she makes it sound. The following response by a male to the question Where do you live? demonstrates the complexity of the concept:

Right now I'd give you this address [in-town trailer], but we always try to keep an address out there [on the reservation]. . . . I'm from [a town about 160 miles away from his current in-town address]. [My wife] has a P.O. box [where her family is from], and we share that one, and then I have my own [where I'm from] that I've had since I was a child. That's actually my home, which is my parents' house. And then the post office [where I'm from] has a box that is more or less a family P.O. box. As we grew up, some of us got our own P.O. boxes [elsewhere], but mine has remained the same. We plan our trips there [160 miles each way] around things that need to be done. One of the things we do when we get to the Rez, actually, the very first thing we do when we get there is we check the mail!

The liberal use of box numbers has implications for such agencies as the census because one cannot assume that the box indicates the region in which the person resides or spends most of her or his time. Nor can it be assumed that people can be tracked or reached according to box numbers. Post office boxes are simply a way in which people can receive some or all of their mail, some or all of the time.

I Live Here, but I'm Not from Here

For many Navajos, the physical address or structural dwelling is not what is important when describing where one is from or where one lives any more than the post office box has that meaning. One says,

For me if an older Navajo asks where I'm from then I would say that they are meaning where I came from and for me that would be my place on the reservation [where the trailer is]. After "Where you're from," they ask, "What are you?" That means what clan you're from, and then you give them your four clans, and then they ask you what family you're from, so it's always about where you're from, what are you, and who you are. It's always been that way.

Most Navajo people I spoke with consider the question of where one lives to imply where one is from. When I asked someone else the question Where do you live? she also wondered if I wanted to know where she lived or where she was from. Another respondent said,

We're here [in an off-reservation town], but we're not from here. We're here for a job. To say where you live, you have to describe where your maternal side is from. I'd say where my reservation place is, that's how I'd describe it, because you always say where you originated but now we're just here for a job.

NAVAJO HOUSEHOLDS

Households from the Navajo Perspective

In very few of the 25 original in-depth interviews did the people I interviewed immediately know how many people lived in their home. Initially, this seemed incomprehensible to me. However, part of the problem ultimately proved to be with use of the word "live," as I will explain. Navajo people also have a unique and flexible manner of moving between households, and it is the combination of these households that actually creates cooperating residential units. It is the social and/or economic interdependence of family that defines household, rather than the parameters of the physical edifice. Therefore, it was not so easy to state how many people lived in a household. Respondents perceived a household as consisting of people who are (1) linked through kinship, (2) share commodities like sheep, vehicles, gas, propane, and income (including disability or other government support), and (3) share daily chores and household maintenance, including child care, sheep chores, and wood cutting. Water, like everything else, is a scarce commodity on the reservation due to minimal rainfall, fostering cooperation among family members as a key to Navajo survival. In sum, Navajos share social and economic capital.

Navajo households, despite seeming fragile and fluid from an etic perspective, have a stable core or foundation that consists of at least one person (usually the grandmother, but if not, often one of her daughters) residing in one place on one area of land (usually passed down from the grandmother). The rest revolve around this core. Most respondents agreed with Leo's comment cited earlier that there really is no Navajo word for household. When I asked people to describe a household, a typical answer was,

> Hogan could mean house or home. House is just descriptive and home carries emotion. . . . Home is composed of family, whereas house is just a tool or something that is used. What would be closest to household would be a functioning home.

To many, home is not necessarily the place where they are currently residing but, rather, the place where the maternal grandmother is located.

> When we go home, we go up there [indicating the remote reservation land where the maternal grandparents lived and where the traditional parents now live]. We go home.

Conjoined Households

As discussed, Navajos do not analyze their household or family structure the way that social scientists do. They certainly do not use the words "nuclear," "conjoined," "complex," or "multiple dwelling." For the sake of clarity, I will describe two types of living situations that I found common among the Navajo people I interviewed. Both situations are what I will term *conjoined households* with each taking different forms. The first type contains multiple members living under one roof but actually containing "subunits" of families. From my perspective, these households consist of two or more small families, or parts thereof, living together and operating as one household. To illustrate, I present the case study of one family living in a single-roofed, single-entrance hogan, with electricity and outhouse, but without running water. On the day of my interview, 10 people had been sleeping there. However, they told me that when they were interviewed on the actual Census Day in 2000 about three months earlier, they had listed themselves as a family of three: 50-year-old parents with a single adult son. Therefore, it appeared to be a noncomplex, nuclear family. However, during the interview, I learned that they had neglected to list their two grandchildren who "live" there but belong to an absent daughter. One grandchild was several miles away sleeping at the boarding school that week "because they provide meals, and he likes it there." They had not thought to list the other one because he was "little"; they did not know if he "counted."

More importantly, they did not include their adult daughter and her four children who were residing in the house on Census Day and were still living there when I met with them. Why? "Because they have a separate refrigerator next to ours and they keep their money separate and because we have separate P.O. box numbers."

This householder said she was waiting for the government to determine if and when they might be able to build a cinder block house nearby so that the aforementioned daughter and her children could move into it and live next door, freeing up more room for everyone. Therefore, I suspect that they did not include the daughter and her four children as part of the household on the census form because they expected them to move eventually, even though the process may easily take in excess of a year. All 10 people shared the one outhouse and appeared from an outside vantage point to be living together as an extended family "complex" household.[12] That was not, however, how it was perceived by this family.

The second type of conjoined household I encountered consists of multiple dwellings within close proximity. The residents commonly share meals, often eating together in a separate, centrally located structure or kitchen. Family members freely go back and forth between dwellings but typically sleep in a designated location. In other words, there may be two or more hogans, houses, or trailers, but the members consider themselves to be part of one household.

An example of this is the case of a married woman, whose husband is away in another state in the armed forces. She lives with her two daughters by different fathers, neither of whom is her current husband. They seem to constitute a partial nuclear family, and yet, the woman feels that her elderly father, who lives alone in an adjacent hogan a few hundred feet away, is part of her household and vice versa, as she cooks for him and he watches TV with her (he does not have electricity). She was told by the local Navajo Census Bureau enumerator to list them each as separate households, but she believes that they are one household and were incorrectly counted. Other family members live equally close in neighboring homes and trailers, and yet, there is clearly a line separating them from these two houses as she did not include them in her household. This suggests that "emotional links" (across separate housing units) may be a factor some respondents use in deciding whom to list on official forms as household members.

I present another actual example of a conjoined household of members who live under separate roofs but could be considered part of one household. This is an extreme example but is used to demonstrate how complicated this breakdown can be and how fluid Navajo households are. Leo and I conducted an interview close to midnight with Ella, whose family consists of married householders, their five children, the live-in boyfriend of one of the listed daughters, that daughter's child, and the elderly mother of the female, married householder. The elderly mother lives with another daughter when she is sick. This mother also maintains a hogan 10 miles from the interview house. During our dialog, visitors came and went. We were confused where the elder actually lived, as it was after midnight and she was still there. When I asked directly if she lived there, the woman householder answered "yes," the man said "no," and the children replied "sometimes." She also eats there, "unless she's at her hogan or living with her other daughter, which is about half of the time."

Since she was currently there and had eaten there, and they told me that she slept there, I assumed that this was, for census purposes, her home. When I asked for clarification about where she really slept, they informed me that she slept in their house but that she "went home" at night. They explained,

> We take her home around midnight each night. Then, she usually stays up weaving or doing her work and then we go and pick her up around 7:00 a.m. and bring her over here for breakfast. She spends the day with us, mostly sleeping.

Therefore, she eats and sleeps at the house of her daughter, Ella (the householder), and "lives" at her own hogan. On Census Day 2000, she was sick and being cared for at the home of her other daughter in another region, and she was counted there in the census. Nevertheless, my respondent included her on the mock census form as of our interview day for she was currently in their house, and they had not taken her "home" yet. Where does this woman really live?

Navajo Households versus Government Forms

To the Navajo, although most seem to take the census count very seriously and truly want to be included, the census form, itself, is perceived as simply just another government or bureaucratic form. Most do not even remember or know that the census takes place every 10 years. People on the reservation are barraged by tribal forms such as Indian Health Service forms, school forms, forms for services on the reservation, forms to transfer the custody of a child to the grandparents while the parents are away, forms for grazing permits, and internal census forms. Many do not really differentiate among them. My sense is that most will complete all forms in a manner that grants them the most advantageous position for being awarded what they are attempting to gain.

Taxes   Several respondents said they would complete forms in certain ways based on whether or not it was tax season, indicating a logical desire to gain the most benefits. The decennial census always takes place around tax time but most Navajos again did not differentiate between this and other government forms. In completing the mock census form for me, most wanted to know if it was supposed to be tax season. Since this seemed important, I asked a respondent how she would determine a household for tax season versus another time of the year. From an etic point of view, she lives with her hus-

Figure 3.3   Multiple dwellings of one "conjoined" household on the Navajo reservation

band, her single son, and a daughter and her children. Despite this, she says that during tax season she would list only herself and her husband on any form, including the census form. Her son files his own taxes, and she says he "thinks of himself as separate." (Apparently the daughter does the same.) Therefore, seasonality affects how the census form may be completed.

Households versus Head of Household   Another issue involving misinformation on government forms flows from the concept that most Navajos confused the terms *household* and *head of household*. Some thought that they were synonymous and that the word "household" implied the "head of a household." Since the Navajos have a word for neither "household" nor "head of household" or a concept of either, other than family or one's mother's land and her home, the words seemed equally irrelevant and interchangeable to them. Many people interviewed had seen the phrase "head of household" on government forms and automatically completed that part incorrectly, often writing what they believed white people wrote for that term, and that was to list the male. In actuality, in true Navajo tradition, the head of a household is always a woman. Regardless, the word "household" still perplexed many. After some discussion, people did understand what I was asking, although who was included in a household was somewhat dependent on who was asked. One householder, whose family was conjoined with another as one household (although they lived in two separated dwellings), responded, "Sometimes we're together as one unit and sometimes we're separate, but either way we're one household." Another respondent explained,

> When someone like white people come around with some forms, they would consider my mom to be a separate household because she gets her own old age check and then my sister gets her old age check. The government sort of separates them out when they should be together.

Yet another said, "Whatever is around my house, that hogan, that shack, everything, and everyone around in my family is my 'household.'" Someone else added, "My mom would call herself the head of the household because the men go where the women are residing." I asked why she listed her husband as the primary householder on my form if she is actually the head of the home. She replied, "I just did that because that's how white people do it," and proceeded to laugh! She confirmed that the house is really hers, on land that her mother always used. She pays the bills in her house. However, her neighboring daughter says that in her own house, her husband brings in the money, and they could not live at the level they do if her husband were not working hard and making money. The daughter consequently views him as the head of her household.

Census Concerns

There is clearly a difference in perception between the Navajo and the surrounding Anglo definitions of "household," "head of household," and "family." This presents problems for accurate representation on census forms. For example, Navajo lifestyles and kinship systems cannot be accommodated by federal forms developed from a Euro-American perspective. Even their dwellings are not accurately represented by forms such as the U.S. census form.[13] The issue of how and where people should be "counted" concerned many Navajos. Some worried that miscounting would affect how monies are allocated to regions. Misplacing people in households can lead to a discrepancy in head count and affect the distribution of job-development programs, schools, social services, and health care. Birth and death rates may be inaccurately reported. For the Navajo, miscounting might affect building, as well as the provision of water and electricity in certain regions. Other implications of miscounting are numerous. There may actually be more single-female-headed households than thought, for example, but due to a belief that a white form should be completed in the "white" way, some female Navajos list a man's name first on the census form to imply head of household. Additionally, Navajo people are not always counted in the place where they perceive themselves as being, potentially leading to negative consequences for them.

> Mother: We're counted here [in a border town] because we work here. So, all of the Navajo people who work in the cities have the funding going to the cities, but really it should go to their chapter areas or where they're from. Those areas are not getting the money they should. Their business and life is out on the reservation.
> Daughter: They should count people by where they are a voter.
> Mother: We both vote there for the tribal chapters because that's where our grandmother is from. Chapters for council and tribal delegates are out there [on the reservation]. We have the Navajo voting. But white county voting is in [this town]. . . . You would think that when the census counts us, they'd tell us to go to our chapter to get counted. That would get everyone who is partly in [this town on the reservation] counted.

A male respondent in a separate interview elaborated on how misreporting in conjoined-appearing households can be erroneous.

> If [the census] is trying to figure out who is where, then they're wrong. If they came and counted us when we were with my grandma or cousins, they'd put us together, but we're three separate households.

NAVAJO RELATIONSHIP CATEGORIES
VERSUS CENSUS CATEGORIES

Relationship terminology is important because it determines and expresses how and why people are connected to one another. Vocabulary is not consistent cross-culturally. If one were not aware of the semantic differences, one could conceivably misconstrue family structure. Envision a family that appears as a nuclear family of four—a couple and two children. They seem to be married and perhaps are considered by the census as married householders with children. In reality, the family consists of a woman, a boyfriend, her biological child by a previous partner, and her niece. From a Western perspective, their household type would not be nuclear at all. But she would probably refer to her partner as her husband, her niece as her daughter, and her other child as her daughter. One would not know enough to probe and would therefore record this family incorrectly.

In zeroing in on the differences, I found seven primary sources of semantic gaps that cause confusion on the census forms.

Issue of "Grandchildren"

The census category of "grandchild" was insufficient for the Navajo respondents because the word "grandchild" does not translate well for Navajo people. Navajos do not call their matrilineal and patrilineal grandparents by parallel terms. One's mother's father and his brothers are called che'ii and one's mother's mother is called *ma'sani*. These are most equivalent to what most Americans would refer to as the maternal grandfather, great-uncle, and grandmother. If one were to ask a Navajo about her or his grandparents, it would be assumed that the question pertained to the maternal grandfather, great-uncle, and grandmother only. The paternal grandparents of both genders are each called *nali*. There would be no connection between this question and the paternal grandparents' generation, clearly confusing the outsider, since "grandparents" are not universally equivalent. Some of the Navajo terms for grandchildren are similar to, or the same as, the words used for both sets of the grandparents. Therefore, under the relationship choice of "grandchild" on the census form, people first have to know if the grandchild is a grandchild of a ma'sani, che'ii, or *nali*. The grandchild of one's son is a nali, and the grandchild of one's daughter is a *tsoi* or *tsui*, depending on regional spelling (Goossen 1986). Without knowing which is intended, most Navajos cannot even answer the census relationship question. When the category of "grandchild" was checked, it inevitably meant the child of one's daughter, or a tsui, and never a nali.

Issue of "Other Relative"

On the census form, there is a place to mark the category of "other relative" and then to write in the relationship of that person to the householder. This gave me great insight into the general Navajo view of relationships. Many who were not literate in English asked Leo to write in the added words "nali" and "tsui" to differentiate between a maternal or paternal grandchild under the category of "other relative" when they wished to list grandchildren, as so many grandparents and grandchildren reside together.

Many respondents have nieces or nephews residing with them, and many said that these warranted their own categories and should not have been part of "other relative." Often the terms for nieces or nephews are interchanged, and in one instance, rather than list a child as a nephew, the respondent wrote in "brother's kid." When I asked for a definition of "uncle" in English, the answer was always *d'ai,* which people translated to mean "uncle on my mom's side." The father's side uses the word for paternal aunt, or *bizhi.* Paternal uncle can also be *ye yazhi,* which translates to "little son." If Navajos had to list uncles on a form, they would only write the maternal uncles unless specifically asked for their father's brothers, which would need to be a separate category. Clearly, there is a gap between the Navajo emic and the standardized (etic?) terminology on the census form.

Issue of "Siblings"

Siblings are identified by Navajo words that indicate whether the sibling is older or younger than oneself, signifying the importance of birth order. A maternal aunt, or "little mother," nearly always refers to her sister's children as son or daughter. Such children are traditionally known to the maternal aunt's biological children as true siblings, but for clarity with outsiders, who would consider them first cousins, many Navajo children will refer to them as "cousin-sisters" or "cousin-brothers." Today, nearly all maternal, as well as paternal, first cousins refer to one another as cousin-brother or cousin-sister, or just simply brother or sister.

Issue of "Aunts" and "Uncles"

A distinction is made between the children of one's brothers and the children of one's sisters. A woman's sister's children are often regarded as one's own and called as such. The sister of one's mother is often called "little mother," or *ma yazhi.* This is generally reserved for the older sister of a woman but can be used for any of a woman's sisters, depending on emotional closeness. Paternal aunts were never brought up under this listing, and to inquire about them, I had to specifically ask for an aunt on the father's side. One's maternal uncle is usually referred to as "little daddy" and takes on such a role. Even more confusing to me, maternal nephews are often called "little uncle" (see also Young and Morgan 1987, 1994). Paternal aunts are considered *bizhi* (Goossen 1986). These are not parallel to the ma yazhi maternal aunts and demonstrate the strength of the matrilineal linguistic system.

Issue of "Child"

Likewise, the daughter of a woman is identified as a *chee* and the daughter of a man is called *tsi*. The son of a man is a *ye'*, and the son of a woman is a *yaazh*. Also, Navajo people would never refer to someone as a stepdaughter or stepson, although etically these may be appropriate terms. These words are considered derogatory; such a child would be considered as one's own.

Issue of "Spouse"

Unmarried partners are often referred to as spouses. The Navajo have no literal translation for spouse: a rough translation is "the one I make my living with," which represents the role of two partners in traditional culture before Western-style civil marriages were performed. It does not always imply that there has been a civil marriage in the way the words "husband" and "wife" do in the Anglo-American tradition. One woman I interviewed is not married to her spouse and files taxes as a single person, but on other forms, she lists her unmarried partner as her spouse. Most Navajo interviewees seemed to like the word "spouse" better than "husband" or "wife" because "it takes into account the Navajo lifestyle better."

In one traditional hogan, an 87-year-old man resides with his 65-year-old spouse. Both have long since been widowed. They may or may not be legally married. He refers to her as his "companion" and as his "mother" because "she takes care of me and cooks for me." After their respective spouses passed away, a medicine man arranged for this couple to live together so that they could "take care of each other," or, in other words, "make their living together." Clearly, subsistence and maintenance are still viewed in a traditional and pragmatic manner on many parts of the reservation.

Issue of "Unlisted" Categories

The common-law partner of a son or daughter living in a parent's house is referred to as a daughter-in-law or son-in-law. Sons-in-law and daughters-in-law are often called sons or daughters by the unmarried partner's parents. The word "mother-in-law" is often confused with "mother," depending on how emotionally close the relationship is. The word "brother-in-law" is also obviously confused with "cousin-in-law" because of the "cousin-brother" issue as described above. I believe that since many Navajo people on the reservation are not accustomed to having nonrelatives living with them, and many do not have roommates or boarders living with them, they attempt to fit people as closely as possible into relationship categories so that they become members of the family and "belong."

As explained earlier, Navajo people have an extensive network of clan relatives, and within their culture, such relatives are often referred to by the terms just described. For instance, one might be introduced to someone as a brother when in actuality that individual would be a clan brother with no obvious biological relation. In Navajo culture, clan relations are not capricious but, rather, are viewed as true kin, similar to one's immediate relatives.

CURRENT LIFESTYLE ISSUES: "GOING BETWEEN"

Challenges and Coping Mechanisms for Bilocated People

In 1990, more than two-thirds of the working-age population on the Navajo reservation had less than adequate income from wage labor.[14] As unemployment continues to rise on the Navajo reservation, more young and middle-aged individuals and portions of families are creating lives that involve some time spent off the reservation. Some regularly move back and forth between neighboring border towns and the reservation, while others temporarily relocate to another state, often far from the reservation, where they work portions (or even the majority) of the year at higher paying jobs. Regardless of distance, however, all feel they have an obligation because of clan, kinship, and family responsibility to help out other relatives who might be suffering economically or in other ways. Often this takes precedence above all else.

Those Living Close to the Reservation   Those with operable vehicles living in border towns or within a 100- to 200-mile radius of their reservation homeland are frequently asked by those without vehicles for rides to various places. This makes it challenging for people with jobs to meet their employment obligations, such as showing up at the right time and not missing workdays. It is difficult for those who live a more traditional or subsistence life to recognize and accept the obligations of those with steady employment. The generation that is in transition, attempting to live in a somewhat traditional world while working in a Western or white environment, must constantly struggle with contradictory expectations. Living between two discrete cultures takes its toll on many.

> Sister 1 (who resides in a trailer in a border town): Every weekend we travel. That's the way our lifestyles are. We're here Monday through Friday at a desk job. Saturday and Sunday is a labor-intensive weekend [at her grand-mother's place on the reservation]. At one time or another for all of us, it's like that. We do that to try to keep our culture that way.
>
> Sister 2: We live between the cultures, and we go between. We go back and forth and back and forth all the time. It's exhausting. Sometimes it's hard to know which world we're in.
>
> Sister 1: We work all week . . . taking care of our children and doing laundry and shopping and everything we have to do to live. And then on the weekend, we have to go home out there and do labor and take care of the livestock and the place for my parents.

Many elderly Navajos who have never lived off the reservation find it difficult to understand why the middle generation cannot spend more time or do more work out at the rural hogans.

> Sister 1: My parents can't understand that I have a home here [in town]. It isn't validated in a cultural sense, and a lot of times we're expected to be out home [at the parents' home], and our place here [off-reservation] isn't val-idated. It's because they never lived in two such different places like that, except back when they moved their sheep camps. As soon as Friday comes, they say, "When are you going to be home?" It's hard because we don't have a day off.

Those Living Away from the Reservation for Lengthy Stays   I found that many of the people who work off-reservation in labor industries such as weld-ing or construction often do so in other states. It is more common for a male to find this type of work, and he will sometimes stay for long periods, which can extend up to a year, in a motel or in a small apartment near the worksite. Sometimes, immediate family members will join him intermittently. In between and on holidays, they all generally return to the home of the wife or of the maternal grandmother. Interestingly, many who temporarily work in the situations described above make an effort to replicate their lifestyles on the reservation by seeking to live near other blood or clan relatives with whom they feel a sense of connectedness in their "away" work environment.

> Male respondent: I lived in Utah for a long time. . . . A lot of Navajos go up for the beef plants and also the steel plants. There are a lot of welders, and they go to weld. There is a section of town with little apartments, and all the Navajos

just seem to go there so they call it the little Rez [laughter]. The thing about it is that with them being so far from home that when they get into clans and kinship, they are all connected there. . . . When they came for work, they had some sort of family that they were plugged into.

Actually, those who live in border towns seem to use similar adaptation skills. Two sisters who live several trailers apart in one border town (although both have roommates to defray living costs), share child-care responsibility and often prepare and eat their evening meals together, hanging out in each other's homes. Another family who had recently moved into a trailer in that town reported a similar need to find a neighbor to connect with. The man described the following:

We met the people three trailers down. He came over and assisted [with my car], and the first thing he asked me was where we were from. I answered the town where I grew up. I gave my clans. He and I are related back a few generations, so there was that natural kinship that was struck, and he is like my brother, my clan brother. So, after that, we felt more at home and more comfortable with each other. It made us more connected here.

Regardless of the distance they travel from the reservation or length of time they spend away, I feel that I can make the generalization that the majority will still list their home (and certainly view their home) as being on the reservation. This home is nearly always affiliated with the maternal land. Despite the census rules stating that one's address should reflect where one lives most of the time, this is not what I saw Navajos actually do. To most, "How long you stay away somewhere doesn't matter. It's all in how you feel."

Children and Grandchildren Going Between   Grandparents play an important role in the lives of Navajo children. Although young people are those most commonly influenced by the surrounding white culture, they are also strongly affected by their elders and grandparents, who often live traditional lifestyles and share in the upbringing of youngsters. Children (biological, step, nieces, and nephews), as well as grandchildren, are often shuttled back and forth both between the parents and grandparents and between the mother and the maternal aunt. Therefore, household numbers also frequently change. This occurs for a variety of reasons. If a vehicle is not running well or if varying weather conditions have caused a road to become muddy, sandy, snowy, or flooded, making it difficult to drive children to a school bus stop, the children may be relocated to the home of another relative so that a different route can be taken. High school children have a choice of attending several day and boarding schools, and they often move between boarding and day schools, consequently choosing housing based on school choices and vice versa.

The number of accidental deaths on the reservation, often involving drinking, is 6.5 times the rate for all races in the United States (Briand 1993). If a parent dies, the children are sometimes moved to the home of a grandparent, aunt, or uncle to be raised for a while or indefinitely. I encountered many homes in which grandparents were raising the children of absent or deceased sons and daughters. In one extremely remote household, three unmarried siblings were raising the children of another sibling who had been killed. They were also raising the children of one of the present, now single, sisters. Many children, regardless of their home situations, like to be near their traditional grandparents on weekends, holidays, and summer vacations so that they can be outdoors, riding horses and herding sheep. Likewise, some widowed grandparents move back and forth between houses so that they can be cared for. Because of this shuffling around of household members, I believe that it is challenging to enumerate many people, especially children, and that, consequently, many are at risk of being miscounted.

Some have practical reasons for moving back and forth between houses. During two of my interviews, I found that one husband and wife maintain separate residences a few miles apart, one a traditional hogan headed by the male and the other headed by the female in NHA housing. They felt that they were all one family, which was not evident until I had conducted interviews in both households and found that the list of approximately 14 or so members of each was very similar! One middle-aged woman told me,

> The grandchildren spend time with us to shower and to sleep because we have water, and then we go to the place out there on the land and stay because they have electricity and TV and so we go back and forth to share.

The ease and fluidity with which Navajo grandchildren, children, nieces, and nephews move among various family members is not commonly seen in mainstream white culture.

As mentioned, I found the use of vignettes to be an extremely enlightening tool in eliciting otherwise unattainable information. I created fictitious, but plausible, scenarios that reflected Navajo family structure and told a story about a certain "family." I then asked where a child really "belonged" or should be "counted." In one vignette, I gave an example of a child who had been at her grandmother's house for many months to attend a school of choice, although her parents lived in the general area. My goal was to find out if Navajos considered this child a member of the parents' or the grandparents' household. I was told that because most people begin their lives at or near the maternal grandmother's, the child would be "from the grandparents' anyway and, so, 'belongs' with the grandparents."

I proceeded to give a variety of circumstances, including ones in which the parents worked away in another part of the country for part of the year and the child stayed with the grandparents. In one example, the parents, who were living away, were still considered by Navajo respondents to be part of the reservation because they were only temporarily staying in California, Wyoming, or wherever they were working, although they might be there for as long as a year. There was no sense of permanence about the job, and there was intent to return to the reservation. Therefore, there remained an affiliation with the grandparents. Whether the children stayed with the parents in Wyoming or with the grandparents on the reservation, the parents, as well as the children, really "belonged" back at the grandparents' anyway. Therefore, according to respondents, they should be considered part of that household or family.

There were other instances in which children actually resided with parents but were registered as being with the grandparents for the purposes of gaining more economic benefits from programs such as Women, Infant, and Children Services. In the end though, nearly all felt that since they are descended from the maternal grandparents and maintain close ties with them, everyone is ultimately just part of "grandma's family." They also expressed that the Anglo need to divide households and families along stringent lines was entirely contrary to their way of thinking and unnecessary. One person added, "You just can't categorize so clearly."

THE MEANING OF "LIVE" VERSUS "STAY"

It should be obvious at this point that even if Navajo people are not actually officially relocating from one place to another, there is a great deal of movement between homes and households. In fact, from my perspective, they were truly bilocal. A significant finding from my fieldwork is that there initially appeared to be no differentiation in the Navajo language between the words "to live" and "to stay." In fact, Leo and I found ourselves frequently using these terms interchangeably. With the respondents who spoke English, I learned that they, too, commonly interchanged the words. But I soon began to specifically ask people what they meant by "live" and "stay" and found that they held meanings rather different from the common Anglo definitions of these terms. A Navajo friend has since confirmed this:

> There just isn't one word to describe "stay" in Navajo. You have to describe
> the action of "stay," which means "sitting." It conveys that the place you stay

isn't permanent. "Live," however translates to "the place you were born" . . . and it is a permanent place . . . and is where relations live or have ties to. (Rose Denetsosie, personal communication 2004)

It is interesting to note that this person has resided in one trailer for at least 10 years and that she would consider this trailer to be the place where she stays, not lives. The location of her maternal relatives' homeland where the sheep are kept is where she feels she lives. Her post office box address may or may not reflect this, and she may have more than one post office box in more than one location.

The varying concepts of "live" and "stay" have bearing on the census and other calculations because I know there are people in my study who, since they work away most of the year, should have been listed as living in Montana, or wherever they spend more than 50% of their time. And yet, the majority of people who live in this manner included themselves, and were included by others, as living in their "home," or where they feel that they "belong." This concept of belonging is critical to understanding why many Navajos include people in their households who, from the census perspective, seem as if they should not be included. Most who were away from the Navajo land (perhaps across the country) did not record themselves as being where they actually were on Census Day because to do so would negate their sense of identity as Navajo people.

Of those in my study who reside in motels or apartments away from home for their work during the majority of the year, most were listed for me on mock census forms as residing on the Navajo reservation because "Working away is just 'staying.' It's temporary, not permanent. 'Live' is permanent." The consensus seems to be that the word "live" refers to the location of one's maternal grandparent's dwelling or of one's wife's permanent dwelling place, while the word "stay" indicates where one goes for work or other temporary activities. "Stay" is also what people do before they have their own home. People stay in places where they go or bring their family while they are waiting for housing or when there is nowhere else to go. Many adult children and their children stay with their parents in the traditional home, while they are trying to get their own home where they can live. A young couple living in a trailer with their children and the wife's 19-year-old cousin said that although they lived there, the cousin was just staying because

Someday he'll have a place and a family of his own. In the meantime, this isn't really his, even though he's been with us for years. He's just staying. It's just like how it was before we had our own trailer and lived with my wife's parents. We were just staying with them then. Now we live here. When I go out to [the

East Coast] to work, I'll just be staying there. Living is when you're not under anyone else.

Traditionally, there was probably no differentiation between "live" and "stay." Most of the places in which Navajo people traditionally lived, I suspect, were places they stayed, although they viewed a region (generally that of the maternal grandmother) as a homeland represented by family and clan relatives. The entire broader region in which they migrated was where they lived. Therefore, the construct of "household" is malleable. I deduce that this malleability and the fact that there is not really a Navajo perception of the household that correlates with that of mainstream America explain why it was difficult not only for me as an ethnographer and anthropologist but for the Navajo people themselves to determine who was really part of specific households.

WHY NAVAJOS LIVE THE WAY THEY DO

Navajo Perceptions of White Families

It was enlightening for me to hear how some Navajos perceive the way in which white people live. There was general consensus that white families have different values from Navajos and do not live with extended family members. Also, Navajos sense that white kids are turned out of the house when they become 18: "With white kids, once you turn 18, that's it. You're out!" Most Navajos stated that if a relative asked to move in, he or she would be taken in. They do not think whites feel this way:

> I don't see them like us. With white people it's more like, "Yes, I know you as family but no, you can't stay here!" Maybe for a couple of days but after that you're out and on your own. If someone here came and needed to stay for months we'd say yes because they're just family.

A discussion between a mother and daughter is illustrative of Navajo perceptions on this issue:

> Daughter: With white people, you ask where their relative is and they say they haven't seen them in 20 years, or they don't know, or their first cousin lives in Maine, and they haven't seen them in 17 years. Or "Where's your cousin?" They go, "Cousin? Cousin? We don't have any cousins. We have an annual family reunion but I didn't go. I had something else to do!"
> Mother: That's how it is. They only know their sister or their brother.
> Daughter: And they have plenty of animals [tremendous laughter!]. Cats and

dogs, and they all get their monthly shots. That's who they worry about, not grandma or grandpa. That's who they take to the clinic!

Mother: My aunt has observed white people, and that's all they do is watch their animals take a leak while we are worrying about cousins, grandchildren and making sure that everyone is eating or seeing if someone needs a babysitter, and then we have to go and deal with that.

Someone else described going to a nearby town to deliver a message to a white person with whom her husband was working.

It was a small, round street [cul de sac] with houses next to each other, with yards, and all of them lined up. We [she and her small child] waited for hours [sitting outside in her pickup and not knocking]. . . . In all that time, there was no one anywhere. Where we live, there are always people coming and going for the sheep or getting water or visiting or doing chores. Just going in and out and between places. . . . There, there was no one anywhere, and we just kept waiting. It was strange.

Finally he came home and invited us in. [There was] a high ceiling, and I was looking around, and he has stuff and all . . . and there were rooms—small rooms—off on the sides. And then I realized that there was nobody in them. I was sort of thinking when we were sitting in the truck that maybe the people in all the houses weren't going [back and forth] because they were just all inside or something. Then, when I was in this one, and I could tell it was empty . . . it was just strange, and quiet. And so, we were in there about a half hour, and in all that time, no one came. It seemed really sad. And later, after I left and I was driving, I was thinking about him and that maybe he was making dinner all alone and how that would be, and I just couldn't imagine. I was wondering if all those houses were like that. Do *you* live that way?

Many of those who work with white people still have misconceptions about white lifestyles. Another person summed up her view of white people. "They are pretty rich. They'd have to be to pay for land, to have their houses." I explained that we do not get land-use rights and would have nowhere to live if we did not pay for rent or a mortgage, which includes the property. I was reminded that none of my original sample had mortgage payments and stated that many of us often use a proportionately large part of our salary to pay for our homes and land out of necessity. She paused for a long time and then added, "Well, maybe we are pretty lucky then. I never thought about that."

Navajo Perceptions of the Ideal Navajo Family

Navajos have their own sense of ideal in terms of lifestyle and family. One explained,

> An ideal Navajo family would be one that is rich in culture, knowing traditions but also knowing that there's another world past their family. They'd also be bilingual but stronger in the Navajo tradition. That would be perfect. They would live traditionally and make sure the entrance to the home is east. Inside each home would be the immediate family members, mom, dad and children. But close by are other relatives because next door would be grandma and grandpa so that the kids would know their traditions. The grandparents would have their own hogan or house.

Despite the fact that most of the people I interviewed did live with extended family in complex family units and expressed love for them, many also felt burdened by the responsibility to care for so many people. Space was tight, and most said they would prefer to have smaller families residing under one roof with extended families in neighboring hogans, trailers, or houses on or near the same land, as people did "in the old days." One person was frank:

> I take care of my mother. I paid for her for 15 years. The last two years I've paid for her trailer. She just wants more and more and more. I know she's getting old but it seems I take care of everything. I'm the one around.

A young married woman added the following about what is important in living as a Navajo:

> I don't think that it's necessarily about living in a hogan but rather that it's about living without all the other things. . . . For me, it would be a Navajo man and a Navajo woman together [not mixed races as her stepfather and mother were]. . . . It's important to have the language so you can understand your family. My little brothers and sisters can't speak to my grandmother. I would prefer for my children to speak Navajo because I didn't.

The essence of what makes a Navajo family "ideal" is summed up best by this statement:

> I think that the ideal is for people to be able to be functioning not only on the Rez but off the Rez as well. Totally ideal is if you have your ties. For us, that's important. We go home for our ceremonial rites a lot, and if we didn't have that, then it wouldn't be ideal. Even if we were Navajo, we'd still be incomplete.

Conclusion Regarding Why Navajos Live the Way They Do

I attempted to understand from the Navajo perspective why people live the way they do and to learn if they felt that they should continue doing so. They live how they live because they "just do," as they told me on 25 occasions during the initial interviews in 2000. They are not introspective or reflective about such issues. They are a pragmatic people. Most of what they have had to deal with for the last 150 years has revolved around political issues beyond their control. Historically, they also have had to contend constantly with a lack of water and a harsh climate. Consequently, lifestyle is not really a choice in the way that it is for many others in this country.

People said, "How else would we live?" "How could we not live with our family?" One woman seated with her mother (both of whom work off the reservation) said to me,

> We don't know how you white people live all alone and just jump in a car and take off and start new lives and leave your people, your mothers, your family. How do you survive? Where do you get your strength? We would be scared and maybe even go crazy, or at least have nightmares. It doesn't make any sense to us.

Indeed, it would not.

One young female respondent replied, "Family is the only thing that keeps us going. I need their help." Another older woman said, "It's been like this so long [living with her extended family], I wouldn't know any other way to live." An elderly woman commented, "I've raised my sheep here, I know the land. How could one not live here with family?" Yet another participant stated, "We're like a growing tree with branches that need roots nearby. That's why we all live with each other." A man felt similarly: "You can't just break up a family. There is no other way to live." Finally, a young woman summed it up: "I always come home [to the reservation]. I always will."

The same feelings arose from another question I asked: If you could live however you want, with whom would you live and how would you live? Not a single respondent in my entire first-phase sample of 25 answered that he or she would live any differently than he or she did now. I gave examples such as, "If money or politics or housing problems were not issues, how would you like to live?" People were extremely perplexed by the questions, and I was astonished by their answers. The fact is that all of the above are issues, so they could not envision a situation without their current parameters. I would then ask them to envision a scenario in which they could have sheep or go back to their homeland or move to Phoenix or live with other relatives, asking what they would like most for themselves. Their answers repeatedly were, "But we can't go back because the Hopis [or the U.S. government] took the land." Or "the land over there is now dry, and I can't have sheep and live in my old hogan." In other words, there was no room for imagination because life is lived and not imagined.

To several people, I said, "If you had a lot of money, would you have water or electricity or a phone?" They would usually smile and then say, "Well, at first I thought I'd say yes and then decided that I like it how it is now without any of that because I wouldn't want any more bills." There was no considering "if money were no object" because money is an object. One woman said that she would like more money. She said that the first thing that she'd do is buy a big chain-link fence so that the animals would not keep getting out, and she would not have to spend her evenings chasing them around! Another who lives in a solar-powered trailer with many amenities (that use too much power to be plugged in) said that if he could live any way that he wanted, he'd like to insulate the trailer and put in thermal windows so that it would not be so hot in the summer and so drafty in the winter. In other words, people did not imagine moving into a mansion in a city. The majority of people over age 60 said they would most like to return to the old lifestyle and spend all of their time out at the old sheep camps, without water or electricity, herding sheep or weaving and eating better foods and living a healthier life.

SUMMARY OF KEY RESULTS

There are 10 key results from this study. First, and perhaps most significant, Navajos remain a nomadic people in certain respects, and they define where they live in a unique way. The maternal land area is still referred to as home, regardless of who (if anyone) is actually "living" there, regardless of time spent away from the reservation or "staying" in another location or reservation residence, and regardless of whether there are even any dwelling structures on this homeland location. One is always welcomed back there, even if to a temporary hogan or sheep camp. The Navajo define the place where they live independently from the census definition of structural dwellings in which people live and sleep. A flock of sheep will often still be retained at this homeland, and one need not actually reside there to know it is home.

Second, the obligation that Navajos feel to care for elders keeps the younger generations returning to the rural reservation. At times, grandchildren will stay with grandparents to tend to them, although they are usually included in their biological mothers' households. The majority of people who resided away from the reservation for more than 50% of their time included themselves, and were included by others, as living at their homes on the reservation, where they feel they belong. Most of those residing away did not record themselves as being where they actually were on Census Day. To do so, would have negated their sense of identity as Navajo people. Navajo bilocality may cause a miscount of population in a census. In other words, the movement of people back and forth, on and off the reservation, as well as between the grandparents' hogans and the homes of other family members, often causes outsiders to not know where people actually live.

Third, the ideal Navajo household is that of a "nuclear family" living together in one dwelling with other, related nuclear families living nearby in a compound or a homesite area. However, the nuclear family unit from the Navajo perspective differs from that of the Anglo-American concept. Navajos can include members who might be nieces, nephews, grandchildren, grandparents, aunts, uncles, cousins, and partners who are not married.

Fourth, lack of suitable income causes many nonelders to leave the reservation to seek employment. These people may make daily commutes, leave for seasonal work, or depart for large portions of the year. However, as permanent and reliable jobs away from the reservation become more available, and as the rate of unemployment remains unacceptably high on the reservation, extended family ties are being threatened. If the extended family vanishes, Navajo culture and households as described in this chapter will inevitably and irreversibly change (Bailey and Bailey 1986). Despite the importance of tradition and the desire to continue to maintain a Navajo lifestyle, language, and connection with reservation life, many people in the younger generation are feeling the tremendous stress and burden of living in two worlds. Tension in meeting impossible economic and emotional demands often came through in the interviews. There seems to be no solution to this dilemma.

Fifth, political constraints on building and relocating cause some people to live with those with whom they might not otherwise choose to live. They also perpetuate the back-and-forth movement of family members, as those without electricity may spend some days at the homes of those who do have it. Other family members without water may go back and forth between their own homes and the homes of relatives who do have it, and so on. This leads to the adaptive measure of creating at least two types of "conjoined" households. In the first type, more than one family or part thereof can live under one roof, yet hold separate post office boxes, maintain separate finances, and file separate income tax returns. They may consider themselves separate units or households, but the census counts them as just one. This seems to indicate a coping mechanism of one of the new and evolving household types in the area. In the second type of conjoined household, there are separate dwellings, but the residents often have reciprocal arrangements with adjacent family members, and some include them in their households. Navajo lifestyles that appear so unfamiliar to outsiders make it difficult for non-Navajo people to decide who lives where.

Sixth, the importance of tribal elections and their ability to influence decisions regarding grazing land, health care, educational reform, and other relevant issues causes most people to retain post office boxes on the reservation regardless of where they actually live. People may feel more strongly about grazing issues and permits where their livestock resides on a grandmother's land, for instance, than they feel about the issues where they currently stay. Having a post office box in the grazing region allows a person to vote there. Therefore, the retention of the post office boxes allows people to use certain regional or tribal benefits but may give a misleading picture of the number and demographic characteristics of people. Conversely, if the tribal record of voters is inflated because those in border towns or areas farther away are falsely considered to be living on the reservation, then the economics of who gets water, what schools are funded, how funds are dispersed to clinics, and so forth, become skewed.

Seventh, addresses may have little connection to where people actually sleep and eat and may not accurately represent what people call home. Counting people based on addresses or "mapspots" from census listing operations could lead to some inaccuracies and possibly influence the adjudication of regional funds.

Eighth, despite the fact that it appears externally as if households are fluid, I suspect that a core of stability focused around the grandmother's homestead remains. A lengthy longitudinal study might support this and demonstrate other repeated patterns.

Ninth, there is a tremendous semantic gap in relational terminology between the supposedly objective, etic categories of the census and the emic categories of the Navajo, themselves, which may cause more confusion regarding who is actually in the household. The problem with the terminology is based on the fact that the Navajos live according to a matrilineal system; consequently, the terms for the paternal and maternal family members are not parallel. Maternal nieces and nephews are often referred to by the same term used for one's children. Traditionally, maternal first cousins were referenced by the terms used for siblings. Today, it is common practice for first cousins on both sides to refer to each other as siblings. The maternal aunt can be called the same as one's mother. A nephew can be called "little daddy" or "little uncle," as seen above. Sons-in-law and daughters-in-law are often called sons and daughters. Grandchildren raised by grandparents are sometimes called by the terms for son and daughter.

Paternally related kin have a different set of kinship terms from the maternal ones. Stepchildren are viewed as one's own. The word "spouse" does not imply civil marriage. This is a world apart from mainstream American kinship structures and terminology. It may prove impossible to truly reconcile Navajo kinship terminology with census forms aimed at collecting standardized relationships for nearly 300 million people. As a result, the household structure of the Navajo, as determined from standardized census and survey relationship categories, may be distorted to some extent.

Finally, Navajos in this study seem to see white people as wealthy, educated, and easily able to move away from extended family members. Whites are viewed as neither physically nor emotionally close to kin. The perceptual gap between Navajo and white lifestyles may be as great as the actual gaps between their cognitive orientations to the world. The narrow physical boundary separating Navajo and white cultures on maps does not do justice to profound differences in their history, lifestyles, and worldviews.

CONCLUSION AND RECOMMENDATIONS

I believe that the heart of the issue of where Navajo people actually live and how they define the word "household" can be found in examining their definitions of "to live" and "to stay." If these concepts could be easily summarized and if there were no fluidity of movement in Navajo society, the Navajo might fit nicely into that Euro-American box that many would like to create for these nomadic people. Within the context of their culture and their families, they maintain functioning lifestyles while they continue to place so much of their energy into bridging the increasing gap between the Navajo and white worlds. They gain their knowledge, support, and emotional nourishment from their families. From a practical perspective, they live near one another because domestic function and social capital are more important to many Navajos than actual structural dwellings. Living with or beside relatives provides built-in child care. This also provides a venue for caring for others, especially elders, in times of illness or need. For those unable to live near extended families, their interconnectedness is sometimes invisible and glimpsed only when cash is passed between one visiting relative and another. It is not imperceptible to those who feel tremendous responsibility across great distances to those back home.

Hopefully, this work contributes to a richer and deeper understanding of how Navajo people on the reservation live and perceive their households and families. "Knowledge is co-created by social dialogue; it is never owned by an individual" (Martinez 1993, iv), as is clearly evidenced by communal Navajo culture. In order to recommend policy change, we must have a better understanding of whom we are representing (Angrosino 1998), for culture helps us create a framework for our worldview and lends parameters within which we operate. A more profound comprehension of how this quarter of a million people live can result in less of a mismatch of knowledge between such projects as the census and other programs that ultimately impact the Navajo people. It is my hope that this study and the voices of local people can provide a setting and context in which to better understand the Navajos. And so, I end with the wisdom of a local resident:

> Tradition and understanding of our structure gives stability and shows me where I can turn for things of greater knowledge concerning religion and beliefs. We have no written ceremonies and so we have to know who to go to in order to learn or have them done. In order to get the best knowledge our race can provide, we need our terms, our words and our knowledge.

NOTES

1. *Diné* means "the people" in Navajo and is how Navajo people refer to themselves.

2. "Born to" indicates the matrilineal, or mother's, heritage, and "born for" describes the patrilineal, or father's, heritage.

3. *Etic* refers to an objective, scientific category system. It is often used to refer to the perspective of a culture from an outsider's (supposedly) objective scientific point of view. *Emic* refers to meaning. It is often used to refer to the perspective of a culture, seen from the perspective of those sharing that culture.

4. By "complex," I mean households that contain anyone other than (or in addition to) a husband, wife, and their biological children, including distant relatives, nonrelatives, and more than one nuclear family.

5. In my sample, the householder was the person whom the respondent tended to believe the government forms would identify as the primary manager of the household. Many identified a male or both husband and wife, when, in actuality, it should have been a female. But, as one respondent said, "We just figured you wanted us to say it the white way." Others identified the person speaking with me as the householder. Note that in the census, the householder is simply the first person who is listed on the census form. The only instruction to respondents is to start with the name of any one of the owners or renters.

6. Border towns are those located on the edge of the Navajo reservation.

7. The method we used for collecting mock census data in this study—asking Navajos living on the reservation to read and fill in a self-administered census form—is not the method that was used in the actual census. In Census 2000, Census Bureau enumerators fanned out across the Navajo reservation and conducted personal interviews with household respondents to collect census data as they were mapping and listing households. If someone was not home, a message was left to call, and the interview was conducted by phone or repeat visit. Most of these enumerators were Navajos themselves, so if respondents had problems with questions, the enumerator could potentially provide assistance during the interview. This "update/enumerate" operation was used in areas of the country where standard, city-style addresses are rare, and the self-administered, mailout-mailback census short form would not be appropriate for nonstandard addresses; census forms are not mailed to

post office box numbers. An "update/leave" operation is used in areas with more of a mix of standard and nonstandard addresses.

8. For a discussion of the use of vignettes in qualitative research, see E. Gerber, T. Wellens, and C. Keeley (1996).

9. Navajo is an oral language for the Navajo people. The written form has been created by Anglos. My spellings are approximations.

10. Homesite leases will be explained in the following section.

11. This is the Navajo word for white person.

12. All but one household in my original sample of 25 met the criteria for the category of "complex household."

13. Many Navajos I met with felt they owned little of value and expressed to me that there was confusion during the census because local enumerators often told the respondents to list the kitchen, living room, and bathrooms under the category of "bedroom," making some homes seem huge and therefore implying that people were wealthier than they were. Under "types of residences," it was suggested that the term "hogan" be included as a type of dwelling, maybe even replacing "condominium," which no one comprehended because they had never seen one. Many Navajos felt that simple wording on forms can affect accuracy in portraying lifestyles and, at a minimum, make people feel that they and their cultures are valued.

14. The Navajo median family income in 1990 was $11,885; the per capita income was $4,106. More than half of the housing units on the Navajo reservation lacked complete plumbing (Dames and Moore, Inc., and Bell 1993).

REFERENCES

Aberle, D. F. 1981a. "Navajo coresidential kin groups and lineages." *Journal of Anthropological Research* 37: 1–7.

———. 1981b. "A century of Navajo kinship change." *Canadian Journal of Anthropology* 2: 21–36.

———. 1983. "Navajo economic development." In *Handbook of North American Indians: Southwest*, ed. W. C. Sturtevant and A. Ortiz, Vol. 10, 641–58. Washington, DC: Smithsonian Institution.

Angrosino, M. V. 1998. *Opportunity house: ethnographic stories of mental retardation.* Walnut Creek, CA: AltaMira Press.

Bailey, G., and R. G. Bailey. 1986. A *History of the Navajos: the reservation years.* Santa Fe, NM: School of American Research Press.

Bellah, R. N. 1952. *Apache kinship systems.* Cambridge, MA: Howard University Press.

Benedek, E. 1993. *Wind won't know me: a history of the Navajo-Hopi land dispute.* New York: Vintage Books.

Briand, X. 1993. "Drugs and alcohol still threaten Indians." *Arizona Daily Sun* (Flagstaff). May 16.

Dames and Moore, Inc., and C. Bell. 1993. "Redevelopment of Diné land and lifeway on the former Bennet Freeze Area: a planning and project delivery process." The Navajo

Nation, the President's Statutory Freeze Redevelopment Task Force. Report written for the Office of Navajo-Hopi Relocation in Flagstaff, Arizona, December 30.

Etsitty, D. 1993. *Statistical abstract of the Navajo Nation.* Window Rock, AZ: Division of Economic Development Support Services.

Farella, J. 1993. *The wind in a jar.* Albuquerque: University of New Mexico Press.

Francisconi, M. J. 1998. *Kinship, capitalism, change: the informal economy of the Navajo, 1868–1995.* New York: Garland.

Gerber, E., T. Wellens, and C. Keeley. 1996. "Who lives here? The use of vignettes in household roster research." In *1996 Proceedings of the American Statistical Association, Section on Survey Research Methods.* Alexandria, VA: American Statistical Association.

Goossen, I. 1986. *Navajo made easier: a course in conversational Navajo.* Flagstaff, AZ: Northland Press.

Kelley, K. B. 1986. *Navajo land use: An ethnoarchaeological study.* Orlando, FL: Academic Press, Harcourt, Brace, Jovanovich.

Martinez, F. G. 1993. "Familism in acculturated Mexican Americans: patterns, change, and perceived impact on adjustment to U.S. society." Ed.D. diss., Northern Arizona University.

Perine, K. 2000. "Clinton visits the lands that tech forgot." Industry Standard Communications, Inc., April 17.

Roessel, R. Jr. 1983. "Navajo history." In *Handbook of North American Indians: Southwest,* ed. W. C. Sturtevant and A. Ortiz, Vol. 10, 506–23. Washington, DC: Smithsonian Institution.

Redoly, M. A., ed. 1995. *Statistical record of Native Americans.* 2nd ed. New York: Gale Research.

Shapiro, R. J. 1998. *Statistical abstract of the United States.* Washington, DC: The National Data Bank, U.S. Department of Commerce, Economics and Statistics Administration.

Shepardson, M., and B. Hammond. 1970. *The Navajo mountain community: social organization and kinship terminology.* Berkeley: University of California Press.

Spicer, E. H. 1954. "Spanish-Indian acculturation in the Southwest." *American Anthropologist* 56: 663–78.

Tamir, O. 1991. "Relocation of Navajo from Hopi partitioned land in Piñon." *Human Organization* 50 (2): 173–78.

U.S. Census Bureau. 2001a. "Total population: Navajo alone or in any combination." Census 2000 SF-2, PCT1 for the Navajo Nation Reservation and Off-Reservation Trust Land: Arizona, New Mexico, and Utah, at www.census.gov (accessed September 1, 2005).

———. 2001b. "Total population: Navajo alone or in any combination." Census 2000 SF-2, PCT1 for the United States, at www.census.gov (accessed on September 1, 2005).

U.S. Soil Conservation Service. 1938. *Statistical summary, human dependency survey, Navajo and Hopi reservations. Navajo District Region 8, Section of Conservation Economics.* Washington, DC.

———. 1990. *1990 Census of population and housing, summary tape, file 3A.* Washington, DC: Bureau of the Census Data, User Services Division.

Vecoli, R. J., ed. 1995. *Gale encyclopedia of multicultural America.* Vol. 2. New York: Gale Research.

Witherspoon, G. 1983. "Navajo social organization." In *Handbook of North American Indians: Southwest*, ed. W. C. Sturtevant and A. Ortiz, Vol. 10, 524–35. Washington, DC: Smithsonian Institution.

Young, R, W., and W. Morgan. 1987. *The Navajo language: A grammar and colloquial dictionary*. Rev. ed. Albuquerque: University of New Mexico Press.

———. 1994. *Colloquial Navaho: a dictionary*. New York: Hippocrene Books.

• 4 •

Household Adaptive Strategies among the Iñupiat

Amy Craver

THE STUDY, THE ETHNIC GROUP, AND THE SAMPLE

$\mathscr{F}$ew ethnic groups in the United States have experienced more changes in the past 200 years than the Iñupiat.[1] During the nineteenth century, practically everything needed for survival—food, clothing, houses, equipment—came from local materials.

Within a relatively short time period, Iñupiaq household dwellings changed dramatically, going from large numbers of people (10–20) inhabiting a single, semisubterranean structure (Langdon 1988) to fewer people living in modern American housing units. Today, most Iñupiaq communities rely on imported goods and services. Although some are beginning to receive water and sewer hookups, many others continue to lack the modern amenities of flush toilets or running water. Yet, in other ways, these communities are considered quite modern. Most homes have cable, which transmits worldwide news, Los Angeles Lakers basketball games, and Hollywood music videos. Local grocery stores sell frozen, Mexican TV dinners, soda pop, and shopworn iceberg lettuce and tomatoes from California. Snow machines built in Illinois and all-terrain vehicles from Japan are parked outside the Washeteria, where people use coin-operated showers and commercial washers and dryers.

Contemporary Iñupiat are increasingly combining elements of traditional and modern culture. Even though such changes have altered domestic life, the traditional social structure of Iñupiaq culture has survived fundamentally unchanged. One explanation for the persistence of Iñupiaq social structure is that the Iñupiat continue to rely on a subsistence lifestyle and implement kin-ship networks as they harvest, process, and distribute local foods. Further, Iñu-piat maintain sharing networks today because year-round employment opportunities are few in most rural Iñupiaq communities. Because it is difficult to find full-time work in rural Alaska, some Iñupiat are forced to leave their communities to find work, and most people are only able to work sporadically. Although the basic Iñupiaq family structure has changed little, Iñupiat house-holds nowadays have significant traits that did not exist historically. One distin-guishing feature of contemporary Iñupiaq households is grandparents raising grandchildren without the middle generation (the grandparent's offspring) present in the household. This is known as a *skip-generation household*. The younger, middle generation is often missing because its members are residing in another community, either working a wage job or attending school. Gener-ally, it is the women who leave their children with their families while they pursue wage jobs or higher education. In some cases, there are social problems associated with this middle generation, in part because its members were sent to boarding schools and did not spend their formative years in a family envi-ronment.[2]

In 17 of 25, or 78%, of the complex households in this study, the middle generation are missing, which means the grandparents are raising their grand-children. In these households, the female offspring have left the household and community for employment, education, or personal reasons, while their chil-dren remain in the grandparents' households. Although offspring leave the household, it is important to emphasize that their ties to the natal household remain strong.

Another unique contemporary characteristic of Iñupiaq households included in this study is the high proportion of single adult men living with grandparents, parents, siblings, or alone. For example, in 12 (48%) of the households in this study, adult single men lived with a grandmother, parent, or sibling. Due to disproportionate female migration, men are more likely than women to be unmarried and living in their parents' or grandparents' house-holds (or sleeping in a nearby building) after reaching maturity.

The high number of single adult men is due in part to Iñupiaq men and women having had different patterns of outmigration for education and employment (Kleinfeld 1981). According to a recent study, Alaska Native women are more likely than Alaska Native men to seek full-time jobs, attend college, or move to cities (Hamilton and Seyfrit 1994). Employment statistics confirm that Iñupiaq women are moving into skilled occupations, while Iñu-piaq men are more likely to combine part-time, intermittent blue-collar work with traditional subsistence activities (Kleinfeld 1981).

One explanation for this disparity is the different roles Iñupiaq men and women play in subsistence activities. Iñupiaq men today continue to be actively involved in and respected for their subsistence hunting and fishing contributions, giving them a persuasive reason not to leave their community or to work a full-time job. As a result, Iñupiaq men often combine subsistence activities with part-time employment and decline the opportunity to relocate to an urban center to pursue a steady career. In contrast to the high esteem lavished on contemporary Iñupiaq men for their role in subsistence activities, women's traditional subsistence activities, such as food preparation, have less present-day appeal and receive less acknowledgment (Fogel-Chance 1993). Contemporary equivalents of these tasks, such as sewing and cooking, can be accomplished as well or better in more urban communities, unlike men's hunting and fishing activities. Often women's jobs help support men's activities, like buying a snow machine or boat.

Today's Iñupiaq families and households are forced to reconcile their desire to live off the land with the need to earn wages. Ironically, cash has become mandatory for living a traditional subsistence way of life. Rural Iñupiaq people face the continual challenge of trying to balance wage earning with living a subsistence lifestyle. This challenge is ongoing, due to constant changes in the wage economy, the types of jobs available, and the amount of money households need. Virtually all hunting, fishing, and trapping activities require store-bought items (Magdanz, Utermohle, and Wolf 2002).

Necessary subsistence equipment includes snow machines, rifles, ammunition, traps, motors, boats, tents, nets, camp stoves, and many other items. There are also increasing demands for money to pay for the onslaught of new items and services being introduced into the villages. For example, in the past 20 years, new prefabricated houses have been introduced into the communities, thus indebting each family for a period of 10 or more years. Other expenses, such as electricity, running water, and sewage, all contribute to the need for steady cash.

Prior Work upon Which This Study Is Based

The history, ethnology, and current socioeconomic conditions of the Iñupiat are well documented (good, widely cited references include Anderson et al. 1977; Burch 1975, 1980, 1998; and Giddings 1951). An abundant literature includes recent studies of kinship and social organization, supporting the generalization that the typical Iñupiaq household consists of those people who occupy a structure (or structures) and share some form of domestic function. *Domestic function*, the primary criterion for describing Iñupiaq households, includes shared activities with other relatives, often living in other dwellings, such as pooling income and food, as well as babysitting and other reciprocal behaviors. Domestic functions, such as providing clothing, shelter, food, child rearing, and labor, are associated with independent households in the dominant Western culture. In Iñupiaq culture, however, these functions are very frequently accomplished by the efforts of relatives living in two or more houses (Bodenhorn 2000; Jorgensen 1995; Wenzel 2000).

In brief, the concept of the household in Iñupiaq culture implies both coresidence and domestic function. The concept of the family implies kin relationships that may include coresidence and shared domestic functions.

The Iñupiaq social structure has always been based on the bilateral extended family, with kin on both sides being equally important. Recognizing kinship connections through at least three generations on both the maternal and paternal sides of the family provides an interwoven pattern of kinship linking family units together. Through economic partnerships, the Iñupiat may extend cooperative ties to nonkin as well.

Local Family and Domestic Units

In order to describe the dynamics of Iñupiaq households fully, it is necessary to build upon E. S. Burch's distinction between local family units and domestic family units. According to Burch, Iñupiaq society in nineteenth-century northwest Alaska was organized around the local family, which he defines as "a family whose members occupy different dwellings"(Burch 1975, 237, 241). Burch believed that the two most common types of households consisted of (1) aged parents with one or more adult children, adult children's spouses, and grandchildren, or (2) two or more adult siblings and their families of procreation (Burch 1975, 239). It was common for two or three households to make up the local family unit, which functioned as a single cohort. An important adaptive aspect of Iñupiaq social organization was how well their affiliation strategies matched subsistence strategies (Burch 1975, 250). The scattering of kin groups over a wide territory allowed for maximal harvesting of unpredictable wildlife resources.

Anthropologists who worked in the Iñupiaq region may have failed to appreciate the importance of the local family unit, both because they assumed the household as a unit of analysis and because the Iñupiat themselves had no specific term for a local family unit (Burch 1975, 240). While the *domestic family unit* is a set of family members who occupy a single dwelling or household, the *local family unit* is an aggregate of households who consider themselves related and who live nearby each other in adjacent dwellings. Burch's definition of the local family unit is similar to June Helm's notion of a "local band" (Helm 1965). Both domestic and local family units existed in traditional times, forming the basis of both settlements and societies (Helm 1965). Local family units are made up of several households choosing to live together because of kinship, economic, and subsistence ties. This setup made sense historically because "everyone in most villages used to belong to a single local family, which is the precise context in which generalized reciprocity did occur" (Burch 1998, 109).

A 1998 study on subsistence food production in Alaska showed that a distinguishing feature of Iñupiaq communities is that they are made up of local family units that cooperate in subsistence activities (Magdanz, Utermohle, and Wolf 2002). J. Magdanz, C. Utermohle, and R. Wolfe's study supports Burch's finding that multiple family units commonly cooperate in harvesting, processing, and redistributing subsistence resources.

The Social Transition in the North (STN) project was a major four-year study of Alaskan and Russian communities.[3] The STN project sought to identify significant domestic household trends over time with regard to composition and size, as well as cultural beliefs regarding relationship roles and family functioning. Data collected from this study indicate that Iñupiat household configurations are volatile. The project results showed short-term changes in the economic and social setting, marked by abrupt shifts in household organizations, indicating that Iñupiaq families were opportunistic, flexible, and creative in their responses to changes in the natural and social environment. The STN project defined domestic transition as changes in household and kinship organization that coincide with other changes (e.g., those affecting subsistence activities, education, employment, and adoption).

Drawing on previous studies, the present research also demonstrates that among the Iñupiaq, a single household seldom accomplishes household socio-economic functioning on its own. Instead, relatives and friends from two or more households frequently form social networks to maintain the socioeconomic welfare of several households. The social interdependence of Iñupiaq households is substantially different from that found among typical households in the United States. In contrast to non-Native households, Iñupiaq households depend on immediate and extended family members for day-to-day support in the form of food, labor, and income. In fact, it is common for two or more households to be linked through kinship and to recognize themselves as a single domestic unit because they prepare and eat food together, share equipment for subsistence activities, and look after children communally.

Another unique characteristic of Iñupiaq households is the fluidity of personnel between the natal and offspring households. Factors that directly influence the stability and dissolution of Iñupiaq households are subsistence activities, employment, education, and care of children and the elderly. Residence is so flexible that in many cases it is often difficult to determine precisely who usually lives in some households. Children go between their parents' household in one community and their grandparents' household in another.

There are also visits and returns from schools and employment sites. Yet, despite all this moving around, kinship bonds remain strong. Each child sees his or her family as an ever-widening circle of relations. Divorce and adoption increase, rather than decrease, the numbers of alliances.

METHODOLOGY

This project is part of the larger comparative study of complex households across the six ethnic groups included in this book, sponsored by the U.S. Census Bureau. For this study, two rural Iñupiaq communities in Alaska were selected, and a purposive household sample was drawn from each. For this project, 25 Iñupiaq Eskimo respondents were interviewed in English. With the exception of one person born in an urban area, all of the people interviewed were born in rural Alaska. Of the respondents, 56% were female. A little over a third (36%) were married, 36% were widowed, five (20%) were divorced, and two (8%) were single. To comply with Title 13, the names and locations of the communities cannot be revealed due to issues of confidentiality.[4] Both communities have small populations of less than 600 people and are only accessible by airplane, boat, snowmobile, or dog team.

I hired one local person in each community to identify and locate appropriate households for my study. This study focused on complex households (i.e., any household configuration that is not solely a nuclear family). During the interviews, I asked about links to other households in order to explore the social ties within and outside the communities.

The two communities were selected because they have a high percentage of Iñupiaq households and because they have a high proportion of complex households typical of Alaska Native communities. Another important reason was the fact that I had experience working in both communities. Both proved to be excellent places to explore extended family networks and interhousehold cooperation.

In April 2000, tribal organizations in the two communities granted permission to conduct research there. Respondents were selected based on their household configurations, and each was paid $35 for participating in this study. Fieldwork took place in May 2000, followed by brief telephone interviews in July 2000. In January 2002, I returned to the communities to conduct additional follow-up interviews and give public presentations on the preliminary study results.

Fieldwork

In May, when I conducted interviews, most people in the villages were engaged in harvesting and processing subsistence foods. Although spring and summer are the most pleasant time of the year to conduct fieldwork in rural Alaska, it is difficult to schedule formal interviews when people are absorbed in subsistence activities. As a fieldworker, it is important to adapt to the daily routines of Iñupiaq communities. For example, a typical day of interviewing during the Alaskan summer usually does not begin until early afternoon when people begin to wake up. It is not unusual to conduct an interview as late as 1 or 2 a.m. with the sun looming on the horizon. Generally, if I am able to talk someone into an interview, it has to be done while she or he is busy preparing dinner, fixing a four-wheeler, or cutting up meat or fish.

Conducting fieldwork in the middle of winter is altogether different from doing so in the summer. In January, it begins to get light at about 10:30 a.m. and is dark by around 3:30 p.m. People are up and around by 10 a.m. and are more than willing to socialize and be interviewed over a cup of coffee after the children have been driven to school by snow machine. The only steadfast rule to remember when socializing and interviewing in the winter is that everything in the villages comes to a standstill at 10:30 a.m. when *The Price Is Right* airs on television. Generally, it is better to avoid interviewing people during this time because they are reluctant to divide their attention between Bob Barker and interview protocols. Because people go to bed early in the winter, it is not appropriate to drop by for an interview after 8 p.m. Dinnertime is more firmly set in the winter and tends to be more formal than during the summer.

In midwinter, it is not uncommon for the temperatures to dip down to −30° to −45°, not including wind chill, as was the case when I was conducting interviews in January. When it gets this cold, most small airplanes are unable to fly and communities cannot receive mail, groceries, or supplies. Transportation around the village is by four-wheeler in the summer and snow machine in the winter.

Conducting fieldwork in Iñupiaq communities is comparable at times to camping. Although water and sewer service are beginning to appear in more rural communities, many communities still lack these facilities except for the Washeteria, the school, and the clinic. This being the case, it is important to arrive fully prepared to be self-sufficient. Even though plans may be made to stay at a designated place, a fieldworker never knows where, in fact, she will be staying until she arrives. It is best to come with a sleeping bag and to bring your own food—preferably freeze dried and instant, requiring only hot water and cooking utensils. Often the facilities provided are a floor in a tribal office, a coffee pot for making hot water, and a honey bucket (a toilet made from a five-gallon bucket) down the hall.

Usually a fieldworker can expect to be invited to a respondent's or friend's house for a dinner of duck soup or caribou stew. In anticipation of invitations, one should be prepared to share grocery items from Anchorage that are either too costly or unavailable from the local native store. I might bring turkey, pork chops, ribs, a five-pound can of Hills Brothers' Coffee, bacon, and cake mixes to share. Gifts such as books, stationery, and puzzles are especially welcome during long winter evenings.

STRATEGIES FOR SURVIVAL: SHARING NETWORKS

Why Do Iñupiaq People Live Where They Do?

It is often difficult for people who do not live in rural Alaska to understand why so many Iñupiaq people choose to live in remote villages where the employment rate is below 50% and the cost of living is twice as much as in Anchorage and three times the U.S. average. Nearly half (48%) of the respondents reported difficulty meeting their household expenses and acquiring store-bought food and clothing for the members of their households with their current income. Over half (60%) stated they have a hard time keeping their house warm during the winter months. Unlike most Americans, who participate in a mobile workforce where employment and standard of living generally determine where a family resides, Iñupiaq people's connections to their family, homeland, environment, and subsistence activities strongly influence where they live. Iñupiaq people's ties to place and kin are profound and enduring, despite the challenges that go with living in a community with an extremely low standard of living compared to mainstream America. Yet, in spite of these challenges, Iñupiaq people are clear about why they continue to live where they do.

Connection to place, family, and subsistence lifestyle were the three main reasons the respondents gave for living where they do. For example, one respondent said that she lives where she does because "This is where we were born and where we have our home. We live here because of the hunting." In most cases, villages are located at strategic hunting and fishing sites. One respondent stated that he lives where he does because it is easy for him and his family to get out into the country to go hunting, berry picking, and fishing. Another respondent (#305) stressed that his local foods tie him to his community. "I can't live without living here. When I go to other villages, I don't get to eat my own food. I must eat my Eskimo food!" People also choose to live where they do because, in many cases, they already have relatives—parents, siblings, children—living in the same community.

Complex Households and Social Nodes

An Iñupiaq household residing in one dwelling is rarely independent, either economically or in other ways. Many Iñupiaq households could not function economically without the assistance of other households. The average per capita annual income for this study's households was $8,537,[5] below poverty level. The mean household wage income was $23,429,[6] and the mean household net income was $24,710.

For example, respondent #319 spent approximately $36,000 last year on utilities; yet, this household's total income was several thousand dollars less than this. In order for this household to function, it receives resources from another household. In this case, the respondent's two adult sons living next door contribute money to this household from their part-time wages. In turn, the sons take it for granted that they will eat their meals at their father's household, as well as share his equipment, such as a snow machine or all-terrain vehicle. Another example of multiple households pooling their resources came from respondent #315. Since he has more than enough income to meet the basic needs of his household, he distributes money to family members in a nearby town. This household is well off because the two adult sons are employed full time, and the father works part time as a professional.

In a number of cases, adult women living in other communities send money and clothes back to their parents' household to help support their children. Often this money is given directly to the child for personal spending money. It can be said that Iñupiaq households are part of a larger broad economy that ties rural households to hub communities and urban centers.

The socioeconomic functioning of Iñupiaq households is seldom accomplished by a single wage earner or subsistence harvester. Instead, relatives and friends from two or more households frequently form social networks to maintain the socioeconomic welfare of several households. Grandparents provide child-rearing assistance to family members with children. Subsistence food and resources are shared between households. For example, respondent #306, a single mother living with her brother and children, relies on her grandfather (#312) to hunt for her family. In return, she prepares daily meals for her grandfather's household. Her brother delivers the hot meals to their grandfather on a four-wheeler.

The mechanisms of sharing and reciprocity remain deeply embedded in Iñupiaq culture. Regardless of the season, most sharing between households occurs within villages and involves the distribution of subsistence foods, short-term uses of equipment, and small services, such as child care.

Of the 25 study households, 72% relied on subsistence resources for more than half of their diet.[7] It is common for several households to cooperate in the harvesting, processing, and redistributing of subsistence resources.[8] In many cases subsistence activities involving multiple families are pursued outside of the village. Fully 76% reported that their household composition experienced short-term periodicity shifts over the past year due to subsistence activities, such as fishing, birding, caribou hunting, and berry picking. Despite modern conveniences, such as the Washeteria, many daily activities are still oriented toward a traditional subsistence lifestyle.

Sharing also takes place between households in different villages. For example, respondent #317 reported that he routinely mails subsistence foods, such as geese, smelt, ducks, caribou, and moose, to his sister in a nearby community and to his biological parents in another community (he also provides subsistence foods to his adoptive mother, respondent #321). Respondent #326 is also actively involved in distributing subsistence foods to relatives outside his community. For example, while I was interviewing this respondent, he was packaging caribou meat to take with him later that afternoon. When he arrived at his destination, the respondent intended to mail the box of caribou meat to his brother. These brothers have an agreement to exchange caribou for *muktuk* (bowhead whale blubber).

Cultural Perception of Households

Contemporary Iñupiaq people's perception of household is consistent with Burch's notion of "local families," family members who occupy different dwellings but operate in terms of a single overriding family organization. Of the 25 respondents, 50% perceived the term *household* primarily in terms of kinship and the majority of these included intergenerational and collateral relationships as part of their definition of household. According to respondent #306, for example, "A household can be any group of parents and children, aunts, uncles, or brothers, or sisters." Respondent #303 replied, "To me a household is my son, myself, my family, my daughters, and grandchildren." Interestingly, another 33% of the respondents defined household in terms that roughly corresponded with the census definition of household, which defines the word in terms of coresidence in one structure.[9] Examples of respondents' definitions for household relating to residence and structure are "Those people who I live with" (#324), "It is my own house with my own boys" (#326), and "A household includes everyone who is living in my household" (#313). The remaining 17% defined household strictly in terms of domestic function.

Iñupiaq families' perception of household membership is based less on residency issues than on the fact that the person is related in some way to others in the household, either by blood, marriage, or adoption. A person who is considered a household member may live in another dwelling or in another community. For the Iñupiat in this study, an important criterion for determining household membership is whether or not the person maintains a physical presence in the household by leaving personal belongings or even children there. Household members residing in nearby dwellings or in neighboring communities remain close to the other members of the household through visits, meals, and phone calls, as well as by contributing subsistence foods and money to the natal household. Members come together during times of need to help raise children or care for elderly family members.

The Iñupiat concept of household membership contrasts with the census definition of household. For example, in one instance, a respondent included his sons living next door in a separate structure as household members. Iñupiaq children are commonly considered part of more than one household. In another case, it was unclear whether in household #315, the grandson of the respondent, Fred,[10] was a part of Fred's household. The grandson, Jimmy, was not living in this household when his grandfather, Fred, was enumerated sometime around March 2000.[11] Rather, Jimmy was living in his mother's household in the same community. According to Fred, Jimmy's mother counted Jimmy as part of her household in Census 2000. When Jimmy is living with his mother, Fred considers his grandson to be part of his mother's household, and when Jimmy is living with Fred, he considers his grandson to be part of his household. Jimmy began living with Fred when he was an infant while his mother attended school in another community. For the next ten years, Jimmy lived with Fred while his mother went to school, got married, and went to live in a larger hub community. Two years ago, Jimmy's mother moved to a nearby village, and Jimmy left Fred's household to move into his mother's household. After two days of Jimmy's living with his mother, Fred took Jimmy back to live with him because "he was sick with sorrow," missing his grandson so much. For the past two years, Jimmy has primarily lived with Fred but also lives with his mother for short periods. This is an example of a person with more than one residence, who is at risk of either being counted in more than one household or of being missed altogether in the census. The migration pattern of the mother is typical of many women who leave their home community for work and education, get married, settle down, and then return after the relationship or marriage ends.

Another example of unclear household residence is respondent #320's household, consisting of Sally and her two grandsons, Daniel, who is the son of Sally's daughter, Angela, and Robert, another grandson of Sally's. In addition to the three full-time members of this household, it appears that Angela and three other children of Angela's, Patty, Billy, and Sam, are fluid members of Sally's household. Currently, Angela lives with these three other children in a larger hub community where she is employed. According to Sally, Angela will rent an apartment there for as long as her job lasts. When Angela lives there, Daniel leaves his grandmother's household about once a month to visit her.

Between March and May 2000, people moved temporarily or permanently from one household to another in 14, or 56%, of the complex Iñupiaq households in this study. Eleven (44%) of the households retained the same residents between March and May 2000. But between May 2000 and January 2002, fully 18 out of 25 (72%) households in the original study experienced personnel changes. In most cases, the people moving into complex households were children moving between their parents' and grandparents' households, frequently in order to attend school. It is not uncommon for children to go to another village to attend school when problems arise related to school in their home communities.

Adoption was common in traditional Iñupiaq society and continues to be widespread today. In part, this is because the Iñupiat treasure children. It is not unusual for a woman to give away her biological child to a woman or couple who are unable to have children.[12] Adoption is very fluid; typically, adopted children grow up knowing both their biological parents and their adopted parents.

An astounding 60% of my complex household respondents reported coresident informally or formally adopted children. Of these, 40% were grandparents adopting grandchildren, which fits traditional norms. In Iñupiaq culture, it has long been common for grandparents to adopt the first child of a coresident adult child (Burch 1975, 130) and keep that child when its parents move.

Equally remarkable—and different from the norms of the white majority—in 17 of 25 (68%) of the complex households in my study, the grandparents were raising their grandchildren, and the middle generation was missing (i.e., these are skip-generation households). As the previous examples illustrate, in these households the female offspring have typically left the community for employment, education, or personal reasons, while their children remain in the grandparents' households. Although grown women leave the household, they maintain strong household ties through sending money to the household to help support subsistence activities and their children, as well as by making periodic visits.

Complex Iñupiaq Eskimo households are part of an interdependent social network that includes family and friends living in other households. Often, as noted, children go back and forth between parents' and grandparents' households. Although there is a great deal of fluidity of personnel moving in and out of complex households, in both communities complex households serve as a stable foundation for noncomplex households. A householder in this study rarely changes residence unless he or she moves into new housing or leaves to help a family member in another household.

Grandparents provide child-rearing assistance to family members with children. As noted, food and resources are shared among households. For example, Dennis lives with his grandson. He babysits and fixes breakfast for his daughter's young children on weekdays, while she works and watches the older grandchildren after school for two hours. On weekends they often stay overnight and watch videos.

In contemporary Alaska, the mechanism of sharing remains deeply embedded in the native's economic system. Although this leads to a great deal of fluidity in complex Iñupiaq households, as noted, the householder remains quite stable: no whole household moves were reported from March to May 2000. When respondents were asked if they had plans to move from their households, only a few of them replied that they were considering a move. These respondents would consider moving into a newer house if more housing were available. Respondent #309 said she would like to move from the community where she is living, either to live in the now-abandoned place where she grew up or to find an apartment in a larger community where she would live with her granddaughter. However, in order for her and her granddaughter to leave, two of her three adult sons now living with her would have to find full-time work outside their community so they could support themselves. Currently, this household relies on the respondent's daughter for support: when the respondent's daughter and her husband have extra money from working a part-time seasonal job, they contribute store bought food and supplies to this household. In exchange, the respondent is raising the first child of her daughter and her daughter's husband.

SOCIAL ORGANIZATION

Householders

The majority (56%) of the 25 householders in my sample of complex households are women. Of the householders, 52 (52%) are older, between 62 and 80. Of the remaining households, 28% were 48 to 61 years old, and the remaining 20% were 27 to 47. There are several reasons why complex households in this study tend to have older householders. One is that elders generally fit the Alaska Housing Authority's[13] low-income criteria for housing needs and, therefore, may be disproportionately represented as householders in complex households. Another factor is that elderly Iñupiats' lives tend to be more stable than their younger cohorts. Elders are also held in high regard and revered.

The respondents' education levels varied from those who had not finished grade school to those who had attended college or technical school. About one-fourth (24%) of the respondents had completed high school, 12% had not finished grade school, and 12% had completed some vocational training or college. The low proportion of high school graduates is related to the high number of older respondents. Prior to Alaska statehood in 1959, Western education was not a priority for Alaska Natives. Instead, the Iñupiats' educational goal was promoting traditional education, passing on the traditional knowledge and wisdom of a subsistence lifestyle to the next generation. Shortly after statehood, regional and boarding schools were opened for Alaska Native students; more children could attend school.

Household Organization and Division of Labor

Generally, Iñupiaq sex roles and division of labor are not rigidly defined. If a husband is disabled, the sons or wife will become the family's hunters. An unmarried woman with children will often hunt to feed her family or rely on a brother or relative to provide for them. A husband takes on the responsibility of cooking and child care when his wife leaves temporarily to care for an elderly relative elsewhere.

In most of the households in this study, the overall responsibility for household functioning rests with the grandparents. Traditionally, elders were highly esteemed in Iñupiaq culture and continue to be respected today. Elderly men and women provide leadership and guidance to their families and community. Although many of the complex householders are advancing in age, elders maintain considerable physical activity around their homes, as well as assist other households with tasks like cooking and cleaning, babysitting, paying bills, hunting, fishing, camping, and picking berries and greens.

Following the birth of a child, it is not uncommon for a single mother or young couple to reside with the parents or grandparents of the young woman or man. This arrangement was present in four households. This setup helps ease the economic and child-care responsibilities of the single woman or couple, while assisting them in learning the proper skills for raising a family.

Subsistence Activities   As children get older, they take on more responsibility by observing and participating in subsistence activities. Boys accompany the men when hunting and fishing, and girls are expected to assist with berry picking and food processing. As children get older, they make greater contributions to the family's subsistence harvest. When family and friends travel up the river or coast to subsistence camps, grandparents and parents instruct children on harvesting and processing subsistence foods.

Household Activities   Generally, girls' main household duties include taking care of younger siblings, cleaning the house, washing dishes, and mopping and sweeping the floor. Boys are responsible for helping to hunt and for outside activities. When children grow older and become parents and grandparents themselves, they will be looked after by their children, grandchildren, nieces, and nephews.

Women's household tasks include tending children, washing dishes and clothes, cleaning, cooking, getting water, and processing subsistence foods. Women are also involved in fishing and berry picking. Men assist in some household tasks when need be, but they are primarily responsible for hunting and fishing.[14] Men also work outside building drying racks for meat and fish, making windbreaks for butchering meat, and fixing equipment.

Historically, the household division of labor for economic tasks was sharply determined by gender. Women handled food preparation and storage, mended and sewed clothing, kept the oil lamp burning, and fetched wood. The husband hunted, fished, made tools, and "loafed" (Burch 1975, 85; Spencer 1959, 183). Men spent most of the rest of their day at the men's house (*qazgi*), a kind of community social center for the males of the family. Wives usually cooked one hot meal a day (R. Spencer [1959, 375] says two) and brought it to husbands or other relatives at night; the men would return to the household to sleep (Burch 1975, 85; Spencer 1959, 55, 187). Today, for both men and women, the household division of labor is balanced between a subsistence and cash economy and is far more flexible than it was in the past.

Household Types and Case Studies

Skip-Generation Households   An overwhelming number of households in the study (17) were classified as skip-generation households. This household type is significant because the middle generation is missing. Household #321 is an example of this household type. Daisy is in her early eighties and extremely active and fit for her age. She is the matriarch of a very large extended family. Daisy's household draws a steady stream of friends and family throughout the day to visit, help cut up meat, or prepare a meal.

In May 2000, Daisy's household included the following people: two biological granddaughters, Martha and Sarah (both of whom had been adopted as daughters); Martha's husband, Bill; a biological grandson, John; and a friend's child, Loren. By January 2002, household personnel changes included John moving out to live with his mother in another community and the birth of Martha and Bill's son, Bill Jr.

Martha and Bill assist Daisy in maintaining her household. Although Daisy is active for her age, she does need assistance taking care of her younger adopted grandchildren and preparing meals. During the day, Martha works locally, while her husband stays home and looks after Daisy and the children. Bill sometimes works as a temporary worker. Daisy's main responsibility in this household is to oversee the processing of meat and fish. Martha and her sister,

Sarah, share cooking and household responsibilities. Daisy's nonresident sons and sons-in-law provide the household with large amounts of unprocessed meat and fish. Daisy processes the meat and fish for her own household use and redistributes some processed food to other households. According to Daisy, what keeps her young is her strong work ethic. "I like to work everyday when I am not sick. I enjoy cutting up meat, and when I don't have anything to do, I like to sew *mukluks* and parkas."

Daisy has lived in her house for almost 50 years. Her three-bedroom house is without telephone, water, or sewer. In general, Daisy is satisfied with the condition of her house, except that her floors get cold, and it is drafty. Compared with other households in the community, this household could be considered average because two members contribute a steady year-round income to the household (Martha with her job and Daisy with her Social Security). Other than shared subsistence foods, this household relies on little outside support. The household provides processed foods, meals, and child care to children and extended family members living in other households.

Household #303 is another example of this skip-generation household type. Dennis is a 60-year-old man who traveled widely while in the military and lived in places around the United States before returning home. Occasionally, he is involved in local politics, but he devotes most of his time to caring for his grandchildren.

In May 2000, Dennis considered his household to include himself, his adopted son, Dennis Jr. (his biological grandson), and his oldest son, Harry. When Harry is not working out of town, he alternates between staying at his father's house and his girlfriend's house in another community. Dennis considers Harry a member of his household because Harry keeps some belongings in Dennis's house, and Dennis expects him to continue returning to his household for visits and family hunts.

Dennis babysits for his daughter Anna's four kids during the week, when his daughter and his son-in-law are working. The grandchildren eat snacks and lunches at Dennis's house five days a week, and often they eat dinner and sleep over at his house.

By August 2000, household personnel changes included Dennis's adopted son, Dennis Jr., leaving the household to attend boarding school outside the region. Dennis Jr. remained in school for three months, then returned home for the holidays and never returned to boarding school because he was homesick for his friends from home. According to Dennis Sr., if other children from this community attended the same school, his son might consider attending again.

Dennis Sr. feels he contributes to his household by making himself available to his children when they need help. According to Dennis,

> My daughter can rely on me to look after her kids. When my other daughter
> needs me, I drop everything. I moved in with my second daughter to help her
> out after her husband passed away. I helped her get back on her feet.

Generally, Dennis does his own hunting, but when he is unable to hunt due
to his health, his half-brothers and friends provide meat and fish to his household. The Tribal Elders program also provides this household with subsistence
foods. This program pays hunters for fuel, time, and ammunition; in return,
the hunters provide elders and needy families with subsistence foods. Dennis
often shares subsistence foods with his aunt in a nearby community. Because
he receives an income from the regional health corporation for taking care of
his grandchildren, he feels he has enough income to meet his basic needs. If he
did not receive subsistence foods, it would be more of a struggle to maintain
his household.

Although Dennis was offered a new house by the Alaska Housing
Authority, he thinks he will remain in his current house because he likes it and
considers it his home. His house was built in the 1970s and has more than one
bedroom and running water. Since Dennis replaced his old heating system, it
is much easier for him to keep his house warm. Because his old stove did not
heat his entire house, Dennis had to sleep in the living room and shut off his
bedrooms during the winter. Although the new system is more efficient, it
does use more electricity. As a result, Dennis's electricity bills are substantially
higher than they were with the old system. Ideally, Dennis would like to live
with his immediate family: his biological son, Harry; his adopted son, Dennis
Jr.; and his adult daughters and other grandchildren.

An example of a fluid household that slips into or out of a skip-generation
pattern is household #314. Les is 60 years old and a well-respected hunter. Les
and his wife, Ally, enjoy living in a household with lots of children. According
to Les, an ideal household "is living with a husband and a wife with grandkids
and children. Before we got our foster children, it was too quiet around here,
so we had to get some more kids."

In May 2000, Les's three-bedroom house domiciled eight people: Les; his
wife, Ally; one son, Kevin; two daughters, Clarissa and Elizabeth; one adopted
daughter, Sena; and foster children, Lee and Justin. In September 2001, Clarissa
moved out of this household to live with her boyfriend, who works in transportation in another community. Clarissa continues to maintain close physical
ties to the household by coming home to visit every two weeks. Although she
lives in another community, Les still considers her part of this household until
she gets married. During the past year, Les's other daughter, Elizabeth, and her
two children moved into his household, while Elizabeth's husband is working
elsewhere. When Elizabeth's husband returns, she plans to move with her children to another part of the country to live with her husband. Les's adult son,

Kevin, recently cleaned up a small building next door and is staying there but continues to eat all of his meals and watch television in Les's household.

Les has completed elementary school and works part-time out of his home. Ally works in a school. Kevin works as a laborer and also helps his father. According to Ally, when everyone in the household works, there is enough money to meet the basic needs of the household. Ally considers their household to be average in terms of its physical and economic condition. Ally and Les consider it "easy" to keep their home warm on cold days because they save money by cooking mostly subsistence foods in the winter. According to Ally, "Our first priority is to have money for fuel oil and supplies to pursue subsistence activities." Supplies include gas, boats, good boots, nets, and camping supplies. All of the adults and children who make up this local family, regardless of where they live, give their Alaska Permanent Dividend checks[15] to Les so that he can pool the family's money to buy the necessary equipment needed for subsistence activities. This equipment includes snow machines, sleds, boats, all-terrain vehicles, guns, fuel, and ammunition.

Les and Ally consider Kevin to be a member of their household, despite the fact that he sleeps in another building. Although his bedroom is detached from Les's household, in every other way, this son is a member of their household. Kevin spends the morning helping his father, eats all of his meals in his parents' house, and spends most of his free time there.

Three-Generation Households   Four households (16%) proved to be three-generation households. This household type is made up of a divorced or widowed grandparent and includes both a biological child and grandchild.

An example of a three-generation household is #310. In May 2000, Larisa's household included herself, her ex-husband, Jerry, their son, Donald, and Larisa and Jerry's grandson, George. Larisa is a woman in her sixties with a severe disability. When Larisa became too disabled to live by herself safely, her ex-husband moved from a nearby community to live with her so that he could help with her household. By January 2002, significant changes occurred in this household. Jerry was no longer able to care for Larisa because he became ill; so, Larisa and Jerry's grandson, Tom, moved in. Together, the two grandsons, Tom and George, as well as the son, Donald, looked after Larisa and Jerry. Tom's adoptive father, Andrew, still considers Tom to be a member of his household, and in fact, Tom goes back and forth between Larisa's household and Andrew's household. After Jerry passed away, several family members living in other communities came to live with Larisa for several months.

Larisa's daughters live in nearby households with their immediate families and use Larisa's four-wheeler and snow machine to do Larisa's errands, as well as their own. The daughters contribute berries and fish to this household, and two local hunters regularly provide this household with ducks and geese. When Jerry was alive, he provided his daughter with fish, *ugruk* (bearded seal), and caribou. Larisa prefers to have her family around her but also accepts that her children must leave because of the lack of jobs:

> Here it seems like my kids live in my house all the time until they start working and then they get their own place to live. I never tell them to leave. They just do it and then they start having kids and that is it. All my kids move out and have their own house. Well, see, three of my daughters have kids but they are not married. I just keep hoping they will have more jobs in here so my kids can stay nearby.

Single-Adult-and-Child-with-Other Households   Four households (16%) fell into the category of single adult and child with other (e.g., a divorced or never-married parent with children and a sibling). Household #306 is one example of this type. In May 2000, Sherry's household included her younger, single brother, James; her two daughters, Rachel and Janet; and her son, Gerald. Sherry is in her early thirties, divorced, and fairly well educated. Sherry's other brother, Mike, had lived in this household for several years prior to March 2002 but left to find work in another community. By January 2002, Sherry had moved her family to a larger community where she is employed in a helping profession. Sherry's job takes her away from her community quite frequently. Generally, she is away from her household one to two weeks per month, during which time, her brother, James, is responsible for taking care of her children.

Before Sherry moved her household, relatives came by her house for meals about once or twice a week. Sherry's grandfather, Emil, provided the household with a substantial amount of subsistence foods. After Emil hunted, Sherry processed the meat with her friend Polly. Generally, Polly and Sherry split the processed meat between the two of them. In exchange for Emil's hunting, Sherry prepared daily meals for her grandfather, which James delivered.

One financial strategy Sherry has adopted is to discontinue receiving water or sewer in the winter. To save money, she relies on her brother to haul ice from a nearby river. Although Sherry finds it difficult to meet her household's basic needs, she considers her household to be about average for her community. Her house was built in the 1970s; during the winter, it is very drafty, especially when the wind is blowing.

POLICY IMPLICATIONS FOR THE GENERAL SOCIAL SCIENCES AND RESEARCHERS

Considering that the Iñupiat rely on extended kinship-based networks of households, one might expect researchers to analyze employment, income, harvest, and other data from the perspective of such multihousehold networks. However, data collection efforts have rarely, if ever, taken a multihousehold approach. For example, data–gathering instruments, such as census forms, are designed for the more typical, independent, nuclear households of mainstream America. Throughout the nation, census data are collected and analyzed on an individual or household basis. But when Iñupiaq households are categorized as if they were conventional American households, the data collected are inaccurate and incomplete, for this approach does not account for the Iñupiats' special understanding of household, family, and domestic function. Since standard surveys fail to account for interhousehold relationships, some of the most unique and critical aspects of rural Alaska's domestic economy—rich and complex economic relationships among cooperating households—are not accounted for and are ignored. Suggestions for future research include developing effective methods for identifying and describing multihousehold networks.

This study indicates that the majority of households in two Iñupiaq Eskimo communities share some domestic functions with people living in other residences. The social interdependence of Iñupiaq households differs substantially from the typical relationships among most U.S. nuclear households.

Exploring and making more visible the ethnic diversity of America's families provides a better understanding of current ethnic household trends in the United States. One cannot assume that all people live the same way, and through an ethnographic study of ethnic households, one can gain a perspective to better understand the various cultural contexts of household formation. The extended family remains important among some cultures, such as the Iñupiat, both as a living arrangement and as a support group. It may contain several generations, or siblings and their partners and even parents. It is important for the Census Bureau to take into account the range of cultural variation in households, even if some patterns are not widespread within the United States today.

NOTES

1. *Iñupiat* means "the people" in the Iñupiaq language. The Iñupiat are the Inuit Eskimo-speaking people of the northern region of Alaska, and a small part extend to northwestern Canada. *Iñupiaq* means "Eskimo person" (singular), while *Iñupiat* is plural, meaning "Eskimos." Iñupiaq is also the language spoken by the Iñupiat. In Alaska, the Iñupiat are categorized into four main groups: Bering Strait people, Kotzebue Sound people, North Alaska Coast people, and Interior North Alaska people. Alaskan Eskimo languages include Iñupiaq, Central Yup'ik, and Siberian Yup'ik. Thirty or more years ago, the word "Eskimo" was regularly utilized to describe Arctic peoples of the entire circumpolar north.

Today, the more common usage in Canada and Greenland is "Inuit." However, in Alaska, "Eskimo" is still actively used to distinguish Iñupiat and Yup'ik populations from other Native groups, such as Aleuts, Athabaskans, and Tlingits.

2. In 1931, the Bureau of Indian Affairs (BIA) sent the most intellectually advanced Alaska Native youths to boarding schools for vocational education; one aim of the federal policy was to assist Alaska Native youth in assimilation and acculturation. By 1947, the BIA opened Mt. Edgecumbe boarding high school in Sitka, Alaska, for Natives from across Alaska and sent some youth to BIA boarding schools outside Alaska.

3. In 1993, (now deceased) Steven McNabb, Bill Richards, and Alexander Pika won a National Science Foundation grant to study northwest Alaska, the Aleutian Islands, and two Russian-region communities.

4. This study was funded by the U.S. Census Bureau under Title 13 of the United States Code governing confidentiality.

5. In 1998, the average per capita income for Anchorage, Alaska, was $32,659.

6. This includes Alaska Permanent Fund dividends, Social Security, supplemental income, Northwest Alaska Native Association dividends, pensions, food stamps, longevity bonuses, energy assistance, and unemployment.

7. According to the Alaska Department of Fish and Game, the per capita replacement costs of subsistence foods in one of the sample communities is $3,360 per person.

8. Sea mammals, moose, caribou, duck, fish, and other wild foods continue to provide substantial portions of the Iñupiaq diet. Traditionally, fluidity of movement in and out of extended households was based on labor needs for a subsistence lifestyle. Iñupiaq subsistence activities follow a seasonal round. During the winter, men make daily trips to hunt birds and caribou and to go ice fishing. Between June and August, families gather and process foods together over extended periods, from a few days to a month. They may camp alone or with other families for spring hunting and whaling, summer fishing, and fall berry picking.

9. It is important to note, however, that the respondents were vague about how they defined "living with."

10. All names used in the household vignettes are pseudonyms.

11. We set March 1 as the date to represent Census Day in these communities to be close in time with the April 1 Census Day in all of the other ethnographic studies. Actual enumeration in these communities may have been conducted either before or after March 1, 2000.

12. I did not determine whether the adoptions were legal or informal. Usually, adoption of a grandchild by a grandparent is informal and is legalized only if the parent is in jeopardy of losing the child to the state.

13. Northwest Iñupiaq Housing Authority is a regional subsidiary to the Association of Alaska Housing Authority.

14. Hauling water in the winter months includes traveling a few miles to cut blocks of ice from rivers and bring it back to melt in the house as a way to save money on the cost water. When the temperature dips to −40°, many people rely on wood stoves to supplement their heat stoves. In these treeless areas, gathering wood entails lengthy travel by snow machine to collect driftwood on the beach.

15. The 1980 Alaska legislature created the Permanent Fund Dividend Program to distribute some of the annual fund income to eligible Alaskans. Eligible adults and children got $1,963.86 in 2000.

REFERENCES

Anderson, D., W. Anderson, R. Bane, R. K. Nelson, and N. T. Sheldon. 1977. *Kuuvanmiut subsistence: traditional Eskimo life in the latter twentieth century.* Kotzebue, AK: U.S. Department of the Interior.

Bodenhorn, B. 2000. "He used to be related to me: exploring the bases of relatedness among Iñupiat of northern Alaska." In *Cultures of relatedness: new approaches to the study of kinship,* ed. J. Carsten, 128–48. New York: Cambridge University Press.

Burch, E. S. 1975. *Eskimo kinsmen: changing family relationships in northwest Alaska.* American Ethnological Society Monograph 59. Seattle: University of Washington Press.

———. 1980. "Traditional Eskimo Societies in Northwest Alaska." In *Alaska native culture and history,* eds. Y. Kotani and W. Workman, 253–304. Senri Ethnological Series. Osaka, Japan: National Museum of Ethnology.

———. 1998. *Iñupiaq Eskimo nations of northwest Alaska.* Fairbanks: University of Alaska Press.

Burch, E. S., and T. C. Correll. 1972. "Alliance and conflict: inter-relations in North Alaska." In *Proceedings of the American Ethnological Society* (Supplement), 17–39. Seattle: University of Washington Press.

Fogel-Chance, N. 1993. "Living in both worlds: Iñupiaq woman and urban life." *Arctic Anthropology* 30 (1): 94–108.

Giddings, L. 1951. *The Kobuk River people.* Studies of Northern Peoples 1. College, AK: University of Alaska.

Hamilton, L. C., and C. L. Seyfrit. 1994. "Coming out of the country: community size and gender balance among Alaska Natives." *Arctic Anthropology* 31 (1): 16–25.

Helm, J. 1965. "Bilaterality in the socio-territorial organization of the Arctic drainage dene." *Ethnology* 4 (4): 361–85.

Jorgensen, J. G. 1995. "Ethnicity, not culture? obfuscating social science in the Exxon Valdez oil spill case." *American Indian Culture and Research Journal* 9 (4): 1–124.

Langdon, S. 1988. *The native people of Alaska.* Anchorage, AK: Greatland Graphics.

Kleinfeld, J. 1981. "Different paths of Iñupiat men and women in the wage economy: the North Slope experience." In *Alaska Review of Social and Economic Conditions* 18: 1.

Magdanz J., C. Utermohle, and R. Wolfe. 2002. "The organization of subsistence food production in two Iñupiaq communities, Wales and Deering, Alaska." Technical Paper #259. Nome: Alaska Department of Fish and Game.

Spencer, R. 1959. "North Alaskan Eskimo: a study in ecology and society." Bureau of American Ethnology Bulletin 171. Washington, DC: Smithsonian Institution.

Wenzel, G. 2000. "Sharing, money, and modern Inuit subsistence: obligation and reciprocity at Clyde River, Nunavut." In *The social economy of sharing: resource allocation and modern hunter-gatherers,* eds. G. Wenzel, G. Hovelsrun-Broda, and N. Kishigami, 61–85, Senri Ethnological Studies 53. Osaka, Japan: National Museum of Ethnology.

• 5 •

The Recent Arrivals: Latinos and Koreans

Rae Lesser Blumberg and Laurel Schwede

ASIANS AND LATINOS IN THE NATION

$\mathcal{W}$hen the Statue of Liberty first raised her torch in 1886, most of the immigrants she welcomed were European whites. Even as recently as 1970, as Anna Chan notes in chapter 1, 90% of the foreign born in the country hailed from Europe. But migration streams have changed dramatically since then, and by 2000, three-fourths of our immigrants were Hispanic and Asian. According to Census 2000 data, of the foreign born in this country, 52% were from Latin America and 26% were from Asia; 11.1% of the total population was foreign born (Malone et al. 2003).

The rapid rise in the proportion of Latino and Asian immigrants helped fuel the very fast growth in the numbers of all Latinos and Asians in this country. Between the censuses in 1990 and 2000, the Latino population increased by a whopping 58% (Guzman 2001). Asians also registered dramatic gains: between 48% (counting Asians alone) and 72% (counting Asians both alone and in combination with other races) (Barnes and Bennett 2002).[1] Since Census 2000, the Latino and Asian populations have continued to soar, according to the most recent annual estimates, based on Census 2000 data (U.S. Census Bureau 2005). From April 1, 2000, to July 1, 2004, the Latino population grew an estimated 17%, to just under 41.3 million, catapulting Latinos past African Americans to become the largest U.S. minority group. This is almost four times faster than the 4.3% growth rate of the total U.S. population. Over this period, the estimated Asian population growth rate was almost as fast (16.2%), rising to just under 14 million people.

Who are the Latinos and Asians, and where do they live? A Hispanic (or Latino) is "a person of Cuban, Mexican, Puerto Rican, South or Central

116

American, or other Spanish culture or origin, regardless of race" (U.S. Office of Management and Budget 1997, 17). More than three-quarters of all Latinos reside in the West or South, many in California and Texas. Of those identifying their origin, Mexicans were the most numerous, followed by Puerto Ricans, Central Americans, South Americans, Cubans, and Dominicans. Most Mexicans lived in the West, most Puerto Ricans in the Northeast, and most Cubans in the South (Guzman 2001).

An Asian is "a person having origins in any of the original peoples of the Far East, Southeast Asia or the Indian subcontinent" (U.S. Office of Management and Budget 1997, 17). Asians are concentrated by region: almost half live in the West. They are also concentrated by state: over half live in only three states, California, New York, and Hawaii, and another quarter live in just seven other states. Asians tend to be in coastal or urban counties, with smaller concentrations through the country (Barnes and Bennett 2002, figure 3).[2]

Household and Family Types at the National Level

In addition to having higher growth rates than the overall U.S. population and different residential patterns across the country, Latino and Asian households also differ noticeably in their living arrangements. In comparison with households in the total population, Latino and Asian households are

- Larger, containing 3.62 people per household for Latinos and 3.09 for Asians, compared to 2.59 overall[3]
- More likely (especially Latino households) to be composed of families[4] that also are larger[5]
- Much more likely to include children under age 18[6]
- Much less likely to be nonfamily households consisting of individuals living alone.[7]

Minimum Proportion of Complex Households at the National Level

As discussed in chapter 2, we can use Census 2000 website data tables to find just one type of complex household, those with one or more nonrelatives. This allows us to (1) establish the minimum proportion of complex households at the national and local levels for each of our ethnic groups, and (2) compare these with the minimum proportion of households in the overall populations. Table 5.1 shows that Latino households are much more likely than all households at the national level to be complex because they include one or more nonrelatives (17.9% to 10.6%). Like American Indian and Alaska Native households, complex Latino households with nonrelatives are more often fam-

Table 5.1   Minimum Proportion of Complex Households for Hispanics (Latinos), Asians, and the Overall Population at the National Level (Family and Nonfamily Households with Any Nonrelatives)

National Population Groups	Percentage of Households with Nonrelatives in Family Households[1]	Percentage of Households with Nonrelatives in Nonfamily Households[2]	Minimum Proportion of Complex Households (Households with Any Nonrelatives)[3]
Overall U.S. population	4.5	6.1	**10.6**
Hispanic (Latino) population	11.9	6.0	**17.9**
Asian population	5.0	7.2	**12.2**

1. Calculated by subtracting percentage of nonfamily households with nonrelatives from all households with nonrelatives (PCT 16 − PCT 9).
2. Calculated from Census 2000 SF-2, PCT 9 data.
3. Calculated from Census 2000 SF-2, PCT 16 data.

ily than nonfamily households (11.9% to 6.0%), in distinct contrast to all U.S. households with nonrelatives (4.5% to 6.1%).

On the one hand, Asians (like Latinos) at the national level have a greater proportion of households that include nonrelatives than all households (12.2% to 10.6%). On the other hand, Asians are like all households (and unlike our Latino and Native American households) in having fewer households with nonrelatives fall into the "family" category: Asians (5.0% family and 7.2% non-family) and all U.S. households (4.5% to 6.1%). In summary, we can say that the minimum proportions of complex households at the national level for Latinos (17.9%) and Asians (12.2%) are higher than the minimum for the overall population (10.6%).[8] Latino households with nonrelatives are more likely to be the family type, whereas Asian households with nonrelatives are more likely to be the nonfamily type.

Indirect Clues to Complex Households with Nonnuclear Relatives at the National Level

Unfortunately, for the purposes of our book (as explained earlier), Census 2000 data tables on the website do not provide counts of households that we would consider to be complex because they contain nonnuclear family members, such as grandparents, nephews, and sisters–in–law. But, as also noted, we can get some indirect clues about complex households from the person–level data and analysis of T. Lugaila and J. Overturf (2004) that focus on one special case: children who are related to their householders but are not their biological, step, or adopted children; instead, they are grandchildren or more distant relatives.

Since these data unambiguously show there to be at least one nonnuclear relationship in the household, we can classify it as a complex household. Note that these are relationships of children to the householder (Person 1 on the census form). The children's parent(s) may or may not also live there: these statistics do not tell us that. Also, note the converse: some households with own children of the householder may also have grandparents or other nonnuclear family kin.

This study shows strong ethnic differences. First, Latino children are much more likely to be living with householders who are other than their "own" (biological, step, or adoptive) parents. Although Latino children made up 17% of all children under 18 in Census 2000, they are a disproportionate 21% of all grandchildren of householders and 38% of "other relatives." Second, children marked as Asian alone made up 3.4% of all children and were less likely to be grandchildren (2.4%) but much more likely (4.8%) to be "other relatives" (e.g., brother, niece, cousin, sibling-in-law, or great-grandchild).

In short, these person–level data show that Latino and Asian children are disproportionately more likely than all children to be living with a householder who is not their "own" parent. Even though we cannot directly compare person-level and household-level data (as explained in chapter 2), these are clues that there might be disproportionately more Latino and Asian households that are complex because they include people other than, or in addition to, nuclear family members.

THE KOREANS AND THE LATINOS

This section of the book presents ethnographies of both Koreans and Latinos who do live in complex households (that's how the purposive samples were selected). We chose Koreans to represent Asians in our study, in part because they are one of the fastest growing Asian groups. Their numbers grew 15–fold from about 70,000 in 1970 (U.S. Department of Commerce 1981) to 1,076,872 in 2000 (U.S. Census Bureau 2001), making them the fifth largest Asian American group. Although Korea's economy boomed in these decades, large numbers of Koreans came to the United States to pursue the American Dream. Many of these people established an ethnic enclave in the crowded tenements of Queens, New York. Their lives have not always been easy. Some immigrants found the cost of living very high and formed complex households to make ends meet as they tried to get established. Tai Kang vividly describes how people in some households lived in such cramped quarters that they shared bedrooms and even mattresses squeezed into tiny living rooms (with different people using the same mattress at different hours).

For our Latino case study, we chose Hispanic immigrants to central Virginia. This is a new pole of migration for Hispanics. So far, it has been a veritable promised land, where jobs are easy to get, crime is low, and the nearest office of *la migra* (immigration officials) is far away. Latino immigrants hail primarily from Mexico, with others from Central and South America and the Caribbean, all places with economies far less vibrant than Korea's. Spurred by hopes of economic betterment, Latino arrivals are growing by leaps and bounds. Now, they are spreading to new areas of the United States. As Patricia Goerman (2004) writes, Hispanics once clustered in three to six states and a few cities, but after the mid-1980s, they began moving to many other parts of the country, especially the Southeast. Her chapter paints a compelling portrait of recent arrivals to central Virginia who put up with living in complex households (not their preferred arrangement) because it helps them to get ahead while still sending money home.

To set the context for this section's Korean and Latino ethnographic studies, let's once again zoom down from the national level to a smaller area encompassing our research sites. This enables us to compare the household patterns of our two ethnic groups to the overall population in these smaller geographic areas. We start by comparing Korean households in the Queens Borough of New York to all households there; then we compare Latino households to all area households in central Virginia.

KOREANS IN QUEENS, NEW YORK

Household and Family Types in the Local Study Area

In Queens, where Kang conducted his ethnographic research, Koreans make up 2.9% of roughly 2.2 million people, according to Census 2000.[9] Queens is arguably the most ethnically diverse of all U.S. counties and boroughs. Compared to all Queens households, Korean households in this area were

- Larger, containing 3.06 people per household compared to 2.8 overall[10]
- Much more likely to be family households, particularly of the married couple type,[11] and (especially those of the married couple type) more likely to include children[12]
- Less likely to be one-person households.[13]

Minimum Proportion of Complex Households in the Local Study Area

Table 5.2 shows that the proportion of Korean households in Queens that include nonrelatives is 11.9%. This is our minimum proportion of Korean

Table 5.2 Minimum Proportion of Complex Households for Koreans and the Overall Population in Queens, New York[1] (Family and Nonfamily Households with Any Nonrelatives)

Queens, New York, Population Groups	Percentage of Households with Nonrelatives in Family Households[3]	Percentage of Households with Nonrelatives in Nonfamily Households[4]	Minimum Proportion of Complex Households (Households with Any Nonrelatives)[5]
Overall population	6.4	5.7	**12.1**
Korean population[2]	4.9	7.0	**11.9**

1. The borough of Queens, New York, encompassing the area where the Korean ethnographic research was conducted.
2. Korean alone or in combination with other races.
3. Calculated by subtracting the percentage of nonfamily households with nonrelatives from all households with nonrelatives (column 3 minus column 2) (PCT 16 − PCT 9).
4. Calculated from Census 2000 SF-2, PCT 9 data.
5. Calculated from Census 2000 SF-2, PCT 16 data.

complex households there. In contrast, 12.1% of all Queens households include nonrelatives. Korean complex households with nonrelatives were less likely to be of the family than the nonfamily type (4.9% to 7%), in contrast to the pattern for all Queens households, in which family households with non-relatives were more prevalent (6.4% to 5.7%).[14]

Summary of Korean Household Types in Queens

In comparison to all Queens households, Korean households in that area were larger, much more likely to be family households (particularly married couple family households), and much more likely to include children under 18. They were less likely to be one-person households. Just under 12% of Korean households in Queens were complex in that they included nonrelatives; these were more likely to be nonfamily than family households, as we found earlier for all Asians at the national level. In contrast, for all households in Queens, family households with nonrelatives were more prevalent (the opposite of what was found for all households at the national level). This may be due to Queen's great ethnic diversity.

In his Korean study, Kang deliberately sought out both family and non-family households with nonrelatives, as well as three-generation households. His telling descriptions of their apartments and lives bring you the people behind the complex household statistics presented here.

LATINOS IN CENTRAL VIRGINIA

Goerman compares her selected Latino households with all households in a multicounty area of central Virginia in table 7.1. In Census 2000, Latinos made up 2% of the 199,648 people in this area.

Household and Family Types in the Local Study Area

As compared to all households in this central Virginia area,

- Latino households had a larger average household size (3.03 to 2.45).[15]
- In stark contrast to their pattern at the national level, where they by far have the largest proportion of family households of all our ethnic groups, in this central Virginia area they were only slightly more likely than the overall population to be living in family households.
- These households were less, rather than more, likely to be living in married couple households.[16]
- Latino households, especially those of the married couple type, were much more likely to include children.[17]
- Latino family households, quite interestingly, were more than twice as likely as all area households to be of the "male householder with no spouse present" type.[18]

Minimum Proportion of Complex Households in the Local Study Area

The Latinos in central Virginia show the highest proportion of complex households with nonrelatives of all of our ethnic groups at either the national or local levels (see table 5.3). A stunningly high 25.5% of Latino households in central Virginia include nonrelatives—double the proportion for all households in this area (12.6%). Latino households with one or more nonrelatives were much less likely to be of the family than the nonfamily type (9.7% to 15.8%); this is in the same direction, but much more prevalent, than all area households with nonrelatives (3.8% to 8.8%).[19] Further, Latino nonfamily households with two or more unrelated people were twice as likely as those of the overall population (9.2% to 4.6%) to be of the male-householder type, just as we found with Latino family households (7.6% to 3.4%).[20]

Summary of Latino Household Types in Central Virginia

In sum, the distinctive profile of Latino households in central Virginia shown here from Census 2000 data—disproportionately high numbers of households

Table 5.3   Minimum Proportion of Complex Households for Hispanics (Latinos) and the Overall Population in Central Virginia[1] (Family and Nonfamily Households with Any Nonrelatives)

Central Virginia Population Groups	Percentage of Households with Nonrelatives in Family Households[3]	Percentage of Households with Nonrelatives in Nonfamily Households[4]	Minimum Proportion of Complex Households (Households with Any Nonrelatives)[5]
Overall population	3.8	8.8	**12.6**
Hispanic (Latino) population[2]	9.7	15.8	**25.5**

1. The central Virginia area encompassing the Latino research site.
2. "Hispanic" is an ethnicity, not a race, in the federal system; Hispanics are of any race.
3. Calculated by subtracting the percentage of nonfamily households with nonrelatives from all households with nonrelatives (column 3 minus column 2) (PCT 16 − PCT 9).
4. Calculated from Census 2000 SF-2, PCT 9 data.
5. Calculated from Census 2000 SF-2, PCT 16 data.

with nonrelatives and disproportionately high numbers of male householders in both the family and nonfamily types of households—is typical for new poles of immigration, where early male arrivals anchor a "chain migration" that initially includes a male surplus, according to Rae Lesser Blumberg (2004), Goerman (2004), and others. Latino households in this local area posted the highest minimum proportion of complex households with one or more nonrelatives in our whole study: 25.5%. And, they were about two-thirds as likely to be of the family type. This is in stark contrast to the national-level pattern, where Latino households with nonrelatives are twice as likely to be the family type.

With this background information, let's walk up several flights of stairs in Queens tenements with Kang to talk with Koreans in complex households. Then, Goerman will take us inside a few of the flats and trailers housing complex Latino households in central Virginia, where she found that they were twice as likely to have extra males than females. Her chapter presents their voices about the pluses and minuses of living in complex households in a strange but (thus far) relatively bountiful new land.

NOTES

1. The minimum growth rate for a race group is based on those reporting one race alone; the maximum is based on those reporting more than one. Latinos have no range; they are not a race in the federal statistical system.

2. Of all people reporting as Asian, 49% lived in the West, 20% in the Northeast, 19% in the South, and 12% in the Midwest (Barnes and Bennett 2002).

3. Statistics in this section are from Census 2000 SF-2 custom tables: average household size from PCT 8.

4. In the overall U.S. population, 68.1% of households are classified as family households. In contrast, 80% of Latino households and 74% of Asian households are family households (PCT 9).

5. The average family size for the overall United States is 3.14, for Latinos, 3.93, and for Asians, 3.60 (PCT 26).

6. Latino and, to a lesser extent, Asian households were much more likely to include "own" children under 18 (51.6% and 40.2%) than all U.S. households (32.8%). An additional 5.3% of Latino households were families with children under 18, all of whom were related to the householder, but not as "own" (biological, step, or adopted) children. The proportions for Asians and all U.S. households are 2.9% and 2.7% (PCTs 27, 28). While these households with children, all of whom are more distantly related than "own" children, are complex, according to our definition, it is not appropriate to add these proportions to the proportions of complex households with nonrelatives due to the risk of duplicating some households.

7. In the overall population, 25.8% of households consist of one person living alone. For Latinos and Asians (alone or in combination with other races), the proportions are 13.9% and 18.9% (PCT 9).

8. Calculated from PCTs 16 and 9.

9. In Census 2000, 63,885 Koreans were counted in the borough of Queens (PCT 1). (All Queens statistics in this section are from Census 2000 SF-2 custom tables on the website for Korean alone or in combination.)

10. Calculated from PCT 8.

11. In Queens, 79.3% of Korean households were family households, compared to 68.7% overall; Korean households were more likely than all area households to be married couple households (63.2% to 46.9%).

12. In Queens, Korean family households with "own" (biological, step, or adopted) children under 18 made up a larger proportion of all Korean households than all area households (37.8% to 31.5%). An added 2.4% of Korean households had young related children who were not "own" sons or daughters but more distant relatives, compared to 3.9% for Queens overall (PCTs 27, 28). Korean households are more likely than all households to be married couple households with "own" children (33.2% to 22.4%) (PCT 27).

13. In Queens, 13.7% of Korean households were single people living alone, compared to 25.6% overall.

14. Subtracting the proportion of nonfamily households with two or more people (PCT 9) from that of all households with nonrelatives (PCT 16) yields the proportion of family households with nonrelatives.

15. Calculated from PCTs 6 and 7 for the central Virginia area.

16. In the overall U.S. population, 80% of all Latino households were classified as family households, far and away the highest of any other group. In contrast, in central Virginia, Latino households were much more similar to the overall population in the incidence of

family households (65.6% to 64.6%). At the national level, Latino households were more likely than all households to be of the married couple type (53.9% to 51.7%), but in this central Virginia area, they were less likely to be this type (48.3% to 50.7%) (PCT 9). The lower proportions of family households here is another indicator of a new migration pole.

17. Latino family households in central Virginia were more likely to include "own" (biological, step, or adopted) children under 18 (38.5% to 29.5%), and more of these were married couple households (29.3% to 21.5%) (PCT 27). An added 3.1% of Latino households in this area had only "related" children who were not "own" children, compared to an added 2.4% of all households (PCTs 27, 28).

18. Among Latinos in central Virginia, 7.6% of households with families were classified as male householder, no spouse present, compared to less than half of that percentage (3.4%) overall. Female-householder family households were less prevalent among Latinos than among all households (9.6% to 10.5%) (PCT 9).

19. Calculated from PCTs 16 and 9. Interestingly, the disproportionately high proportions of Latino nonfamily households with two or more people found among central Virginia Latinos contrasts sharply with the national-level picture, where Latinos do not differ in this regard from the overall population.

20. PCT 9. There were also more female-householder nonfamily households among Latinos than among all area households (6.6% to 4.2%).

REFERENCES

Barnes, J., and C. Bennett. 2002. "The Asian population: 2000." Census 2000 Brief C2KBR/01-16, issued in February.

Blumberg, R. L. 2004. "Ethnicity and complex households among Latinos and Asians: an exploratory study emphasizing the foreign born." Contract report prepared for the U.S. Census Bureau, Washington, DC.

Goerman, P. 2004. "The promised land? The gendered experience of new Hispanic 'proletarian immigrants' to central Virginia." Ph.D. diss., University of Virginia.

Lugaila, T., and J. Overturf. 2004. "Children and the households they live in: 2000." Census 2000 special reports CENSR-14, issued February 2004.

Malone, N., K. Baluja, J. Costanzo, and C. Davis. 2003. "The foreign born population: 2000." Census 2000 Brief C2KBR-34, issued December 2003.

U.S. Census Bureau. 1981. "Census 1980 summary file 1." Washington, DC: U.S. Department of Commerce.

———. 2001. "Census 2000 summary file 1." Washington, DC: U.S. Department of Commerce.

———. 2005. "Table 3: Annual estimates of the population by sex, race, and Hispanic or Latino origin for the United States: April 1, 2000, to April 1, 2004" (NC-EST2004-03), at www.census.gov/popest/national/asrh/NC-EST2004-srh.html (accessed September 1, 2005).

U.S. Office of Management and Budget. 1997. "Revisions to the standards for the classification of federal data on race and ethnicity: notices." *Federal Register* 62 (210): 58781–59790.

• 6 •

Household Structure and Its Social and Economic Functions among Korean American Immigrants in Queens, New York: An Ethnographic Study

Tai S. Kang

INTRODUCTION AND RESEARCH OBJECTIVES

*M*r. K, who is in his sixties, lost his wife in a car accident four years ago. He remarried a lady from his church, with the support and encouragement of his adult children. Mr. and Mrs. K reside in a small, two-bedroom apartment within a large apartment building near a subway station. Upon entering the building, you recognize a large number of Asian surnames on the mailboxes. Paint on the walls in the small lobby area at the front entrance has peeled off in many places. A florescent light in one of the two building elevators is flickering, leaving the elevator rather dim. Mr. and Mrs. K's apartment has a 10′ × 12′ living room with a kitchen near the front door to one side and a bed to the other side, and two bedrooms beyond the living room. Mr. and Mrs. K rent each bedroom out to a nonrelative, a Korean restaurant worker and a Korean store employee. The elderly couple uses the bed in the living room. Mr. K describes his living conditions with a long sigh:

> I and my wife just cannot afford to keep an apartment of our own without taking in housemates to share our rent. Around here a two-bedroom apartment goes for about $1,900 a month. I lost SSI [supplemental security income] and food stamps when I received some insurance money for losing my ex-wife [former wife] in the car accident. The money from the insurance is deposited in a bank. I have a small sum of monthly interest from it. Even with housemates sharing the rent,

126

my son and daughter pitch in to help us keep this place. Of course, the building management would not lease the apartment to a person like me with no financial credit. My son leased the unit under his name, so we can live here.

This research explores a Korean American immigrant population in New York. It focuses primarily on 25 complex households and compares them with 10 noncomplex (largely nuclear) households. Definitions of household and household composition, as well as the use of relational terms, serve as clues to important operational norms within social groups. They reflect cultural history and social values at work under changing conditions requiring adaptive living situations.

Goals of the research include an understanding of the following issues: (1) how the social and economic functioning of both complex and noncomplex households emerges and develops, (2) how the culture of the ethnic community affects the social and economic functioning of households, (3) how and to what extent relational terms used among household members reflect or influence the social and economic structure and functioning of the households, (4) how these households are embedded in the social network and socioeconomic life of the community, and (5) how the social and economic functioning of households affects attitudes and responses to both U.S. censuses and survey research conducted in the community.

The results of this study should assist policy makers and administrators in various governmental and private organizations to plan and implement culturally appropriate social and economic programs in this rapidly expanding group. Furthermore, the study will suggest culturally sensitive and appropriate ways for researchers to conduct social research, be they ethnographic or survey types of work.[1]

Typically, the most recent immigrants tend to form complex households (i.e., units containing people who are not members of the nuclear family) as they attempt to establish themselves, so a study of these households provides an excellent opportunity to examine the adaptation process at work. During a five-month period from February to June 2000, I conducted in-depth ethnographic research among 25 such complex Korean households. Complex households in this study encompassed the following types: (1) coresident three- or four-generation families, (2) nonrelated individuals coresiding in an apartment, and (3) families with at least one coresident nonrelated individual. From January to February 2002, I conducted a new study with a sample of 10 noncomplex households from the larger urban community to serve as a comparison group. These noncomplex households included these household types: (1) married couples, (2) married couples and their children, and (3) single parents with children.[2]

The comparison between complex and noncomplex households allows us to examine differences in how interviewees themselves define "household" and "family" and how their definitions of these words differ from general definitions used in the majority society. In other words, we compared the insider's cultural view, the *emic*, with the general definitions in the larger society that may seem to be standard and objective, the *etic*.

A BRIEF OVERVIEW OF KOREAN CULTURAL THEMES AND INFLUENCES

Historically, China provided a significant influence upon Korea in many areas of life, from scholarly traditions to the importation of Confucianism. In the 1900s, and particularly during World War II, Japan also exerted its cultural traditions within Korean society. After the middle of the twentieth century, Korea experienced dramatic, often turbulent, political, economic, social, and cultural changes. These changes included political and military tension surrounding the Korean War, urbanization, rapid industrialization, gross national product and per capita income growth, as well as a vastly expanded public-education system, dramatic declines in fertility, and wide acceptance of the ideology of democracy.

Consequences of these increasingly rapid social and economic changes are evident in many areas of Korean life. The Korean economy has maintained a high level of growth over the last four decades with about an 8% average increase of the gross domestic product in 1990 prices in U.S. dollars: 4.9% in 1961, 8.3% in 1990, and 8.8% in 2000 (United Nations Statistics Division 2002). Now, South Korea is one of the "four Tigers" of Asia, a newly industrialized country, or NIC, that exports steel, automobiles, ships, electronics, and other advanced manufactured products. By the middle of the 1990s, the per capita income of South Korea had reached over $10,000 (Min 1998). The literacy rate among Koreans over the age of 15 is remarkably high (97.76% in 2000). The illiteracy rate showed an amazing decline—from 7.12% in 1980 to 2.24% in 2000 (United Nations Statistics Division 2002). In major urban metropolitan areas, with limited housing space and a scarcity of affordable housing, the proportion of complex, extended households (comprised of an older couple and at least one married son and his family) has continued to decline. Today, apartment buildings are the dominant housing form in large cities, and the great majority of urban people live in noncomplex households with only members of their nuclear families. The average household size has noticeably decreased, from 5.2 in 1970 to 3.7 in 1990 (United Nations Statistics Division 2002). The rural population of South Korea has steadily decreased over the last several decades. A recognizable annual rate of loss to the urban areas started in early 1970 (–0.39% in 1970), and the decline continued (–2.19% in 1980, –4.91% in 1990, and –2.83% in 2000). Also, during this period, many rural youths left for cities and urban centers, leaving their aging parents behind (United Nations Statistics Division 2002), and female labor force participation has increased markedly. The fertility rate has declined drastically, while the divorce rate has crept upward (United Nations Statistics Division 2002). During this modern period, the military, political, economic, and cultural influences of the United States on Korean society have increased dramatically, particularly after the Korean War (Min 1998).

In traditional Korean culture, the essential foundation of social interaction is rooted in *Sahm Gahng*, meaning three basic levels of social structure, and *Uh Rewn*, meaning five fundamental social and cultural norms. The three basic levels of social structure consist of relations between a king and his subjects, between a father and his sons, and between a husband and his wife. The five fundamental social and cultural norms, which govern relationships, consist of loyalty/duty between a king and his subjects, affective benevolence between a father and his sons, hierarchical role differentiation and separation between a husband and his wife, hierarchical order between an older person and a younger person with respect and deference to an older person, and trust between friends.

In the cultural tradition of Korean families, these basic levels and norms become mirrored in the patriarchal, patrilineal, and patrilocal Korean family system. The family structure tends to exhibit the dominant authority of the father over his children, the subordinate status of the wife to her husband (or to her oldest son if she is widowed), filial piety for parents and grandparents, respect and deference for older people, the subordinate marginal social status of females, and separation of paternal and maternal relatives.[3]

KOREAN AMERICAN IMMIGRATION

General Background

The liberalized immigration law of 1965 in the United States opened the door to Asian immigrants and resulted in a chain migration pattern that increased the Korean American population fivefold from 70,000 to 355,000 between 1970 and 1980 (U.S. Department of Commerce 1981). Once initial immigrants became somewhat settled, a migration cycle or chain often began when an immigrant sent for his or her spouse, children, or parents ("second preference" relatives in immigration-law terminology). Then, after obtaining citizenship, an immigrant became eligible to send for brothers and sisters ("fifth preference" kin). These siblings in turn often invited their spouses, children, and the spouse's parents, thereby starting migration cycles of their own. By 1990, the total number of Korean Americans was 798,849 (U.S. Census Bureau 1991). In Census 2000, the Korean American population had increased to 1,076,872, to become the fifth largest Asian American group (U.S. Census Bureau 2001).

Since 1980, approximately 32,000 to 33,000 Koreans have immigrated to this country annually. Most have urban, middle-class backgrounds. They tend to concentrate in a few states where large metropolitan areas provide relatively favorable economic opportunities for newcomers. In 1990, California attracted 32.5% and New York 20% of Koreans (U.S. Census Bureau 1991). In 2000, California and New York accounted for 43.2% of all Korean immigrants, where California received 32.1% and New York 11.1% (U.S. Census Bureau 2001). In contrast to other Asian American groups, however, Koreans do disperse more widely across all states.

Specific to the Research Site

The 1990 Census showed that 51.3% of the 95,800 Korean Americans in New York State resided in Queens, a borough of New York City (U.S. Census Bureau 1991). The present study focuses upon the Queens area, which contains a particularly dense population of Korean Americans. Two groups of early Korean immigrants came and settled in this area. The first group came to participate in the 1964 World's Fair held in Flushing Meadow and consisted of Korean government employees and business personnel. A core number of these people decided to stay in the country rather than return to Korea. They joined an already established corpus of Asian businessmen attracted to the Queens area for its affordable rents and convenient access to the transportation system (Foner 2000; Sanjek 1988).

The second group of Koreans to settle in this area consisted of professionals who came to the United States under the liberalized 1965 immigration law. Part of this group consisted of a large contingent of professionals who immigrated into the United States by way of West Germany. During the 1960s, the Korean government sent a large number of miners and nurses to West Germany. Many nurses married overeducated, but underemployed, Korean miners in Germany. A substantial number of these Korean nurses took advantage of the 1965 law, which gave preference to foreign medical professionals, and immigrated to the United States. Then, they brought over their husbands, children, and often their parents, contributing to the rapidly accelerating migration cycle. Since the 1970s, some large apartment complexes near hospitals have consisted entirely of Korean nurses and their families (Kang 2001).

SELECTION OF RESEARCH SUBJECTS AND
SOLICITATION FOR RESEARCH PARTICIPATION

I initiated groundwork for the field study during February and March 2000 by conducting a general demographic survey of the research site, reviewing literature on the ethnic community, researching major community organizations, and identifying influential community leaders. As the principal investigator, I solicited support for the research from a number of major community organizations: three large Korean American churches; one Buddhist temple; and four important Korean American community organizations, namely, the Korean American Association of Greater New York, the Korean American Social Service Center, the Korean American Census Awareness Project, and the Korean American YWCA of New York; and an association of Koreans from the northeastern region. In meetings with the leadership of these organizations, I discussed the political, social, and economic importance to Korean Americans of participation in the U.S. census. I explained my research project as a part of the continuing efforts of the Census Bureau to encourage participation in the census and to improve accuracy in census response. I also stressed the stringent safeguards of confidentiality and the noncoercive nature of the interviews. Community leaders expressed support for the project and acknowledged the importance of participating in the census for the Korean American community. The leaders also facilitated a series of meetings during which my research team visited churches, a temple, a YWCA, and a Korean American Senior Citizens Nutrition Program to explain the objectives and goals of our research project.

During the course of meetings to promote the research project, my research liaisons and I asked for a show of hands from the audience to indicate their willingness to participate in our interviews. Few people raised their hands. Our reassurances about confidentiality of information and emphasis on the noncoercive nature of the study simply did not work. These difficulties correspond to findings on the general reluctance of Asian Americans to participate in the decennial census and to respond to survey studies in general (Kang 1982, 1992, 2001). Refusal or reluctance to participate in interviews stems from cultural views related to social status and historical experience with governmental authorities resulting in the following attitudes: a deep distrust of authorities, be they governmental or business; fear of losing face by revealing less than socially acceptable aspects of life in one's household; and legal insecurities concerning residence status, modes of income, means of employment, and lease restrictions related to housing composition (such as limits on which people, or how many people, are permitted to live in a residence).

Given our understanding of these cultural views and their connection to low rates of participation in research studies, we used special efforts designed to increase our success rate. First, I recruited several influential community leaders as paid liaisons to introduce our research to potential interviewees. I asked the liaisons to accompany me to interviews and conducted interviews in the privacy of the respondents' homes. We also offered a small compensation ($35) to each interviewee. Using these efforts, we visited 30 complex households and successfully obtained 25 completed interviews. For the study of non-complex (nuclear) households, we visited 12 households and completed 10 interviews. On the whole, our special efforts met with moderate success.

Despite our use of respected people as liaisons, the privacy of interviews, payments to interviewees, and assurances of confidentiality, fear and distrust did hamper the research to some extent. Perhaps one example of these refusals can best illustrate the difficulties encountered by researchers or social-service providers working with this immigrant group. In the following description of household #501, note the internal family dispute over cooperation, reluctance to reveal family situations to outsiders, and underlying hidden economic motives, coupled with fear of authorities. This pattern generalizes, in fact, to the other cases of refusal.

The elderly couple lives in an apartment, consisting of two small bedrooms and a living room, leased by their daughter and her husband. The apartment is in a large complex with several multistory apartment buildings. The place is clean with simple, yet tasteful, curtains in the windows. The young couple has two children: a boy and a girl. The old couple's daughter graduated from a well-known university with a business degree and works in Manhattan. The interviewee refused to discuss the type of work his daughter performs. The interviewee's son-in-law is a graduate student. The grandparents take care of the grandchildren while the daughter and son-in-law are at work or at school. When the liaison and I walked into the apartment, the elderly potential interviewee was quite friendly. He offered us coffee as we sat down. After exchanging social pleasantries, complimenting him on his apartment, admiring a graduation picture of his daughter and other family pictures, I once again explained the objectives of our work, the confidentiality of census-related work, and the voluntary nature of participation in the research. Then, I asked him for permission to tape the interview. The old man's facial expression immediately turned stiff. With an embarrassed smile on his face, he said he should ask his daughter whether it would be all right to do a taped interview. The old gentleman telephoned his daughter. I could hear her raised voice over the phone. He kept saying, "Yes, yes, . . . I will not . . ." into the phone. When he returned to the table, he said, "I am sorry, but I don't think I can continue our interview." I responded, "Taping is strictly a voluntary thing, so we won't tape it. However, if it is all right with you, we could do the interview without taping it." He said,

> There are certain things that I don't think should be in written or recorded reports. As you know, in our culture there are certain things you don't want to tell outsiders. You understand, don't you? I am truly sorry that you have come all the way out here, but . . . let's have coffee.

As we came out of the apartment, my liaison explained,

> You see, the grandmother looks after a few neighborhood Korean children—babysitting work. She gets paid for the work under the table. They don't want people to know about the underground economy that they are a part of.

This illustrates the problem of attempting to research sensitive topics with vulnerable, culturally conservative populations. More specifically, inquiring about another's work, income, share of household expenses, and share of rent is considered culturally inappropriate in Korean society. If a researcher raises those questions without great care and caution, he or she risks an abrupt termination of the interview. I circumspectly phrased those questions. For example:

> Rents around this area are much higher than rents for comparable apartments or houses in Buffalo, New York, where I live. I don't know how people could afford to live in New York. When I was a student, I had many different types of part-time work: a store clerk, bus-boy, and hospital orderly. It was hard to get settled in a new place, new environment; it takes a long time.

In social interaction, saving "social face" is of vital importance in Korean culture. If a person has a less than socially desirable occupation or place of residence, he or she will show great reluctance to reveal the situation to an outsider.

HOUSEHOLD TYPES AND GENERAL LIVING CONDITIONS

Complex Households

Since previous research (Kang 1992) indicates that Korean complex households often consist of the most recent immigrants and that these provide the greatest resistance to participating in the census, initial efforts focused on this subpopulation. Participants reflected three types of complex households: (1) nonrelated people living together in one apartment ($n = 8$); (2) families with coresident, nonrelated people ($n = 5$), and (3) three-generation families ($n = 12$). It should be noted that the third type, the multigenerational family, most closely resembles the traditional patrilocal family living arrangements in Korea, which were more prevalent when that country was still primarily rural and agrarian. But, as shown below, these multigenerational families in the United States are not necessarily related on the father's side.

All three of these complex types of households usually contained what some demographers term a "slice-and-split" arrangement, where two or three people share a bedroom or two or three people make use of mattresses or beds placed in a small living room (Kang 1992, 2001). Indeed, fully 22 out of the 25 complex households contained slice-and-split arrangements of sharing a bedroom, a mattress or bed, or both.

Two-thirds of the households lived in a one-bedroom apartment. Yet, the average size of these households was 4.6 individuals. The size of each subtype of complex household breaks down as follows: (1) nonrelated coresidents (average 3.6 residents); (2) families with coresident, nonrelated individuals (average 3.8 people), and (3) three-generation families (average 5.6 people). Each of the three-generation families included a child or two (average of 1.76). In three-generation families, grandparents usually joined their busy adult children's households to help them take care of young grandchildren and to help out around the house—cleaning, cooking, and doing laundry. More often, adult children asked grandmothers rather than grandfathers to join the household because of their domestic skills. In other words, formation of three-generation families frequently occurred when adult children sent for their parents to care for young offspring, freeing both adult parents to work and to work longer hours. Furthermore, the wife's mother was more likely to have moved in rather than the husband's. In other words, the coresident three-generation families were not a re-creation in Queens of a traditional patriarchal, patrilocal Korean family. Part of the reason reported by respondents is that sons tend to get along better with their mothers-in-law than their wives do with their mothers-in-law—so the young couple often sends for the grandmother who will make the most harmonious addition to their tiny, cramped quarters.[4]

The main reason respondents gave for living in complex households centers on economics. On the one hand, these people are struggling economically, and their complex living arrangements help them cope. Of the 25 households, 21 fell into a lower-low or low category for standard of living. For example, seven of the eight households comprised of coresident nonrelatives had a lower-low standard of living.[5] On the other hand, high rents also contribute to people clustering in complex households in small apartments. With rapidly rising real estate prices in New York City, new immigrant groups have to compete to find affordable accommodations in a tight market for low-rent apartments. Queens offers new immigrants relatively affordable housing, unskilled job opportunities, convenient transportation networks, and a high concentration of established, inclusive, ethnic businesses and organizations.

Two examples of complex households illustrate the typical life style.

A Household Comprised of Nonrelatives Living Together in One Apartment (Case #516)   The apartment is within walking distance of a subway station, banks, public buildings, a rapidly expanding Chinese business district (with restaurants, supermarkets, Chinese herbal medicine stores, law offices, and barbershops), and a few dozen Korean businesses.

This one-bedroom apartment is quite small. A 9′ × 15′ room serves multiple purposes with a small kitchen at one end of the room, a dining table with four chairs in the middle, and two beds on the other end. The only bedroom is for a female student in her twenties. Two separated women, Ms. C (in her fifties) and Ms. L (in her thirties), use the two beds in the living room. One works in a nail salon, the other, in a beauty salon. The three housemates share the rent. When I mentioned, "Rent in this area seems to be very high compared to the rent we pay in Buffalo, New York," Ms. C replied,

> A one-bedroom place around here goes for about $900 to $1,000 a month. I put a "housemate wanted" ad in local ethnic Korean papers whenever I have a vacancy. That's how I could pay for the apartment. Ms. P, the young female student is supported by her father in Korea for her education. On weekends, we all share the cooking and cleaning together. However, I do most of the household chores.

The two employed women manage a very meager level of living. Observing the cramped living arrangements in the apartment and hearing the description of their lifestyle underscores the economic reasons why many people live in a complex household.

A Three-Generation Household (Case #509)   The one-bedroom apartment is on an upper floor of a large apartment complex. Names on the mailboxes at the front entrance indicate that a majority of residents in the building are Asian. The hallways are dimly lit and narrow. The door to the apartment opens directly into the living room. The living room contains a mattress in one corner, one small, well-worn couch, a 19″ TV set, a short coffee table, which doubles as a dining table, and a small desk with two chairs at the other end of the room. Mrs. R (the interviewee) is a divorcée in her sixties. She resides in the apartment with her daughter, her son-in-law, and two young grandchildren. Mrs. R and her toddler grandson sleep on the mattress in the living room.

The daughter, son-in-law, and a young infant daughter sleep in the bedroom. On the desk in the living room are a Korean Bible and a large open notebook. Mrs. R explained,

> I have been copying the New Testament into these notebooks. Now I am copying the Bible for the third time. This is my prayer to God in seeking his help for the success and welfare of my daughter and her family. My husband left me for a younger woman, so I came to the United States in the 1980s. My daughter and son-in-law followed me to the United States a few years later. As you can see, we have not done too well so far. My son-in-law works in a local store, and my daughter has been a student for years to keep her foreign student [F-1 Visa] status. This way, the family can maintain legal status for staying in the country. My daughter often has part-time retail jobs. I don't know if we can ever get out of our rut. [It should be noted that, almost certainly, both her son-in-law and her daughter's jobs were "off the books."]

When her daughter and son-in-law work, Mrs. R takes care of her two grandchildren. She also babysits several young children of her neighbors. In addition, Mrs. R cooks and does most of the household chores for the family. When I commented that rents in the area are quite high, she said, "In this neighborhood, a one-bedroom apartment generally goes for about $900 a month. You know, in this area the demand for apartments is so high that rents have steadily increased over the last few years." She continued, "All three members of the family work and contribute to household income. We have been working hard to improve our lives, but we barely make enough to live." Asking a direct question about the share of household income each person contributes would have been culturally inappropriate. However, inferring from the different income sources, it seems that Mrs. R's son-in-law is the major provider for the family and that Mrs. R and her daughter help supplement that income.

Noncomplex Households

In the second round of fieldwork, I successfully completed interviews in 10 of the 12 noncomplex households identified for the study. The breakdown by household type is as follows: seven married couples, one married couple with children, and two households consisting of a single parent with children. Concerning the single-parent-with-children households, this research lends support to the findings of many previous surveys of Korean Americans showing that this household type tends to result from divorce or widowhood. The divorce rates both in Korea and in Korean American communities have steadily increased in recent years (Min 1998). Interviews with divorced-single-parent-with-children households remain difficult to conduct in this ethnic community because of people's reluctance to reveal this situation due to the cultural stigma and loss of face created by divorce.

Two noncomplex households depict the living situations I observed in the community:

A Married Couple Household (Case #531)   Mr. S and his wife reside on the first floor of a small apartment building in an old, quiet neighborhood near a park. The apartment is located amid several dozen interlinked row apartment houses. Mr. and Mrs. S are in their sixties. Both of them received a college education in Korea and were teachers. Mr. S's older brother is a health care professional who sponsored Mr. S's family's immigration to the United States in the 1980s. Mr. and Mrs. S and their daughter stayed with Mr. S's brother for two months before they found their current apartment through a Korean church member. The apartment has a long, narrow, rectangular shape, with two bedrooms, a living room, and a small kitchen. Mr. S has a caretaker's job with a Korean enterprise. Mrs. S babysits two or three young Korean American children during the day. Their daughter graduated from college and has a professional job. They expressed a number of quite traditional concerns about their daughter. Mr. and Mrs. S said,

> You are a college teacher, right? If you have a nice Christian Korean young man in your graduate program, please remember our daughter. We raised her in a traditional Korean way. She turned out to be a bright attractive young lady. We are afraid that she may be getting too old to find a good husband.

When I asked them about their daughter further, Mr. S replied,

> Yes, she is doing just fine. Her students like her; her colleagues seem to like her and her work as well. She comes up here often; it takes only a few hours to get here by train. She tries to help us out financially, but we manage all right by ourselves. So, we have encouraged her to set up an investment account of her own.

He turned to his own situation, saying he works full time and his wife babysits for children in their apartment. "We have just enough income to pay for rent, keep our 15-year-old car, and pay for other living expenses." In response to a question about his ideal living arrangements, Mr. S said,

> Just the two of us—an old couple together. Nowadays, old parents should not think of living with their adult children, not even in Korea. Eventually, sometime in the future, we would like to own a place of our own, be it a condo or

co-op. But, we know that we are now too old to save enough money to do that [he said with a resigned smile].

A Single-Parent-with-Children Household (Case #533)   Mrs. P, a widow in her sixties, lives in a partially rent-controlled, one-bedroom, Manhattan apartment with her unmarried son, who is in his thirties. Mrs. P uses the bedroom, and her son uses a futon bed/couch in the living room. The rooms have small windows and appear dark even during the day. Mrs. P and her husband came to the United States in the 1980s. A year later, their son joined them. Both Mr. and Mrs. P have a college education, and they owned a moderately successful business in Korea. Several years after moving to the United States, Mr. P got ill and passed away. Mrs. P's son gave up his graduate work and began working in a Korean store. Mrs. P worked as a part-time receptionist for four hours a day, five days a week. She did most of the household chores: cooking and cleaning. Her son helped her with grocery shopping. Mrs. P gave her paychecks to her son, and he managed the household finances. I asked her, "What does your son do at the Korean store?" Mrs. P just smiled and said,

> Certain things are not supposed to be talked about. I am getting worried about my son. Around here, it is not easy to find an eligible young Korean American girl, so he tells me. When he gets financially settled down, maybe we should find someone in Korea for him.

DEFINITIONS OF "HOUSEHOLD" AND "FAMILY" AND USE OF RELATIONSHIP TERMS

In the census, as well as in other research on families and households in an ethnic community, it is of essential importance to understand culturally appropriate *emic* (their own) definitions of family and household, as well as their use of relationship terms within the household and in the ethnic community. I researched the following questions: (1) how do Koreans define "family" and "household," (2) what categories of people fall inside or outside these structures, (3) how do people use kinship terms, and (4) does the use of kinship terms reflect changing social structure?

Definitions of "Household" and "Family"

Korean Americans confine their definition of "family" (*kahjock*) to those individuals who are related to each other within two or three generations of paternal or maternal relations or through one's own marriage. Included in a family are those kin (*eelkah*) who reside in the same housing unit. A strong, family-centered definition of "household" exists within the Korean American community. Most Korean Americans I interviewed refused to include nonrelated individuals residing in the same housing unit in their definitions of "members of their households." Conversely, they often insisted on including family members who resided in other locations in their definition of "household."

Mrs. S, a woman in her sixties, lives with her adult son, a daughter-in-law, and a nine-year-old grandson in a small, two-bedroom apartment. One bedroom is for the grandmother and her grandson, and the other is for her adult son and daughter-in-law. Another young son of Mrs. S used to stay in the same apartment; however, the place was too small for five people. The elderly lady said,

> My younger son rents a room in a neighbor's apartment. He just sleeps in that rented room. He spends most of his time with us—he watches Korean TV programs and has all of his meals with us here. He is a member of our family and he is a member of our household. That's why he is included in our census report.

Mrs. C, a 75-year-old widow, provided her own definitions of "household" and "family."

> I have all three adult children—two sons and a daughter—and their families living within a few blocks from this house. They are my family—*kahjock*. A household—*Sae-dae*—includes members of a family living in the same housing unit. I would not include nonrelated persons in my *Sae-dae* even when they may live with us.

Problems Concerning Definition of Terms

The last example above leads to discussion of one problem I discovered during fieldwork. Several Korean words can be used as a translation for "household," but they carry the potential for variations in meanings. These words are *Sae-dae*, *Sik-coo*, and *Kah-coo*. The term *Sae-dae* is the most widely used for "household"; however, when written in Chinese characters, the word "Sae-dae" can be written in two different ways, one that means "household" and another that means "generation."[6] When I asked interviewees to define the word "Sae-dae," most interviewees were confused as to which meaning I intended. I had some difficulty eliciting interviewees' own definitions of what they included in a household without contaminating or inserting my own definition of "Sae-dae." I attempted to avoid confusion by saying they should not consider the written form meaning "generation."

"Sik-coo" means "mouths that share meals" (people who share meals together), a word with an origin in the old agrarian economy in Korea. Mr.

and Mrs. O, an old couple who live in a one-bedroom apartment in a six-unit apartment building responded that,

> "Sik-coo" could include everyone living in the same housing unit with the same address, but generally excludes nonrelated roomers or housemates, even when they share meals with you. It generally includes those members of a family who share meals together in the same housing unit.

"Ka-coo" literally means "mouths in a house," again, a word with origin in the old Korean agrarian economy. Mrs. L, an elderly widow with a college education, defined the word as follows:

> I would say the word means people living in the same house. I include in Ka-coo those living in the same housing unit, whether they are related to each other or not. But in general use of the term, we do not include nonrelated individuals in Ka-coo, do we?

The Korean Americans defined all three terms within the confines of related members of a family. The difficulty in applying these terms toward a definition of "household" became even clearer in the second phase of research with the noncomplex household residents. One interviewee in this group was a social worker for a community group. Mr. S remarked, with an exaggerated expression of surprise,

> I found a truly amazing definition of "household" in this country. I helped an older Korean American couple to apply for Medicaid and SSI benefits. I accompanied them to the local Social Security Administration office [SSA]. A counselor in the SSA office told us that if the couple met the means tests to qualify for welfare benefits for the elderly, they could claim that they have a separate household of their own, even when they reside with their adult children in the same addressed housing unit. Just think . . . the same apartment, the same housing unit, and the elderly could claim that they form a separate "household!" How do you like that?

Terms Used in Addressing Nonrelated People in the Household

In Korean culture, any distinction between the words "roommate" and "housemate" often becomes muddy. Roommates or housemates occur in Korea as products of urbanization and modernization, seen in college towns and factory neighborhoods. Koreans use the term *hah-sook-inn* (a person who shares the housing unit) to denote these two categories of nonrelated coresidents. In this country, the Korean version of the Census 2000 form does not translate "roommate" and "housemate" into Korean. The census form presents these two terms in Korean phonetic symbols for the English pronunciation.

My research examined how nonrelated individuals residing in the same apartment address each other. We can learn this from the household of Mr. K, described at the beginning of this chapter. Mr. K and his wife live in a two-bedroom apartment leased by his son, who lives elsewhere. The two bedrooms were rented out to two housemates, while the old couple slept in a bed placed in one corner of the living room. When asked about the housemates, Mr. K replied,

> We had to take in hah-sook-inn after I lost my government benefits. We barely can make ends meet, even with the rent money we get from the two hah-sook-inn and some financial help we get from my son and my wife's daughter. One roommate eats elsewhere. The other person shares meals with us.

Asked about any differences between the words "roommate" and "housemate," Mr. K responded, "I really don't know the difference. Roommate is a nonrelated person who shares meals with the family; housemates do not share meals with us, perhaps?"[7]

I asked Mr. K, "How do you address your housemates?" Mrs. K chimed in, "We just call them Mr. so and so" (the last name of the person). I asked, "What other forms of address would you use to call your 'housemate' or 'roommate'?" Mr. K said, "When a roommate or housemate is a much older person, you could address him as *Hal-ah-bojee* [grandfather] or address her as *Hal-mo-nee* [grandmother]." These fictive kin terms show friendly social deference for the aged with no real necessary kin relationship implied. For those just a few years older, one could use terms such as *Hyung-neem* (older brother) for a man and *Un-nee* or *Noo-neem* (older sister) for a woman. Again, we use these terms as fictive kin terms with friendly social connotations.

Adopted Children, Stepchildren, and Foster Children in a Family or Household

Almost all Korean adoptions take place within the family. An adoption from outside of one's own kin group seldom occurs. When people get remarried and bring children from previous marriages, stepparent-stepchildren relationships result. When such relationships exist, the family only reluctantly reveals these relationships to outsiders.

Mrs. M, a 46-year-old woman, works for a Korean agency. She and her husband have two young children. Mrs. M's elderly parents reside in their daughter's two-bedroom apartment. Two young grandchildren share a bedroom with their grandparents. I asked Mrs. M, "How would you address an adopted child, or a stepchild, if you had one?" Mrs. M, with an embarrassed smile, replied,

> As you know, in Korea, an adoption generally takes place within a closely related kin group—then only in special situations, like when a couple does not have a child of their own, particularly a boy who would carry the family name, or when children of a very close family member become orphaned. At any rate, an adoption does not occur too frequently in Korean society. Until recent years, the divorce rate in Korea was quite low, and remarriages of widows were frowned upon; stepparent and stepchildren relationships in a family seemed like a pretty rare phenomenon. I would be very hesitant to reveal to outsiders adopted or step status of those children in the family. I would call them by their first names, just as I would call my own children by their first names. Since they would have our family name, the outsiders would not know our relationships unless we tell them. As for foster children, I don't think we have that system in the Korean family.

All of the interviewees in both complex households and noncomplex households presented much the same responses for defining these three relational terms—adoptive, step, and foster relationships. Because the foster-care system goes unrecognized in Korean culture, I raised the following hypothetical question to each interviewee: "A very close friend of yours in Korea asks you to take care of his or her son while he attends a college in the United States. Would you consider him a member of your household?" Out of the 35 households I interviewed, only one person would include the young man in his household.

GENERAL FINDINGS AND IMPLICATIONS OF THIS STUDY FOR FUTURE RESEARCH

General Results

Except for one each, among the 25 complex households and the 10 traditional households, all interviewees had a restricted family- (kahjock-) centered definition of household: Sae-dae. In their view, the household consisted of members of a family residing in the same housing unit. Respondents considered a nonrelated individual residing with a family as a roommate or a housemate but not a member of the household. Even in the households of nonrelated individuals, people defined their coresidents as roommates or housemates living under the same roof but not members of the household, or Sae-dae.

As noted above, 21 out of 25 complex households had a low or lower-low standard of living. All five families with coresident, nonrelated individuals had a lower-low level of living. Among the households of nonrelated individuals, seven of eight maintained a lower-low level of living. Housing formation and people's roles within the unit are largely associated with economic conditions. Nonrelated individuals in complex households share rent and utility expenses with the family or other housemates or roommates. In seven of the nonrelative households, the residents of the apartment shared meals together. Each member was assigned work around the apartment: cooking, cleaning, and washing dishes after meals. In three households of young, nonrelated males, everyone had his own assigned work around the apartment, such as cooking or cleaning. When occupants shared meals, each member of the household contributed his or her portion of the grocery expenses, generally a fixed sum of money each month. Some housemates and roommates had odd work schedules that conflicted with dinner hours for the household, and some housemates and roommates worked for restaurants where they had their meals. They used the apartments as a place for lodging only.

Among the noncomplex households, female household members cooked for the family and did most of the chores. In every case, all family members put their financial resources into a common pool to meet the household-related expenses. In two families, adult offspring of elderly interviewees kept their own separate bank accounts after contributing a fixed sum for household expenses.[8]

Only interviewees from three complex households and two noncomplex households had any recognizable degree of regular social or business contacts with members of the majority society. Such contact mainly occurred through their work in deli shops, corner grocery stores, social work agencies, or nail salons. An overwhelming majority of individuals interviewed in both complex and noncomplex households managed their lives primarily within the ethnic community. They shopped in Korean-owned grocery stores, ate in Korean restaurants and bakeries, used Korean travel agencies, read ethnic papers, listened to ethnic TV and radio, used Korean hair stylists, received treatment for illness by Korean doctors, including herbalists and acupuncturists, and attended ethnic Korean churches and Buddhist temples. They could manage their lives without using English.

For most of the recently immigrated Koreans, their lives literally revolve around their churches, which provide places for socializing with other Koreans and acquiring information and knowledge to manage their lives in the new, alien society. This includes information on job opportunities, apartment availability, and government benefit programs. Churches and a few select ethnic organizations provide valued social, affective, and instrumental resources (financial, legal, educational, medical, and social-service information) to new Korean immigrants.

Implications of This Study for Future Research

Cultural Aspects to Consider   Historically, Koreans have long exhibited a distrust of authorities, even in the old country. In the United States, some new immigrants may have good reason for their fear and distrust of the interview process. Some recipients of government benefits (SSI, Medicaid, food stamps) understandably may not want to reveal their financial resources and their sources of income, particularly those with unreported income from underground economic work. A reluctance to reveal housing arrangements may stem from the fact that complex households may violate housing codes or leasing agreements by having more than the permitted number of residents in their homes. Some immigrants may have an ambiguous legal status (e.g., they may be working full time on a student visa). These marginal conditions increase the natural cultural reticence toward responding to surveys and questions. With deep-seated distrust of outsiders and authorities, taping interviews was completely out of the question for this study. The research subjects in this community viewed assurances of confidentiality with great skepticism.

The concepts of saving social face and maintaining social desirability in responses work hand in hand to keep outsiders at a distance and to protect a sense of integrity for the individual and family. Maintaining a respectable social face plays a central role in everyday social life for Koreans. As a consequence, they sometimes protect their sense of self-worth by embellishing their educational and occupational status. A large number of my interviewees refused to reveal the type of work done by different members of their households because these people worked at menial jobs. Similarly, Koreans make a great effort to avoid revealing less-than-desirable living conditions to outsiders. Cohabiting partners do not wish to reveal their partnership arrangements in order to protect face and maintain the facade of culturally acceptable social desirability to others. Divorced individuals or families with a disabled person tend to hide their situations in order to avoid loss of face. These aspects of face and social desirability may apply to Korean responses to face-to-face interviews with researchers, where interviewees might say what they think the interviewer wants to hear.[9]

Unique Korean definitions of "household" and "family" could result in key participants being overlooked in research and in social-service provision. Social services or programs for nonfamily coresidents need to cast a broader net to reach these people effectively. Many new immigrants live in complex households under less-than-ideal conditions. As new Korean immigrants arrive in this country, their social networks and social support systems are pretty much confined to the ethnic community. To study the socioeconomic functioning of the households and social life of these individuals, one must examine their social networks and support structures, including their range and dimensions, as well as the type of networks and variety of support therein. Korean Americans use Christian churches and Buddhist temples for a wide range of social needs. Along with key social-service organizations, these organizations can serve as useful avenues to provide service and information to the Korean American community.

Suggestions to Improve Survey Research in the Korean Community

In order to conduct census and survey research within a Korean American community successfully, an in-depth understanding of the ethnic culture is required. For example, culturally appropriate norms of behavior might require age and gender matches between interviewees and interviewers to increase response rates and the trustworthiness of the data. The success of census or research work in this community requires appropriate use of honorifics and recognition of respected cultural value systems in this highly hierarchical social structure. After three consecutive failures to complete interviews in the pretesting phase of this research study, I modified my research protocol to emphasize my affiliation with a university, my advanced degree, my mature age, my contacts with trusted liaisons in the community, and my Korean ethnicity. These elements addressed culturally important values and increased the number of responses and the quality of those responses.

To conduct research in this community, one must identify community leaders, influential religious organizations, and community service organizations and secure their support for the research. Of Korean Americans, 75% are Christians, 10% are Buddhists, and the remainder consists of followers of other religions or nonbelievers. These preachers and priests have enormous influence in the community; they have wide social networks and command respect and trust. They have influence through formal organizations and through informal social networks. Support and sponsorship for census or other research from trusted community leaders and religious organizations are of critical importance to open doors to the community.

Listings of Korean households in most communities are not available. Often, the accumulation of data will take a much longer time than anticipated. The researcher might have to resort to snowball methods in order to initiate the research. For such efforts, I recommend getting a list of households from churches or community organizations, selecting individuals from the list, and then asking these contacts to provide additional lists of households that meet identified research criteria. Of course, the snowball method of sampling limits the generalizability of research findings, but it provides an entrée into the community and can build a platform for wider research efforts.

Research instruments in English should have a conceptually equivalent (gestalt) translation rather than a literal, word-by-word, direct translation. Even after going through several back translations (back and forth between two languages) to prepare research instruments, the equivalency of meanings for words used in the two different languages may not match. For example, the term *foster children* does not exist in Korean. Verbose expressions should be avoided in trying to develop precise definitions of terms. For example, the census expression used to identify the householder—"the person living here who owns, is buying, or rents this house, apartment, or mobile home"—was too convoluted to be meaningful.

Publicizing the importance of census or survey research in the community will assist to some extent, but this technique does not necessarily reduce or eliminate the barriers toward increasing the response rate and the accuracy of responses. Appropriate incentives should be offered to leaders who provide positive support for the census or other research in the community. For example, social or political recognition through letters of appreciation or plaques from notables, such as the governor, mayor, or borough presidents, will provide needed encouragement to those with limited opportunities for respectable recognition in the majority community. These incentives should assist research efforts.

NOTES

1. This study was funded by the U.S. Census Bureau.

2. I used *etic* (an outsider looking in) definitions in my dichotomy of household structures in this Korean American immigrant study. Certainly, the multigenerational family household is a widely accepted traditional household type in Korean culture. It almost invariably involves patrilineally related kin: grandparent(s), adult son(s), and any spouse(s) and offspring. However, in the majority U.S. culture, the nuclear family household may be more prevalent. In my study "Complex Households and Census among Korean Americans in Queens" (Kang 2001), the funding agency (the Census Bureau) included the multigenerational-family household as a complex household. To keep consistency among the chapters, I classified Korean multigenerational-family households as complex households.

3. Of course, the structures and functions of Korean families are not homogeneous and uniform. I used an ideal-type description of Korean families by extracting salient characteristics of Korean families. Internal diversities in family structures and functions exist among families in different social, economic, and cultural environments. These are based on differ-

ences in socioeconomic status, stages of life course development, and historical or cultural surroundings.

4. As in other immigrant groups, the majority of new immigrants from Korea have been young. For most recent arrivals, it takes long, hard work and considerable economic and social hardship to achieve a stable economic status in the newly adopted country. When the young newcomers attain somewhat sustainable economic status, they marry and start raising new families or bring their spouses from Korea. With the added burden of raising children, along with managing their economic activities, they often need another family member to help take care of household chores and the children. Their old parents are often invited to join the family in the United States to fill this family need. For reasons of family harmony, the person most likely to be invited is the wife's mother, despite the traditional, patri-oriented, Korean kinship system.

5. The standard of living for each household described in the study was based on subjective evaluation of the following items: (1) the size, locale, appearance, and condition of the housing unit, (2) the number of residents relative to the size of the unit, and (3) the furnishings in the unit, such as kitchen facilities, TVs and audio sets, tables and desks, sofas and chairs in the living room, and beds or mattresses in the living room.

6. Chinese culture has had a pervasive and dominant influence over Korean culture for many centuries. Koreans use several thousand Chinese characters, along with their own phonetic Korean characters.

7. When such ways of accommodating nonrelated individuals in a "family-oriented household" in urban areas become widely accepted and acknowledged, Koreans will find it less difficult to differentiate between a roommate, a housemate, a roomer, and a boarder.

8. The traditional (patriarchal) Korean family functions as a collective social and economic entity.

9. Where self-administered or mail surveys are used with the assurance of anonymity and confidentiality of responses, the measurement reliability issues associated with social desirability and social face are generally much less serious (see Kang 1994; Koh et al. 1986).

REFERENCES

Foner, N. 2000. *From Ellis Island to JFK*. New Haven, CT: Yale University Press.

Harrison, R., and S. Rolark. "Summary tape file 1a, press release CB91-215." Washington, DC: U.S. Department of Commerce.

Houchins, L., and C. Houchins. 1972. "Korean experiences in America, 1903–1924." In *The Asian Americans,* ed. N. Hundley. Santa Barbara, CA: Clio Press.

Kang, T. S. 1982. "Korean American elderly: access to resources and adjustments to life change—an exchange approach." Special Studies Publications No. 151. Buffalo: State University of New York.

———. 1992. "Ethnography of alternative enumeration among Korean Americans in Queens." Report No. 15. New York: Center for Survey Methods Research, Census Bureau, U.S. Department of Commerce.

————. 1994. "Mental health status of Asian American elderly." In *Mental health and minority elderly*, ed. D. K. Padgett. Westwood, CT: Greenwood Press.

————. 2001. "Complex households and census among Korean Americans in Queens, New York." Final Report. New York: Center for Survey Methods Research, Census Bureau, U.S. Department of Commerce.

Koh, S. D., T. M. Ceca, T. H. Koh, and W. T. Liu. 1986. *Mental health and stresses in Asian American elderly*. Chicago: Pacific/Asian American Mental Health Research Center.

Min, P. G. 1998. "The Korean-American family." In *Ethnic families in America*, eds. C. H. Mindel, R. Wright, and R. W. Habenstein. Upper Saddle River, NJ: Prentice Hall.

New York Times. 1991. "Queens, doorsteps to the whole wide world," May 3.

Patterson, W. 1979. "A profile of early Korean immigrants to America." Paper presented at the 31st Annual Meeting of the Association for Asian Studies, Los Angeles, California.

Sanjek, R. 1988. "The people of Queens from now to then." Working Papers Series. Queens, NY: Asian/American Center, Queens College, City University of New York.

United Nations Statistics Division. 2002. "Statistical databases," at http://unstats.un.org/unsd/databases.htm.

U.S. Census Bureau. 1981. "Census 1980 summary file 1." Washington, DC: U.S. Department of Commerce.

————. 1991. "Census 1990 summary file 1." Washington, DC: U.S. Department of Commerce.

————. 2001. "Census 2000 summary file 1." Washington, DC: U.S. Department of Commerce.

Making Ends Meet: The Complex Household as a Temporary Survival Strategy among New Latino Immigrants to Virginia[1]

Patricia L. Goerman

INTRODUCTION

$\mathscr{A}$ccording to Angela,[2] being a stranger in a new land is like being

> a little bird that [builds] a new nest. He doesn't know if it's going to rain or not. That's our situation. We don't know, maybe tomorrow we'll be out of work and we'll have to leave [the United States]. . . . So, right now we're trying to establish some savings, what little we can.[3]

Angela lives with her husband, their two children, her niece, and her niece's husband and child in a small apartment in central Virginia, the focus of this study. Angela and her husband are working hard to get established in this country after selling all of their belongings in Mexico to pay $6,000 to cross the border as undocumented immigrants. Her niece plans to move to her own apartment with her husband and child as soon as they have the money, but everyone benefits from dividing the rent and bills in the short term.

Much of the literature on complex household living among Hispanic[4] immigrants in the United States focuses on explaining household formation based on economic, cultural, and life course factors. There is little agreement as to which, if any, of these factors best explains complex household formation. Hispanic immigrants, particularly those who are undocumented, can be considered part of a "hidden" group in the sense that the general public is often unaware of the circumstances of their lives. Our economic system is becoming increasingly dependent on new immigrants to fill the lowest positions in the workforce, and immigrants often live side by side with native-born U.S. citizens. The voices and daily experiences of these new arrivals are often obscured even in academic studies.

This study aims to examine complex household living through the voices of Hispanic immigrants themselves. Research on complex household living has identified a variety of motivational factors involved in household formation, but little research has been done on how Hispanic immigrants actually feel about living with residents other than nuclear family members. I find evidence for economic, cultural, and life course explanations for complex household formation, with a particularly strong emphasis on economic motivations. Most importantly, I find evidence that although complex household living can function as a survival strategy for Latino immigrants, many immigrants dislike these arrangements and hold the nuclear family household as an ideal.

This chapter is based on a subset of data from two in-depth ethnographic interview studies of Hispanic immigrants in central Virginia conducted in 2000 and 2001. The first study was done in conjunction with the Census Bureau, and I interviewed additional respondents later as a part of my dissertation research. In this chapter, I focus on 49 respondents from the two studies.[5] Both of my samples were "purposive" in nature and are not representative of the overall population of Latino immigrants in Virginia or in the United States. Due to the fact that much of the Hispanic immigrant community in central Virginia consists of new or temporary residents, and many are undocumented immigrants, it was not possible to delineate the entire population in order to obtain a representative sample. On the other hand, both studies provide rare, in-depth insight into people's views on complex household living. This study is also unique in shedding some light on the living conditions of new Hispanic immigrants in central Virginia, a population about which very little is known.

To gain an understanding of respondents' views on complex household living, I looked at a variety of factors. I asked respondents to discuss their definitions of "home" and "family"; their criteria for determining household membership, which often differed from those of official organizations, such as the Census Bureau; their ideal living arrangements; their plans for the future; and factors that led to the formation, stability, and dissolution of their households in the United States.

THE LITERATURE ON COMPLEX HOUSEHOLDS AND HISPANIC IMMIGRANTS IN THE UNITED STATES

As T. K. Burch and B. J. Matthews (1987) note, overall trends in developed societies such as the United States point to a progressive decline in average household size with a corresponding decline in the number of households containing nonnuclear relatives and nonrelatives. These overall trends include lower fertility rates, later first marriages, increased cohabitation and divorce rates, and an increase in the number of people living in one- or two-person households and in single-parent families. At the same time, many researchers point out differences by race, socioeconomic status, and immigrant status in people's propensity to form complex households.[6] For example, using the nationally representative 1976 Survey of Income and Education, R. Angel and M. Tienda (1982) compared households of Hispanics, blacks, and non-Hispanic whites. They found that, in general, minority-headed households and female-headed households were more likely to contain extended family members than were non-Hispanic white and married couple households. Using 1990 Census data and data from the 1990 Panel Study of Income Dynamics, J. E. Glick (1999) found that Mexican immigrants were slightly more likely than Mexican Americans, whom she defined as having been born in the United States, to live in extended family households in general. Further, she found that Mexican immigrants were more likely to live with nonnuclear relatives from their own generation, such as cousins and adult siblings, which Glick, F. D. Bean, and J. V. W. Van Hook (1997) call "horizontally extended households" and anthropologists call "laterally extended households." Mexican Americans in Glick's (1999) study, on the other hand, more often lived in "vertically extended households" (Glick, Bean, and Van Hook 1997) with relatives from multiple generations, such as grandparents and grandchildren. The term used in anthropology is *lineally extended households.*

Three different theoretical perspectives are often used to examine complex household formation in the Latino immigrant community in the United States: economic, cultural, and life course explanations (Blank 1998; Glick 1999). Economic explanations often assert that immigrants form complex households to compensate for limited economic opportunities in the United States. High rents, low incomes, the desire to accumulate savings, and the responsibility to support kin in the country of origin can encourage people to increase the number of residents in a household.

Cultural explanations often propose the idea that Latino immigrants traditionally have a strong sense of "familism," or a reliance on and valuing of kinship networks (Tienda 1980). Under this explanation, extended family households are often viewed as a cultural preference and the fact that immigrants residing in the United States for longer periods tend to choose simple, or nuclear family, household arrangements is attributed to cultural assimilation into mainstream U.S. norms and values (Blank 1998; Blank and Torrecilha 1998; Burr and Mutchler 1993).

Finally, life course explanations for complex household living emphasize the idea that opportunities and resources vary at different stages in the life course and that events and circumstances, such as marriage, childbirth, and old age, are strong influences on household composition (Blank and Torrecilha 1998; Glick 1999). According to Blank (1998), the need for economic and social support and the desire for privacy vary along with people's stages in the life course. Factors that often encourage the establishment of simple, nuclear family households are (1) financial independence, (2) marriage, and (3) family reunification through the migration of spouses and children. Families with children under age six or with elderly family members needing care are presumably more likely to form extended households (Blank and Torrecilha 1998). At the same time, S. Blank (1998) emphasizes that normal life course stages are often interrupted by migration; typical patterns are not always predictable for recent immigrants. It can also be argued that migration is itself a stage in the life course for many Latin American immigrants.

There is little agreement about the relative importance of these three explanations for complex household formation. J. A. Burr and J. E. Mutchler (1993) find support for both economic factors, measured by income and cultural assimilation factors, which they examine through English-language proficiency. Based on an analysis of 1980 Census data, they find that low English-language proficiency is linked to complex household living for older Mexican American and Puerto Rican women at lower income levels, but the relationship is much weaker for women of higher economic standing. S. Blank and R. S. Torrecilha (1998) stress the importance of life course explanations for extended family living among Mexican, Puerto Rican, and Cuban immigrants. Using data from the nationally representative 1990 Panel Study of Income Dynamics—Latino National Political Survey, they find no significant relationship between extended family living and cultural or economic indicators, but they do find that Puerto Rican, Cuban, and Mexican immigrant families use extended family living as a "resource generating strategy" to care for children under six and for elderly adults.

Blank (1998) finds economic resources and life course explanations to be the most supported in her study of extended family living among Mexican immigrants and Mexican Americans but finds little support for cultural explanations. She bases her findings on data from the nationally representative 1990 Panel Study of Income Dynamics, Latino Sample. Regarding recent arrivals to the United States, she hypothesizes that specific goals and responsibilities, such as saving money or sending remittances to relatives still in Mexico, may hold even greater importance than cultural and life course explanations for household composition. In short, there is little consensus about the interplay of these three factors and whether one offers a better explanation than the others with respect to complex household formation in the Hispanic immigrant community. Comparison is made difficult by the fact that different researchers often operationalize the three factors differently.

Aside from these three factors, many researchers have found differences in immigrants' propensity to form complex households based on national origin and legal status (Blank and Torrecilha 1998; Burr and Mutchler 1993; Chavez 1990; Glick 1999). Glick (1999) finds that the living arrangements of Mexican immigrants tend to be more temporary in nature than those of U.S.-born Mexican Americans. This finding is consistent with the conclusions of both Blank (1998) and L. R. Chavez (1990). Blank compares the household structure of recent Mexican immigrants who have been in the United States less than 10 years with both immigrants present for more than 10 years and U.S.-born Mexican Americans. She finds that recent immigrants are significantly more likely to live in simple, nuclear family households the longer they reside in the United States. For longer-established immigrants and Mexican Americans born in the United States, increased years of residence do not increase the likelihood of simple-household living.

Chavez (1990) examines the situation of undocumented Mexican and Central American immigrants. Through in-depth interviews of a nonrepresentative sample of immigrants residing in Dallas, Texas, and San Diego, California, Chavez finds that complex household living was common upon arrival in the United States as a survival strategy, but the longer immigrants lived in the United States, the more likely they were to live in nuclear family or single-parent arrangements. He considers "coresidence," or complex household living, as a form of resistance and survival for immigrants who are in a particularly vulnerable position vis-à-vis the host society. Variation in living arrangements for undocumented immigrants is, in essence, making use of friendship and family networks as a social resource in an often-hostile environment.

Some researchers emphasize the need to examine the characteristics of the specific receiving communities in which new immigrants reside as a part of their decisions to live in complex households (Chavez 1990; Mutchler and Krivo 1989). For example, Chavez (1990) finds that undocumented Central American immigrants in Dallas in his sample were more likely to live in complex households than were their counterparts who had been living in San Diego for similar periods. He attributes this finding to the fact that more Central Americans in Dallas than in San Diego appear to be in the United States without their nuclear family members. J. E. Mutchler and L. J. Krivo (1989) point to the importance of examining "community level factors," such as the availability of affordable housing in a region. A trend evident in one part of the United States may not hold true in other areas.

Most of the aforementioned studies of complex household formation make use of large data sets to examine issues of complex household living.

Although their findings have the advantage of being representative of larger populations, there are also some shortcomings. First of all, as Tienda and Angel (1982) point out, knowledge of the mere presence of nonnuclear family members in a household says little about the dynamics within the household. For example, when examining economic factors influencing complex household formation, many researchers report the total combined income of adult household members. Income levels say little about different household members' willingness to pool resources within a household.

Cultural factors influencing household formation are notoriously difficult to define and measure. Chavez (1990) stresses the importance of taking the national origin of immigrants into account. It cannot be assumed that immigrants from different countries and socioeconomic backgrounds will share cultural preferences with regard to household formation. While many Mexican immigrants in his sample give economic and social reasons for migrating, many Central American immigrants migrated due to political turmoil; for them, formation of complex households may be related to helping relatives or friends escape political conflict or violence in their home countries, rather than being any sort of cultural preference.

Although many researchers talk about extended family households as a cultural preference in Latin America, there is evidence that nuclear family households are the norm in industrialized or industrializing nations in general (Blank 1998). For example, the National Institute of Geography and Informatics of Mexico reports that 73.8% of Mexican households were comprised of nuclear families in 1995. A number of my respondents from Mexico, El Salvador, and Honduras expressed the idea that nuclear family living is the ideal and the norm in their countries as well.

The present study has the advantage of rich information from in-depth interviews with people currently or previously residing in complex households. In this chapter, I describe types of complex households, explore respondents' conceptions of "household" and "home" (*hogar*), derive criteria for determining household membership, identify ideal household structures, and analyze the functioning of complex households, as well as people's feelings about their living arrangements and their future plans.

In recent years, the Hispanic immigrant population has been fanning out to new regions of the United States. A study of one such region, central Virginia, may be useful in learning about the experiences of people living in the context of relatively small immigrant communities in other new regions.

RESEARCH SITE

Central Virginia is a research site that provides valuable insight into the recent dramatic increase in Hispanic migration and settlement into a new pole of migration: the southeastern United States. States such as Alabama, Florida, Georgia, Kentucky, Louisiana, Mississippi, North and South Carolina, Tennessee, Virginia, and West Virginia have seen a rapid increase in their Hispanic immigrant populations in recent years (Pressley 2000).

In 1990, Hispanics were the fastest growing ethnic group in Virginia (Tolson 1997). There is a decided lack of accurate data available on this population. Hispanics, particularly recent immigrants, have been a notoriously undercounted group; nevertheless, Census 2000 has confirmed high rates of growth in the Hispanic population in Virginia. The Census Bureau reported that out of the total population in Virginia in 1990, 2.6% was Hispanic (see table 7.1). By 2000, the Hispanic population had risen to 4.7% of the total population. There was a 14.4% increase in the overall Virginia population between 1990 and 2000. For Hispanic residents, a staggering 105.6% increase in population was reported (U.S. Census Bureau 1990, 2000).

The Census Bureau reported that Mexicans were the largest Hispanic national group in Virginia in 2000, making up 22.4% of the overall Hispanic population. After Mexican immigrants, Salvadorans made up the second largest Hispanic national group, composing 13.2% of the total Hispanic population, while Cubans constituted 4.7%, and Hondurans made up 0.5% of the Hispanic population (U.S. Census Bureau 2000).

Large numbers of Hispanic immigrants, particularly Salvadorans, have lived in northern Virginia outside Washington, D.C., for many years (Tolson 1997). Agricultural migrant workers, mostly Mexicans, have traveled and lived throughout the entire state, mostly during summer months when there is demand for agricultural laborers. Hispanic immigrants have recently begun to settle on a more permanent basis in central Virginia. In order to illustrate the growth of the Hispanic community in central Virginia, I provide statistics on a multicounty area in the central part of the state (see table 7.1).[7]

Table 7.1   Population Increases in Virginia and Central Virginia from 1990 to 2000: Overall Population and Hispanic Population

	1990	2000	Percent Change
Virginia total population	6,187,358	7,078,515	+14.4
Virginia Hispanic population	160,288	329,540	+105.6
Hispanics as percentage of total population	2.6	4.7	
Central Virginia[1] total population	164,210	199,648	+21.6
Central Virginia Hispanic population	1,610	4,054	+151.8
Hispanics as percentage of total population	1.0	2.0	

1. This table provides data on a multicounty area in central Virginia.
Source: Data from U.S. Census Bureau (1990, 2000).

In 1990, the Census Bureau reported that Hispanics made up 1% of the residents of this part of central Virginia. By 2000, the Hispanic population had increased by 151.8%, as compared with the 21.6% growth rate in the overall population, bringing Hispanic residents to 2% of the population in this region (U.S. Census Bureau 1990, 2000). Mexican immigrants made up 45.6% of the Hispanic population in this part of central Virginia, while Salvadorans accounted for 13.2%, Cubans for 2.5%, and Hondurans for 2.4%. Given that Hispanic immigrants are a consistently undercounted group, the actual numbers may be significantly higher.

In the past, Hispanic migrant workers have tended to be disproportionately young and male, but former migrants are increasingly "settling out" from or leaving seasonal farm work and are remaining in nontraditional southeastern states and bringing their wives and families to join them. Through my research, I have found that word about job opportunities and good living conditions in Virginia has also spread through immigrant networks, starting a new chain migration pattern.[8] Many immigrants now work in the service sector in restaurants, construction, gardening, and domestic work (Goerman 2004).

METHODS AND SAMPLES

As previously noted, this chapter is based on information from two different rounds of data collection. For the first study, done in conjunction with the Census Bureau, I interviewed 25 Latino immigrants living in complex households in central Virginia.[9] For the purposes of the study, we defined complex households as those consisting of people other than, or in addition to, nuclear family members (spouses and their children) living together in one housing unit. The complex households included both extended family members and nonrelatives.

Subsequently, I conducted a second round of interviews of 42 married or cohabiting Latino immigrants in central Virginia as a part of my dissertation research. Although I did not focus on complex household residence in my recruiting, over three-quarters of the 42 respondents happened to be living in complex households at the time of their interviews. Of the remaining eight respondents, five had lived in complex households in the past, and I interviewed them about past experiences. Only three respondents reported never having lived in a complex household, and I therefore exclude them from the present analysis. In 14 of the households in my second sample, I conducted two separate interviews, one of each partner in a married or cohabiting couple. In order to retain the household as my unit of analysis in this chapter, I exclude the second person I interviewed from these 14 households.[10] Finally, I exclude one respondent from the second sample since he had participated in both studies.[11] Excluding these 18 respondents from the second study, the total number of respondents from both studies is 49 people.

I attempted to recruit as diverse a sample of respondents as possible for both studies. I recruited respondents by making announcements at church services and Mexican Embassy–related gatherings, approaching people in a hospital waiting room, and leaving flyers at Hispanic businesses. In addition to public appeals for volunteers, I employed a "snowball" sampling technique in which I asked each respondent to recommend friends or family whom they thought might be interested in participating in the interview. I also made use of contacts who worked or volunteered with the Hispanic community to meet potential respondents. I contacted the vast majority of respondents, 82%, directly.

The census interviews were conducted from May to June of 2000, and I carried out my dissertation interviews between May and December of 2001. Both rounds of interviews were semistructured. I personally conducted all of the interviews for both studies, most often entirely in Spanish. All but four of the interviews took place in the respondents' homes. Additionally, I interviewed two respondents at their workplaces, one at a restaurant and one at a medical facility. Since the majority of respondents lived in complex households with an average of 5.8 residents, other household residents were often present during the interviews. This occasionally seemed to have an effect on our discussions, particularly with respect to issues such as a respondent's feelings about living with nonnuclear family members. It was quite common that respondents needed to care for small children during the interviews. Other household members, children in particular, often made a great deal of noise and interrupted the interviews. I attempted to conduct the interviews in private if at all possible. Due to the respondents' understandable nervousness, particularly when I was representing the Census Bureau, I did not deem it appropriate to insist that other household residents leave during the interviews.

Experiences in the Field

Working in the field was a very positive experience, but it also involved a number of challenges. People were extremely gracious when I showed up at their churches, workplaces, and other gatherings and explained my research. When I introduced myself as working for the Census Bureau, some respondents were initially nervous about providing personal information, and these interviews were more formal than my second round of interviews. Despite this fact, I had very good rapport with my respondents, and there were most likely a number of factors involved. I introduced myself to the respondents as a graduate student. One woman said that she wanted to help me in the hopes that people would help her children if they did similar projects in the future. With many respondents, I also discussed the fact that I have relatives by marriage from Mexico and that I have spent time abroad in both Mexico and El Salvador. Potential respondents who were unable or unwilling to participate rarely said so directly. I came to realize that a person's saying that he or she was busy more than twice probably indicated an unwillingness to participate. This happened in fewer than 10 instances overall.

As discussed by M. Hammersley and P. Atkinson (1995), there was most likely some interviewer effect involved in my interactions and rapport with respondents due to my age and gender as a young woman. Because many respondents saw me as an unmarried student, they often took a protective and helpful attitude toward me. For example, when I asked their advice about places to meet new respondents, a few people told me about social events, such as dances, but advised me not to attend them since they can be dangerous for a young woman, with alcohol and occasional fighting. Many people offered me special drinks and foods from their countries. A number of respondents, particularly women, said that they would like to stay in touch and remain friends after the interview. I often spent time with respondents after the interviews and conversed about topics not related to the study. In addition, many respondents asked for help with things such as interpreting for them during medical and legal appointments, sending money orders, making calls to their landlords to resolve problems, and providing transportation. I was always happy to help with these situations.

Often, the most challenging part of an interview was locating the respondent's home. I was usually given directions in Spanish over the telephone, and these directions often did not include street names. Some respondents lived in rural areas that were not included on maps. One man could only give me his address as "trailer number three," along with a description of nearby landmarks. In the end, he waited outside, and I drove around until I saw him. While on the road, I relied heavily on my mobile phone and called many respondents more than once in an effort to locate their homes.

I only had one negative experience related to my fieldwork. Unbeknownst to me, one of my female respondents went to a domestic-violence shelter a short time after our interview. Her husband found my name and telephone number among his wife's belongings and called me repeatedly, trying to discover her whereabouts. He suspected that his wife was staying with me and demanded to have my address so that he could come to my home. I did not give him my address, but I was concerned that he might discover it on his own. Due to the strict confidentiality that I had promised my respondents, I struggled with what to do if the man became threatening. In the end, the man discovered that his wife was in a shelter, and he called me to apologize. I later learned that she had returned home with her husband.

Demographic Characteristics of the Respondents

Table 7.2 provides a summary of my respondents' demographic characteristics. Of my respondents, 61% are female.[12] They range in age from 17 to 65, with an average age of 33 years. The educational level of my respondents ranges from having had no formal education to 17 years of schooling, with an average of 8.6 years.[13] The majority, or 63%, of my respondents were from Mexico. Salvadorans were the second most numerous group, making up 25% of the sample. There were four respondents from Honduras, one from Cuba, and one second-generation Mexican American.[14]

The majority of my respondents, 71%, were employed. Of the 35 employed respondents, the most common occupations for both men and women were in the service sector, doing restaurant and domestic work. Factory work was another common occupation for both men and women. Many men worked in construction, and a number of women worked in hotel housekeeping. A few women respondents were small-business owners, sharing ownership with their husbands.

Table 7.2   Respondents' Characteristics Summary Table

Respondent's Characteristics	N = 49	Number	Percent
Gender	Men:	19	39
	Women:	30	61
Nationality	Mexican:	31	63
	Salvadoran:	12	25
	Honduran:	4	8
	Cuban:	1	2
	Mexican American:	1	2
Employment status	Employed:	35	71
	Homemakers:	9	18
	Retired:	2	4
	Unemployed:	3	6
Age	Range:	17–65	
	Mean:	33	
	Median:	31	
Education	Range:	0–17	
	Mean:	8.6	
	Median:	9	

Of the 14 respondents not working outside the home, 9 were house-wives. Additionally, there were two retirement-age women. One of them lived with 11 others in a small apartment and helped care for her grandchildren. The other was a wealthy, retired woman living with a servant and the servant's young child. Her situation was not typical in comparison with the rest of the respondents. There was one man who reported that he did not work because he was in the United States on a tourist visa and did not wish to break the law. There were two men who had recently lost their jobs, but I later learned that both had secured new employment soon after their interviews.

In many respects, recent Hispanic immigrants seem to be isolated from the Anglo population in central Virginia.[15] Although many respondents lived and worked alongside native-born U.S. citizens, they seemed to spend the majority of their free time with other Hispanic immigrants. I spoke with many of my respondents about the nationality of their friends in Virginia. A number of respondents said that they had North American friends, but upon further questioning, most explained that these friends were coworkers with whom they did not socialize outside of work. Low English-language proficiency was a major barrier to socializing with Americans. Most of my respondents reported difficulty communicating and said that they had minimal English-language skills. Close to 15% of respondents said that they spoke no English at all, but another 15% described themselves as fluent in English.

As previously mentioned, a number of theorists have found that complex household living arrangements are most common among recent immigrants as a temporary survival strategy (Chavez 1990; Glick 1999). The majority of people in my sample were relatively recent arrivals to the United States, which lends support to this theory. A total of 44 of my respondents were living in complex households at the time of their interviews. The median amount of time that these people had resided in the United States was four years. I spoke with 36 of these respondents about how long they had resided in Virginia; they had been there for a median of two years. It is likely that the relatively recent arrival in Virginia of many of my respondents accounts in part for their complex household arrangements.

RESULTS

Description of Complex Households

There were four broad types of complex households in my two samples, all with varying combinations of nonnuclear relatives and nonrelatives. First, there were married and cohabiting couples living with their children and additional residents. Second, there were complex households maintained by married couples without children present. Third, there were households headed by men with varying combinations of relatives and nonrelatives. Finally, there were a small number of households maintained by women with additional residents.

The modal complex household was comprised of a married or cohabiting couple, their children, and additional residents, most often other nonnuclear relatives. Following the terminology of Glick, Bean, and Van Hook (1997), these households were typically "horizontally extended," including siblings or cousins of an adult householder. Andrea, for example, lives with her husband, their two children, her sister-in-law, and her sister-in-law's two children (her nephews). Some households were "vertically extended," including parents of an adult householder.

The married or cohabiting couple with additional residents other than children was another common household type. For example, Roberto lives in an apartment with his cohabiting partner, Gema, his brother, and three other men. They live as two relatively separate groups of three. He, Gema, and his brother share one bedroom, and the three men share another bedroom.[16] They did not know the men before moving to Virginia. Roberto and Gema left their young children in Mexico and planned to work in the United States to save money before returning to Mexico to reunite with them.

Another common type of complex household was comprised of a male householder living with both relatives, such as siblings and cousins, and nonrelatives, such as friends and acquaintances. Carlos, for example, lives with seven other men. There are sets of brothers from two unrelated families in the household; three brothers from one family are living with two brothers of another (unrelated) family. The other men are friends or acquaintances, and many did not know each other prior to coming to Virginia. In fact, the three people present during the interview were not even able to name one of the other men who lived there, and we referred to him as "Person X" during the interview. Carlos explained that the number and specific residents in the household varies and is determined by their landlord. He said that often there are fewer than the eight current residents and that it is hard to keep track of who lives in the household, as people come and go. Some of these men have wives residing in their home countries.

Finally, I interviewed a small number of female householders living with either relatives or nonrelatives. Marlena, for example, lives with her two young, adult sons and an adult male friend of one of her sons. Marlena came to the United States with her two sons after separating from her husband. They invited the male friend to live with them temporarily to share the rent and to help him get established.

Types of Dwellings

Most of my respondents lived in either apartments or trailers. Relatively few occupied entire houses, and a small number of respondents lived on just one floor or in one section of a house. In some of these cases, other relatives or friends lived in the other section of the house. One respondent lived in a house that was divided among different families by the landlord, who was also the employer of many of the adult residents. Just over 10% of the respondents lived in housing owned by their employers. These were mostly people engaged in agricultural labor who were provided housing by their employers as part of their wages. Houses tended to be small in size and densely populated.

Many of the homes I visited were sparsely furnished and had a temporary feel to them. In other homes, it was obvious that the residents had put some effort into the décor. It was common to see family photographs hanging on the walls in the living rooms. Some respondents informed me that the pictures were of absent family members, often their own young children, whom they had had to leave behind in their home countries due to the danger and expense of crossing the border as undocumented immigrants. Others had religious symbols, such as crosses and pictures of Catholic figures, on display. In one home, children's dolls hung on the walls, and in another, a display case was filled with model cars. Some respondents had beautiful lace curtains on the windows, and one had a hammock, which she used to put her toddler to sleep, suspended across the living room. I never saw much evidence of overcrowding, even with the family who had 12 people living in a two-bedroom apartment. Most homes were neat and well ordered. Some homes appeared to be quite well established with more-expensive-looking furnishings and electronics equipment.

To gain a more complete picture of the respondents' views of complex household living, the next sections examine their understanding of the concepts of *hogar* (home) and *familia* (family), as well as their criteria for determining household membership. These examinations lend support to the theory that many Hispanic immigrants prefer nuclear household living but form complex households on a temporary basis for a variety of social and economic reasons.

Conceptions of Home and Family

People in my sample reported a strong mental association between the concepts of home and family. This is important for census purposes in collecting data on complex households. When people record the number of residents in their household on a census form, if they view a home as tied to a nuclear

family, they might omit temporary or nonnuclear residents. Also, understanding respondents' definitions of home and family reveals a great deal about their
views of complex household living.

Overall, the word "hogar," translated as either "home" or "household,"
seems to have strong sentimental meaning to many respondents. When asked
about the meaning of the word "hogar," the majority of respondents discussed
the idea of family in general, but nuclear family members more specifically.
Manuel lives with his wife, four children, a grandchild, and a friend. He
described the word "hogar" as follows: "Well, for me hogar means family. For
example, when I speak of my hogar, I'm talking about my children and her
[referring to his wife], my hogar, my family." He then went on to include his
young grandchild in his definition, but not the unrelated friend who was living
in the household.

A smaller number of respondents discussed the idea of "hogar" as being
related to the term *casa* (house). For example, Roberto, who lives with his
cohabiting partner, Gema, a brother, and three friends, said, "Well, in the first
place, in the material sense, hogar is a casa, to have good stability, I mean,
somewhat in a religious sense. An hogar is to be in good standing with God,
with yourself and with other people." Gema[17] says, "We have a small hogar in
our room, my brother-in-law, my husband, and I. We eat together, I make
food for the three of us, and they make food for me. And, well, sometimes we
go out together. Well, we're a little family now, and we all depend on each
other." Although a number of respondents discussed the idea that a hogar
could include extended family members, there seemed to be a consensus that
the word itself implies parents and their children living together, and unrelated
people were rarely considered to be members of a hogar.

Because nuclear families are often separated due to the migration of some
of their members, some respondents consider themselves to be part of, or connected to, households in their countries of origin. Fernando lives with his wife
and a nephew on one floor of a house. They left their three children, ages 5 to
17, in Mexico to spare them the dangers of crossing the border. They are
working to be able to establish their own home in Mexico and plan to return
as soon as possible. When asked to define "hogar," Fernando responded,

> Well, I don't know, right now it's like I don't have one because my children
> aren't here, but when I was in Mexico I went to work at . . . three o'clock in
> the morning and I returned at about ten o'clock at night. But I would say, ay,
> how I long to be in my casa, in my hogar, with my family.

In addition to having implications for filling out the census form, the idea
of a person's being a member of more than one household also has strong policy implications, which I discuss below.

A number of respondents described hogar as *lo máximo* (the most important thing) to them. Alejandro said,

> My God, it's lo máximo, to me. Do you understand? There's an abyss of differ-
> ence between an hogar and a casa. The casa is the building. The hogar is what
> we construct, the elements of each family, no?

Many respondents listed values that they feel are essential in a home, such as
understanding, responsibility, love, sharing, and respect.

I discussed the situation of nonfamily groups living together with a number of my respondents as well. Many people said that the word "hogar" would
be inappropriate to describe a group of nonfamily members living together.
Benita lives with her husband, her young child, her mother, and her husband's
parents. When asked to differentiate between the words *hogar* and *vivienda*
(dwelling), she describes a vivienda as

> your casa. The vivienda [is] to have a roof over your head. But here . . . a group
> of people, as is the case here [in the United States] out of necessity, a group of
> cousins, neighbors, friends live in an apartment. Sometimes up to 12 people live
> together to share the rent . . . but an hogar for a family, a vivienda for a group
> of people.

When I asked them to consider nonfamily members, a few respondents did say
hogar could be used to describe nonfamily members living together if they
functioned as, and considered themselves to be, like a family.

Since many respondents discussed the idea of family as being important
to their definition of a home, I also asked them to define the term *familia* (family). The majority of respondents said that when they mentioned the word
"family," they were referring to nuclear family members. Manuel said, "Family
for me means . . . where a person focuses his love. With his children, his wife,
well, family." Other respondents mentioned other nonnuclear family members
as well. Teresa lives on one floor of a house with her husband and children,
and her mother lives nearby with other family members. In a discussion of the
word "family," she said,

> I have everything. My husband and my children, they are the people I love the
> most. My mother is also nearby, and when I want to, I bring her [here]. If she's
> sick, I have her here. If not, I go to visit her [where she lives], or if my brothers
> take her for a few weeks, we also go and visit her there.

Felix said that for him, family "is my wife, my daughter, my brother, my parents-in-law; they are my family." Other respondents spoke of family as being

related to the term *hogar*, as pertaining to people who share a common interest, and as being related to love.

The overwhelming association of the word "hogar" with family, either nuclear or extended, and with values, such as harmony, love, respect, and understanding, shows that respondents do not necessarily consider that just any group of coresidents constitutes an hogar just because they live together under one roof. This has important implications for filling out questionnaires such as the census form. If a respondent does not consider every resident of his or her household to be a member of his or her home, it is possible that not everyone will be counted.

Criteria for Determining Household Membership

Respondents used a number of criteria to define household membership, and these did not necessarily match those of the Census Bureau. Often, people living in complex households actually considered themselves to be members of separate households living together under one roof. One particularly strong example of this was Beatriz's household. Beatriz lives in a house owned by her husband's employer in which three different families live on two separate floors. On one floor, with one entrance, there are two unrelated families in one housing unit, one consisting of a husband and wife with their two children, and the other, a man, his mother, and his two children. The second floor has a separate entrance, and one nuclear family lives there. The family living alone on the second floor is related to one of the families on the first floor, and members of all three families spend a lot of time together. The two related families reported sharing child care and occasional meals, but they do not live in the same housing unit. Nevertheless, it is important to note that the two families living on the same floor and sharing a common entrance see themselves as two completely separate households, keeping separate finances and preparing meals separately. In addition, these two families reported having filled out two separate census forms in 2000. However, according to Census Bureau rules these two families would be considered one household.[18] This is a clear example of the respondents' views of a household not matching those of the Census Bureau.

Some respondents also considered permanency of residence as a factor in defining household membership. Mariana lives with her husband, her three children, her sister, and her brother-in-law. When she filled out the mock census form during our interview, she omitted her sister and brother-in-law from the form.[19] Through additional probing, Mariana told me that they were in fact residents but that they were just staying with the family temporarily until they were able to establish their own household. She said that she had not included them on the census form since they had only been in the household a short time and were going to be leaving soon.

Some households had members whose residency was ambiguous, as they could have been considered members of more than one household. Raquel lives with her husband, their three children, two of her husband's brothers, and a nephew. During the interview, she told me that she has an additional brother-in-law who was not currently in the household but who often lives in the house for up to two years at a time and whom she expected to return in the next month or two. All three of her husband's brothers have wives and families in Mexico, and they work in Virginia for about a year at a time, then return to Mexico for five or six months to be with their families. Depending on which of these brothers happened to be present at the time of the census, the household would look very different on the census form. These men could be considered members of households in both Mexico and the United States.

The division of household expenses is also important in determining household membership. In the majority of cases in my sample, all of the working adults contributed equally to the household expenses. For example, Ruben lives with two nephews, two cousins, and a friend. He and his roommates divide the rent, electricity, telephone, and grocery bills in six equal parts. In many other cases, the bills were split evenly between two families living in the same residence. Flora lives with her husband, her young son, her cousin, and her cousin's wife. Flora is currently caring for her son full time. Financially, they live as two separate family units, dividing the bills in two equal parts. She and her husband and son are one family unit, and they are responsible for half of the rent and other bills; the other couple pays the other half. Flora says that the two families keep their finances and savings separately, and the other couple is also responsible for the support of their children who remain in Mexico.

In a large number of cases, some of the adults in the household contributed to the household expenses, and other adults did not. The noncontributor in these cases was generally a woman, such as Flora, who was caring for young children, a very recent immigrant who was not yet working, or an elderly relative. Benita lives with her husband, their young child, her mother, and her parents-in-law. Benita and her husband, Gerardo, are business owners. Their parents help with both the business and child care. Benita and Gerardo pay all of the household expenses and do not ask their parents to contribute anything. They are grateful for their parents' support and want to help them save money for their eventual return to their country of origin.

In a smaller number of cases, all adults contributed, but not at an equal level. Juanita lives with her cohabiting partner, their child, her child from a previous relationship, her partner's cousin, and a female friend of Juanita's. Because her partner owns the trailer, he pays most of the bills and does not ask the others to contribute equally, although they do pay a small amount of rent. The two women split the telephone bill since they are the only ones who use the phone. Juanita buys the food for her family, while the other residents buy their food separately.

In two cases, one household member was the sole earner in the family. One of these was Rafael, who lives with his cohabiting partner, Carmen, and her biological child and grandchild, who are not related to him.[20] Carmen cares for the children, and Rafael supports the family. In the other case, Camila lives with her husband, their young child, her sister, and her sister's newborn child. Both women are caring for their children, and Camila's husband is the sole earner in the family. In one final case, nobody worked outside of the home due to the high economic status of the household. This home consisted of a wealthy, retired woman, her live-in servant, and the servant's child. In general, people divided the rent and household bills among all working adults, and separate individuals or families kept the remainder of their earnings, either for remittances to family in their home countries or for personal expenses and savings. This type of arrangement may contribute to families' or groups' viewing themselves as separate households under one roof.

In addition to cases of separate households under one roof, there was clear evidence of connections between distinct households both across national boundaries and within the United States. Concerning connections between respondents and households in their countries of origin, all 33 respondents with whom I spoke about this issue reported either sending money to family members on a regular basis or having done so in the past. The most common relatives receiving remittances were the parents of the respondent or his or her spouse. Many people also reported sending money for the support of their children who remained in their home countries, most often with grandparents. In some cases, the respondents sent money to their siblings and various other relatives, particularly in cases of emergency, such as to pay unexpected medical bills.

Although I found few examples of monetary support between households within the United States, there was a strong sense of community and mutual aid in activities such as looking for jobs, allowing friends to stay while going through hard times, and sharing transportation.[21] A number of respondents also discussed sharing child care with friends and relatives in other households free of charge, providing an economically valuable service. One respondent in particular, Alejandro, discussed differences between U.S. and Latino cultures in this respect. He said that, in his experience, Hispanic families would rarely use a stranger as a babysitter.

In addition to the mutual aid and financial ties discussed above, the division of labor in a household, including housework and child care, can be a factor that respondents use to define household membership. In most of the households in my sample, women residents did the majority of the housework. For example, Lupe lives with her cohabiting partner and another cohabiting couple. She reports that she and the other woman, who both have full-time jobs, do virtually all of the cooking and cleaning. Her partner, Alberto, helps occasionally, but the other man never helps and, in fact, teases Alberto when he sees him doing housework. As was the case in many other households, the two couples buy groceries and prepare meals separately.

In some cases, respondents reported that the housework was shared equally among all adults. This was particularly true in households with no women residents. Ruben lives with five other men, who are nephews, cousins, and friends. He reported that they have a housework schedule, and every third day, a different man is in charge of cleaning the apartment. They also take turns cooking for the group. They make an effort to do equal amounts of housework.

Some respondents reported that men and women share equally in the housework. One man said that he does half of the housework in his home. He lives with his wife and child, two other women, and a man. He says that everybody looks around to see what needs to be done and pitches in, and it is a very nice arrangement.[22] Interestingly, I spoke with his wife separately, and she had an entirely different view of the situation. She complained that her husband does not clean much and, in fact, creates more housework for her by leaving messes around the house. She reported that she does the vast majority of the housework. In summary, it seems likely that respondents who live as groups or families, taking care of their meals or other housework separately from other household residents, may see themselves as members of separate households living under the same roof.

Ideal Household Structures

In order to further investigate respondents' views of household structure, I asked them to discuss their ideal living arrangements, their satisfaction with their current household arrangements, and their plans for the future. Due to the nature of complex households and the fact that I interviewed most respondents in their homes, it was often impossible to carry out the interviews in private.[23] The presence of others most certainly had an effect on some of the respondents' discussions of their ideal living arrangements, as a person would be hesitant to express dissatisfaction in the presence of other residents. Despite this, many respondents did express dissatisfaction with living in complex households.

I spoke with 32 respondents about their views of the ideal household structure. The vast majority of them, 91%, mentioned a nuclear family arrangement as their ideal household structure. Luz lives with her husband and her three children but has lived in complex households in the past with both her husband's brothers and with nonrelatives. She says,

> I told my husband, look, we already have the house in Mexico. We already have what we wanted. I don't want to live with anybody. The goal has been achieved. We won't be any richer or poorer if we pay the rent ourselves. And it's such tranquility. Oh, we live so much better.[24]

Just 17% of those respondents expressed that their ideal might include living with both nuclear and extended family members. Milagros lives with her husband, her husband's brother, her sister, her father, and a friend. When asked to name her ideal household structure, she listed her daughter who was currently residing in Mexico, her parents, and her siblings as ideal coresidents. It should be noted that her husband and sister were listening in on the interview.

Only one respondent mentioned the possibility of living with nonrelatives when asked about his ideal situation, but even he expressed nuclear family living arrangements as his first choice. Roberto said, "[I'd like to] live with my children and my wife, all others come after them. . . . We might live with other people as we're doing now, no? Well, yes, we'd live with friends, but not if we could make it alone." Once again, other people walked in and out of the room during Roberto's interview. It is clear that nuclear family living was the overwhelming preference among these respondents.

Although most respondents said that they were not currently living in their ideal type of household, many of them said that they were happy with their current living arrangements for various reasons. Victoria lives with her husband, his cousin, and a married couple of no relation to them. She says that she is happy with her current situation and compares it to a previous complex household in which she and her husband and his cousin had lived. She says,

> Where we are now is the best house, the best *hogar* that we've been in [in the United States] because here you can come home and you know that nobody is going to mess with you. Nobody will say, "Hey, you did this or that wrong." Here everyone is respectful of each other. We're a couple, and the other couple that lives here, if they have a problem, they take care of it without our intervention because it's none of our business.

Victoria and her husband, Enrique, plan to return to Mexico in the next few months to establish a business and reunite with their extended family members. Like many others, they seem happy with their current living situation because it is helping them advance toward their objectives of saving money and establishing themselves as an independent nuclear family at some time in the future.[25]

The majority of respondents did not perceive their current living situations to be permanent. I spoke with 41 of the 44 respondents currently living in complex households about this issue. Fully 76% anticipated that they would not live with their current coresidents permanently. In some cases, this was related to the fact that they planned to remain in the United States only temporarily. Others who planned to remain here indefinitely reported living in complex households either to receive help or to help others get established in the United States. For example, Silvia, who lives with her husband, their two children, her sister, and another couple and their child, says, "It's nice to have fewer people, who wouldn't like that? You feel at times that you have to support people, help them when they are in need because it's the right thing to do." Silvia and her husband, Gumersindo, had invited the other couple to stay with them since they were friends from the same village in their home country, and they had arrived in Virginia without a place to stay. The couple planned to stay with Silvia and Gumersindo indefinitely until they could afford to move into their own place. In 7% of the cases, respondents reported that they were uncertain of their future plans, which, again, might have been related to other residents being present during the interview.

I asked 13 of the respondents currently living in complex households whether they felt it would be common to live with their current coresidents in their home countries. All 13 replied that they would not expect to be living with these same people. Some respondents discussed the idea that they perceived nuclear households to be the norm in their home country. Elena lives with her cohabiting partner and two male friends she met through her job. When asked if she thought that it was common in El Salvador to live with nonfamily members, she said,

> No, there it's not very common because, whether it's a nice house or a bad one, every person has his or her little house. . . . There, only family members live together, like the mother and father, the children, and sometimes an uncle. But no, the majority of people, when they get married, they form their own separate household. On the other hand, here it's necessary to [live] with other people because the rent is more expensive; there, the majority of people have their little house, so they don't have to pay rent. You buy it and don't pay rent. . . . [D]epending on where you live, if there's electricity you only pay for electricity or water.

Respondents from Mexico and Honduras also emphasized this idea. P. Hondagneu-Sotelo notes that historically in rural Mexico, for example, it has been common for a young couple to live with the husband's parents while working to establish themselves independently, although matrifocality and neolocality are becoming increasingly common (1994, 13). Some women in my sample discussed having lived with their husband's parents in their home countries.

Migration to the United States, whether temporary or permanent, is often the easiest way to achieve the goal of establishing an independent household. Teresa, a woman who lives with her husband and children in the United States, says,

> Here he who works has [a future] and in Mexico even if you work you don't have anything . . . If you want to build yourself a house or something, I think that you won't ever be able to do it, only one made of straw or poles . . . because to make yourself a house of good materials, working in Mexico you'll never do it.

Respondents from Honduras and El Salvador expressed similar views.

FACTORS THAT LEAD TO HOUSEHOLD FORMATION, STABILITY, AND DISSOLUTION

I spoke with 42 respondents about their reasons for living in a complex household. Many people discussed multiple motivations. The majority, 62%, cited economic reasons for living in complex households. For example, Flora lives with her husband, their child, her husband's cousin and his wife. When asked how they had come to live together, she responded, ". . . What happens is that when someone is married he or she tries to live with another couple to help each other with the rent. There are times when one couple doesn't earn enough [to cover everything]."

Just over half, 52%, also explained that they lived with their other household members simply because they were family. Ana[26] lives with her husband, two adult children, a son-in-law and a grandchild. When asked how they all came to live together she said, "we've never been separated, mother and siblings" and explained that it was logical that they should all live together. In some cases my question about how respondents had come to live together sounded strange to respondents because they felt that it was obvious that they were living with family members. This finding lends support to the idea of "familism" and the importance of kinship networks in settling in the United States. While nuclear family living arrangements were the overwhelming preference in my sample, when faced with the possibility of doubling up on housing to make ends meet, my respondents demonstrated a preference for extended family arrangements over living with friends or acquaintances.

Of the respondents who cited economic reasons, many discussed the idea that they had invited people to stay with them temporarily in order to help them get established in the United States. Others had taken in people who had nowhere else to go or who had shown up unexpectedly. Fernando lives with his wife and a nephew. In describing how they came to live with his nephew he said,

> One day they [other family members] called me here . . . and told me that he was coming here, and I said, "Where is he coming from?" And well, he was already coming . . . nobody told him to come, he just said, "I'm coming" . . . [he asked] if we could meet him here and here he's stayed.

Gumersindo[27] discussed the idea of being obligated to help friends and family and conflicts that can occur if one is not able to accommodate everyone who arrives. He lives with his nuclear family in addition to his wife's sister and a married couple with a child. He said,

> if I don't have space, what am I going to do? I can't [invite people to stay], and then the friend can interpret the situation badly, right? "He didn't want to give me a place to stay," but sometimes you just can't.

Two respondents had sent for family members from their home country to help them establish a business or to help them care for young children. Silvia said that she had paid for a sister to come to help her with child care. After her sister got married and moved out of her house, Silvia sent for another sister, who is now caring for her children. This finding lends support to life course explanations for complex household formation.

Remedios[28] brought up the additional issue that although she would like to get her own place it would be extremely difficult since she lacked valid U.S. identification, which would be required by many landlords. Clearly the availability, including constraints for undocumented immigrants, as well as the affordability of housing in a region have a strong effect on the formation of different household types.

In order to examine household dissolution I asked respondents to describe some of the problems that they had experienced in complex households. Problems with housework, cramped living quarters and a lack of privacy were the most commonly cited complaints. Hondagneu-Sotelo reports that women respondents in her study often complained about the increased domestic burdens involved in hosting male visitors (1994, 107). Similarly, a number of women in my sample complained about male household members who refused to participate in housework or who left the residence in disarray.

Gisela[29] lives with her husband, Fernando, and his nephew. She discussed her previous negative experience living with her husband's siblings and a different nephew:

> They started to drink a lot . . . here on Saturdays and Sundays when they were off. They left a big mess for me, and they played very loud music all the time. They started doing this on Fridays, and we [she and Fernando] have to work on Saturdays and Sundays. . . . They also brought lots friends to the house, and they made even more of a mess.

Teresa discussed her problems with cramped living space when her husband's cousins stayed with her family for nine months.

> At that time, I had three children, two boys and a girl, and the house only has three bedrooms. My daughter slept in one bedroom, my sons were in another, and the other one was for us [Teresa and her husband]. So, when they came, I had to take my sons and put them in my bedroom to make space for the others, and that's a little bit difficult.

Lack of privacy was a common complaint. Ana described a time when a man from her church had stayed with her family until he could find his own place. She typically gets up at five o'clock in the morning to prepare lunch for her son to take to work. While the man was sleeping in the living room, she had been unable to cook without getting dressed first. Her husband eventually asked the man to leave, saying, "Mine should be the only pants in the house."

Some respondents discussed lifestyle differences as a problem in complex households. The drinking behavior of coresidents and their bringing unwanted visitors into the home were common complaints. Many people also discussed differences in schedule as a problem. Milagros talked about a previous living situation and the difficulty of many people wanting to use the bathroom at the same time in the mornings. She also said that residents who were on different work schedules made a lot of noise at times when she was trying to sleep.

Respondents cited other issues with less frequency. One such problem was fears about personal safety with respect to other housemates. Victoria reported that in a previous household where she had lived with her husband and a number of single men, she spent all of her time locked in her bedroom while her husband was working. The men were always drinking and acting rowdy, and she felt unsafe. Luz told a story about a female housemate's mistreating her child. The woman had been providing child care for Luz, but a neighbor later informed her that she was shutting Luz's child in the bathroom when he cried. Flora talked of other residents acting as a bad influence on her spouse and encouraging him to drink more than he had in the past. People discussed these issues both as reasons for leaving households in the past or for why they were unhappy in their current situations.

Although it was not a specific question in my interviews, 20 respondents offered their opinions on the benefits of complex household living. The most commonly cited benefit, in 57% of the cases, was economic help. Many people talked about social support, 14%, and help with housework and child care, 11%. Finally, a few respondents discussed the ideas of not being alone and of having someone to stand up for you against your spouse in times of conflict. Overall, it seems that the benefits of living in a complex household can outweigh the difficulties for many new Hispanic immigrants, at least in the short term.

Dominant Residence Patterns in the United States versus Trends for New Immigrants

As described by Burch and Matthews (1987), in developed Western countries, the overall trend has been a decline in average household size and a decline in complex household living. Recent Hispanic immigrants, on the other hand, face a number of disadvantages as new arrivals in the United States. I did not specifically ask my respondents about their legal status. However, less than one-fifth of my respondents specifically identified themselves as legal residents or U.S. citizens. Chavez (1990, 32) discusses the plight of undocumented immigrants as "outsiders" who are "victims of state policies which limit, or attempt to limit, their participation in state programs such as health care, education and housing." Due to their illegal status, they face barriers against finding and maintaining employment. They also face the threat of being apprehended and even expelled from the country (Chavez 1990). The formation of complex households truly can be seen as a way of using social networks as a resource in the face of barriers to social and economic incorporation into the new country.

CONCLUSION AND IMPLICATIONS

Overall, the experiences of the respondents in my two samples most strongly support economic explanations for complex household living. For people in these samples, there is evidence that complex household living, both with extended family and nonfamily members, is not a cultural preference. In fact, many respondents felt that nuclear family living was the norm in their countries of origin. The majority expressed nuclear family living as their ideal. At the same time, a small number of respondents did express extended family living as their preference, and thought it strange when I asked them why they were living with their current coresidents.

There was also evidence to support life course explanations in that a small number of respondents with young children and small-business owners had sent for extended family members from their countries of origin to live with them temporarily to help them get established. Migration itself can be considered a part of the life course, with many people spending time working in the United States in order to get established either in the United States or in their home countries. Many of my findings support Blank's (1998) idea that specific goals particular to the context of early migration, such as the desire to establish a household or support relatives in the home country, play a strong role in the household formation of recent immigrants.

There is evidence of an association between the concepts of home and family for the majority of my respondents. The Census Bureau definition of household emphasizes the physical building and assumes that a structure intended for occupancy as separate living quarters will necessarily correspond to one household. In the complex households in my two samples, there is evidence that simply sharing a living space with others does not automatically constitute household membership for many people. A number of respondents view themselves as members of one household among multiple households within a single structure. There is also evidence that many respondents consider themselves to be continued members of households in their countries of origin. Many people have left nuclear family members behind, including their own young children, and many are responsible for the economic support of households in their countries of origin. Overall, respondents did not regard complex household living in Virginia as an ideal or permanent situation.

Additional study of these issues is in order. Many of the insights gained may be of use in examining new immigrant receiving areas, such as those in the southeastern United States. As the Hispanic population increases in states such as Virginia, an understanding of the way in which these new immigrants are living will become increasingly important.

There are a number of policy implications related to complex household living among recent Hispanic immigrants. First of all, there is an association between complex households and issues of undercounting in the census (Blumberg and Goerman 2000; de la Puente 1993). A number of people in my census sample incorrectly omitted household members from their mock census forms because they did not consider them to be permanent or actual members of their households. A more complete understanding of complex household living should aid in reevaluating questionnaires such as the census form, taking cultural conceptions of the meaning of the words "household" and "family" into account.

Businesses and communities in the United States reap many benefits from the presence of Hispanic immigrants. Immigrants contribute to the U.S. economy through their labor, their consumer activities, and their payment of income and sales taxes. They bring many cultural contributions to their communities as well. The prevalence of ethnic restaurants and food products, festivals, and holiday celebrations are some of the many examples. Immigrants also participate in religious and political organizations, and they forge personal bonds with members of their new communities. At the same time, many new immigrants do the least desirable work in our society, often for extremely low pay, lacking health insurance, job security, retirement benefits, or job-advancement possibilities. New immigrants in this situation face many challenges.

When the number of new immigrants in a state is underestimated, inadequate government resources will be allocated to that particular area. Resources sorely needed by immigrants that could potentially be provided through government policy include more affordable housing, health care, educational services, access to affordable child care, increased public transportation, and greater facility in obtaining driver's licenses.[30]

New Hispanic immigrants often live side by side with longer-term residents of Anglo communities in the United States. Often, due to a language barrier, there is a lack of understanding and communication between the two groups. There are a number of misconceptions about complex household living. Many people assume that it is a cultural ideal and that immigrants are in fact continuing traditions from their countries of origin. A number of my respondents discussed having had misunderstandings with Anglo-Americans, including incidents in which neighbors have attempted to have them evicted for having too many residents in their homes. With a greater understanding of people's reasons for living in complex households, we can better understand their needs and objectives. The fact that many immigrants are contributing to the support of households in other countries is an extremely important factor.

Any policies designed to reduce or regulate complex household living will have far-reaching effects across national boundaries. While complex households are far from the ideal living situation for many new immigrants, they do serve as a temporary survival strategy, enabling people to get established in the United States or save money for an eventual return to their home countries.

NOTES

1. I presented an earlier version of this chapter at the 2002 Southern Sociological Society Annual Meeting in Baltimore, Maryland. I would like to thank Rae Blumberg for her

collaboration on the first project. I would also like to thank Laurie Schwede, Anna Chan, Rae Blumberg, and Sharon Hays for their insightful comments; Paul Schroeder for his feedback, assistance with data analysis, and support; and Marjorie and Charles W. Goerman for their support and encouragement. The U.S. Census Bureau and a University of Virginia Graduate School of Arts and Sciences Dissertation Year Fellowship provided research support.

2. All names used in reference to respondents are pseudonyms.

3. I have translated all of the respondents' comments from Spanish to English.

4. In 1978, the Office of Management and Budget began to use the label "Hispanic," which the office defined as "a person of Mexican, Puerto Rican, Cuban, Central or South American, or other Spanish culture or origin regardless of race" (Marín and Marín 1991, 20). I adhere to this definition, but since immigrants in my sample referred to themselves as both Hispanic and Latino, I use the two terms interchangeably.

5. See the "Methods and Samples" section for more information on my samples.

6. Some researchers focus only on extended family households, while others examine households with nonrelated members as well.

7. I provide general information on a multicounty area as an illustration of Hispanic population trends in central Virginia. To maintain the confidentiality of my respondents, I do not provide the exact location.

8. A chain migration pattern is one in which "the concentration of immigrants in certain destination areas create a 'family and friends' effect that channels later streams of immigrants to the same places and facilitates their arrival and integration" (Massey 1999, 306).

9. Rae Lesser Blumberg and I collaborated on the original project (Blumberg and Goerman 2000).

10. I include comments from some of these 14 secondary respondents in this chapter; in those cases, I indicate that the spouse of a primary respondent made those comments.

11. In tabulating summary characteristics for my sample, I use only the information that this respondent gave me in his first interview. Interestingly, this respondent was unemployed and living in a complex household at the time of his first interview in 2000. When I reinterviewed him in 2001, he was a small-business owner living in a simple, nuclear family household.

12. I made no attempt to choose respondents based on their gender. In general, I interviewed those who signed up when I visited churches or businesses and the people whose names I received through contacts or through snowball sampling. It did not seem that either men or women were more willing to participate.

13. In Mexico, the educational system is structured as follows: Primary school consists of six years and secondary school of three years of schooling. This is followed by three years of preparatory school and an average of four years of university studies. Other Latin American countries have similar systems. In my sample, the mode was six years of schooling (27% of respondents), and another 22% had completed secondary school (nine years). Of my respondents, 18% had not finished primary school, while 12% had completed the equivalent of a university degree.

14. I include this last respondent in my analysis because her husband and coresidents in her complex household were foreign born.

15. The relative lack of connections between my respondents and the wider Anglo community is most likely due, in part, to the fact that most of my respondents were relatively recent arrivals in the area.

16. Whether or not there was a partition dividing the bedroom shared by Roberto, his female partner, and his brother was beyond the scope of my inquiry.

17. Gema is the cohabiting partner of one of the 49 principal respondents in this chapter.

18. According to the Census Bureau, "a household consists of all the persons who occupy a housing unit. A house, an apartment or other group of rooms, or a single room, is regarded as a housing unit when it is occupied or intended for occupancy as separate living quarters; that is, when the occupants do not live and eat with any other persons in the structure and there is direct access to the outside or through a common hall" (2003, B14).

19. For my first round of interviews, the census cases, I asked respondents to fill out a mock census form on which they were instructed to list all of the people living or staying in their household.

20. Carmen's child and grandchild (the child of a nonresident adult daughter) were both minor children.

21. Only two of the 25 respondents in the census sample reported receiving monetary support from nonhousehold members within the United States. One young married woman reported that her mother occasionally gave her a few dollars, and another woman reported that friends of the family sometimes ate meals in her home and left a little money in exchange.

22. This man is the spouse of one of the 49 principal respondents in this chapter.

23. Many times, other household residents walked in and out of the room where the interview was taking place, and in a few cases, other residents even sat down to listen or participate.

24. While many immigrants come to the United States with the intention of remaining temporarily, plans often change, and people settle more permanently in their new communities. Luz and her husband's original goal was to save money to establish themselves in Mexico, but they had recently purchased a home in central Virginia and no longer had specific plans to return to Mexico. (For more discussion of this issue, see Goerman 2004.)

25. While some respondents hoped to establish an independent household in their home countries, others wanted to establish themselves permanently in the United States.

26. Ana is the spouse of one of the 49 principal respondents in this chapter.

27. Gumersindo is the spouse of one of the 49 principal respondents in this chapter.

28. Remedios is a secondary household resident and not a primary respondent.

29. Gisela is the spouse of Fernando, one of the 49 principal respondents in this chapter.

30. Since the terror attacks of September 11, 2001, there has been a great deal of debate about the issue of undocumented immigrants' access to driver's licenses. In March 2003, Virginia governor Mark Warner signed a law prohibiting undocumented immigrants from obtaining driver's licenses in the commonwealth of Virginia (Wood 2003). Unfortunately, this type of law causes many undocumented immigrants to drive without valid licenses or automobile insurance. It remains to be seen whether a system can be devised that will both strengthen national security and prevent unlicensed and uninsured driving. (For more information on this debate, see Dinerstein 2002.)

REFERENCES

Angel, R., and M. Tienda. 1982. "Determinants of extended household structure: cultural pattern or economic need?" *American Journal of Sociology* 87: 1360–83.

Blank, S. 1998. "Hearth and home: the living arrangements of Mexican immigrants and U.S.-born Mexican Americans." *Sociological Forum* 13: 35–59.

Blank, S., and R. S. Torrecilha. 1998. "Understanding the living arrangements of Latino immigrants: a life course approach." *International Migration Review* 32: 1–20 (retrieved February 20, 2000, from InfoTrac Web Expanded Academic ASAP. A55207898).

Blumberg, R. L., and P. L. Goerman. 2000. "Family complexity among Latino immigrants in Virginia. an ethnographic study of their households aimed at improving census categories." Report submitted to the U.S. Census Bureau.

Burch, T. K., and Matthews, B. J. 1987. "Household formation in developed societies." *Population and Development Review* 13: 495–511.

Burr, J. A., and J. E. Mutchler. 1993. "Ethnic living arrangements: cultural convergence or cultural manifestation." *Social Forces* 72: 169–79.

Chavez, L. R. 1990. "Co-residence and resistance: strategies for survival among undocumented Mexicans and Central Americans in the United States." *Urban Anthropology* 19: 31–62.

de la Puente, M. 1993. "Why are people missed or erroneously included by the census: a summary of findings from ethnographic coverage reports." Paper presented at the Census Bureau's Research Conference on Undercounted Ethnic Populations, Richmond, Virginia, May 5.

Dinerstein, M. 2002. "America's identity crisis: document fraud is pervasive and pernicious." Center for Immigration Studies, April, at www.cis.org/articles/2002/back302.html (accessed December 1, 2002).

Glick, J. E. 1999. "Economic support from and to extended kin: a comparison of Mexican Americans and Mexican immigrants." *International Migration Review* 33 (3): 745–66 (retrieved February 20, 2000, from InfoTrac Web Expanded Academic ASAP. A56021149).

Glick, J. E., F. D. Bean, and J. V. W. Van Hook. 1997. "Immigration and changing patterns of extended family household structure in the United States." *Journal of Marriage and the Family* 59: 177–91.

Goerman, P. L. 2004. "The promised land? The gendered experience of new Hispanic 'proletarian' immigrants to central Virginia." Unpublished Ph.D. diss., University of Virginia.

Hammersley, M., and P. Atkinson. 1995. *Ethnography: principles in action.* 2nd ed. New York: Routledge.

Hondagneu-Sotelo, P. 1994. *Gendered transitions: Mexican experiences of immigration.* Berkeley: University of California Press.

Massey, D. S. 1999. "International migration at the dawn of the twenty-first century: the role of the state." *Population and Development Review* 25: 303–22.

Marín, G., and B. V. Marín. 1991. *Research with Hispanic populations.* Newbury Park, CA: Sage Publications.

Mutchler, J. E., and L. J. Krivo, 1989. "Availability and affordability: household adaptation to a housing squeeze." *Social Forces* 68: 241–61.

National Institute of Statistics, Geography and Informatics, Mexico (Instituto Nacional de Estadística, Geografía e Informática, Mexico). 1995. "Households and family indicators." www.inegi.gob.mx/difusion/ingles/fiest.html (accessed August 19, 2002).

Pressley, S. A. 2000. "Hispanic immigration boom rattles South: rapid influx to some areas raises tensions." *Washington Post*. March 6, A03.

Tienda, M. 1980. "Familism and structural assimilation of Mexican immigrants in the United States." *International Migration Review* 14: 383–408.

Tienda, M., and R. Angel. 1982. "Headship and household composition among blacks, Hispanics, and other whites." *Social Forces* 61: 508–31.

Tolson, D. J. 1997. "Increased immigration: an asset for Virginia." *Virginia Newsletter* 73 (3) (April), at www.ccps.virginia.edu/publications/NLtrs/Mar97NL.pdf (accessed January 15, 2000).

U.S. Census Bureau. 1990. "American FactFinder detailed tables: census summary tape file 1-100-percent data, tables: P001 persons, P008 persons of Hispanic origin," at http://factfinder.census.gov/servlet/BasicFactsServlet (accessed March 15, 2002).

———. 2000. "American FactFinder detailed tables: census summary file 1-100-percent data.tables: P1 total population, P11 Hispanic or Latino, and PCT11. Hispanic or Latino by specific origin," at http://factfinder.census.gov/servlet/BasicFactsServlet (accessed March 15, 2002).

———. 2003. 2000 Census of population and housing, technical documentation, www.census.gov/prod/cen2000/doc/sf3.pdf (accessed March 15, 2002).

Wood, D. B. 2003. "Should illegals be given driver's licenses? Advocates say IDs are for road safety, but others say they reward those in the US illegally." *Christian Science Monitor.* April 28, at www.csmonitor.com/2003/0428/p02s02-usgn.htm.

• 8 •

African Americans and Whites

Laurel Schwede and Rae Lesser Blumberg

AFRICAN AMERICANS IN
THE OVERALL POPULATION

$\mathscr{B}$efore 1970, when changing immigration patterns started creating a rainbow of diversity and changed the colors in which the portrait of the United States was painted, our country's people were depicted largely in white and black. In Census 2000, 12.9% of the U.S. population reported as African American or black alone or in combination with another race (this was still slightly higher than the Latino population, which, by 2003, had become the largest ethnic minority). The terms *African American* or *black* refer to people with origins in any of the black racial groups of Africa (U.S. Office of Management and Budget 1997).

From 1990 to 2000, the African American population grew faster than the overall U.S. population: between 15.6% and 21.5%,[1] as compared to a 13.2% population growth for the nation as a whole (McKinnon 2001). Geographically, a majority (54%) of African Americans live in the South, distributed in a loose arc across the coastal and lowland areas from East Texas through Maryland and into Delaware. The Northeast and Midwest each account for a little under 20% of blacks, and the remaining 10% reside in the West.[2] Blacks made up the majority of the population in Gary, Indiana, and Detroit, Michigan, as well as in at least eight cities in that southern arc from New Orleans, Louisiana, to Baltimore, Maryland. Significant numbers of African Americans also live in large cities, such as 2 million in New York City and more than 1 million in Chicago. The black population, however, is still highly concentrated; in just under two-thirds of all counties, they made up less than 6% of the county population (McKinnon 2001, figure 3 map).

From Census Day in 2000 to July 2004, the African American population grew 5.7% to 39.2 million people. This was faster than the 4.3% growth of the overall population, but a fraction of the Latinos' 17% growth rate (U.S. Census Bureau 2005a).

Household and Family Types at the National Level

In comparison to all U.S. households, African American households are

- Larger. There are 2.74 people per household for African Americans, compared to 2.59 overall.[3]
- Almost as likely to consist of families as compared to the overall population, but with a very different breakdown by type. Specifically they are
- More than 2.5 times more likely to be of the female-householder family type, to a lesser extent, of the male householder family type, and, concomitantly, much less likely to be married couple units[4]
- Much more likely to include children under age 18[5]
- The least likely of all six ethnic groups to be living in nonfamily households with others.[6]

Minimum Proportion of Complex Households at the National Level

As discussed in the introduction to the Navajo and Iñupiat, households containing nonrelatives are complex by our definition and we can identify them at the national level using Census 2000 tables on the website. As table 8.1

Table 8.1   Minimum Proportion of Complex Households for African Americans, Whites, and the Overall Population at the National Level (Family and Nonfamily Households with Any Nonrelatives)

National Population Groups	Percentage of Households with Nonrelatives in Family Households[1]	Percentage of Households with Nonrelatives in Nonfamily Households[2]	Minimum Proportion of Complex Households (Households with Any Nonrelatives)[3]
Overall U.S. population	4.5	6.1	**10.6**
African American population	7.2	5.1	**12.3**
White population	3.2	6.3	**9.5**

1. Calculated by subtracting percentage of nonfamily households with nonrelatives from all households with nonrelatives (PCT 16 − PCT 9).
2. Calculated from Census 2000 SF-2, PCT 9 data.
3. Calculated from Census 2000 SF-2, PCT 16 data.

shows, African American households are more likely than all U.S. households to include nonrelatives (12.3% to 10.6%). Recall that these are of two types: (1) family households with nonrelatives, and (2) nonfamily households of at least two people. Like American Indians, Alaska Natives, and Latinos at the national level, black households with nonrelatives are more likely to be of the family than the nonfamily type (7.2% to 5.1%); the opposite is true for all U.S. households (4.5% to 6.1%).[7]

Indirect Clues to Complex Households with Nonnuclear Relatives at the National Level

As discussed in the earlier section introductions, clues from the person-level data indicate that African American children are more likely than children in the overall population to be living in complex households where the householder is a relative, but not their parent: African American children represent 15% of all children recorded by Census 2000, but about "32% of all grandchildren, 35% of all foster children, and 29% of relatives of the householder other than sons, daughters, and grandchildren" (Lugaila and Overturf 2004, 7). Unfortunately, we cannot convert person-level data to household-level data from website data tables. This means that we cannot identify and count the number of African American households that are complex because these children are living with people who are nonnuclear relatives.

WHITES IN THE OVERALL POPULATION

In Census 2000, 77.1% of the total population, 211.5 million people, were reported as white, alone or in combination with some other race(s).[8] "White" refers to people with origins in any of the original peoples of Europe, the Middle East, or North Africa, including Arabs (U.S. Office of Management and Budget 1997). High proportions of whites are found in the majority of U.S. counties, especially across the northern half of the country, with some projections southward (see Grieco 2001, figure 3 map). But note that in federal data collections, the "white" category includes Hispanics who classify themselves as white.[9] If those classified both as Hispanic/Latino and as white are taken out of the white count, then the proportion of the total U.S. population in 2000 that was non-Hispanic white is only 70%, not 77.1% (Grieco 2001).

From 1990 to 2000, the population growth rate of whites was between 5.9% and 8.6% (Grieco 2001). This is the only population group in this comparative study that increased more slowly than the overall population (13.2%) during this time period.

This trend of the white population growing more slowly relative to other U.S. ethnic populations continued in the four years following Census 2000. According to the most recently released estimates (U.S. Census Bureau 2005a), from April 2000 to July 2004, the white population grew by 3.6% to 239.9 million, less than the 4.3% growth of the total population. If we exclude (1) those who reported another race in addition to white, and (2) those classified as white and listing Hispanic ethnicity, then the remaining "white alone, non-Hispanic" population increased by just 1.2% during this three-year period to an estimated 197.8 million (U.S. Census Bureau 2005a). This was a much lower rate of increase than for any other ethnic group in this book.

Part of the reason this subpopulation is increasing at a slower rate than any of our other groups is its age structure: on average, non-Hispanic whites reporting one race make up the oldest of our ethnic groups, with a median age of 40.0 years in 2004, compared to 36.0 for the whole population and 26.9 for Latinos (U.S. Census Bureau 2005b–d). They are disproportionately more likely to be in the 65 + age group than any other ethnic subpopulation[10]; this difference will become even more pronounced as the disproportionately large baby boom generation moves into the retirement years. In our rural white study, we visit complex households with elderly people.

Household and Family Types at the National Level

As compared to all U.S. households, white, non-Hispanic households in Census 2000 are

- The smallest, containing 2.43 people per household, compared to 2.59 for all households[11]
- The least likely to be living in family households and the most likely to be living alone[12]
- The least likely of any group to be of the "female householder, no husband present" type
- More likely than the average, but less likely than the Asians, to be married couple households[13]
- The least likely, by far, to include children under age 18,[14] and, related to that, the smallest in terms of family size, consisting of 2.97 people compared to 3.14 for all households

Minimum Proportion of Complex Households at the National Level

Table 8.1 shows that at the national level, white, non-Hispanic households are less likely than all households to be complex because they include nonrelatives

(9.5% to 10.6%). In fact, this is the lowest proportion at the national level among all six ethnic groups in this volume. In contrast to the households of African Americans, American Indians, Alaska Natives, and Latinos at the national level, non-Hispanic white households with nonrelatives are less likely to be of the family type than the nonfamily type (3.2% to 6.3%), reflecting the same pattern for all U.S. households (4.5% to 6.1%).[15]

Indirect Clues to Complex Households with Nonnuclear Relatives at the National Level

Non-Hispanic white children are more likely to be living with a householder who is their "own" (biological, adoptive, or step) parent than others: they made up 61.1% of all children, but just 39% of all grandchildren, 23.8% of "other relatives," and 40.8% of foster children (Lugaila and Overturf 2004). It should be stressed that "parent" includes biological, adoptive, and stepparents, so we cannot determine from this report how many of these white, non-Hispanic children living with a parent are actually living with a stepparent in a blended family, which we would classify as a type of complex household.

AFRICAN AMERICANS IN URBAN, COASTAL VIRGINIA

Bernadette Holmes conducted her study of African American complex households within the Census Bureau's "urbanized area" of Virginia Beach, Virginia. This area includes roughly 1.4 million people who live in Virginia Beach, Norfolk, Hampton, and the surrounding areas. In this area, Census 2000 recorded 32.9% of the population as African American, alone or in combination with other races.

Household and Family Types in the Local Study Area

In comparison to all households in this Virginia Beach urbanized area, African American households in this area are

- Larger, containing 2.73 people per household, compared to 2.60 for all area households[16]
- Just slightly more likely to be family households, but with nearly double the proportion of female-householder family households and considerably more male-householder family households[17]

- Considerably more likely than all households in this area to have children under 18[18]
- Somewhat less likely to live in nonfamily households with others.[19]

Minimum Proportion of Complex Households in the Local Study Area

Table 8.2 shows how many complex households we can identify from census data for this Virginia Beach area. In this area (as at the national level), African American households were more likely than all households to include nonrelatives (12.8% to 11.9%). Also, as at the national level, these African American households with nonrelatives were more likely to be of the family than the nonfamily type (6.8% to 6%), while all households in the area showed the opposite pattern (4.9% to 7%).[20]

Summary of African American Household Types in the Virginia Beach Urbanized Area

To recap, compared to all households in this local urbanized area, African American households were larger. While they are just slightly more likely than those in the overall area population to be family households, they are nearly twice as likely to be female-householder family households and somewhat more likely to be male-householder family households, while much less likely to be of the married couple type. In addition, they are more likely to have

Table 8.2   Minimum Proportion of Complex Households for African Americans and the Overall Population in Coastal Virginia[1] (Family and Nonfamily Households with Any Nonrelatives)

Coastal Virginia Population Groups	Percentage of Households with Nonrelatives in Family Households[3]	Percentage of Households with Nonrelatives in Nonfamily Households[4]	Minimum Proportion of Complex Households (Households with Any Nonrelatives)[5]
Overall population	4.9	7.0	**11.9**
African American population[2]	6.8	6.0	**12.8**

1. The "urbanized area of Virginia Beach, Virginia" that encompasses the area where the African American ethnographic research was conducted.
2. African American alone or in combination with other races.
3. Calculated by subtracting the percentage of nonfamily households with nonrelatives from all households with nonrelatives (column 3 minus column 2) (PCT 16 − PCT 9).
4. Calculated from Census 2000 SF-2, PCT 9 data.
5. Calculated from Census 2000 SF-2, PCT 16 data.

children under 18. About one-eighth (12.8%) are complex households with one or more nonrelatives, which are somewhat more likely to be the family type, as compared to all area households with nonrelatives (these are more likely to be of the nonfamily type).

As Holmes writes in her chapter, African Americans long have gotten "bad press" for having a family system that some view as deviant compared with the rest of the United States. Our findings show that with respect to household complexity, African Americans are not alone out in left field. Rather, they look more like other ethnic minorities. This is the case even though some of the specifics of their pattern (especially family households with female householders and no husband present) are at one end of the six-group continuum. But Navajos are not far behind African Americans for female householders nationwide (25.6%[21] compared to 30.7% for African Americans). Interestingly, these are the two groups with long histories of female economic power and autonomy (see chapter 11).

NON-HISPANIC WHITES IN UPSTATE NEW YORK

The most recently released estimates for the population as of July 2004 show that non-Hispanic whites make up a disproportionate share of people in the age 65 + cohort as compared to the overall U.S. population (15% to 12%) (U.S. Census Bureau 2005). Thus, it was very fortuitous that our original ethnographer for the white, non-Hispanic population, Sharon Hewner, had a special interest in gerontology. As a result, she deliberately selected a number of complex households for this study that either included, or revolved around, elderly people. She interviewed respondents in complex family households who brought elderly relatives into their own homes, and she also talked with respondents who had either partially or totally left their own households to move in and take care of elderly relatives. Often, the most stressful part of that arrangement was that no one knew whether it would be short- or long-term. You will be struck by the poignancy of the living situations of these adult caregivers who are betwixt and between two households, not fully belonging to either, when you read the results of Hewner's interviews, analyzed and written for this book by Jennifer Hunter Childs. Childs describes another variation on the theme of elderly caregiving: several complex households that have taken in elderly nonrelatives for board-and-care or for board alone.

The study of rural whites was conducted in four upstate, western counties. According to Hewner, in recent years, both agriculture and industry have declined in this area, offering fewer economic opportunities for young adults.

They have been leaving the area in search of work elsewhere, leaving behind an older population that may be in need of assistance and services.

Since the ethnographic study focused on rural whites, rather than whites overall, we have taken an additional step in defining our geographical comparison area: comparing only the rural white, non-Hispanic households to all households in the four-county area in upstate New York. In this area, 16.3% of all households are rural, and virtually all of them are white, non-Hispanic households. In fact, 86.4% of all (urban and rural) households in the four counties are those of non-Hispanic whites.[22]

Household and Family Types in the Local Study Area

In comparison to all households in these four counties, rural, white, non-Hispanic households are

- Larger, containing 2.68 people per household, compared to 2.43 overall[23]
- Much more likely than all local-area households to be classified as family households
- Dramatically more likely to be of the married couple type (63.6% to 47.9% for the four-county area and 54.2% for the total United States[24]) as well as more likely than all area households to have children under 18[25]
- Much less likely to be living in nonfamily households than all households in this area (which is concomitant with their being more likely to live in family households).[26]

Minimum Proportion of Complex Households in the Local Study Area

Our minimum estimate of complex households is the proportion of households containing one or more nonrelatives, which we can identify directly from Census 2000 data tables on the website. It turns out to be extremely low for the rural, non-Hispanic whites in the four upstate New York counties where this research was conducted: 8.3% (see table 8.3). In fact, this is the smallest proportion encountered in the whole book, below both our "benchmark" minimum of 10.6% for all U.S. households and even the 9.5% figure for all (urban and rural) white, non-Hispanic households in the country. As at the national level for all white, non-Hispanic households, rural, white, non-Hispanic households with one or more nonrelatives in this four-county area were less likely to be of the family than the nonfamily type (3.8% to 4.5%),

Table 8.3   Minimum Proportion of Complex Households for Rural Non-Hispanic Whites and the Overall Population in Upstate New York[1] (Family and Nonfamily Households with Any Nonrelatives)

Upstate New York Population Groups	Percentage of Households with Nonrelatives in Family Households[3]	Percentage of Households with Nonrelatives in Nonfamily Households[4]	Minimum Proportion of Complex Households (Households with Any Nonrelatives)[5]
Overall population	3.6	5.5	**9.1**
Rural, non-Hispanic white population[2]	3.8	4.5	**0.3**

1. Four upstate New York counties encompassing the area where the rural, non-Hispanic white ethnographic research was conducted.
2. Rural, non-Hispanic white alone or in combination with other races.
3. Calculated by subtracting the percentage of nonfamily households with nonrelatives from all households with nonrelatives (column 3 minus column 2) (PCT 16 − PCT 9).
4. Calculated from Census 2000 SF-2, PCT 9 data.
5. Calculated from Census 2000 SF-2, PCT 16 data.

exhibiting the same pattern as all area households (3.6% to 5.5%),[27] of which they are the majority.

Summary of Rural, White, Non-Hispanic Household Types in Upstate New York

These rural, non–Hispanic whites are similar to all non–Hispanic whites at the national level in having the lowest proportion of households with nonrelatives, and in these households with nonrelatives' being more prevalent in nonfamily- than family-type households. Only the Asians at the national level showed the same pattern of households with nonrelatives being more prevalent in nonfamily than family households.

However, in terms of other family household types, rural, non–Hispanic whites in these upstate New York counties differ from all non–Hispanic whites at the national level in being (1) more likely to be in family households, (2) especially of the married couple type, and (3) more likely to have young children. These patterns are like those of our other ethnic groups at the national level, though not as pronounced.

At least two factors mentioned by Hewner (2000) before census results became available might potentially contribute to these differences. One is that the cultural patterns of rural people may be diverging from those of urban people, and these may affect how households adapt to demographic and economic pressures. The second is that there are some Amish households in upstate New

York, which are quite likely to consist of a very high proportion of family households of unusually large sizes, often extended, with large numbers of children. Unfortunately, we have no way of identifying Amish households from the census tables. None of the respondents in the ethnographic study was Amish.

SUMMARY: MINIMUM PROPORTION OF COMPLEX HOUSEHOLDS BY ETHNIC GROUP

In our three section introductions (chapters 2, 5, and this one), we have presented the minimum proportions of complex households for each ethnic group at both the national and local study-area levels. For the country as a whole, the minimum proportion of complex households was 10.6%, but this was much higher for some ethnic groups than for others. The results from the national level for all six groups are presented in table 8.4.

We emphasize that these are the minimum proportions, since only one of the types of complex households we have identified in this book can be identified unambiguously from Census 2000 data tables on the Census Bureau website: households with one or more nonrelatives. These Census 2000 tables that we used as data sources for this book are not constructed in a way that allows

Table 8.4   Minimum Proportion of Complex Households for the Six Ethnic Groups at the National Level (Family and Nonfamily Households with Any Nonrelatives)

Ethnic Group[1]	Percentage of Households with Nonrelatives in Family Households[2]	Percentage of Households with Nonrelatives in Nonfamily Households[3]	Minimum Proportion of Complex Households (Households Containing Any Nonrelatives)[4]
American Indians	8.6	6.9	**15.5**
Alaska Natives	8.9	7.3	**16.2**
Asians	5.0	7.2	**12.2**
Hispanics/Latinos	11.9	6.0	**17.9**
African Americans	7.2	5.1	**12.3**
Non-Hispanic Whites	3.2	6.3	**9.5**
All U.S. Households	4.5	6.1	**10.6**

1. Statistics calculated using data on "Race alone" in combination with other races, for all groups except "Hispanic/Latinos," which is not a race in federal statistics.
2. Calculated by subtracting the percentage of nonfamily households with relatives from all households with nonrelatives (column 3 minus column 2) (PCT 16 − PCT 9).
3. Calculated from Census 2000 SF-2, PCT 9 data.
4. Calculated from Census 2000 SF-2, table 16.

us to identify and count other types of complex households, such as those that are (1) lineally extended (multigenerational households with grandparents and grandchildren), (2) laterally extended (with adult siblings, aunts, nephews, and the like), (3) blended (including stepchildren), (4) including in-laws, (5) comprised of more than one family, or (6) some combination of these.

Throughout our section introductions, however, we have identified indirect clues or hints from person-level data on relationships to householders that these might be more prevalent among some ethnic groups than others, but, as noted, we cannot translate person-level data from the website into counts of complex households.

If we were able to identify and count these other types of complex households, we believe the total proportion of complex households for each of our groups, and for the country as a whole, would be much higher than the minimums presented in this table. As noted in the American Indian and Alaska Native introduction, it would be possible to develop a more complete estimate of the proportion of complex households for ethnic subpopulations by writing programs to identify different types of complex households and running them with the full Census 2000 database. That is beyond the scope of this book but a topic for future research.

Why is it important to estimate the proportions of complex households for different ethnic groups and for the country as a whole? As summarized in chapter 2, previous research has shown that certain subpopulations are at higher risk for coverage error in censuses: complex households (e.g., de la Puente 1993), ethnic minorities (e.g., U.S. Census Bureau 2003; National Research Council 2004), and nonrelatives. Therefore, we assert that studying the various types of complex households among different ethnic groups, with their array of nonrelatives, nonnuclear relatives, or multiple families, is important. It provides data that may be used to develop better methods to improve coverage and accuracy in future censuses and provides a more complete picture of how household structure varies by ethnicity and other factors.

Finally, let us turn to our ethnographic studies in black and white, the last set of comparisons. Holmes takes us inside African American households located in the growing urban sprawl along the humid Virginia coast, while Childs introduces us to white, non–Hispanic respondents in complex households in a rural upstate New York area with decreasing economic opportunities and deep winter snows. The whites are somewhat defensive about living in complex households, and the blacks are somewhat defensive about how their complex households are perceived by others in our society. The reasons why may help to complete our picture of the distance many in our land have traveled from the once-modal "Ozzie and Harriet" household of father, mother, and their biological offspring.

NOTES

1. The minimum and maximum growth rates are based, respectively, on the number of people in Census 2000 recorded as African American alone, compared to the composite of African American alone and African American in combination with one or more other races. See chapter 2 discussion.

2. Of those marking African American either alone or in combination, 53.6% lived in the South, 18.8% in the Northeast, 18.9% in the Midwest, and 9.6% in the West (McKinnon 2001).

3. The average household size data come from Census 2000 Summary File 2, Quick table DP-1 for African Americans alone or in combination with another race and for the total population. All other statistics in this section are for African Americans alone or in combination with another race, unless otherwise specified.

4. In the United States, 68.1% of all households are family households; African American households are almost the same: 67.9%. However, the distribution of African American family household types is very different from that of all households: female householder, no husband present (30.7% to 12.2%); male householder, no wife present (5.8% to 4.2%); and married couple (31.4% to 51.7%) (Quick table DP-1).

5. At the national level, African American family households were much more likely than all U.S. households to be family households with one or more "own" (biological, step, or adopted) children under age 18 (38.3% to 32.8%). An added 6.7% of African American family households had related children under 18, all of whom were other than "own" children, compared to an added 2.7% for all U.S. households (PCTs 27, 28). See note 9 in chapter 2 for a discussion of why it is inappropriate to add this type of complex household to the number of households that are complex because they include nonrelatives.

6. Only 5.1% of all African Americans lived in nonfamily households of more than one person, compared to 6.1% for the overall population (PCT 9).

7. Proportions of households with nonrelatives were calculated from SF-2, PCT 16. Proportions of nonfamily households with two or more people were calculated from PCT 9. Proportions of family households with nonrelatives were derived by subtracting the latter from the former.

8. In Census 2000, 75.1% reported white alone, and another 2% reported white with one or more other races (Grieco 2001).

9. In federal data collections, Hispanic/Latino is an ethnicity, not a race. Though Latinos can be of any race, most are classified in the census as white. In Census 2000, 18.8 million people were classified as white and Hispanic (Grieco 2001).

10. Of non-Hispanic whites reporting just one race, 15% are age 65 and above, compared to just 12% for the country as a whole and just 5% for Latinos (U.S. Census Bureau 2005a).

11. The data for this section were obtained from Quick table DP-1 at the national level, for non-Hispanic whites who marked one or more races and for all households.

12. White, non-Hispanic households were the least likely of any subpopulation we have considered to be of the family type (66.4% to 68.1% for all households) and the most likely to consist of individuals living alone (27.3% to 25.8% for all households) (Census 2000 Summary File 2, Quick table DP-1).

13. White, non-Hispanic households are the least likely to be classified as female-householder (no spouse present) family households: 8.8% to 9.6% for Asians and 12.2% for all households. White, non-Hispanic households are more likely than all households, but less likely than Asian households, to be characterized as married couple households (54.2% to 51.7% to 59.3%).

14. At the national level, just 29.5% of all white, non-Hispanic households are family households with one or more "own" (biological, step, or adopted) children under age 18, compared to 32.8% for all U.S. households. This is the lowest proportion for all of the ethnic groups in this book at the national level; the second lowest group is Alaska Natives at 38.1%, with Latinos being the highest at 51.6% at the national level (PCT 27). An additional 1.7% of white, non-Hispanic households are family households with young children, all of whom are other than the "own" (biological, step, or adopted) children of the household, compared to an added 2.7% for all U.S. households (PCTs 27 and 28).

15. See note 7 for the method used to calculate these proportions.

16. Statistics in this section were calculated for the Virginia Beach, Virginia, "urbanized area" overall and for "African Americans alone or in combination." Average household size is from SF-2 PCT 8.

17. The breakdown of African American households to all households in this urbanized area is as follows: all family households (69.9% to 69.1%), female-householder family households (29.2% to 15.3%), and male-householder family households (5.2% to 3.9%) (PCT 9).

18. In this urbanized area, 40.9% of African American households were family households with one or more "own" (biological, step, or adopted) children under 18, compared to 35.7% of all area households. An additional 6.1% of local African American households had children under 18, all of whom were related, but not as "own" children, compared to an added 3.3% for all area households (PCTs 27 and 28).

19. While 6% of African American households in this urbanized area consisted of non-family households with two or more people, which we label "complex," 7% of all households were of this structure.

20. Calculated from SF-2, PCTs 16 and 9.

21. Calculated from SF-2, PCT 9 for Navajos alone or in combination at the national level.

22. All data in this section are from custom tables run for the rural areas of the four upstate New York counties and just for non-Hispanic whites alone or in combination. Calculated from PCT 6.

23. Calculated from PCTs 6 and 7.

24. In this area of New York State, 75.3% of rural white, non-Hispanic households were classified as family households, compared to 64.8% overall. These rural, white, non-Hispanic households were more likely than all area households, and than white, non-Hispanic households in the whole country, to be of the married couple type (63.6% to 47.9% to 54.2%) (PCT 9).

25. Of all rural, white, non-Hispanic households in this area, 33.9% were family households with "own" (biological, step, or adopted) children under age 18, compared to 30.1% for all area households. An additional 1.8% of rural, white, non-Hispanic households had young related children, none of whom was an "own" son or daughter, with the same proportion of these added to all area households (PCTs 27, 28).

26. Rural, non–Hispanic whites were less likely than the overall population in this four-county area to be living in nonfamily households: alone (20.3% to 29.8%) or with others (4.4% to 5.5%) (PCT 9).

27. Calculated from PCTs 16 and 9.

REFERENCES

de la Puente, M. 1993. "Why are people missed or erroneously included by the census: a summary of findings from ethnographic reports." In *Proceedings of the 1993 Research Conference on Undercounted Ethnic Populations*, 29–66. Suitland, MD: U.S. Census Bureau.

Grieco, E. 2001. "The white population: 2000." Census 2000 Brief C2KBR/01-4, issued August 2001.

Hewner, S. 2000. "Ethnographic research on complex households in western New York State: impact of migration and economic change on the complexity of household composition among rural Caucasians." Unpublished final contract report on the Complex Households Study for the U.S. Census Bureau, Suitland, MD.

Lugaila, T., and J. Overturf. 2004. "Children and the households they live in: 2000." Census 2000 Special Reports CESNR-14, issued February 2004.

McKinnon, J. 2001. "The black population: 2000." Census 2000 Brief C2KBR/01-5, issued August 2001.

National Research Council. 2004. *The 2000 Census: counting under adversity*, ed. Panel to Review the 2000 Census, D. F. Citro, D. L. Cork, and J. L. Norwood, Committee on National Statistics, Division of Behavioral and Social Sciences and Education. Washington, DC: National Academies Press.

U.S. Census Bureau. 2003. *Technical assessment of A.C.E. Revision II*. Washington, DC: U.S. Census Bureau, issued March 12.

———. 2005a. "Table 3: Annual estimates of the population by sex, race, and Hispanic or Latino origin for the United States: April 1, 2000, to April 1, 2004" (NC-EST2004-03), at www.census.gov/popest/national/asrh/NC-EST2004-srh.html (accessed September 1, 2005).

———. 2005b. "Annual estimates of the population by age and sex of white alone not Hispanic for the United States: April 1, 2000, to July 1, 2004" (NC-EST2004-04-WANH), released on June 9, at www.census.gov/popest/national/asrh/NC-EST2004-asrh.html (accessed September 1, 2005).

———. 2005c. "Annual estimates of the population by sex and five-year age groups for the United States: April 1, 2000, to July 1, 2004" (NC-EST2004-01), released on June 9, at www.census.gov/popest/national/asrh/NC-EST2004-asrh.html (accessed September 1, 2005).

———. 2005d. "Annual estimates of the population by age and sex of Hispanic or Latino origin for the United States: April 1, 2000, to July 1, 2004" (NC-EST2004-04-HISP), released on June 9, at www.census.gov/popest/national/asrh/NC-EST2004-asrh.html (accessed September 1, 2005).

———. 2005e. "Hispanic population passes 40 million, Census Bureau reports." Press

Release CB05-77, dated June 9, at www.census.gov/Press-Release/www/releases/archives/population/005164.html (accessed September 1, 2005).

U.S. Office of Management and Budget. 1997. "Revisions to the standards for the classification of federal data on race and ethnicity: notices." *Federal Register* 62 (210): 58781–59790. Also available at www.whitehouse.gov/omb/fedreg/1997standards.html.

· 9 ·

African American Households in Transition: Structure, Culture, and Self-definition

Bernadette J. Holmes[1]

BACKGROUND AND OVERVIEW

$\mathcal{A}$merican households and families in general, and African American households and families in particular, are undergoing major structural changes. These changes include declining rates of marriage, high rates of divorce and remarriage, and an increase in female-householder households. According to the U.S. Census Bureau (2000a, 200b), 36.4 million, or 12.9%, of the population is African American alone or in combination with other races; there are 13 million African American households.

African American households and families have been the subject of academic and popular debate. More often than not, the experiences of African American families have been studied and viewed against the "mythical dominant ideal." The image of a husband, wife, 2.5 kids, and a dog is the basis of the presumed cultural norm. The dominant conception of households and families shapes the discourse and resulting social policies. Minorities are consistently judged based on this traditional ideal. In particular, this view has resulted in societal misconceptions and stereotypes that characterize African American household structures as "disorganized," "dysfunctional," and "breaking down." A *stereotype* is a "rigid, oversimplified and often-exaggerated belief that is applied both to an entire category of people and to each individual within it" (Johnson 1995, 282). Stereotypical images of black households and families are pervasive in the dominant culture. More often than not, the dominant characterization frames popular debate, attitudes, and policy. Most "mainstream" social science research on black households tends to be "problem focused," using white middle-class households as the norm.

196

Unquestionably, all households and families are experiencing change. I contend, however, that this transition is reflective of the broader structural and institutional changes taking place in society. As M. L. Andersen (2000, 178) notes, although certainly many African American families struggle with problems of poverty, unemployment, and violence, those problems stem from the social-structural locations of families in a race-, class-, and gender-stratified society, not from something inherently problematic in households maintained by women or in African American values.

Clearly, like all households, black households are not immune to wider societal changes and challenges. Why, then, is there a consistent portrayal of African American households as being in crisis and chaos? I challenge this assumption and explore the diversity of African American households in the context of broader structural changes and from the cultural perspective of the households themselves.

I examine the contemporary structure of African American households in the context of culture and self-definition, which serve as the basis for understanding complex households. Specifically, I explore and analyze structural transitions taking place across a broad range of household forms.

African American households and families are not monolithic; this is especially important given that most social science research on African Americans focuses on poor black families (Billingsley 1992; Staples 1999). I contend that the unique historical and cultural experiences of African Americans underscore structural arrangements characterizing diverse household structures and frame the self-definition of blacks. The interpretive framework of ethnography gives voice to this study's households. Finally, while not exhaustively, I discuss broader policy implications.

REVIEW OF THE LITERATURE

African American Households

A sociological perspective examines African American households and families in relationship to the broader societal context. In this view, the family, as an institution, reflects the changes in society, resulting in structural changes in households. I argue that all knowledge, behaviors, and institutions occur within a cultural framework and within a structural context. Thus, what constitutes a household and a family reflects the unique cultural experiences of that group. Key research questions are, What are the expectations of household membership? How do families and households function? What factors contribute to the establishment of complex households?

The extended family network is an integral part of black family structure.

Generally speaking, extended families are large groups of related kin, parents, and children, who may or may not live together in the same household (Andersen and Howard 2000). Extended family networks tend to be more common among ethnic minorities. E. P. Martin and J. M. Martin (1978, 1) define the black extended family as a multigenerational, interdependent kinship system that is welded together by a sense of obligation to relatives; it is organized around a "family base" household, is generally guided by a dominant family figure, extends across geographical boundaries to connect family units to an extended family network, and has a built-in mutual aid system for the welfare of its members and the maintenance of the family as a whole.

Consequently, in many communities, the extended family includes a network of individuals, both relatives and fictive kin, who make interconnected households. C. Bagley and J. Carroll (1998, 8) note, "The extended family retains a primary role in the black family and functions as a cooperative network. The extended family can be extensive: parents, grandparents, cousins, nieces, nephews." For African Americans, the kinship network serves as the basis of family relations and has been shown to be a central component of family relations and functioning (Stack 1974). For example, 22% of African American households were extended, compared to 10% for white households (Staples 1999). W. Allen (1979), examining the U.S. population as a whole, found that the extended family structure was more prevalent among lower socioeconomic groups and served as the basis of survival. By contrast, J. Johnson (1981) reported extended family structures across all African American socioeconomic groups. As such, she views this structural variation as part of the cultural experience of most African Americans.

Conceptual Framework

The conceptual and analytical framework for understanding African American households and families is based on the assumption of cultural relativism. Cultural relativity assumes that America is a multicultural society and that differences in black and white families are largely accounted for by variation in cultural backgrounds and experiences (Billingsley 1968; Hill 1972; Dobson 1988). This approach begins with the assumption that

> Black American culture and family patterns possess a degree of cultural integrity that is neither related to nor modeled on White American norms. . . . This school traces the origins of these cultural differences back to black America's African cultural heritage, and all tend to focus on the "strengths" of black families. (Dobson 1988, 77)

Thus, this conceptual framework of African American households and families directly challenges the culturally ethnocentric view that sees black families as pathological and dysfunctional. In general, ethnocentrism refers to viewing one's own group as superior to all others. This culturally ethnocentric approach is represented in the works of Daniel Patrick Moynihan. In his highly publicized report, *The Negro Family: The Case for National Action* (1965), Moynihan characterized the black family as a "tangle of pathology" that retarded the economic and social advancement of the black community. Rather than focusing on systematic discrimination and institutional racism, he blamed the black family for its condition. In particular, he blamed black female-headed households and viewed them at the core of this "tangle of pathology."

In contrast, my research draws heavily on the scholarship of researchers who represent a major paradigm shift in family studies. The interpretive framework of this study directly challenges misconceptions and stereotypes of African Americans and does not view the experiences of black American households and families as monolithic. This conceptual and analytical distinction is imperative for understanding the statistical trends and patterns in African American households. Statistics, like households, do not occur in a vacuum.

RESEARCH METHODOLOGY

The Research Process

To gain the support of the research community and potential respondents, as the first step in our study, I made a brief presentation at a meeting of the local branch of the National Association for the Advancement of Colored People. After our introduction and overview of the research project, I answered questions for more than 45 minutes. There was a great deal of enthusiasm that "we" [black scholars] were undertaking this research about our families and that a historically black college and university was involved in a study with a major government agency. However, participants were quick to note, "They [white scholars] don't know anything about our families." This sentiment was expressed in various statements and questions regarding our role as black researchers in this project.

Also, the connections between contemporary household structures and slavery were noted. One member said it directly: "Our families are different, and they had to be because of slavery." That evening, several members of the audience provided contact names in the community and said they would spread the word about the study. After adjournment, questions and comments continued for 20 minutes. One person wanted to know if I could go to another state to interview her family members!

Later, a student came to my office, stated that she had heard about the research, and asked if she "could be interviewed because a single mother had raised her, and she had made it." This college student stressed her desire to tell her story about a "successful" single mother. (While her story would have been interesting, her household did not fit the complex household definition, so she was not included.)

Further community support was solicited by visiting local churches and calling community leaders. Since the university is a very visible and highly respected community institution and has established partnerships there, I felt it was very important to network and interface with the community.

Sample

I relied on contacts in the community and snowball sampling to obtain a purposive sample of 25 households. The households were selected on the basis of their unique characteristic: they were complex households as defined in this U.S. Census Bureau research project. I used the snowball method in four cases. In these cases, people I had previously interviewed directed us to the respondents. Both selection procedures are nonprobability methods. The researchers were aware of the major limitation of this method: the inability to generalize the findings. Nonprobability sampling procedures, however, are well suited for qualitative research that focuses on a small sample, permitting an intensive examination of respondents' knowledge, attitudes, and activities.

I also recognized the class diversity in the African American community and tried to include respondents from different economic levels, assessed qualitatively. Four households were classified as low-low, three as low, six as low-average, nine as average, and three as high. Household size ranged from two to seven residents, with a mean of three (table 9.1). Respondents' ages ranged from 29 to 70, with a mean of 47; 20 were female, and 5 were male.

Method of Data Collection and Analysis

The data collected were qualitative in nature. Semistructured personal-visit interviews were conducted with respondents. The instrument used was a questionnaire designed by the U.S. Census Bureau. Additional questions developed by the researchers relating to the objectives of the study were included. These questions focused on the structure, culture, and self-definition of households and families.

Additionally, observational and interpretive analyses were employed. These multimethod approaches enabled us to document and understand households from the vantage point of the respondents. All of the interviews

Table 9.1 Characteristics of African American Complex Households

Type of Household	Number of People in Household	Qualitative Assessment of Economic Well-being
Married householders, stepgrandson [grandmother has legal custody]	3	Average
Divorced female householder, 2 children	3	Low low
Widowed female householder, son, householder's sister	3	Average
Single female householder, 2 sons, 1 niece [aunt has legal custody]	4	Low low
Married householders, 2 granddaughters	4	Average
Single female householder, 2 children[2]	3	Low low
Married householders, 2 adopted sons [nephews], 2 grandsons [legal custody]	6	Low average
Single female householder, mother, nephew	3	High
Female householder and son[3]	2	Low
Widowed female householder, separated son, grandson	3	Average
Widowed female householder, adopted daughter, granddaughter	2	Low average
Widowed female householder, daughter, son-in-law, 3 grandchildren, 1 unrelated child [legal custody]	7	Average
Married householders, mother, mother-in-law	4	Low average
Single male householder, nephew, male roommate	3	Low
Female householder, sister, their 2 daughters	4	Average
Married householders, daughter, and stepson	4	Low low
Widowed male householder, 3 children[4]	4	High
Married householders, wife, foster child, and son	4	Average
Married female householder, boyfriend, 2 children, 1 adopted child	5	Average
Married householders, 2 children, and 2 stepchildren	6	High
Married householders, 1 grandchild, mother of respondent	3	Low average
Single female householder, cousin, cousin's child	3	Average
Widowed female householder, nephew [aunt has legal custody]	2	Low average
Married householders, 2 grandchildren [grandmother has legal custody]	4	Low average
Single female householder, her sister [householder has legal custody of younger sister] roommate, aunt [of the 2 sisters]	4	Low

1. The mother had custody of her two children from two relationships. However, when the daughter turned 18, she would "stay" with her biological father.

2. The boyfriend appeared to be attached to this household. However, there are residential rules regarding public housing (Section 8).

3. The respondent has spent time in a shelter. During this time, her son had stayed with his grandmother. However, at the time of the study, this mother and her biological son did not fit the definition of a complex household.

4. An adult niece from a nearby university periodically stays in the household to assist with the children.

except three were conducted in respondents' homes. The exceptions were requested by the respondents to accommodate their schedules. The formal interviews lasted about 60 to 90 minutes; however, many informal aspects of the interview lasted 20 to 45 minutes, with one lasting for two hours. In many instances, the informal interviews contributed intriguing insights into the research process itself and cultural expectations surrounding our role and responsibility in the process. Both researchers conducted 15 interviews together, and the female researcher alone conducted 10.[2] Interviews were audiotaped, providing rich, contextualized data.

FINDINGS

Definitions of Household

The respondents' definitions of households and families reflect a self-definition, or emic view, rooted in the unique cultural experiences of African Americans. The collective voices of the respondents represent several salient themes. Households and families, as conceptualized by the respondents, integrate both *instrumental* and *expressive* functions. The theme of survival and racial identity underscores this definition. The saliency of these themes transcends socioeconomic status. As one single, professional, African American female, who is raising a nephew, explains,

> A household is any group of people who have consented to live as a family. . . .
> I think, given a lot of what exists in African American communities, that our definition of the family is not the Ozzie and Harriet mode. Our definition of family tends to mean a close, loving relationship of people who live in the same house. . . . [T]hese relationships may or may not be biological, but at the same time, there are parental and child roles. . . . [R]elationships exist where people in the household are committed to taking care of each other and depending on each other for their survival. As a result, more and more African American families are looking like that. It is not dysfunctional in the manner that society would ascribe to the way our families are functioning. In many ways because African American families are more than willing to take on the responsibility of other members of the family, it has a tendency to be very smoothly functioning, and it works for a lot of our families. As a result, this has become and always has been a survival technique in our community. This is one of the ways that we can ensure that our children can grow up to be productive adults, and our neighbors' children become productive adults. It never has been within our culture to operate as nuclear families.

A divorced mother raising two children defines households and families in interchangeable terms: "A house is a group of people living together in a unit base. A group could be extended family or relatives who live day by day." Similarly, a single female living with her sister and nephew states,

Traditionally, I would say a husband and a wife with their children or maybe just a wife. But I guess anyone who lives together could be a household. . . . If they are sharing and contributing and buying stuff together, they are a household. Sharing is what makes a household.

This respondent went on to point out that when she was younger, she had a roommate whom she "considered family." Both the expressive and instrumental aspects of household are pointed out by a widowed father raising three children:

The term household means a place where you stay, where you keep your belongings, where you have family-related activities, where you rest, relax, where you have income, a place where you invite friends. But most importantly, I think it is a place where you . . . call your own, you are paying, you are renting, or you are buying to own. That is a household.

In all cases, the definition of household extends beyond a dwelling place per se and focuses on how people live. The definition also denotes a sense of sharing economically and emotionally. There is a clear expectation that individuals should contribute both in expressive and instrumental terms. Working together, pooling resources, and sharing responsibilities are central to this definition. "Surviving" and "making it work" frame the definition of households. As one respondent remarked, "It doesn't matter what you contribute, but you must contribute."

Regarding the social functioning and division of labor in these households, the majority of the respondents noted that they did not make distinctions in terms of household responsibilities. In fact, most made the point that everyone had a responsibility to make things work. Several of the respondents noted that it was indeed important not to make distinctions regarding the division of labor. In cases involving children, the respondents expressed the view that children should contribute to the household based on the age appropriateness of the tasks. For example, cleaning one's room, washing dishes, or taking out the trash were some of the tasks cited. There was no gender distinction made in this regard.

Additionally, several of the respondents noted that a primary responsibility for children in their household was to concentrate on getting good grades in school. In three of the households with elderly parents, the parents often did the cooking for the family. However, all emphasized sharing and negotiating as central to household functioning. As one respondent noted, "In this household, whoever sees what needs to be done, does it." Similarly, another respondent stated that there should be no difference in who contributes to the household based on gender. She noted, "With fast food, no one really cooks much any more," but "everyone living in the household should do their part."

Despite strong, positive self-definitions of household and family and flexible social functioning, when asked whether they thought members of the dominant (white) society view black households and families negatively, all believed they do. They articulated the impact of racism on the societal conception of household and family. A few made reference to the fact that similar problems (i.e., divorce, single-female households, and drugs) are occurring in other communities; yet, African Americans are viewed and treated differently. As a married grandmother raising her grandchildren observed,

> Most of them [members of dominant society] feel that there is only the women in the house raising the children. Or most of the time, women are out working, and the children are raising themselves. . . . I think that they are not being fair with us. It seems that they want to think that we are not capable of raising our families the way they are capable of raising theirs. They also do not think that we are in an environment that is suitable. That is not true.

This grandmother proudly pointed out that her husband is very involved with his grandchildren. She further emphasized the grandfather's role:

> My husband and I stepped in. We talked to a lawyer who asked us if we would consider adopting the children and whether anyone would object to that. I said I did not think so because, since I had them, no one had stepped forward to get them. So, we adopted them.

This retired grandmother and grandfather went back into the labor force in order to provide needed financial support for their grandchildren. They were willing to make the sacrifice to ensure the economic well-being of the household and provide the emotional support these children needed.

To reiterate, our respondents pointed to the strengths of many black households and noted that African American households are typically viewed negatively. As a divorced mother, who is disabled and raising two children, commented, "Even if you have a degree, we are viewed negatively, lazy, and low. It does not matter what the circumstances are, we are not given a break." This former middle-class nurse and ex-military spouse now "struggles to make ends meet." She is particularly distraught about her current financial and living conditions because, as she noted, she had once lived in a nice, middle-class neighborhood. Similarly, a single mother raising her two young sons and a niece became particularly emotional as she discussed how single mothers are viewed. This respondent made repeated comments that she knew that people "looked down" on her and her circumstances. She poignantly stated, "Single black mothers do not get respect." Society only focuses on the "bad things" about single black mothers. She added, "No one looks at the fathers, just the single mothers."

Although the majority of the respondents were female and clearly articulated that African American women and, by extension, households and families are viewed negatively by the dominant society, they were also sensitive to and concerned about the image of the "absentee" or "invisible" black male. As such, most female respondents pointed to the importance of the involvement of nephews, uncles, brothers, grandfathers, and nonrelated males who are positively assisting their households. As one respondent noted, "African American fathers are invisible." In many ways, there is a "societal perception that all African American men are not involved with their families and children." She identified this perception problem as a "systemic" problem and noted that it is "part of the social and political fabric of this society." Many respondents noted that the media perpetuates these images. However, their lived experiences and collective voices reject this characterization. One male respondent noted,

> Everyone is talking about single-parent households. . . . I mean, you have mothers, fathers, and the extended family that are already there. . . . [I]t's not a single-parent household; it might be absent a parent, but it's not a single-parent household.

Extended Families and Social Networks

The role of the extended family is critical to the social functioning of these complex households. Embeddedness in extended families and social networks provides complex households with psychological and emotional support and assistance with parenting children. For single mothers, these support systems also provided financial assistance. This support is particularly evident in the comments of a married grandmother raising her teenage granddaughters due to the death of their mother:

> We have my sister-in-law and also my daughter. . . . Sometimes, when we feel that we can't reach these girls, we have to call someone else in. Maybe they do not feel that they want to talk to me at that time about what the problem is. So, I will call those two people and ask them can they talk with them?

This pattern of support was evident at all income levels. As a single, professional female noted, she truly has an "extended village" to assist her with balancing her professional and family obligations in a household with an elderly mother and a nephew. Similarly, a professional male who is widowed and raising three children discussed the role of extended family, noting,

> If it wasn't for the outside help that I get, it would be almost impossible for me to keep things well in here sometimes. . . . Because my children are involved in so many extracurricular activities . . . I oftentimes need someone to drive them some place or to pick them up from some place. And, I have been fortunate, no, I have been blessed, to get people to help me that way. . . . So, I have a very helpful extended family. . . . I have a niece who occasionally comes out and helps me with the children. . . . But I have people who are not biologically related who have been of extensive help to me.

Similarly, a married professional male with a blended family noted the importance of extended family. He stated, "I couldn't imagine doing it without the extended family . . . everything from working late in the office and other forms of help." More importantly, he emphasized the emotional and psychological support that his household receives.

From a financial standpoint, single mothers in the sample were the most financially vulnerable and received more financial assistance. One single mother relied on friends for extra financial assistance, such as giving clothes to her kids and giving her rides to run errands. Another single mother reported, "Family and friends provide support. Like when I don't have it for my children, they will come through."

Regarding the role of the extended family networks, these respondents articulated a sense of obligation and sacrifice. For example, a single, female professional indicated that bringing her mother and teenage nephew to live with her from another state relieved her of the "stress of worrying about their circumstances." She explained that she had a "moral responsibility" to ensure that her nephew had a positive environment to grow up in and that she would "not be able to live" with herself if she did not help, given the economic resources she had. Similarly, another respondent wanted her teenage cousin to live in a "better" environment and felt she had a "spiritual responsibility" to assist her cousin and her cousin's son. This sentiment reflects the African American adage "Lift as you climb," which encapsulates a cultural expectation: you have a responsibility to assist others in the extended family.

In most instances, women in this study were central to extended families and social networks. The respondents often referred to female best friends as sisters and the children used the word "aunt" to refer to these close friends. As one single mother noted, in her apartment complex, "if you are kind to children, most will call you aunt." One female respondent illustrated the concept of fictive kin:

In the neighborhood where I grew up, the terms "aunt" and "uncle" and "cousin" were used to refer to older neighbors and your parent's friends. . . . [I]t is an issue of respect.

In particular, the word "aunt" is viewed as a term of endearment for close female friends. Similarly, another respondent's comments echoed the importance of fictive kin in the black community. She noted, "Aunts provide moral and financial support," and "play mamas" and "play mothers" all serve as "surrogate mothers" in the community. She said that a white roommate living in the household with her and her nieces now calls her "aunt." She attributes this to her age (46) and the guidance she offers.

With the exception of one separated male, all others expressed similar views regarding the role of extended family and extensive social networks in providing an array of support for their households. Even in the exception, the respondent noted that his brother "drops in" to help out.

More importantly, respondents listed numerous tasks and responsibilities regarding women's involvement in these households. For example, aunts, grandmothers, sisters, and sister-friends offer support in a wide range of tasks, such as driving children to academic and sporting events and medical appointments, bringing meals in when the parent has to work late at the office, and counseling children or troubled family members. In essence, the extended family and social networks are central to the functioning of these households. The African American proverb "It takes an entire village to raise a child" is more than a cliché. For these complex households in the African American community, it is a lived experience and underscores a shared sense of collective identity.

Reasons for Complex Household Formation

Our respondents had formed complex households for varied and often interrelated reasons. These households emerged out of such circumstances as divorce and separation, single parenthood, death, the blending of families, economic conditions, drugs, and incarceration. The primary factor in the formation of complex households in this study was some sort of family crisis. Of the 25 households studied, 10 had experienced problems related to addiction. However, I suspect that the number of such cases in this study may be slightly higher. More often than not, the respondents were very candid and open regarding a relative's use of or involvement with drugs. In two instances (foster child living in a home), a nonrelative's drug addiction was cited as the reason for the formation of the household. However, in some cases (i.e., separation, divorce, and single parenthood), specific reasons were not always given. For example, one single mother, who is raising her niece because of her sister's death, merely noted that her sister "had problems," while others spoke about someone being "unstable."

In most cases, a direct confluence between family problems and economic conditions necessitated the formation of complex households. One interview in particular stands out in this regard. A recently unemployed, single female with an advanced degree, who had moved in with relatives while selling her own home, eloquently discussed the economic and psychological impact of unemployment. Afterward, she smiled and wrote on a piece of paper that her sister was unstable and had a drug problem. The respondent's teenage niece was present during this interview. This is significant because it illustrates the importance of protecting and shielding children from the harsh realities of parents who are unstable. And it illustrates the economic precariousness of the black middle class. After exhausting her savings, this respondent had moved in with a relative. This unemployed, middle-class professional sought refuge with family when experiencing economic difficulties. She commented that she could have exercised other living arrangements, such as having a housemate, but she felt more "comfortable" staying with family. In fact, she noted that in the past, she was the one in her family who had "taken in" several relatives when they were experiencing economic difficulties. She characterized her current living situation as "ironic" and provided insightful commentary about the economic restructuring of the economy and downsizing, as well as its impact on the middle class.

In contrast, regarding the financial status of the middle class, two single sisters living with their young daughters noted that they lived together to "share bills and cut down on costs." They see the situation as only temporary, and it allows them to save money for future plans. They both have "good" jobs, but indicated that it is difficult for many in the middle class to get ahead financially. They described their relationship as "very close," indicating that their daughters, who are actually cousins, call each other "sister." Sharing the responsibility of parenting was important to this household.

Significantly, grandparents, and especially grandmothers, were central in 6 of the 10 households where a relative had a substance-abuse problem. Also, the term *legal custody* emerged in eight cases.[3] Only one of the legal-custody households involved a nonrelative. This is a particularly intriguing factor in the formation of African American complex households. In essence, grandmothers, aunts, cousins, and siblings are assuming legal responsibility for raising relatives (i.e., nieces, nephews, sisters, brothers, and grandchildren). This unique legal status appears to occur in crisis situations involving the courts and social services. Caring for kin is not a new phenomenon in the black community.

Generally, however, it has been informal, often referred to as "informal adoption."

In one case in our sample, a nonrelated child was literally taken in from the streets by a middle-class family. This family was experiencing economic difficulties because of major medical expenses arising, in part, from the care of their own disabled child and from the temporary disability of the husband from a work-related injury. In order to alleviate the family's financial stress and to assist an aging parent, this nuclear family had moved out of their home and moved in with the respondent's mother. The respondent noted that this arrangement had been working well. Then, in an unexpected twist, the respondent explained the circumstances around and the issue of assuming legal custody of a child who was homeless:

> This one particular time this little boy was out, this little seven-year-old boy was out after 10:30 at night, and it was pouring down raining. My daughter came and told me. . . . [S]he asked if she could bring him home. He was just out in the street. . . . We bathed him, fed him, my husband went out that night and bought underwear. . . . He [the child] had on pants that belonged to an adult and shoes that were two sizes too small. . . . We bathed him, fed him, and put him to sleep.

The respondent went on to note that a Child Protective Services worker showed up at her home the next day, and they were in court within 24 hours. Discussing her lack of knowledge regarding the legal process, she explained, "At the time I was ignorant of the meaning of the terms and was awarded permanent legal custody." Later, as she sought services and support for this child, she discovered, "I was not a blood relative, I was not a foster parent. . . . [I]t is so ironic, I receive the least amount of support." Despite the added economic strain and the legal and bureaucratic nightmare that had ensued, she indicated that if she could go back in time, she would do it again.

By contrast, in another case, married householders with their own child had taken in a foster child. This female respondent, along with several others in the study, was quick to point out that she considered labels such as "foster" and "adoptive" to be negative and insensitive, and she felt that they should not be used, particularly in the presence of children. She noted,

> However, in the family unit, when we go out, my daughter doesn't like to be called a foster child or she doesn't like me to be referred to as her foster mother. To call her my foster daughter denotes separation.

A respondent from a household consisting of a grandmother, an adopted daughter, and her adopted daughter's teenage child expressed a similar sentiment. The 70-year-old grandmother in this multigenerational household noted that everyone in her immediate family knew that her daughter was adopted, but in her generation, people did not discuss such issues. This adoption involved a teenage relative.

A married homemaker, who is caring for her mother and mother-in-law, both over 80 years old, in separate households, noted that she wanted them to be "well taken care of." Despite the stress of her caretaking responsibilities, she feels good about caring for them in their homes and is resolved that they will not go into an institution. However, she became emotional as she described the difficulty of her caretaking responsibilities. Similarly, another grandmother, who is caring not only for her grandchild but also for her own mother, who is over 90, exemplifies adaptability and this commitment to caring for relatives. In this particular household, the respondent's elderly mother cycles among her household and those of her three siblings at four-month intervals. This unique arrangement helps alleviate the stress of the responsibility of caring for the elderly parent. The respondent also expressed the desire to ensure that her elderly mother would not be institutionalized. As she shared her story, she was overcome with emotion.

In essence, these families find unique and creative ways to make their households function. The complex and multifaceted character of many of these households and families reflects a willingness on the part of African Americans to rescue and save children, keep them out of "the system," and offer assistance and support to others in need. For example, as one grandmother explained, if she were to give up the child she's caring for, she could have more "spending money" because she could qualify to live in a senior citizen's complex, given her age and disability. However, she noted that her adopted grandson would not be able to live with her, and she did not want him to go into the system. She stated, "Even though he is not my biological grandchild, he is my responsibility now that my son is gone. . . . I had to do it." This grandmother had assumed legal custody of her stepgrandson prior to the death of her son and the incarceration of the child's mother. She pointed out that during the "difficult times" [when they were using drugs], her son and daughter-in-law were "in and out" of her home, but she always kept a room for this child.

From the perspective of the dominant society, complex African American households are often viewed as inherently problematic and unstable. However, I contend that although each case is unique in its circumstances, there is a unifying theme regarding household complexity among these respondents. In all cases, there is a strong sense of obligation, duty, sacrifice, and commitment. As such, in many ways, they represent flexibility, adaptability, and resiliency, despite the institutional and individual challenges they face. The confluence of history, culture, and social and economic conditions influences household structure and functioning. Clearly, despite the precipitating events that led to the establishment of these complex households, these households stress the importance of working together and trying to make the best out of a difficult situation.

The Centrality of Spirituality and the Role of the Black Church

Finally, how do complex households and families negotiate, manage, and cope with the challenges and realities of their experiences? Of the 25 respondents, 24 noted that spirituality was significant in dealing with everyday demands and challenges. Even a woman from a household with one of the worst economic situations in our sample stated that she was "blessed." Another respondent remarked that she had a "spiritual responsibility" to assist a family member experiencing economic difficulty during her divorce. She commented, "Family should be supportive. . . . Overcoming adversity is how a household works." Many respondents indicated that they received emotional support and, in some instances, financial assistance from the church. One noted,

> I feel that if you have God in your life, the household will be pretty stable. If you teach the children about God, take them to church every Sunday, and have love in your house, there will be stability. Going to church is important in my family. I make sure every Sunday morning, they get up and dress and I take them to the bus, which takes them to Sunday school. The three older children are involved in church activities. When we did not have money to take the children to some of these activities, someone in the church always paid for them.

The role of spirituality and the church in providing services and support was a central theme among the respondents. Respondents repeatedly referred to the power of spirituality in dealing with the crises and problems that many had faced. Faith, prayer, the church family, and the spiritual family were identified as sustaining forces in their lives and households.

Also, several of the respondents referred to members of their church as "sister" or "brother." One respondent remarked that her "spiritual mother" was supportive in her life. In several instances, the church had provided direct support, both emotionally and financially, when household members had difficulties. More importantly, there was an expressed "hope" from the "church family" that family members would "get their lives together" through the support they received.

Researchers have documented the role religion plays in the well-being of African Americans, as well as the social functions of the black church (Billingsley 1992; Collins 2000). For example, M. Thomas and B. J. Holmes (1992) found that the major determinants of life satisfaction and subjective well-being for African Americans, irrespective of income, were closeness to family and religion. The buffering effects of family and church have historical roots in the African American experience. Despite material conditions or challenges, this is the case for these complex households and families. The voice of one "invisible" grandmother put it best: "You have to believe in something higher. I believe in God, faith. If it were not for faith, the black community would be destroyed."

CONCLUSION AND IMPLICATIONS

This chapter has examined the complexity of African American households and families. Rethinking the myopic conception of the meaning and functioning of diverse households and families requires analyses that reflect the perspective of the African American community. The voices of the respondents provide a glimpse of the cultural and structural factors, as well as the challenges, facing complex households. What emerges is a definition of households that rejects the dominant society's view of the monolithic family ideal as the only functioning model. As one person stated, "Most black people share a sense of family. Not all families are torn apart. There are lots of stable families."

In general, households and families reflect the broader structural changes occurring in the larger society. As A. Billingsley (1992, 45) has noted, "The key to understanding African American family structure is to see the whole picture with its many variations and to note its flexibility." Grandparents raising grandchildren and other relatives assuming responsibility for children in the family, caring for the elderly, and pooling economic resources are survival strategies that have historically shaped how people live. While in a number of cases a crisis precipitated complex household formation, these households are instructive regarding expectations, responsibilities, role flexibility, and mutual support for kin and nonkin alike. The self-definition of a group that has been marginalized and survived systematic oppression provides innovative and practical strategies as demographic shifts result in complex households and families across race, class, and gender lines.

Research and public policy must move beyond the "family values" rhetoric and stereotyping that have often served as the basis of analyses and critiques of African American households, families, and communities. In one respondent's words, "The government is only concerned with counting people, not how people live." Respondents expressed the concerns of most Americans, articulating the need for "better jobs and wages," "affordable housing," "assistance with escalating medical costs," "better schools for children and better child care," and "more services for the elderly." There was a particular concern about drugs and crime. One disabled respondent would settle for "reliable" public transportation.

The culturally unique self-definition of households and families articulated by the respondents in this study in no way suggests that they are naive regarding the serious problems confronting the African American community. In fact, in every case, the respondents voiced concern and a clear understanding of the devastation and despair that many households and families are experiencing. Indeed, they demonstrated an insightful "sociological" understanding and analysis of the impact of drugs, single parenting, poverty, and the weakening of the extended family, personal accountability, and values. Yet, these respondents also rejected the dominant view that characterizes all African American households and families in a negative and stereotypical way. Moreover, the most positive attributes and qualities that exist in the African American community are often "invisible" and "distorted" by mainstream scholars, the media, and the society at large. In this regard, the respondents gave voice to their experiences and provided a collective identity that accentuates the flexibility and adaptability of complex households.

I contend that just as there is no universally accepted definition of family or household, so is there no single policy initiative that will address the complexities of African American households and families. While it is beyond the scope of this discussion to develop exhaustive policy recommendations, several key implications are identified here.

First, there is a clear need for coordinated and comprehensive approaches to providing support and services to households and families with adopted or foster children. For example, several of the respondents who had assumed responsibility for children reported that it was a bureaucratic nightmare getting information, let alone services, from the courts and social service agencies. In many instances, this void of information clearly limited the financial assistance and other services that were critically needed to assist these children. This concern was voiced particularly by the grandmothers raising grandchildren and other family members' children. Moreover, the issue of legal custody was germane in eight of our complex households. This legal category warrants further exploration, given the number of children being raised by relatives.

Second, the pervasiveness of drug-related crises impacting families in our sample is noteworthy. Given the destabilizing effect of drugs on all communities, our national priorities must go beyond the "just say no" campaign and the "lock them up" mentality. Well-planned and coordinated efforts focusing not merely on the criminal justice system are a major challenge facing this society.

Third, there is a relationship between poverty, unemployment, and underemployment and the precarious status of many African American males. In general, the economic marginality of African American males has a negative impact on their attachment to and involvement in households and families (Hudgins, Holmes, and Locke 1991). Systematic policies related to education and job training are needed if we are to address inequality and despair. Although often rendered invisible by this society, black males are involved as fathers, uncles, brothers, and role models. The importance of this fact should not be underestimated as a survival strategy in many complex households.

In a similar vein, poor mothers need job training and skills to lift themselves out of poverty. Indeed, policies are needed that move beyond stigmatization to empowerment. The growing "feminization of poverty" is not exclusive to the African American community (Hudgins and Holmes 1989). At the same time, black women carry the societal stereotypes of the "matriarch" and the "Welfare queen," which serve as ideological justifications for inequality and contribute to African American women's continued objectification. Research has documented the pervasiveness of the negative, stigmatizing, and controlling images of black women in popular culture and the impact of such images on shaping social policy (Collins 2000; Jewell 1993; St. Jean and Feagin 1998). Declining economic conditions impact all households and require real solutions, not blame.

Fourth, the shifting demographics of an aging population will require greater household and family responsibility in caring for the elderly. Currently families provide 80% to 90% of long-term care for the elderly (Andersen and Taylor 2000). Moreover, the additional stress and responsibility of elder care disproportionately affects women. This gender difference impacts all communities and requires the expansion and development of national policies that reflect this growing trend, the "graying" of America. Clearly, more support services are needed to assist households in caring for the elderly.

Finally, the role of the black church in formulating policy and providing services must be addressed. The black church is one of the most powerful institutions in the African American community. With one exception, all of the respondents in this study identified and accentuated the role of spirituality in meeting the challenges of their households and families. Hence, faith-based institutions and comprehensive services must be responsive to the current social conditions confronting the African American community in general, and African American households and families in particular.

In summary, policy makers, researchers, and social scientists must move beyond statistics and develop methodologies and theories, as well as programmatic and institutional policies, that reflect how households and families really live. A better understanding of complex households may assist in more accurate analyses and the development of effective social policies. Hope, resiliency, and perseverance, grounded in the cultural realities of people's lives, are the starting point. As a society, we must refocus our priorities on building healthy communities so that all households and families may thrive.

NOTES

1. The support of the U.S. Census Bureau for the funding of the project that served as the basis for this chapter is appreciated. I wish to thank the respondents for their participation and the editors and other colleagues for their useful comments and suggestions.

2. Dr. Charles Amissah participated in the initial phase of interviewing

3. In Virginia, "Legal custody means a legal status treated by court order which vests in a custodian the right to have physical custody of the child, to determine and undetermine where and with whom he shall live, the right and duty to protect, train and discipline him and to provide him with food, shelter, education, and ordinary medical care, all subject to residual parental rights and responsibilities" (Commonwealth of Virginia, Virginia Family and Juvenile Laws and Rules Annotated. Virginia Administrative Code. Richmond, VA: Matthew Bender Co., 2001).

REFERENCES

Akbar, N. 1984. "Afrocentric social sciences for human liberation," *Journal of Black Studies*, 14: 395–414.

Allen, W. 1979. "Class, culture and family organization: the effects of class and race on family structure in urban America." *Journal of Comparative Family Studies* 10: 301–13.

Andersen, M. L. 2000. *Thinking about women: sociological perspectives on sex and gender.* 5th ed. Boston: Allyn and Bacon.

Andersen, M. L., and F. T. Howard. 2000. *Sociology: understanding a diverse society.* Belmont, CA: Wadsworth Publishing Co.

Bagley, C. A., and J. Carroll. 1998. "Healing forces in African-American families." In *Resiliency in African-American families*, ed. H. I. McCubbin, E. A. Thompson, A. I. Thompson, and J. A. Futrell, 117–42. Thousand Oaks, CA: Sage Publications.

Billingsley, A. 1968. *Black families in white America.* Englewood Cliffs, NJ: Prentice Hall.

———. 1992. *Climbing Jacob's ladder.* New York: Simon & Schuster.

Collins, P. H. 2000. *Black feminist thought: knowledge, consciousness, and the politics of empowerment.* 2nd ed. New York: Routledge.

Dobson, J. 1988. "Conceptualizations of black families." In *Black families*, ed. H. P. McAdoo, 77–90. Newbury Park, CA: Sage Publications.

Esterburg, K. G. 2002. *Qualitative methods in social research.* New York: McGraw-Hill.

Flaherty, M. J., L. Facteay, and P. Garver. 1994. "Grandmother functions in multigenerational families: an exploratory study of black adolescent mothers and their infants." In *The black family*, 223–40. 5th ed. Belmont, CA: Wadsworth Publishing Co.

Herring, C., and C. Amissah. 1997. "Advance and retreat: racially based attitudes and public policy." In *Racial attitudes in the 1990s: continuity and change*, ed. S. A. Tuch and J. K. Martin, 121–43. Westport, CT: Praeger Publishers.

Hill, R. 1972. *Strengths of black families*. New York: Emerson Hall.

Hudgins, J. L., and B. J. Holmes. 1989. "Black women: pillars of strength, a report to the women's bureau." Presented at the Eleventh Annual Black Family Conference, Black Family Institute, Hampton University, Hampton, Virginia, March 1989.

Hudgins, J. L., B. J. Holmes, and M. E. Locke. 1990. "The impact of alternative family structure variations among black families on the underenumeration of black males—part I: a review of literature." Report prepared for the U.S. Census Bureau. Washington, DC: U.S. Census Bureau.

———. 1991. "The impact of family structure variation among black families on the underenumeration of black males—part II: focus group research." Ethnographic Exploratory Research Report 14. Washington, DC: U.S. Government Printing Office.

Jewell, K. S. 1993. *From mammy to Miss America and beyond: cultural images and the shaping of U.S. social policy*. New York: Routledge.

Johnson, A. G. 1995. *The Blackwell dictionary of sociology: a user's guide to sociological language*. Malden, MA: Blackwell Publishers.

Johnson, J. J. 1981. "Urban black Americans." In *Ethnicity and medical care*, ed. A. Howard, 37–129. Cambridge, MA: Harvard University Press.

Martin, E. P., and J. M. Martin. 1978. *The black extended family*. Chicago: University of Chicago Press.

Moynihan, D. 1965. *The Negro family: the case for national action*. Washington, DC: U.S. Department of Labor.

Ladner, J. A. 1998. *Ties that bind: timeless values for African American families*. New York: John Wiley & Sons.

Reinharz, S. 1992. *Feminist methods in social research*. New York: Oxford University Press.

St. Jean, Y., and J. R. Feagin. 1998. *Double burden: black women and everyday racism*. New York: M. E. Sharpe.

Stack, C. 1974. *All our kin*. New York: Harper & Row.

Staples, R., ed. 1999. *The black family: essays and studies*. 6th ed. Belmont, CA: Wadsworth Publishing Co.

Staples, R., and L. Johnson. 1999. *Black families at the crossroads: challenges and prospects*. San Francisco: Jossey-Bass Publishers.

Taylor, R. L., ed. 1999. *Minority families in the United States: a multicultural perspective*. Upper Saddle River, NJ: Prentice Hall.

Thomas, M., and B. J. Holmes. 1992. "Determinants of satisfaction for blacks and whites." *Sociological Quarterly* 33: 459–72.

U.S. Census Bureau. 2000a. "Facts for features." CB02-FF.01. Available at www.census.gov/Press-Release/www/2002/cb02ff01.html (accessed August 23, 2005).

———. 2000b. "American families and living arrangements: March 2002." Current population reports P20–537. Available at www.census.gov/population/socdemo/race/black/ppl/tab04.txt (accessed August 23, 2005).

10

Not the Typical Household:
Whites in Rural New York[1]

Jennifer Hunter Childs

INTRODUCTION

*S*ophia[2] and her husband seem like prototypical wealthy retirees. They spend seven or eight of the colder months in Florida, then return to their home in western New York in May for the summer. The complexity of their situation stems from the extra members of their household in New York. Jessica, their daughter-in-law, and their two grandchildren are living in Sophia's New York home year-round. Jessica's husband, Mark, who is Sophia's son, left New York to take a job in the South nine months ago. According to Sophia, Jessica and the children were going to join him after school ended that year, but Jessica is now "refusing to move." Sophia hopes that Jessica and her children will move out soon, though she doubts they will because it would be hard for Jessica to afford a place of her own. Because Sophia and her husband own the home in New York, Jessica is only responsible for paying the utility bills.

Tensions run high during the four months when all of the household members are present in the New York home. Here is how Sophia described the living arrangements:

> We each cook our own meals because cooking together on occasion works out, but not that often. I take care of the downstairs and I don't go upstairs to see what Jessica is doing. I try not to, let's put it that way.

Mark makes a substantial economic contribution to the household. He is trying to help pay off Jessica's credit card debt. Jessica is currently working and contributes to the household by paying the utility bills. Mark calls daily to talk to his children. When asked how they ended up in the current situation, Sophia replied,

> Well, we thought we were giving Mark a chance to put it all together. Right now it's sort of falling apart. We thought, well, we'll make it a little easier, but maybe we made it too easy. I don't know.

Although Mark is clearly tied both emotionally and economically to the household, he is physically absent. Sharon Hewner, the ethnographer who conducted the interviews, noted, "He is emotionally like a long-distance trucker, very much part of the household from a distance."

This story demonstrates several of the themes that run through the current ethnographic study of whites living in rural New York. Sophia and her husband travel south in the winter and return to their northern residence for the summer. They represent one type of residential mobility, which leads to the creation of fluid, complex households. Mark represents another type of residential mobility, one that begins as a temporary move. He moved to take a job in another state with the idea that his family would join him if it worked out, and if it did not, he would return to their home in New York. What began as a temporary separation for this family is becoming more permanent as time passes.

Before Mark's journey away from the household, he was living with his family in his parent's home. Sophia and her husband are well established and were able to help Mark and his family when he was struggling economically and emotionally. This represents a complex household established due to economic and psychological distress.

The final key characteristic of this household is that people outside the household support it economically. Sophia and her husband own the home and allow their daughter-in-law and grandchildren to live there throughout the year, even though they themselves are only present for four months of the year. Mark also supports the household from a distance, sending Jessica money to help pay her bills.

Through the course of this chapter, you will meet several families like Sophia's who live in complex households of different sorts. This chapter describes the findings of 25 ethnographic interviews commissioned by the U.S. Census Bureau and conducted by Dr. Hewner with rural, white complex households in western New York. The households in this study were predominantly middle-class. Before examining this study group, one might ask why it is of interest.

Often cultural research ignores white, middle-class households, perhaps because they are assumed to consist of mostly typical nuclear families (for an overview of research into the working middle class, see Overbey and Dudley 2000). However, as you will see in this chapter, these "typical," white, middle-class Americans do not necessarily live in typical nuclear households. In the United States, since perhaps the 1950s, an emphasis on the nuclear family has been pervasive in cultural values and norms. More recently, alternative family and household structures have become more common. This change in society's ideals has been mirrored by a change in the types of families we see on television. In the 1950s and 1960s, there were *Ozzie and Harriet* and *Leave It to Beaver*, both of which involved married parents and two biological sons. On television, until very recently, we had *Frasier*, in which the title character's father, Martin, has moved in with him, along with his home health-care provider, Daphne, after an injury. In another popular show, *Friends*, Ross and Rachel were an unmarried couple raising their child together. Complexities abound in middle-class, white America, both on television and in real life.

It is important to recognize this shift in the way people live. In many ways, society has adopted the nuclear family as the norm. However, the simple nuclear family is becoming less predominant. Data from the Current Population Survey (CPS)[3] show that the proportion of married couple family households is decreasing, while the proportion of other types of family households and nonfamily households is growing.[4] In 1970, 70.6% of all households were maintained by a married couple with or without children (Fields and Casper 2001). In 2000, this number had dropped to 52.8% (Fields and Casper 2001). As the proportion of married couple households drops, the potential proportion of nuclear family households drops as well, because nuclear families are one subset of the married couple household category.[5] In order to understand the household structures that are emerging, we must take our focus away from the nuclear family and turn it toward more complex households.

According to Census 2000, 5.2% of all households were unmarried partner households[6] (Simmons and O'Connell 2003). This statistic most likely understates the true number of unmarried partnerships, in part because cohabiting respondents do not always identify themselves as such. This chapter examines the dynamics of unmarried partner households in our rural, white, New York sample and whether they are reported as such on a census form.

Of the reported unmarried partner households in Census 2000, 43% included at least one child under the age of 18 (Simmons and O'Connell 2003). In these cases, the child may be the biological offspring of both partners, of only one, or of neither. L. L. Bumpass and H. Lu (2000) estimate that approximately 40% of all births to unmarried mothers are actually births into unmarried partnerships. Another goal of this chapter is to examine the composition of unmarried partner families through ethnography to make recommendations for further research into nonnuclear households.

The multigenerational household is another alternative to the simple nuclear family household. Nationally, at least 3.7% of the population live in multigenerational households, that is, households that include a householder living with his or her child and grandchild, a householder living with a parent and child, or a householder living with a parent, child, and grandchild (Simmons and O'Neill 2001; U.S. Census Bureau 2001). In New York State (the location of the study site), 4.4% live in multigenerational households; of these, 57% are householders living with a child and grandchild, 41% are householders living with a parent and child, and 2% are householders living with a parent, child, and grandchild (nationally these numbers are 65%, 33%, and 2%, respectively; U.S. Census Bureau 2001). While these households may contain nuclear families, adding members to the household greatly changes the dynamics. This research aims to provide a glimpse into the nature of these households and how they function.

METHODOLOGY

Dr. Hewner, an anthropologist with research interests in nursing and gerontology, was commissioned to conduct 25 interviews with rural, white, complex households. The households spanned approximately a 200-mile radius in four counties in upstate New York (one of the snowiest regions in the United States). The interviews were conducted in May and June 2000. Hewner contacted community leaders in the area to request help in locating households that met the definition of "complex" for this study. "Snowball" sampling was also employed; that is, she recruited the family and friends of respondents who identified other complex households. The study group was neither a random nor a representative sample of rural, white households. Hewner's special interest in health care and caring for the elderly was reflected in the study group that she chose, which consists of households containing grandparents, parents-in-law, and unrelated caregivers. This research provides a glimpse of household complexities primarily in middle-class, rural, white America.

Characteristics of Respondents

In 24 out of 25 cases, the respondent was female. Respondents ranged in age from 36 to 83, with a mean age of 54. The age of the respondents is higher than one might expect, given national averages. However, one focus of this research was to examine complex households that contained an elderly member and the relationships and circumstances surrounding these situations. Rural areas have a higher proportion of elderly people than urban areas (see Glasgow 2000; Rogers 2000). There are also particular problems surrounding the elderly in rural America. Elderly folks in rural areas are more likely to be poor and less likely to have access to health care than those in urban areas (for a review, see Rogers 2000). To compound matters, they are also more likely to have poorer health; thus, it becomes necessary to have family or friends nearby to care for them, especially in areas like the study site where the abundant snowfall can have detrimental effects on someone who is not physically able to shovel snow.

All respondents in this study either were currently, or had previously been, married. This was not one of the selection criteria but resulted from searching for complex households, including blended families and unmarried partners. Interestingly, of the nine households with cohabiting unmarried couples, all respondents were separated or divorced. Of the 25 respondents, 9 were married, 9 divorced, 6 widowed, and 1 was separated. Their educational level was above average—half of the respondents had at least some college education. Only 2 had less than a high school education, 10 had completed high school, 5 had some college, 3 had college degrees, and 5 had at least some graduate education. All respondents were native-born whites; none reported Hispanic ethnicity.

In Hewner's subjective assessment, the households were predominantly middle-class. She classified 4 households as having low socioeconomic status, 5 were low-average, 10 were average, 3 were high-average, and 2 were high. Note that no household with a low-low economic status was included in this study. Again, this is a result of the convenience sampling procedure and is not necessarily representative of rural America. However, it does provide an insightful glimpse into middle-class, rural whites, who have often been ignored in research like this because of their presumed typicality.

Of the 14 respondents who were employed, 9 reported working full time, 3 were self-employed, and 2 reported being employed part-time. Of those respondents who were not working, six were homemakers, and five were retired. No respondent reported being unemployed because they could not find work. Respondents were employed in various occupations ranging from factory workers to bankers. Those who were self-employed owned small businesses.

Household size ranged from 1 to 6 members, with a mean of 3.6 members. Two single-person households were included that represent elderly women who have a social network of friends and family to provide them with support. While these two respondents were not considered to be living in complex households, they were able to speak about times in which they had lived in complex households in the past, and both had adopted children. Aside from the two single-person cases, only one other case was a nonfamily household. In that one, a widow provided home health care to several other elderly women. Five of the study households were three generational. Two others were skip-generation households with a married couple raising a grandchild. The remaining households were one- or two-generation households, comprised mainly of unmarried partners or adoptive or foster members.

Fieldwork

Most of the interviews took place in the respondents' homes at their convenience. Some of the respondents' homes were in need of renovations or finishing, but most were small, cozy, single-family homes. Many of these homes were located in quite out-of-the-way places. During one interview, the milkman even came to deliver milk!

One respondent lived in an old trailer located on top of an unpaved hill. Because the location was so difficult to get to, the interview took place in town in a small office. The respondent was afraid that the ethnographer's car would not make it up the hill to her trailer.

In another case, the interview took place at the respondent's place of business. Here is how the respondent described her home:

> Well, it's on a back road in the country. It's the only house on the road, and, really and truly, we do not have no electricity there. If we want electricity there, we have to use a generator. . . . It was a cabin but it has been converted, it's been winterized, so we live in it all year round. We checked on electricity when we first bought it 15 years ago, and at that time, it was going to cost $16,000 to have electricity run up to that place. And we thought that was too much.

The attitude of the respondents toward these interviews differed greatly. Some respondents prepared for the interview by making coffee for the ethnographer and setting aside some time to spend with her. Others forgot about the meeting, which was then conducted in an impromptu fashion. Two interviews were actually conducted with respondents in their robes. Interviewing conditions varied from an uninterrupted discussion at the kitchen table to a very hectic environment with children and pets running around and telephones ringing. During one interview, the respondent's two-year-old son, who was being toilet trained, had an accident due to all the excitement. During another, the respondent's 11-year-old son was frantically trying to finish a school project in the kitchen, where the interview was taking place.

RESULTS

Conceptions of "Household"

The interviews elicited three basic conceptions of the term *household*. The first was the physical structure. This was sometimes referred to as a place of comfort, meaning the same as "home"; at other times, it was defined in contrast to a home, as a physical structure without the emotion associated with a home. The second commonly given definition of a household consisted of the people who live in the physical structure at that point in time. For respondents whose household composition changes frequently, this term can be used for the people who live there currently. This definition is most closely associated with the definition that the Census Bureau uses for household membership.

When asked what the word "household" means to her, Emily began by reciting the names of family members who physically live in each house at this moment in time. She first described her household as herself, her partner, Joe, and one of his biological children. Then, Emily went on to say that her oldest son lives in a household with her parents (his grandparents). Emily's ex-husband's household consists of his new wife and daughter. Joe's other children live in a household with his parents (their grandparents). She described each household as those people who are currently in it, although there had been considerable movement between households in the past. However, she said that she would like to include all of her children and all of Joe's children in her household, if she could. This ideal household that she presented is an example of the third meaning of "household," which is much broader and encompasses people who have lived in the structure (or with the residents) who are no longer present.[7] In some cases, the nonresidents have passed away, and in others, they have moved out. This extended definition of household is similar to that of "family." Elderly respondents sometimes include their nonresident children and grandchildren as part of this larger concept of household. Ruth, one of the widows in the study who lived alone, began defining "household" by describing her household when she was first married. She lived in her father's home with her husband and her father. She raised her family there and lived in that home for almost 40 years. Now, she is living alone in an apartment, but she thinks of her former household as her household.

What constitutes a household? To some rural white respondents in this study, it is the building in which they live. To others, it is the people with whom they live. And to others, it is family, no matter where they live, or if, in fact, they are still living. These differences in meaning are critical when one asks the question "Who lives in this household?" and expects to get an accurate response.

Connections to the Household

There are several types of people who are very connected to a household but who are not considered permanent residents, according to the census residence rules. College students fit in this category because they are emotionally, and often economically, tied to the household; yet, they may live seven or eight months of the year at another residence. One respondent said that her college-student daughter was part of her household because "she hasn't established a house of her own; she doesn't have her permanent apartment." By saying this, she implies that every person needs a household to which he or she belongs, whether it is that person's primary residence or not. College students are often financially supported by their parents and are claimed as dependents for income tax purposes, even if they do not live at home. Many college students also maintain their parents' address as their permanent residence for purposes of drivers' licenses, bank accounts, and taxes. This results in conflicting definitions of "residence," such as a permanent residence used for most official paper-work, a place of usual residence for census forms,[8] and a concept of belonging-ness that is used for personal, social, or emotional classification.

People who travel for their jobs are also often considered part of the household, although they do not live there most of the time. Two respondents included their husbands as household members although they were on the road most of the time as truck drivers. According to census residence rules, these people who are away temporarily for work purposes are to be included in the household.

In one case, Debbie lives with her boyfriend, Roger, whom she describes as "an over-the-road truck driver." Roger stays in the cab of his truck most nights and comes home every weekend for one or two days. Roger stays at the house seven or eight nights a month at most. He spends the majority of the month in his truck. Debbie schedules her own activities around Roger's sched-ule so that they can spend time together when he is home. Emotionally, Roger is very much a part of the household. He is also the primary breadwinner. This case clearly indicates that household membership stems from something more than spending most of one's time there. Emotional and financial attachment to the household define membership for Debbie and Roger, much as they do in the case of the college student. However, Roger's financial attachment is even stronger than that of a college student. Rather than being financially depen-dent, he has considerable financial responsibility in the household.

The example that introduces this chapter also demonstrates this type of attachment. Sophia still considers Mark a part of Jessica's household[9] because he still supports his family financially, and the separation is thought of as tem-porary. Mark still calls to talk to his children every day, so the emotional attach-ment is there as well.

In a third type of situation, a nonresident financially supports the household but is not considered part of the household. Megan and Sam are divorced, but Megan receives about 75% of her income from Sam to support herself and the children. Due to the physical, emotional, and legal separation, Megan does not think of Sam as a part of her household, but her household could not function without his financial support. In this case, the economic unit is not equivalent to the residential unit. A glimpse into this household based on residential structure shows that Megan and her sons can support themselves. However, a closer look will show that a key component of the economic unit lives outside the household.

Division of Labor

Most respondents have traditional ideas about the roles of men in the household. Men are seen as the primary breadwinners; their household chores consist of outside and heavy-duty work. However, most women in the study are expected to work outside the home to help support the household financially and also to raise children and maintain the house. This reflects more modern ideas about women in the workforce, but also places more pressure on women to work for pay and manage the household.

Children are also often given chores to help around the house. The extent of the chores varies greatly. In some cases, children are raised to learn to take care of themselves at an early age. Natalie, who is married with biological and foster children, described her philosophy of raising children:

> Growing up, my children had to do everything by themselves. They had to make their own lunches, or they weren't going to school. They had to make their beds. They had to do the dishes. They had to do the laundry. And that was because when my mom came home [from her nervous breakdown during Natalie's childhood] we felt pretty hopeless and helpless. When [my mother] had her eighth child, she had a relapse. . . . [W]e knew we had to function so I had it in my mind that my kids were going to know how to do everything so that if I died, the only thing they would do was miss me. . . . So, with [the foster child], she's being trained to take care of herself. I think it's important, I think it gives her a lot of self-worth.

In other cases, parents "let kids be kids" and do not expect them to do much work around the house. Nancy, who lives with her elderly father, Jay, and her sons, said that she does most of the work around the house. When asked if anyone else helps out, here is what she had to say:

> Very rarely. The boys are very busy and I get criticized by neighbors and family
> and friends for not making them pitch in and help me, but they're going to be
> older and adult longer than they're ever going to be children, and this is their
> time for no responsibility. I give them freedom that most parents probably don't.

Most respondents fell somewhere in between these two parenting strategies, expecting children to do some chores around the house.

Nonresidents are sometimes involved in the division of labor when the residents are elderly. It is fairly common to find an adult son who comes to his parents' house to help with the outside chores, such as shoveling snow, a survival necessity in this part of the country. One of the widowed respondents who lives by herself receives help from her son with the outside work or hires help when he is not available.

In rural households, child care is sometimes provided informally by another family member or neighbor. In the three-generation households, it is common to see the grandparent caring for the children while the parents are at work. This situation serves the dual purpose of providing child care for the parents and having someone around in case the grandparent falls or needs assistance. When there are no grandparents at home, children sometimes go to a neighbor's house to receive care while their parents are at work. In one case, the respondent cares for her neighbor's foster child for a few hours a day until the neighbor gets home from work. She described this as a "social support" network that they had established when the neighbor decided to join the foster-care system.

Household Relationship Structures

Of the 25 householders, 19 were in either married couple or unmarried partner relationships. Other members of the households included adopted and foster family members, in-laws, grandchildren, children from a previous relationship, and elderly nonrelatives. This section examines the different household structures found in these complex households and the terminology used by respondents to describe these relationships. The following categories are not mutually exclusive; sometimes a single household falls into several of these categories. For example, in one household, an unmarried couple lives with their two adopted daughters and the former foster mother of one of the daughters, who was a nonrelative to all other household members. In this household, we find adopted children, an unmarried partnership, fictive kinship, child care, and care for the elderly.

Adoptive Families   Nine of the respondents had adopted family members of some sort. Cases varied from families with adopted children to a couple who lived with the biological and adoptive mothers of the husband. Two more respondents reported considering fictive kin to be adopted relatives, though in neither case was the "adopted" kin living in the household.

In this study, adopted children, particularly those adopted at birth, were considered part of the family with kinship terms being extended to include them as natural-born kin. In fact, in one interview, the respondent did not mention that she had been adopted into her family until she was asked about the term *adoptive parent* almost three quarters of the way through the interview. Even when describing the relationships within her adopted family, she used only natural-born kinship terms. When probed, she said that there was no difference between an adopted and a natural-born child.

One respondent, Hannah, whose adopted daughter had grown up and moved out of the household, had a strong negative feeling toward forms such as the census form that distinguish between biological and adopted children. Hannah said,

> Now you know that bothers me, because [my daughter] picks up one of those forms that asks for a list of the children and asks if they are adopted. I have never thought of [her] as an adopted child and I don't put adopted on forms. It's none of their business.

While Hannah expressed a strong aversion to this distinction, most other respondents did use the appropriate categories on the census form but referred to their adopted children as sons and daughters. Adopted siblings were referred to as brothers or sisters with no regard to biological kinship. Respondents considered the child of their adopted child their grandchild, without reference to biological or adopted origin.

At the end of one interview, a respondent, Grace, confessed that her "adopted" daughter, Maria, had not been legally adopted. As a newborn, Maria was given to the midwife because her mother did not want to keep her. Grace was a friend of the midwife and took Maria in. On Maria's birth certificate, Grace and her husband are listed as her biological parents, but they told family and friends that they had adopted her. Although this is a very unusual case, it demonstrates the fine line that distinguishes biological and adopted children. Maria was raised from birth as Grace's daughter. Is Maria Grace's biological daughter? Their DNA does not match, but they possess legal documents that state this is the case. Could one say that Maria is Grace's adopted child? There was no legal adoption. The relationship, technically, is fictive kinship, but few people actually know this fact about Grace's family.

Whether a child is called biological or adopted or even fictive kin is based on a principle that could have nothing to do with the child's life. It is a distinction that is sometimes based purely on the child's genetic makeup. While this distinction may be important for certain purposes, many adoptive parents go to considerable lengths to avoid it. Adoptive parents in this study expressed that natural-born and adopted children were raised equally, with no distinction between the two. In many cases, parents raised their adopted children from infants as their own, with only their DNA distinguishing them from natural-born kinship. As in Hannah's case, sometimes asking parents to distinguish between natural-born and adopted children is seen as insulting.

In another household, a married couple had lived with the husband, Jack's, biological and adoptive mothers. Jack was raised by Dorothy, his adoptive mother, but he had also become acquainted with Alice, his biological mother, who had no other children. When Alice became unable to care for herself, she moved into Jack's home. Two years later, Dorothy's husband died, and she also came to live in Jack's home. However, this living arrangement ended just prior to the interview. Alice was sent to live in an assisted-living facility because there was too much conflict between her and Dorothy. The respondent, Jack's wife, described this situation:

> There was conflict almost right from the start between Alice and Dorothy, but I didn't accept it . . . and as it turned out . . . when push came to shove, Alice was the outsider and Dorothy was the one that we have the background with and the loyalty to. Biologically, it doesn't have anything to do with it. It's really a strange thing when it gets right down to it: Who is the mother? It's the woman who raises you.

This is typical of how adoptive families in this study reacted to the distinction between biological and adopted kinship. Those who raise and support someone are considered "real" family members, not necessarily those who share a common bloodline.

Strictly speaking, adoption refers to a legal process by which custody of a child is transferred. However, respondents did use other, more liberal definitions of adoptive families, such as raising, or helping to raise, a child who is not legally your own. This type of "adoption" involves fictive kin. For example, Rachel talked about her adopted family as being a friend's family who took her in when she was having problems with her own family as a teenager. Although Rachel lived with them for only three years, she developed a bond with the family—she felt they were there for her when her biological family was not. Though legally this was not her adopted family, Rachel identified them as such. After describing her biological family, she described her fictive adopted family:

There's my adopted family too. They kind of adopted me, not legally, but I have another family. They are not related at all, they just kind of adopted me when I was 17. I lived with them from 17 to 20, and I still have real close ties with them. There was a mother and father, but my dad died, I consider him my dad. . . . I have a very close relationship to them, these kids, to me they are brothers and sisters.

Under etic definitions Rachel's other family would be nonrelatives; however, she feels strongly that they are more than that. She uses natural-born kinship terms when describing her relationships with them and has emotional ties that are as strong as, if not stronger than, those to her biological family. Another respondent, Karen, lives with her fiancé, Jim, her two adopted daughters, and Janet, the former foster mother of one of her adopted daughters. Janet raised Trisha as a foster child from the time she was four months old until she was four years old, when she was adopted by Karen. Though there is no kinship between Karen and Janet, Karen described Janet as an adopted grandmother and listed her on the census forms as an "other relative" and wrote in "adopted grandmother."[10] After Karen adopted Trisha, Janet was living with her son in the area and coming to Karen's home daily to help her with her children. Karen said that it eventually became more convenient for Janet to move in. Karen thinks of Janet as a mother figure to both herself and Trisha. However, since she fills more of a grandmother role in the household and is in her seventies, she is described as an adopted grandmother.

Karen's family also represents a family who adopted older children. Karen has two adopted daughters living with her. The youngest age at which any one of her children was adopted was four years old. Even though the daughters have memories of times when they were not a part of the family, Karen considers them her daughters, and they consider her their mother. The girls think of each other as sisters, and they all think of Janet as a grandmother. Karen made this comment about the relationships between the five members of her household:

The two rabbits are related. That's it. But if we're talking about two people who have a connection to each other, we're all related. . . . The girls call [friends of the family] aunt and uncle. So, I mean, I think that makes them a relative.

Using etic classification, the only family in the household is Karen and her adopted daughters, yet this household functions very much as a family unit. Janet functions as a grandmother, helps with the child care, and receives help as she needs it. Karen's fiancé, Jim, is taking on the role of stepfather as well.

Grandparent Caregivers   The two cases of grandparents as caregivers in this study also happened to be cases of adoptive families. In both cases, the respondents were caring for the children of adopted daughters. The adopted daughters (the biological mothers of the children) could not or did not want to care for the children, so the grandparents had stepped in. In one case, the grandparents had legal custody of their grandchild.[11]

When a grandparent fills the role of a parent, there may be some confusion in the terms used to classify them. One grandmother caretaker, Grace, said that she feels like both the child's parent and grandparent. While the child's biological mother, Maria, is technically his mother, Grace thinks Maria is unfit and does not deserve that title. Grace defines a mother as "someone who *has children* and *takes care of them and meets their physical and emotional needs*" (emphasis added). According to this definition, Maria fits only one of the three criteria. Grace meets the other two. This sentiment is identical in nature to feelings expressed by adoptive parents. Those who raise the children are considered parents. Biology is not considered to be a very important factor from the perspective of some of these respondents, although it is a critical factor in etic classification systems, such as those used by the Census Bureau.

Foster Families   Three families in this study had foster components. Two were married couples with foster children. The third was Karen's household, as previously discussed, with an unmarried couple, adopted daughters, and the former foster mother of one of their children. The nature of foster families makes them temporary situations, although, on occasion, the child may be adopted by the family or may become a permanent foster child. One respondent defined a foster child as a "child in custodial care." Another referred to her foster children as "temporary family members." A third described the relationship in terms of their needs: "As a foster parent you give more to kids than regular parents . . . because they need more."

Sometimes foster children in this study refer to their foster parents as "Mom" and "Dad," but they are not usually considered relatives. Other children in the household sometimes dictate the relationship terms that foster children use for their foster family. For example, if a foster child has a foster sister who talks about her uncle, aunt, and grandparents, the foster child may also use these terms. However, in most cases, the respondent notes that the foster children are not related to the family.

Natalie joined the foster-care system because she had been in the system as a child and wanted to help other children as her foster family had helped her. Natalie had taken in several foster children, then decided to adopt her most recent one. Natalie describes the decision to adopt her foster child:

We didn't plan on it. That wasn't in the plan at all. But she's a very, very strong-willed child, very determined, opinionated, forceful, and we had one of them,[12] so we just decided we were the best thing for her. We know—oh, she's precious, this kid is just precious—but we know if you let down your guard for one moment, you've lost her forever.

Natalie encouraged her neighbors to join the foster-care system as well, and one of them has taken in one of Natalie's former foster children as a permanent foster child. Natalie helps her neighbor with this child by caring for him two or three hours a day after school before the neighbor gets home from work.

The technical definition of a foster child is a person under 18 who is placed by a government agency in a household with an unrelated individual to receive parental care (U.S. Census Bureau n.d.). However, not all respondents understood "foster child" in this way. One thought that foster care could include a child in the care of another relative as well. Nancy's ex-husband's son, Luke, was in her care for a brief period and is now in the care of his grandparents. After Nancy and her ex-husband divorced, Luke went to live with his mother. While there, he got into trouble with the law. At that point, he was sent to live with Nancy, where he stayed until recently, when he moved in with his grandparents. Nancy considers Luke a foster child because he was in her care and now is in his grandparents' custodial care. While this is not the official foster-care definition, having legal custody is one emic type of foster care.

The prospect of permanent foster children and fostering leading to adoption presents an interesting perspective for relationships and kinship. From this research, we know that adopted children assume natural-born kinship terms and are considered relatives, but foster children generally are not. It would be interesting to examine when the crossover takes effect. How long must a child be in the network before he or she is considered a relative? Does it happen when the child becomes a permanent family member? This study did not examine this dimension, but it would be a good topic for future research.

Unmarried Partners Of the 25 respondents, the ethnographer identified 9 as being in unmarried partner relationships. Three were more than 60 years of age, two were in their forties, and four were in their mid- to late thirties.[13] The partnerships ranged in time together from less than a year to 30 years. All unmarried partners had previously been married and were separated, divorced, or widowed. Five of these households had coresident children; in all cases, at least one child was from a previous relationship.

Of the seven respondents openly cohabiting in romantic relationships, the categories they marked on the mock census form varied greatly. While the

Census Bureau intends to gather this information in the category "unmarried partner," only four respondents chose it. On the mock census forms, one chose "other relative" and wrote "girlfriend," one marked "wife," and another marked "other nonrelative."[14]

In addition to the seven respondents who were openly involved romantically with their live-in partners, two other respondents were in situations that seemed to also fit this category. One was a male respondent, John, from a household that had been identified in the community as a gay household. He listed his partner, Rob, as an "other nonrelative" on the mock census form. John chose not to identify him as an "unmarried partner" or "housemate/roommate."[15] When asked directly about the relationship between himself and Rob, John said that they were friends. He declined to use the terms "spouse" or "husband" for Rob, but he defined a husband or a wife as a good friend, which is how he identified Rob at the beginning of the interview. It is possible that John chose to conceal the nature of his relationship with Rob. This could be an example of purposeful misrepresentation of the true relationship, possibly because the respondent felt it was not necessary information to give to the ethnographer or that it would lead to uncomfortable circumstances. Alternatively, there may not be a romantic relationship at all, and the community perception may be wrong.

The other potential case of misrepresentation is also ambiguous. Shirley is a widow who lives with a divorced man, Bill, whom she identified as a "roomer/boarder." However, the relationship seemed to extend beyond that of a roomer or boarder. Shirley described their living arrangements:

> Bill gives me $50 per week, and of that, $30 is for—he writes this on the check—$30 is for groceries, and $20 is for board, which you know is laughable, but that's the way he wants to do it, and I don't argue. . . . Well, I love Bill, but that's as far as it goes because Bill doesn't want to get married again.

This is clearly a relationship that Shirley would like to further; however, Bill wants to portray the relationship as a boarder and friend only. Even though the couple travels together frequently and their families are acquainted, because of Bill's wishes, officially, his relationship to Shirley is only that of a boarder.

These are two situations where the ethnographer labeled the relationship as an unmarried partnership, but the respondent did not openly agree. In John and Rob's case, the evasion of that category may have been purposeful. In Shirley's case, she was attempting to accurately categorize an ambiguous situation.

Respondents did not use the term *unmarried partner* in conversation or consistently. Casually, many referred to these partners as boy- or girlfriends or fiancés, if they are going to be married. Others referred to them as husbands or wives, although the title is not legally correct. This could be because they feel some discomfort in the fact that they are living in a nontraditional situation. Finally, some do not wish to express the nature of the relationship and avoid doing so by marking an ambiguous category.

When asked about her living arrangements with her unmarried partner, George, Heather described her views on cohabitation:

> Living with someone is no different than marriage. But I do have my freedom and he has his freedom. . . . I don't need a certificate to tell me who I can or cannot be with or who I can or cannot love. If it ends in marriage, yes, but like I said, I had a bad one the first time around. I'm the one that's reluctant to get married a second time.

This seems to be a common, implicit theme. All respondents in this study who were in unmarried partnerships had previously been married. They had not remarried a second time because either one partner had not completed his or her divorce or at least one partner did not want to remarry because of a bad experience in his or her first marriage. They have chosen to cohabit instead of getting married or until they can get married (see Seltzer 2000). This is in contrast to research on younger cohabiting couples, which often shows that cohabitation is not thought of as an alternative to marriage but as a living situation that just happens (Manning and Smock 2003).

Cohabiting relationships like these are becoming more common in the United States. However, demographers are just beginning to develop measures to capture statistics on these relationships. The Census Bureau uses the term *unmarried partner*; however, as we have seen, this is not a term commonly used by the rural white respondents (see also Hunter 2004; Manning and Smock 2003). In this small study, only four of the nine unmarried couples were identified with this term. Additionally, this measure or term only captures unmarried partnerships of which the householder is a member. L. M. Casper, P. N. Cohen, and T. Simmons (1999) present an adjusted indirect measure of cohabitation and a review of the problems associated with the direct measure of cohabitation (for example, these relationships are often informal, subjectively defined, and difficult to categorize). While the adjusted measure presents a way to deal with existing data, ideally, a direct measure that is more valid and reliable should be developed and used.

Children of Previous Relationships   When a parent remarries or resides with an unmarried partner, a blended family results. Nancy had previously lived in a blended family. She was married to Nick, who had a son, Luke, by a previous marriage. Nick and Nancy also had two children together. Nancy described the difference between raising her natural children and her stepson:

> I was really a stepparent for seven years. . . . You don't have bonding that has taken place that I had with my children, developed from the day that they were conceived. If I had received Luke as an infant, that would have been a whole different bonding. But Luke came to me at age five with all the loss of control and discipline. I would say the first year was probably the easiest. It was after the dust settled that Luke realized that mommy and Nick are not going to get back together and that you are what is standing in the way. You stand between the child and their lost relationship with their parents and their desire to keep their surviving parent to themselves.

The relationship between stepparent and stepchild is complex and definitely not easy to understand, but it is easy to identify. When a person marries someone who has children from a previous relationship, that person becomes a stepparent, and the children become his or her stepchildren. However, if the couple does not marry but live together with the children of only one of the adults, the relationship of the children to the other adult is ambiguous. Four respondents in this study were in such a situation. Some respondents referred to their unmarried partner's children as stepchildren, though this is not the correct etic relationship. However, sometimes the closeness of the personal relationship determines what it is called. If the unmarried partner has helped to raise the children, he or she may assume the role of a stepparent and may be called such. However, if the children are not in the household, the close personal relationship is not there, so they may be considered nonrelatives. To exemplify the difficulty of choosing the proper term, one respondent (who identified her unmarried partner as Person 1 on the mock census form) gave her biological son the designation of her unmarried partner's biological son. During the interview, she talked about him as a stepson to her unmarried partner. Technically, the two share only fictive kinship.[16]

Another respondent, Donna, and her significant other, Jeff, have been together for almost 20 years. Together, they raised Donna's daughter, Jackie. Jackie considers Jeff her stepfather and the grandfather of her child. Donna also has a son, Michael, who is older and does not consider Jeff a relative. Donna describes their relationships:

> As far as my relationship to Jeff, we might as well be married. . . . I'm comfortable with "partner." I think "boyfriend" is silly. . . . Jackie is related to Jeff. He could be her stepfather. He raised her just about. . . . On the census form, it's hard to say what term I would have used if Jackie was still in the household. . . . I would have said "stepfather," even though biologically he isn't. This is tough.

In Donna's case, the relationship of a stepparent is defined by the role that the person has played in the child's life. Jeff is Jackie's stepparent but not Michael's.

Cindy is in an unmarried partner relationship with Doug. Both Cindy and Doug have children who have their own families. Cindy sometimes refers to Doug's son as her stepson or to her children as stepchildren to Doug, but she is not consistent. Cindy's children were not raised by Doug, but they do have a close relationship. Cindy thinks of Doug's family as her "adopted family" instead of a stepfamily. She feels like they "took her in" to their own family. Cindy's unmarried partnership with Doug is not accepted by Cindy's family, so he is not considered a relative of her family, except by her children.

Several respondents in this situation were asked to define "stepparent." One extended the definition to include "the spouse or partner of a real parent." Another respondent said that it was "another adult coming in, kind of in a parallel role to either the parent or mother." People who are not in this situation often do not include children of unmarried partners in the category of "stepchildren." However, it seems fairly common for unmarried partners with children to extend the terms *stepparent* and *stepchildren*. As cohabitation becomes a more common alternative to marriage, more of these blended families are occurring, and these terms are being broadened in order to describe the relationships (see Kreider 2003; Bumpass and Raley 1995; Bumpass, Raley, and Sweet 1995). It is critical for social scientists to be aware of this and to investigate the similarities and differences between blended families resulting from marriage and those resulting from unmarried partnerships.

Caring for the Elderly   Families sometimes take in a parent or parent-in-law who becomes unable to care for him- or herself any longer. In three cases, a married couple lives with their children and the husband's mother. In another, a married couple lives with both the biological and adoptive mother of the husband.

Carol is from a tradition of caring for the elderly members of the family. When she was first married, she lived with her mother-in-law. Carol describes her mother-in-law as "the best person I'd ever known." It was a beneficial experience for her, and it helped her when she needed to move in with her own son and his family because of her own poor health. She described her situation:

> My other two sisters said that I was unlucky to be subjected to a mother-in-law, and I said, "You were the unlucky ones." It was a real privilege. So, that way I felt I was a little bit more able to move in here, because I knew the pros and cons of living together. I never meant to stay this long. . . . [I]t's living together that is difficult because it, it just is. And I know that there are good days . . . but

> I do feel like I shouldn't be here. [My daughter-in-law] is exceptionally good,
> it's just the fact that you have to feel dependent on someone.

Growing older and becoming dependent on one's children is not easy. However, Carol enjoys being able to watch her grandchildren grow, and she cherishes the time she spends with them. She serves as the children's babysitter while their parents are at work. She describes it as a joyous experience:

> The highlight is coming home from school and getting off the bus and grandma
> is here with a special snack. They do enjoy that, and I do too, and that makes
> me feel of some worth. Because actually, it is. [My son and his wife] get home
> late, and I'm always here.

This relationship is mutually beneficial. Carol receives the care that she needs as an elderly adult, and her grandchildren receive child care while their parents are at work.

In addition to the cases of in-laws, two other households were formed to give care to the elderly. In one case, the daughter of a widowed man moved into his house with her children to care for him while he was recovering from surgery. This case will be described more thoroughly in the section on temporary situations.

In the other case, a widowed woman in her sixties, Susan, has converted her home into a private home-care facility. She houses and cares for five elderly women at a time, sometimes on a temporary basis, at other times on a more permanent basis. Some of her boarders only come for weeks or months at a time, but others are there for many years. Susan's attachment to the women is more than just that of a landlord:

> I just figure this is my home, and the ladies, they're here, and they are part of
> my family. . . . I think I'm more or less their support, but after they live with
> you for a long time . . . they get so that you're real close to them, very close. I
> know I lost a lady a while back here. She was with us for ten years. I loved her
> dearly. It's like losing one of the family.

Susan told the ethnographer that she only charged the ladies "a little bit more than $100 per month" to stay with her. This is a very low cost for the type of service she provides, that is, cooking meals, cleaning their rooms, doing laundry, and driving them to doctors' appointments. When asked why she does it, she said, "Oh I love them. I love to take care of people." Susan takes care of these ladies for the joy of helping others. Her relationship to these women is stronger than that one would feel for a boarder, but that is the designation that she chose on the mock census form. The complexity of this household is not captured by the census relationship categories. Although Susan identifies her residence as a household, it actually falls between a household and a small care facility.

Etic versus Emic Relationship Classification

Respondents were asked directly to distinguish between relatives and nonrelatives. This was a difficult task for some. Although they could come up with a definition, their usage of the terms did not always fit this definition. Three levels of relatives appear in these definitions: those related biologically, those related by law, and those related emotionally. While these are conceptually distinct, respondents differ in which levels they use to classify relatives.

Some respondents clearly defined relatives as those who were related by blood or law. Others were very inconsistent in their usage of these terms. For example, one respondent listed herself on the mock census form as an "other relative" and wrote in "girlfriend." However, when asked about these terms, she defined her unmarried partner as a nonrelative but included his children as relatives.

Relationship Terms   Respondents were asked to define several relationship terms during the course of the interview. Many of these definitions are incorporated into the descriptions of the living situations, but some of the larger, more encompassing terms deserve special attention. The technical definitions here are drawn from the definitions used for Census 2000 (U.S. Census Bureau n.d.).

Spouse and Husband/Wife

During the 25 interviews, each respondent was asked to define "spouse," "husband," and "wife." Only one definitive conclusion can be drawn from this activity: definitions for these terms are not commonly held. Some respondents saw no distinction between spouses and husbands or wives. However, even agreeing that they meant the same thing, some respondents did not agree on the common meaning. Some thought both implied a legal bond; others thought that neither was contingent on marriage. Other respondents thought one term indicated a legal bond and the other did not, although which had the legal meaning varied. Overall, the terms *husband* and *wife* seemed to connote more of an emotional attachment for most respondents than "spouse."

Some respondents saw themselves as their unmarried partner's spouse or wife but did not mark this on the form. However, one respondent actually did mark on the mock census form that she was her unmarried partner's spouse.[17]

One might argue that some of these couples are legitimately married under common law. However, only 11 states and the District of Columbia recognize common-law marriages (Legal Information Institute n.d.). New York, where the study site is located, does not. Under these standards, none of these couples is in a common-law marriage. However, several couples used emic definitions of "spouse," "husband," and "wife" that are conceptually equivalent to common-law marriages.

MOTHER/FATHER

Many definitions given by respondents extended beyond legality or biological constraints. Some examples of typical definitions of the word "mother" in this study include "Somebody who was there for me when I needed them," "Someone who has children and takes care of them and meets their physical and emotional needs," and "Someone who raised a child, the primary raiser of the child." There was a clear trend toward defining a mother as someone who raised a child, not necessarily someone who gave birth to a child. In the cases with adopted children, the adoptive parents were more likely to be considered the parents than the biological parents were. Emotionally distant mothers and those considered poor mothers were not subjectively considered mothers by respondents.

Definitions of "father" were more likely to include a biological component than definitions of "mother." However, men who are not biological fathers can also be considered fathers. Several respondents mentioned support as a defining characteristic of a father. Two specifically mentioned financial support as a fatherly duty. Several also discussed the importance of nurturing. Again, respondents in this study considered the person who helps raise and support a child a father.

GRANDMOTHER/GRANDFATHER

These terms serve two functions. One is to identify the parents of parents. This appears to be based on biological distinctions, but extensions of the meaning of the term abound. Adoptive parents are seen as grandparents to the adopted child's children. Lines are also blurred with unmarried partners and the relationship of their children to the partner's family. To exemplify this extension, one respondent said that the children of her unmarried partner are grandchildren to her adoptive parents. These children are fictive kin—they are not related by blood or marriage—but they are considered grandchildren by the respondent's parents.

A second function of the terms *grandmother* and *grandfather* involves more distant relatives or fictive kin. One respondent referred to this as a "lady with white hair and wrinkles" relationship category. She is considered the grandmother to her adopted child's children and stepchildren. Another respondent referred to the mother of her father-in-law as a grandmother. Nonresident nonrelatives who are elderly and close to the family are sometimes called grandparents for the sake of simplicity and respect. Another case is that of Janet and Karen, mentioned previously. Janet is the former foster mother of one of Karen's adopted children. Janet now lives in the household and was marked on the actual and mock census forms as an "other relative," with the write-in answer "adopted grandmother," although she is actually fictive kin.

AUNTS/UNCLES

Biology plays a very different role with these terms than with parent terms according to the respondents in this study. All of those members of the family who are biologically aunts or uncles are considered as such, even if there is no close personal relationship. However, the category also encompasses other family members and fictive kin. Great aunts and uncles are often generalized to the simpler terms. An older cousin is sometimes called an aunt or uncle. Nonrelative friends of the family are also given this title out of respect. One respondent describes this more general definition as including people who are around for holidays and family milestones, "another adult who is part of the extended family, but not part of the household."

Census Categorization

In summary, this research uncovered problems with some of the relationship categories as presented in Census 2000. Adopted kin, unmarried partners, and children of unmarried partners are often accepted into the natural kin network, and the relationship terms reflect that. If extension of kinship terms happens regularly, as it appears to in this study, then the addition of relationship categories on the census form intended to distinguish between natural and fictive kin may be fruitless. At any rate, it should be understood that these changes in word usage are taking place, and the prevalence of these extensions of kinship terms should be examined further.

It should be noted that the extension of kinship terms usually occurred naturally in interviews or when Hewner asked for the definition of relationship terms. In a formal survey or census environment, respondents may be more likely to identify the actual relationship, ignoring these extensions. This research demonstrated this likelihood in the adopted family households. While most respondents referred to adopted children with natural-born kinship terms, when speaking they did mark adopted son or daughter on the form.

Fluid Households

One of the factors that leads to household formation and dissolution is the residential mobility of some, or all, of the households members. In previous ethnographic research, Manuel de la Puente (1993, 19) cited residential mobility as "one of the key features of irregular and complex households." The next sections discuss several reasons for mobility.

Seasonal Residents   Sophia and her husband, from the example that introduces this chapter, are retirees who have a summer residence in the North and a winter residence in the South. Sophia and her husband live in Florida seven or eight months a year and spend the remaining four or five months in New York. Sophia said that she was just beginning to feel like she lived in both her New York and her Florida homes; it had taken several years of living for half of the year in Florida for her to feel like she also "lived" there.

John and Rob also have two residences; however, they only spend about four months of the year in Florida. When asked where he lives, John easily replied that he lives in his cabin in New York; he only stays in his condo in Florida in the winter.

For many seasonal residents, the answer to the question "Where do you live?" depends on the season in which it is asked. Some, like Sophia, feel they have two residences. Others, like John, maintain a primary residence and also have a vacation spot. In many situations, it is not necessary to choose a usual, or a primary, residence. However, for census purposes, this becomes important. Having two residences leads to the possibility of counting the household in both places or not counting it at all.

College Students   College students also present a problem for residence classification in the census. As mentioned, they may only live in the household for three months a year; however, because they are supported financially and emotionally by the remaining household members, they may still be considered part of the household.[18] Patricia described having to exclude her son, Jason, from the actual census form:

> My son migrates between college and home. When I first filled out my census form, I did not realize that at first. I just included him as part of the household. College students were not supposed to be included, so I just filled out my form and had to cross him out.

Patricia thinks of Jason as very much a part of the household, but she realized that the Census Bureau's residence rules meant that she should exclude him.

She did list him on her mock census form for this study because "he's here today."

Another respondent had a similar experience. She did not include her daughter on the actual census form for this study while she was away at school in April, but she did include her on the mock form for this study because she was home at the time of the ethnographic interview in May. Thus, the number of residents reported as living in the household may be contingent on the time of year the census is taken. It is easier for respondents to exclude college students when they are physically not present than when they are home, even if their stay at home is brief.

Children Moving among Households   Grace has custody of her grandson, the biological son of Grace's adopted daughter, Maria. Maria's other child, Sarah, who is only an infant, also stays with Grace every other week for two or three days. Grace says that Maria is not a good mother, and the courts have agreed and have granted custody of one of Maria's children to Grace. However, in her sixties, Grace feels unable to take Sarah, an infant, into her care permanently. So, Sarah spends some time with Grace, some time with her mother, and the rest of the time with her aunt and cousin. Because she cycles among three households, it is not clear where Sarah really lives.

Another situation in which children often move between households is joint custody. Divorced parents may have shared custody with a schedule of visitation; one parent may care for the children for part of the week, and the other for the remainder of it. This may result in children who "belong" to two households. One respondent, Megan, lives with her three children. Her ex-husband, Sam, has visitation rights with the children from Friday evening until Sunday afternoon. Sometimes the children see Sam every weekend, but lately he has been seeing them only every other weekend. Megan has a very clear view that the children belong to her household. However, it is unclear whether Sam would agree that they are members of her, rather than his, household. The ethnographer made a note that people outside this household had given her the idea that the children spend more time with their father than Megan is willing to admit. It is possible that Sam would also claim that the children belong to his household.

Foster Children   As previously discussed, foster children are, by definition, temporary residents of a household. One of the households in this study currently has two foster children with a third on the way. Sandy has had foster children in her home for seven years. When speaking of former foster children, Sandy distinguished between those who were permanent and those who were temporary:

> Two boys were here. The first was here for three months and the second was here maybe a month. . . . Other kids have been here for like two weeks. These are special assignments. . . . They have to evaluate this child before they can do anything with them. . . . The evaluation kids don't stay long enough to become part of the household.

Length of stay may be an important factor in whether foster children are considered part of the household. Those expected to be in the house for just two months may not be considered usual residents and, consequently, may not be included as members of the household.

"Temporary" Situations   There is a conceptual difference between residents who are viewed as temporary household members and those who are viewed as permanent members of the household. This study included examples of both. In most cases where a mother-in-law moved in with the respondent, the situation was viewed as permanent, a situation that would last for the remainder of the mother-in-law's life. Likewise, adoptions are most often viewed as permanent situations that will last until the children grow up and move out.

However, some living situations are created to resolve a temporary problem and will be dissolved once the problem has passed. In one case, a respondent's daughter is staying with her grandparents while they recover from ill health; she expects to get her own place after they recover.

A difficulty in identifying household members sometimes stems from current living situations that seem temporary. Many of these situations are viewed as likely to change at any time. When asked "Who lives here?" a respondent may interpret the question as asking about permanent household members, or those who "belong" in the household, and may exclude others due to their temporary status.

Nancy reported that she had been staying in her father's household at the time of Census 2000, but she did not report herself or her sons on the actual census form because she had thought it to be a temporary situation at that time. Instead, she only listed her father, Jay, at that residence; she listed herself and her sons at their own house (which was actually vacant with the exception of her pets). Nancy's house is just down the street from her father's, so she left her pets there while physically residing at his house. She goes back and forth between houses several times a day to care for her pets. Nancy explained that at the time of the census, she thought her stay at her father's house would be temporary, that he would only need help recovering from his most recent surgery. However, in the months following the surgery, it has become clear that Jay may never be able to live on his own again. Nancy refuses to place him in a nursing home and will stay and care for him as long as needed. This "temporary" living arrangement has changed into a situation that will probably continue through the remainder of Jay's life.

The case study presented at the beginning of this chapter provides another good example of this type of living situation. When Mark got a job in the South, he moved there ahead of his family to see how he liked the job. If all went well, they had planned to join him there. However, nine months had passed, and there was no indication that Mark would be returning or that Jessica and their children would be moving to be with him. This situation remained uncertain. At the time of the interview, Sophia still considered Mark part of Jessica's household[19]; however, he may not be returning to live with them.

The inclusion of these temporary household members in the answer to the question "Who lives or stays here?" depends on the respondent's interpretation of the question. It could be interpreted as an inquiry for either a cross-sectional or a representative picture of the household. The former implies that everyone who is staying there on a given day should be included. This would be equivalent to asking, "On April 1, who was staying here?" This interpretation would gather data on the temporary residents who were there at that point in time, but would omit those permanent residents who were away temporarily.

Another interpretation gathers slightly different information. If the question is interpreted as asking for a representative picture of the household, then temporary residents, who do not "belong" to the household, may be omitted, and other people who are not really current residents may be included because they seem to belong. This interpretation would exclude members of the household who seem temporary and could include nonresidents, such as college students or people with multiple residences. Respondents will give different answers, depending on their interpretation of the question.

CONCLUSION

As nuclear families become less predominant, it is important to make an attempt to understand the complexities of the households of today. In this study of rural whites in New York, we saw complexities of several types. Hewner (2000) has suggested that the reasons for the formation of these complex households were both functional and economic. These households provided companionship, pooled economic resources, and care to those who needed it. Participants in this research were dealing with the out-migration of the younger generation, marital breakups, and the need to have someone in the household to provide care to both children and the elderly (Hewner 2000).

There were multigenerational households, which saw the mutual benefit of providing child care while the parents were at work and care for the elderly who could no longer live alone. There were also skip-generation households where grandparents were raising their grandchildren, functioning as parents. These interrelationships provide an opportunity to examine nontraditional family households.

In several cases in this study, complex households were formed to care for elderly people. While this is certainly not a new phenomenon, it is one that is not well documented. Federal surveys, such as those fielded by the Census Bureau, do not include relationship categories that describe these situations. If a person cares for several elderly people in her household, the only way to designate the relationship on the current census form is "boarder." However, the relationship is much more complicated than that. The boarder's well-being is in the hands of the caretaker, much like a child's life is in the hands of a parent. This relationship is not accurately described or identified by the current relationship categories. A similar situation occurs with a grandmother living in a multigenerational household. From her presence, one cannot infer whether she is a contributing member of the family, being cared for by her children, or both. Without this information, we cannot truly understand the functioning of these households.

This study also examined households with adoptive family members. Within these families, it was noted that kinship terms were often extended to include adopted kin into the natural-born kin network. In fact, people's use of kinship terms demonstrated a preference for social over biological roles in assigning terminology. As one respondent put it, "Who's the mother? It's the woman who raises you."

A similar extension of terms is occurring within unmarried partner households. As cohabitation continues to become a more accepted living situation (see Seltzer 2000), people seem to be adjusting the emic meaning of kinship terms to compensate for otherwise hard-to-describe relationships. The partner is sometimes referred to as a spouse, husband, or wife. The children of one's unmarried partner are often referred to as stepchildren. However, this is not a consistent pattern; some families use these terms, and some do not. The overarching trend in this study seems to be toward using functional, rather than kinship-based, definitions for relationship terms (Hewner 2000). This research provides insight into the ways in which white, rural, household composition and usage of relationship terms are changing. Future research should examine how extensive these changes are.

As the participants in this study demonstrate, the nuclear family may no longer typify the rural, white household. Next door you may find Mom, Dad, little Pete, and Grandma. But looking more closely, you realize that Mom and Dad are not married, and Dad is not Pete's biological father, even though he is the man raising Pete. Grandma has a room in the basement, but she is not actually Mom or Dad's mother. She is a very close family friend, but everyone calls her "Grandma." In this changing world, one must be careful not to assume that any household is a "typical" household, even those in white, middle-class, rural America.

NOTES

1. This chapter is based on research contracted by the U.S. Census Bureau and conducted by Dr. Sharon Hewner in the spring and summer of 2000. Information for this chapter was gathered from the interview summaries, the audio tapes of the actual interviews, the mock census forms, and the other interview materials that Hewner submitted at the closure of her contract. Dr. Hewner was not able to write the chapter for this book due to other contractual obligations.

2. All respondents' names have been changed to protect their confidentiality.

3. The Current Population Survey (CPS) is a monthly survey of about 50,000 households conducted by the Census Bureau for the Bureau of Labor Statistics. "The CPS is the primary source of information on the labor force characteristics of the U.S. population. The sample is scientifically selected to represent the civilian noninstitutional population. Respondents are interviewed to obtain information about the employment status of each member of the household 15 years of age and older. However, published data focus on those ages 16 and over" (Herz 1996).

4. The CPS defines a family household as one in which the householder is related to at least one other member of the household (Weyland 1996). All other households are considered nonfamily households, even if there are relationships between its other members.

5. Married-couple households include nuclear families (a married couple with at least one biological child), as well as childless married couples and married couples living with other relatives or nonrelatives. The Census Bureau does not produce counts of nuclear families per se.

6. In an unmarried-partner household, one of the household members is identified as an unmarried partner of the householder.

7. This is an extended definition of "household," which is probably not likely to be used in completing a survey or census. It is more of an emotionally laden definition that one might use conversationally or to reminisce.

8. According to the decennial census's "usual residence" rule, college students living away from home to attend school are not to be included in their parents' households.

9. It is interesting to note that Sophia talks about a household consisting of Jessica, Mark, and their children rather than about the residential household, which includes Sophia, her husband, Jessica, and Jessica's children.

10. Karen listed Janet this way on the actual Census 2000 form as well as on the mock interview form.

11. Although the daughter in question is identified as adopted, the respondent confessed that this had not been a legal adoption. This is explained earlier, but, technically, both the daughter and grandchild are nonrelatives. They are included here because the respondent claims that they are her relatives on all legal documents.

12. The respondent is referring to her natural-born child with these traits.

13. A unique aspect of this research is the age of the unmarried partners. Most research to date on cohabitation has focused predominately on younger, unmarried partners. This gives us insight into older partners who are likely to have different motivations for cohabiting than their younger counterparts. While many young unmarried partners are on their way to marriage, many of these older unmarried partners seem to have chosen cohabitation instead of marriage (perhaps because of a bad past experience with marriage).

14. Five of these couples could be matched to actual Census 2000 records. Three had used "unmarried partner" on the form, one had used "other relative," and the fifth did not include her partner on the form because he was not residing in the household at that time.

15. However, his partner was listed as a "housemate/roommate" on the actual census form.

16. The correct relationship, that is "other nonrelative," was reported on the actual Census 2000 form.

17. This respondent did correctly identify herself as an "unmarried partner" on the actual census form.

18. See note 8.

19. See note 9.

REFERENCES

Bumpass, L. L., and H. Lu. 2000. "Trends in cohabitation and implications for children's family contexts in the United States." *Population Studies* 54: 29–41.

Bumpass, L. L., and R. K. Raley. 1995. "Redefining single-parent families: cohabitation and changing family reality." *Demography* 32: 97–109.

Bumpass, L. L., R. K. Raley, and A. Sweet. 1995. "The changing character of stepfamilies: implications of cohabitation and nonmarital childbearing." *Demography* 32: 425–36.

Casper, L. M., P. N. Cohen, and T. Simmons. 1999. "How does POSSLQ measure up? Historical estimates of cohabitation." Population division working paper no. 36. Washington, DC: U.S. Census Bureau.

de la Puente, M. 1993. "Why are people missed or erroneously included by the census: a summary of findings from ethnographic coverage reports." Paper presented at the Census Bureau's Research Conference on Undercounted Ethnic Populations, Richmond, Virginia, May 5.

Fields, J., and L. M. Casper. 2001. "America's families and living arrangements: population characteristics." Current population reports, P20-537. Washington, DC: U.S. Census Bureau.

Glasgow, N. 2000. "Rural/urban patterns of aging and caregiving in the United States." *Journal of Family Issues* 21: 611–31.

Herz, D. 1996. "A joint project between the Bureau of Labor Statistics and the Bureau of the Census: CPS overview." Washington, DC: Bureau of Labor Statistics. Available at www.bls.census.gov/cps/overmain.htm (accessed January 24, 2003).

Hewner, S. J. 2000. "Ethnographic research on complex households in western New York State: impact of migration and economic change on the complexity of household composition among rural Caucasians." Unpublished report for Complex Household and Relationships in the Decennial Census and Ethnographic Studies.

Hunter, J. E. 2004. "Are you shacking up? The search for an appropriate measure of cohabitation." Paper presented at the Annual Meeting of the American Association for Public Opinion Research, Phoenix, Arizona, May 13.

Kreider, R. M. 2003. "Adopted children and stepchildren: 2000." Census 2000 special reports CENSR-6RV. Washington, DC: U.S. Census Bureau.

Legal Information Institute, Cornell Law School. N.d.. "Marriage laws of the fifty states, District of Columbia, and Puerto Rico." Available at www.law.cornell.edu/topics/Table_Marriage.htm (accessed January 24, 2003).

Manning, W., and P. J. Smock. 2003. "Measuring and modeling cohabitation: new perspectives from qualitative data." Paper presented at the Annual Meeting of the Population Association of America, Minneapolis, Minnesota, May 3.

Overbey, M. M., and K. M. Dudley. 2000. "Anthropology and middle-class working families: a research agenda." American Anthropological Association Special Publication. Available at www.aaanet.org/gvt/mcwf.htm (accessed February 19, 2003).

Rogers, C. C. 2000. "The graying of rural America." *Forum for Applied Research and Public Policy* 15: 52–55.

Seltzer, J. A. 2000. "Families formed outside of marriage." *Journal of Marriage and the Family* 62: 1247–68.

Simmons, T., and M. O'Connell. 2003. "Married-couple and unmarried-partner households: 2000." Census 2000 special reports CENSR-5. Washington, DC: U.S. Census Bureau.

Simmons, T., and G. O'Neill. 2001. "Households and families: 2000." Census 2000 brief C2KBR/01-8. Washington, DC: U.S. Census Bureau.

U.S. Census Bureau. 2001. "Multigenerational households for the United States and for Puerto Rico: 2000 (PHC-T-17)." Census 2000 special tabulation. Available at www.census.gov/population/www/cen2000/phc-t17.html (accessed January 24, 2003).

———. N.d. "Census 2000 glossary," at www.census.gov/dmd/www/glossary/glossary_a.html (accessed January 24, 2003).

Weyland, G. 1996. "A joint project between the Bureau of Labor Statistics and the Bureau of the Census: CPS basic monthly survey: concepts. Washington, DC: U.S. Census Bureau, at www.bls.census.gov/cps/bconcept.htm (accessed January 24, 2003).

11

Gender, Economy, and Kinship in Complex Households among Six U.S. Ethnic Groups: Who Benefits? Whose Kin? Who Cares?

Rae Lesser Blumberg

INTRODUCTION: SIX TALES OF WEAVING GENDER, KINSHIP, AND ECONOMY INTO A SURVIVAL STRATEGY

*I*n a murder mystery, when the detective assesses the suspects, the big question is, Who benefits? But this question seems less appropriate if we are talking about family and household; culturally, these are supposed to be about love, not material advantage. Yet, the six ethnic groups portrayed in this volume—the Navajo living on the vast "Rez" (reservation) in Arizona, the Iñupiat of northern Alaska, the Korean immigrants to New York's Queens, the Hispanic immigrants to central Virginia, the African Americans from urban coastal Virginia, and the white Americans from rural upstate New York—all manage to cobble together a strategy for living that entails residing in complex households very different from the nuclear "Ozzie and Harriet" household that is the implicit basis of the U.S. census. And all do so in a way that combines both caring and material benefits.

Let us begin with a brief overview of the six samples. First, the households of the original Americans, the Navajo and the Iñupiat, are not only complex but also flexible; individuals may shift back and forth between two or more households as part of a strategy of preserving a cherished way of life. Sharing within and between households is widespread, as is informal adoption or fostering of children. Grandparents (particularly grandmothers among the matrilineal Navajo) are at the heart of this system. And their adult sons and daughters in their prime productive years often voluntarily put their own economic and career advancement in second place in order to support kinfolk's efforts to maintain a beloved subsistence and family system.

Second, the more recent arrivals to our shores, Hispanics in central Virginia and Koreans in the crowded tenements of Queens, have adopted complex household arrangements more out of economic necessity or advantage than for love. Their goal is to get ahead, and part of their definition of the good life, especially among the Hispanics, is moving on up to a nuclear household, where they will not have to live with various and sundry relatives or nonrelatives.

Third, in our samples, urban African Americans in coastal Virginia and rural whites in upstate New York have forged complex households partly to survive structural problems. On the one hand, the African Americans have responded to discrimination, poverty, and their grown children's travails (including drugs) with a highly adaptive matri-oriented system that involves not only complex households but also sharing networks so that children can be raised in loving homes and the worst effects of sometimes dire economic straits kept at the doorstep. On the other hand, the rural white New York sample of aging (average age 54) females (24 of 25 respondents) has adopted complex households to solve the problems of growing old in a region where the population is shrinking and the younger generation is leaving, but the snow still has to be shoveled and the sick succored, no matter what.

The ethnographers use slightly different language to refer to the hypothetical mainstream American family, invoking images of Ozzie and Harriet and middle-class, white, American lifestyles of the 1950s. This has been the qualitative comparison group in all of the ethnographic chapters. The Ozzie and Harriet household has entered our culture as a synonym for white-bread, middle-class, white, American familism. Our quantitative comparison group in this book has been the overall population, which, as we have seen, was 70% non-Hispanic white at the national level in 2000 (Grieco 2001).

Let us now zero in on gender, the main focus of this chapter. In overview, in comparison with the prevailing level of gender stratification in mainstream America, the Navajo are the most gender egalitarian of the six groups, followed by the African Americans and, increasingly, the Iñupiat, where female status has been rising. At the other end of the continuum are the traditionally patriarchal Koreans; the Latinos are a bit less unequal. The Koreans appear to be notably less patriarchal than in their homeland, and the Hispanics perhaps somewhat less so (in part because both groups are living in a more gender-egalitarian culture). The rural whites seemed to consider themselves "modal America."

In order to analyze gender in all six cases, I turn to my general theory of gender stratification (see, e.g., Blumberg 1978a, 1984, 1991, 1998, 2001, 2004a). As it turns out, a number of the hypotheses prove useful in illuminating, comparing, and contrasting each group's gender/kinship system.

Some of my findings and conclusions also have policy implications for the census. Unfortunately, one of the dimensions, which I call "side of house" and which I will try to tease out and analyze, is one not likely to be incorporated into the census at any time soon. Here, I consider whose kin (his or hers) of which gender are involved in those complex households and what difference this makes to individual and familial strategies of getting by versus getting ahead.

The remainder of the chapter is organized as follows: First, I present a summary of relevant hypotheses from my theory of gender stratification. Next, I examine gender in the six cases, grouped in the same pairs of ethnic groups as in the organization of this volume. Finally, I discuss commonalities, contradictions, and conclusions.

SOME HYPOTHESES FROM A GENERAL THEORY OF GENDER STRATIFICATION

My central hypothesis is that the single most important, although far from only, variable affecting the level of gender equality is relative economic power, defined as relative control of economic resources by males and females at a variety of nested levels ranging from the macro (the state) to the micro (the couple or family). (The main focus of my fieldwork has been gender and Third World economic development, and in none of the 40 countries, plus the United States, where I have worked have I ever found a case where women who controlled income proved more subjugated than those who did not.)

Work in productive activities[1] is necessary, but insufficient, to gain control of economic resources. Factors that help women translate work into economic power include:

1. The extent to which the kinship system provides them with advantages.
   a. The most important advantage is inheritance equal to or greater than that of men.
   b. The second most important advantage is living near or with female kin.
2. A high level of what I term *strategic indispensability* (Blumberg 1984, 56–62) as a labor force (e.g., being critical to and irreplaceable in a

key activity, controlling technical expertise, being organized, being competed for by more than one group).

But achievement of economic power is complicated by cultural and structural factors, including *macro-* and *micro-level discount factors* (Blumberg 1984, 1991; Blumberg and Coleman 1989). At the level of the state, these involve the extent to which the political, legal, religious, ideological, and economic systems disadvantage women relative to men. The macro-level discount is much smaller in, say, Sweden than in Saudi Arabia, but at present, it is invariably negative worldwide. At the level of the household, however, micro-level discounts can be negative or positive for either males or females—subtracting or adding metaphorical pennies' worth of economic power from and to each dollar brought into the household by a man versus a woman. Micro-level discount factors relevant for this chapter include male and female members' (1) personal ideologies, including gender ideology, as well as their relative (2) dependence on each others' income, (3) attractiveness, (4) commitment (the less committed have more leverage because the others fear he or she will withdraw), and (5) bargaining assertiveness. (Consider, for example, a rich old man, besotted over a beautiful young wife whose commitment to the relationship is shaky. In this case, his economic power is negatively discounted by his position on the micro-level discount factors so that he gets far less than a dollar's worth of economic power from each dollar of his wealth.)

Two kinds of asymmetry also affect economic power: (1) one gets more clout from control of surplus than mere subsistence (because one has more degrees of freedom in allocating surplus), and (2) unless cushioned by strong ideological or kinship organization factors, a woman's position falls rapidly when her economic power drops,[2] whereas, increased power leads to a slower, less linear rise.

The consequences of greater economic power, once consolidated, I posit, include the following dependent variables: (1) greater influence over other types of power (e.g., more political clout, less likelihood of being a victim of domestic violence—although the more a man feels threatened by a recent rise in a woman's relative economic power, the more likely a short-term spike in violence), (2) greater self-confidence, and (3) greater control over "life options," aspects of one's destiny known to exist in all human societies, including marriage, divorce, sexuality, fertility, freedom of movement, access to education, and household power. Household power, in turn, includes greater say in decisions involving domestic well-being (e.g., how many years of schooling to give sons versus daughters), economic matters, and fertility control. Finally, greater economic power is linked to having more say in household and community land-use decisions and general influence in community affairs. (Various researchers, including myself, have provided empirical support for these hypotheses, but documenting this is beyond the scope and focus of this chapter.)

THE FIRST ARRIVALS: NAVAJO AND IÑUPIAT

Viewing the Navajo and the Iñupiat through the lens of gender enriches their stories. We first note that the Navajo and Iñupiat (see chapters 3 and 4) have different kinship/gender systems. At nearly 300,000 strong, the Navajo are the second-largest U.S. Indian tribe and emphasize mother's side kinship. This is also the case with five more of the eight largest Indian tribes: the Apache, Cherokee (the largest tribe), Choctaw, Iroquois, and Pueblo (including Acoma, Hopi, Laguna, and Zuñi) also have matri-oriented kinship; the other two, Chippewa and Sioux, have male-oriented kinship systems (see Coltrane and Collins 2001, 233, for the tribes and Murdock 1967 for the kinship systems).[3]

Technically, the Navajo are matrilineal (they reckon descent mainly through the mother's side) and matrilocal (the young couple traditionally lives with or near the bride's female kin). More importantly, women are the main inheritors of the most important resources (sheep and land-use rights). In short, the traditional Navajo system gives women both economic power and centrality in kinship organization, a very powerful combination in terms of my theory. Further enhancing their power is the fact that "Navajo women very frequently manage the household money regardless of whether the man or the woman earns the most" (Tongue, personal communication).

In contrast, the Iñupiat give about equal weight to maternal and paternal relatives. They have "bilateral" kinship, the same as the U.S. mainstream. In most bilateral kinship systems, women are neither advantaged nor disadvantaged in either inheritance or where they live after marriage, although in some groups' actual practice, inheritance, or marital residence may favor one gender more than the other.[4] Among the Iñupiat, however, women get no extra economic or other power from the kinship system.

The second thing to notice is that both have quite different traditional ways of making a living—ways very different from that of the U.S. mainstream. The Navajo long have lived as nomadic herders on their semi-arid lands, tending sheep (as well as goats, cattle, and horses); they also may do a little farming on rain-fed plots. In contrast, the Iñupiat long have hunted, fished, and, to a limited extent due to climate, gathered.

The resulting gender division of labor is also quite different. On the one hand, Navajo women tend to be the main herders (doing all the work with the sheep aside from the fencing and heavy labor, with even elders walking miles to herd). This remains true, Nancy Tongue writes, even though the Navajo, on average, have not relied on subsistence for more than 35% of their diet since the Department of the Interior imposed a drastic stock-reduction program in the 1930s. According to Tongue (personal communication), women keep the sheep not only for tradition's sake but because the wool is the basis of women's "job," as they wash, dye, card, spin, and then weave the wool. They maintain their looms and weaving utensils, which are usually passed down from their grandmothers and treasured. The sale of the resulting rugs, even if only sporadically made, contributes extra income. Many women also have home/cottage industries making jewelry, pottery, or other arts/crafts/handiwork, and this fills in financial gaps for their families.

On the other hand, 18 of 25 (72%) in Amy Craver's Iñupiaq sample continue to rely on subsistence resources for over half of their diet, and the key "culture hero" tasks, hunting and fishing, are done mostly by men (Craver does mention cases of women becoming the hunters for their families, however). Women usually spend more of their time on the less glamorous aspects of hunting and fishing, processing the results, although the seasonal berries and grains gathered mainly by women are appreciated for adding taste and variety to the diet. But recent changes in the division of labor have enhanced the economic power and relative position of Iñupiaq women, while having a less gendered effect among the Navajo.

Specifically, Iñupiaq hunting and fishing are expensive under current conditions: snow machines, guns, ammunition, boats, and the like, are costly. It takes cash income to underwrite the much-valued traditional way of life. These days, young women are more likely than their brothers to provide it. As Craver writes, they are more likely to leave the village for school and get the resulting better jobs than the young men. By voluntarily providing much of the surplus that makes possible the traditional Iñupiaq subsistence strategy, the young women have enhanced their relative position in terms of my theory of gender stratification.

One of my theory's hypotheses (see above) argues that you get more power from allocating surplus than trying to stretch subsistence income (Schmeer 2005, 407, provides the most recent empirical support): The young women decide how much of their disposable income (surplus) to send home and when, which raises their power. In terms of my micro-level discount factors, (1) their families (which, as Craver notes, may be scattered over several dwellings) have become more dependent on the young women's contributions, and (2) the families also may worry about the absent young women's continued commitment, which further enhances the women's relative position. Recall that my theory argues that the person perceived as less committed has more leverage, since he or she is seen as more likely to withdraw.

Nevertheless, although young women's position is rising, they still do not get a full dollar's worth of economic power for every dollar they contribute. This is because of two counterbalancing factors. First, the "cultural ideology" discount factor continues to give greater prestige to (mostly male) hunting and fishing. Second, despite their rising status, young women often pay a different kind of price: leaving their child or children behind with their parents. Such practices are culturally well accepted—adopting a first grandchild is an entrenched custom among the Iñupiat. In this purposive sample study of complex households, 17 of 25 households (68%) contain grandparent(s) and grandchild(ren) but are missing the mother of the child(ren). Leaving their kids behind also blunts some of the power these young women could derive from their control of the surplus that they voluntarily contribute to household subsistence hunting and fishing, as well as the leverage they could get from the "relative-commitment" discount factor. The fact that the women's children are in the village helps to insure that they will continue to send money home for hunting, fishing, and child support, and their families need not fret much about their continuing commitment. Even with these caveats, however, there is no denying that, overall, young women's clout has risen. In contrast, the young men tend to hunt, fish, and do sporadic odd jobs but live in their parents' house (perhaps sleeping in a nearby shed).

Among today's Navajo, it is common for some, usually men, to have a blue-collar trade that periodically takes them far away from the reservation; women are more likely to stay in school and then get social service jobs on or near the "Rez." Maternal grandmothers' lands and sheep remain the cultural heart of family resources, but the economic heart comes from job income. Yet, even where men's earnings are greater, women's relative position remains strong. "The women are still in charge," according to Tongue (personal communication). They not only continue to have a disproportionate share of the culturally valued and economically significant land and animals, but they also enjoy "solidarity power" with coresident female kin and an ideology that they are central to family and group life.

Even so, the larger U.S. culture has made a few inroads. First, relocation and shrinking landholdings are a continuing problem. Loss of traditional lands is especially disturbing for women who hold the use rights to those lands—it means they have nothing to pass on to their children. Second, women are not always identified as the census "householder." When Tongue asked one woman, who owns her family's home, why she had listed her husband as the primary householder, she laughed. "I just did that because that's how white people do it." Her daughter's husband brings in the money, so the daughter views him as the head of her household. But this is still atypical. Both the Navajo and Iñupiaq cultures remain remarkably resilient and enduring, given the political, legal, economic, and cultural onslaughts of the more powerful dominant group.

A few other themes that are important in the Navajo and Iñupiaq chapters also prove to have a "gender angle" on closer analysis, as we see in the following sections.

Sharing

Both groups practice sharing, although to different extents and in different, gender-differentiated patterns. First, sharing is a "cultural universal" among hunters and gatherers (see, e.g., Nolan and Lenski 1999; Blumberg 1978a): it evens out the ups and downs in finding food and, thus, acts as survival insurance. Accordingly, it remains a crucial part of Iñupiaq survival strategies. Moreover, as noted, the men still dispense the more valued animal and fish protein, which continues to boost their prestige. Navajo sharing involves pooled herds of sheep, shared vehicles and rides, shared subsistence tasks and purchases (e.g., hauling and buying wood and water, installing and repairing fencing), and shared conveniences (one relative's home may have electricity, another's water, and a third may be close to a school; people may move from one household to another as they need these services). Other than sheep, which tend to belong to women, Navajo sharing seems gender neutral and, perhaps, not quite as important as for the Iñupiat.

Informal Adoption and Fostering

Adoption and fostering are very prevalent in the Iñupiaq sample, as in the Navajo sample. Kids may derive special benefits from living with grandparents. For example, they can learn the most interesting and valued aspects of traditional culture and subsistence: hunting, fishing, and gathering with their grandparents among the Iñupiat, and riding horses and herding sheep on their maternal grandmothers' land among the Navajo. Children may also be fostered with kin closer to school or to help care for an aging relative. In gender terms, adoption and fostering are largely with matrilineal kin among the Navajo. Iñupiaq children, in theory, could go to live with either their mother's or father's parents. But the Iñupiaq "skip-generation" pattern is gendered: it is the children's mother (rather than father) who is likely to be absent, thus tilting child adoption and fostering toward her parents or siblings. In both groups, adoption is formalized only if there's a problem with the state.

Grandparents

Anthropologists recently have come to recognize the benefits that grandparents can provide, even when no formal adoption or fostering is involved. The data tend to show that it is the mother's mother who exerts the most positive influence (Angier 2002), which can include higher rates of infant and child survival. In the Navajo case, the most important grandparent clearly is the maternal grandmother, since she is the source of inherited resources and the "homeland" to which family members return all their lives. Both Iñupiaq grandparents seem important since resources flow from both. But grandfathers get a little extra clout because they are the ones who can teach the most prestigious and important subsistence skills—hunting and fishing.

Spouses

There are distinct patterns in the two groups. The most important difference is that a Navajo man has less formal responsibility to his children if the union breaks up; conversely, mother's brothers are expected to maintain close, loving, and economically supportive ties with their nephews and nieces no matter what. (The relationship with mother's sisters is even closer: they are referred to as mothers and call each others' children sons and daughters, not nephews and nieces.) Navajo do not say "husband" or "wife" but, rather, "spouse," which translates to "the one I make my living with" (Tongue, chapter 3) and they cooperate economically and care for each other. Whether there has been a civil marriage is irrelevant. In contrast, an Iñupiaq husband is closer to his children than are any of his wife's siblings. His obligations to his children continue even if the union ends. In short, we see what we would expect from a matrilineal versus a bilateral kinship system.

    This leads to the question, How do Navajo men feel about their kinship/spousal system? The short answer is that they seem to be as emotionally bound by family as women. Tongue's quotes from men are quite eloquent. For example, her cultural liaison, Leo, resides with his wife on land she inherited matrilineally. Her mother resides next door in a traditional *hogan*, her sister's family lives part time down the dirt road, and her single brother lives "behind the hill next to them." When she asked Leo to describe the people he lives with, he suggested the word *k'é*, which he defined as

> The people I live with who are part of my family and are my people. They are the ones I shake hands with, and the ones I feel good with above, in front, and behind. They are the ones I have peace with. K'é means family group. It also is our word for peace.[5]

The Burden on the Middle Generation

This is most visible in the Navajo because of the sheer size of the reservation. A woman will try to see and help her mother as often as possible. Even if she lives a couple hundred miles away and works Monday to Friday, she'll drive long distances every weekend, frequently feeling pressured and exhausted by the effort. Her husband may accompany her, then make long journeys to his own maternal kin. Among the Iñupiat, those who leave also try to return, at minimum for subsistence "high season," when winter does not rule the land. These patterns maintain both caring and traditional economic patterns but at a high price for the "sandwich generation": beyond losing sleep, they may lose chances for career advancement because of their schedule.

Fit between the Census Categories and Those of the Group: Living Arrangements and Kinship Terms

Whereas many Navajo and Iñupiat live in shifting arrangements that transcend a single residence, the Navajo have an added problem that makes it impossible to represent their kin arrangements accurately with extant census categories. In their matrilineal system, terms for maternal and paternal kin are not parallel. For example, the grandchild of one's son is a *nali*, whereas the grandchild of one's daughter is a *tsui*. If the census term *grandchild* was checked, Tongue found, the grandchild in question was inevitably the child of one's daughter (tsui), never a nali. In other words, the maternal relatives are the Navajo "default option": if not asked to specify "side of house," they will automatically name maternal kin for categories such as uncle, aunt, nephew, niece, or grandchild.

In sum, it is the way of life that precludes the Iñupiat from fitting comfortably into census categories. With the Navajo, it is not only the way of life but also the fact that their way of life is centered on matrilineal kinship. Even their kinship terms do not match those of the census. Yet, Tongue found, not a single respondent wanted to live any differently.

THE RECENT ARRIVALS: KOREANS AND LATINOS

First, let us note that the complex households encountered among the samples of recent immigrants from South Korea and Latin America (the great majority of the Hispanic households were from Mexico, with most of the rest from El Salvador) are not the typical form in their countries of origin. For example, Patricia Goerman (2004) cites data from Mexico's National Institute of Geography and Informatics that in 1995, 74% of households in Mexico were nuclear families. The situation is similar in South Korea, Tai Kang writes. The country has undergone a dramatic transition from an agrarian to an urbanized, fast-growing nation where gross domestic product has been growing at an average 8% a year for 40 years. Now, the great majority of city folk reside in apartments with nuclear family members only.

The second point to emphasize is that, overwhelmingly, both the Koreans and the Hispanics cited economic reasons in explaining their living arrangements. Also, their current arrangements are not their long-term preference: large majorities of the Latinos Goerman studied named the nuclear household as their ideal and said they would not continue living with their current coresidents permanently. But, for now, as they struggle to establish a toehold on the lower rungs of what they hope will be the ladder of opportunity in the United States, such complex household arrangements provide economic advantages.

The third point to emphasize involves gender differences when we compare Koreans' and Latinos' life in the United States with that in their countries of origin. In preview, the gender stratification and kinship system they left provided more structural advantage to males than is the case here.

Among Koreans, patriarchy is woven into the very fabric of everyday life. As Kang writes, one of the fundamental social and cultural norms (*Oh Rewn*) is "hierarchical role differentiation and separation" between a husband and his wife. In the traditionally patriarchal, patrilineal, patrilocal Korean extended family, the wife is subordinate to her husband, and to her oldest son if she is widowed. In general, females have subordinate and marginal social status, and there is separation of paternal and maternal relatives.

Among the Hispanics, although kinship is formally bilateral, a number of the women reported living with their husband's parents in their home country. Goerman writes,

> Elena told me that in her experience it is quite common for a couple to move in with the husband's parents until they are able to establish their own household. Temporary migration to the United States is often the easiest way to achieve this goal (personal communication).

While the traditional systems in Mexico and El Salvador (together, these are the home countries of some 90% of the Latino sample) are far less patriarchal than the Koreans', they are near the patriarchal end of the continuum for Latin America and are far more patriarchal than is typical in the United States. Therefore, let us see how these patterns have shifted under the exigencies of surviving—and, hopefully, advancing—in a strange, new land.

Female Labor Force Participation

Though these small, nonrandom samples cannot be generalized to all Korean and Hispanic immigrants, they merit scrutiny. Let us begin with the Hispanic sample, because for reasons of "face," the Koreans were reluctant to discuss whether they were working and at what. (A number were in the underground, informal economy, something they would not admit to an interviewer who, albeit Korean, represented the U.S. Census Bureau.) Of the 49 Hispanic people in two samples discussed by Goerman, 30 were women. Two were older than "prime labor force" age (18–64) and retired, so they are not counted. All but 9 of the 28 other females were working (68%). The Mexico and El Salvador data are as follows: in 1995–1997, 39% of Mexican and 41% of Salvadoran women aged 15 and older were in the labor force, making up, respectively, 34% and 37% of the total labor force (United Nations 2000, 145).

The 1995–1997 figures for Korea are 50% of women aged 15 and older working, making up 41% of the total labor force (United Nations 2000, 147). It can be inferred, however, that more than 50% of all women in his 25 complex households were earning income (Kang personal communication).

Recall that my gender-stratification theory posits that when women control income, they have more economic power and say in household decisions. It also posits that when women's relative income rises, so does their power, although the path to greater clout is not as smooth, fast, and linear as their drop in power if relative income falls (unless that decline is cushioned by ideological or kinship-structure factors). Here, in the two samples, a larger proportion of Korean and Hispanic women are earning income than in the home country, and in only one case (Kang's description of a 62-year-old widow who gives her paycheck to her son) is there any indication that the woman does not have a say vis-a-vis her own earnings. So, this implies more power for these Korean and Hispanic women.

Whose Kin? Whose Power?

Indeed, in the Korean sample, we find examples of atypical female power. Consider Kang's Case #501: The grandparents were brought over by their daughter (who has a university degree and a job in Manhattan) to take care of her two children (her husband is a grad student). When Kang asked permission to tape the interview, the old man felt he had to call his daughter for her okay. She refused, and her embarrassed father had to abort the interview. Such a direct exercise of power by a daughter would be heresy in traditional Korean culture. Kang's liaison explained, "You see, the grandmother looks after a few neighborhood Korean children—babysitting work. She gets paid for the work under the table. They do not want people to know about the underground economy that they are a part of."

In fact, Kang looked for three-generation families for his sample, and in 12 of the 25 households, a grandmother (or grandparents) had been brought over to help with the children and chores (Kang personal communication). Intriguingly, this involved another reversal of Korean patriarchal practice:

> [T]he wife's mother was more likely to have moved in, rather than the husband's. In other words, the coresident three-generation families were not a re-creation in Queens of a traditional patriarchal, patrilocal, Korean family. Part of the reason reported by respondents is that sons tend to get along better with their mothers-in-law than their wives do with their mothers-in-law—so, the young couple often sends for the grandmother who will make the most harmonious addition to their tiny, cramped quarters.

Among the Latinos no such dramatic reversals of traditional practices were encountered. Rather, more women were living with husband's male kin than with their own female kin. For this article, Goerman and I coded our original census sample of 25 households (Blumberg and Goerman 2000) for side of house. We found the following: of seven households where extended kin were from the woman's side, two included only her female kin; three, both female and male kin; and two, only male kin. In other words, in 5 of 25 households (20%), the woman had a kinswoman living with her. But where the kin were from the man's side, six of eight households included only the man's male kin, and two more included both his own male and female kin. In other words, in no household with husband-side kin did a man live with only his own female relatives. All told, in 8 of 25 households (32%), the man had a coresident kinsman, compared with the 20% of women living with their own female kin. Using a different subgroup of her purposive sample, Goerman found that 86% of 44 households that now or once were complex contained extra men (mean of 2.2 men), whereas only 48% contained extra women (mean of 1.2 women). Such patterns may explain why some women cited not having to pick up after husband's male kin as one reason they looked forward to moving up to the preferred nuclear family household once they were better established.

Summing up, women in both the Korean and Hispanic purposive samples have a higher level of labor force participation than do women in their home countries, thereby boosting their power. As an added power bonus, in the United States, these women seem much less likely to have to live with their husband's parents. Further, now they are living in a culture considerably less patriarchal than that of their countries of origin. There is one area, however, where Korean women clearly gain and Hispanic women clearly lose: in naming practices in the United States as opposed to their homelands.

What's in a Name?

First, let us see why Hispanic women lose when they fill out U.S. forms such as the census questionnaire. In Latin America, naming customs permit women to retain their maiden name all their lives. Here's an example: If a woman named Alicia had a father named Juan Rodriguez and a mother named Susana Gonzalez, her name while she was single would be Alicia Rodriguez Gonzalez, with Rodriguez being her "main" surname (in Latin American naming customs, the father's surname comes first, followed by the mother's). If she married Roberto Cordero Mendoza, she would be "Alicia Rodriguez de Cordero." On formal occasions, she might use all her names—Alicia Rodriguez Gonzalez de Cordero Mendoza. Unfortunately, the U.S. census forms allow space for only one last name. If she follows Latin American custom, Alicia will write "Rodriguez," her "own" name. But if Alicia has been in the United States for a while, she may know that in this country, the custom favors using the husband's name. So, she might write "Cordero," perhaps feeling discomfort or resentment since she's really Alicia Rodriguez.

Next, let us see why Korean women might find this less onerous. According to S. Park (2002, 6), Korea retains the family-registry system (*hoju-je*), which defines the status of each family member in relation to the *hoju*, or male householder. If a woman divorces the father of her daughter and remarries, she is not allowed to register her child with her new husband's surname. Until her daughter marries and is transferred to her husband's family registry, she must remain on her first (biological) father's registry and keep his surname. Sadly, Ji-eun, the daughter in Park's article, was teased mercilessly at school because she and her younger half brother (born to the mother's new husband) do not have the same surname. It gets worse:

> There is a rank order for who may be a householder. If the household has no living father, his son, no matter how small, succeeds to the position. Then follow, in order, his grandson, unmarried daughter, wife, and his mother. Ji-eun's mother is fourth in line to possess legal rights over her own daughter—even after Ji-eun's first father dies.

Ji-eun is registered only as a "cohabitant" in her stepfather's family registry. A male householder can register even illegitimate children in his family registry, despite his wife's objections. Because the family register must be submitted to claim tax deductions, move to a new home, or apply for jobs, it acts as a scarlet letter for people in nontraditional family situations. Not only do single mothers lose rights over their own kids, but adoptees also suffer: they must keep their original surname even after legal adoption.[6]

> Women's groups say the system institutionalizes discrimination against women and delivers the message that a married woman is merely an instrument for the paternal lineage of her husband's family. Above all, the groups argue, the hoju order . . . clearly follows the sexist principle that all men are superior to any woman (Park 2002, 6).

In the United States, Koreans in nontraditional households can use whatever surname they choose. In comparison, it is a much freer arrangement for women.

Adoption and Fostering

The adoption or fostering of children almost never occurs outside the paternal lineage among Koreans. Latino customs are much more open, with informal adoption and fostering being fairly common in the countries of origin. Such children are viewed as part of the household, and there do not seem to be any strong preferences for fostering maternal versus paternal children.

Cohabitation and "Face"

Hispanics also are much more likely to cohabit and say so (throughout Latin America, up to half of poor people, in particular, live in common-law unions). In most instances, these couples consider themselves spouses, causing a potential recording problem for the census. But Koreans will not admit to being in cohabiting relationships. In Korea, it would be a loss of face in the patriarchal system, as well as unaccepted legally, and the Queens respondents also avoided revealing such ties.

The Balance Sheet

Just reading the description of the Korean family registry is enough to lead most people to conclude that Korean immigrant women living in cramped quarters in Queens have had to swim against a much stronger current of patriarchy but that they have made more *relative* progress than Hispanic women who have lived in a much more moderate system of patriarchy in their home countries. There is evidence, however, that Hispanic women, too, appreciate the greater gender equality afforded them in the United States, as well as the greater opportunities for their children. In fact, other studies have found them to be more reluctant than their husbands to take their savings and return home (see Foner 1978 on Jamaican migrants in London; Pessar 1988 on Dominicans in New York; Hondagneu-Sotelo 1992 on Mexicans in California; and Goerman 2004 for further discussion).[7] This sense of enhanced possibility in the United States may be one of the factors that lead Koreans and Hispanics, female and male, to put up with the negatives in their complex households. But for women, there is also the bonus of potentially greater autonomy and economic power, with the resulting increased equality in and beyond the household.

USING COMPLEX HOUSEHOLDS TO SOLVE COMPLEX ISSUES: AFRICAN AMERICANS IN THE SOUTH, RURAL WHITES IN THE NORTH

Two Commonalities

We found two major commonalities between the samples of African Americans from urban coastal Virginia and rural whites from upstate New York. First, both groups have created nontraditional households that help them solve structural difficulties. The problems and the specific types of complex households that ensue are rather different, but both represent ways that people adapt and use gendered kinship systems to enable them to care for each other and, hopefully, survive and thrive.

Second, both samples had a somewhat defensive attitude about the fact that they are not living in Ozzie-and-Harriet-type nuclear families (though Census 2000 data analyzed by Simmons and O'Connell 2003 show that only 52% of America's 105.5 million households were maintained by a married couple, down from over 70% in 1970, per Fields and Casper 2001, using Current Population Survey data). The African American sample seemed defensive about how their households are seen by outsiders, and with reason. African Americans have, indeed, been much criticized for a family structure with substantial proportions of households headed by women rather than married couples. *The Negro Family*, better known as the "Moynihan Report" (1965), makes a controversial argument often considered racist, misogynistic, or both, but it has been influential. Daniel Patrick Moynihan saw the rising rates of female-headed families among poor, urban blacks as a growing "social cancer":

> At the center of the tangle of pathology is the weakness of the family structure. Once or twice removed, it will be found to be the principal source of most of the aberrant, inadequate or anti-social behavior that did not establish, *but now serves to perpetuate* the cycle of poverty and deprivation (Moynihan 1965, 30, emphasis added).

The African Americans studied by Bernadette Holmes strongly reject this view. Instead, they point to the fact that blacks have long lived in flexible, adaptive, "extended family networks," rather than in nuclear units, and that the resulting institution has been a source of strength, not weakness, in surviving structural adversity and disadvantage.

In contrast, the rural whites in New York see themselves as generally epitomizing a nonethnic, all-American identity—and traditional values. So, even though this is a purposive, nonrandom sample, it comes as a bit of a surprise that (1) 9 of 25 households (36%) involve a cohabiting couple (although 100% of the cohabiting rural whites in the sample had previously been married), and (2) 5 of these 9 involve children. According to S. Hewner (2000), who carried out the research, the people in her sample felt a certain stigma that they (of all people!) lived in nontraditional, complex households. For example, only four of the nine cohabiting couples used the "unmarried partner" terminology favored by the census; the others used alternatives ranging from spouse to girlfriend to "other nonrelative" (in the case of a seemingly gay couple still in the closet). But, like the African Americans, they had structural reasons for living in complex households, whether or not they wanted to publicize the fact. Let us now consider African American patterns in more detail.

Sharing among the African Americans

In general, blacks' postslavery economic history has been marked by more downs than ups, the continuing heritage of discrimination and prejudice. Holmes' sample of 25 households represents a wide range of social classes; this is not an "underclass" group. A good proportion of the complex households came about because of problems where they shoulder the burden of caring for someone (usually a child) who might otherwise fall victim to "the system": 8 of 25 households (32%) involved some form of adoption, and 5 (20%) were married grandparents raising a grandchild because of a child's problems (in at least 10 of 25 households, 40%, drugs were a factor) (Holmes and Amissah 2002). But all the children were being cared for, and as Holmes' quotes show, extended kin of both sexes contributed love and various kinds of help. There may not have been a village, but a sharing network was involved.

Sharing Networks in General

Elsewhere (Blumberg with Garcia 1977; Blumberg 1978b, 1993) I have written about the conditions under which sharing emerges. A "feast-or-famine" pattern of fluctuating, less-than-reliable subsistence, in particular, seems to affect the adaptation strategy and family patterns of a group.

1. Environmental uncertainty tends to lead to flexibility in organizational structure. Whether we are considering the research-and-development

department of a large corporation (e.g., Perrow 1967), hunters and gatherers (e.g., Lee 1968, 1969), or economic marginals in wage-labor societies (e.g., Stack 1974; Calley 1956), their adaptive strategies are loosely structured, dynamic responses to fluctuating conditions.

2. Unpredictable fluctuations of scarce resources or inconsistent surpluses tend to lead to sharing and exchange. This strategy smoothes out the fluctuations and spreads risk. J. R. Lombardi (1973) showed that involvement in a sharing network worked for one U.S. household on welfare: without sharing, his input-output analysis showed, the household's net available resources would have dropped below zero for three successive days; with exchange, it never did. (Blumberg with Garcia 1977 present references from Europe and Australia showing that such sharing also occurred with nonblack groups contending with similar uncertainty and resource fluctuations.)

3. Flexibility, sharing, and exchange among groups facing inconsistent surplus extend even to household members. Household units form and reform, and children are shifted or informally adopted, but they generally do get cared for.

There is a price, however: if you share surplus when you have it, you have less for your own advancement in a society such as ours, which promotes individual achievement. Regardless, the African American respondents subscribe to the notion of "lift as you climb." In fact, it appears that the most sharing groups—the Navajo, African Americans, and Iñupiat—tend to stress generosity, sometimes at the expense of individual social mobility.

Gender Matters

In order to better understand the relative position of men and women among African Americans, we have to look at the historical big picture. The high labor force participation of African American women goes back to slavery, when women were as expected to work in the fields and do agricultural work as men. Actually, most of these women came from West African horticultural groups where females tended—and still tend—to be the principal farmers (e.g., Boserup 1970; Saito and Weidemann 1990 show that today's sub-Saharan African women raise up to 80% or more of locally grown and traded food crops). Data are rather sketchy, but it appears that since the end of slavery, African American women have generally been more economically active, with a smaller wage gap, than their white counterparts. For example, J. Jones (1995) writes, "African American wives were more likely to work. In the 1870 Census for the cotton belt states, 4 in 10 African American wives had jobs as field workers. In contrast, 98% of white wives said they were keeping house and had no jobs." D. Spain and S. Bianchi (1996) also note that historically, men and women's work patterns varied by race: black women had higher labor force participation than white women, whereas black men had lower labor force participation than white men.

According to my gender-stratification theory, this would give African American women more power in the household than white women. They would, therefore, be less willing to put up with a bad relationship or one requiring subservience. Also, until the 1996 welfare reform, the United States maintained a "safety net" system (Aid to Families with Dependent Children; see Hays 2003) for more than two generations; this provided a small, added backup that further reduced African American females' dependence on male income.

Black men themselves often were more economically marginal—or unavailable: The U.S. prison population reached 2 million in 2003, the highest incarceration rate and number in the world, with African American men (especially since the War on Drugs began in 1981) disproportionately likely to be locked up. Given all this, blacks' higher divorce rates and proportions of female-headed households are not surprising. (As discussed below in the "Conclusions, Commonalities, Contradictions, and Policy Implications" section, divorce rates and woman-headed families have increased in mainstream white America, too.)

In short, African American women long have had greater relative economic power and autonomy vis-à-vis their men than white women, but their low overall economic position and social status due to racism did not permit them to "go it alone"; hence, these extended kin networks.

Summing up to this point, it is suggested that because of their (1) historically higher labor force participation rate, (2) apparently smaller wage gap, and (3) long traditions of extended family networks, as well as their (4) lower rates of marriage, black women have proved more likely than white women to be householders, that is, the first person listed on the census form. (The Virginia sample, although nonrandom, also had more female than male householders.) Moreover, those women were very likely to be aided by a flexible network comprised of kin (mostly hers but sometimes relatives of a former male partner) as well as fictive kin.

In contrast to the black purposive sample, the rural whites participating in this qualitative study had more couple households (19 of 25, or 76%) and support systems that were less structured than full-fledged sharing networks. Compared to the black sample, fewer women in Hewner's purposive white sample were in the labor force (after all, they were older), fewer were listed as householders (in part because more were married), and fewer emphasized their own side-of-house relatives. But these whites, too, benefited from kin. Let us now examine their patterns.

Complex Households as Adaptive Strategies among the Rural Whites

By design, the sample's average age was high (54) and almost entirely female (24 of 25, or 96%). Most of the respondents earned income (this was primarily a middle-class sample). Why should such people live in nontraditional complex households? In a third of the sample, Childs documents that their complex households came about because someone needed care. In another third, "it just happened." In the last third, respondents said they had chosen it. Most complex households, however, were formed because they addressed the kinds of issues facing an older population that has had to deal with the out-migration of young people, snowy winters, and marital breakups. Creating cooperative arrangements among elderly people was one solution. An example is the woman who tenderly cared for up to five aged women "boarders" for a pittance (about $100 a month per boarder). Indeed, handling elders' sickness and infirmity was a major reason for forming complex households. In sum, the reasons mentioned by the whites varied somewhat from those of the African Americans, but the complex household proved valuable for both groups.

Gender

Not much gender data surfaced in the interviews with the rural whites. But considering that this is an almost all-female group with an average age of 54, the householder's education puts them slightly above the U.S. average: only two had not finished high school, 10 of 25 had finished high school, and the remaining 13 had at least some college. On the one hand, perhaps reflecting their rural background and age more than their level of education, their ideas about gender tended toward the traditional: most saw men as the primary breadwinners, whose chores consist only of outside and heavy-duty work. And they also tended to live in couples (19 of 25, or 76%), even though the number of cohabiting couples (9) almost equaled the number of married couples (10). On the other hand, more in keeping with their educational and labor force participation levels, they stretched their notion of women's traditional role to include working for pay outside the home, along with raising the children and maintaining the house.

Gender and Side of House

The rural whites' kinship system is bilateral, which is the U.S. norm. Interestingly, however, in all four households where a married couple lived with a parent, it was the husband's mother.[8] In one case, presented by Childs, in fact, it was both of the husband's mothers—his adoptive mother who raised him and his birth mother with whom he was recently reacquainted (and who was later sent to an assisted living facility because she and the adoptive mother did not get along). In the other three cases, the household was three generational: the couple, their kids, and his mother. The grandmother helped care for the children while the parents were at work, and the parents helped care for the grandmother. This is part of a pattern of forming complex households to care for older kin and has policy relevance in a nation that is "graying" fast.

What Does It All Mean?

The rural New York white sample's complex households are quite flexible. Boundaries have stretched to include a high proportion of cohabiting couples, and the sample households also incorporated a surprisingly high proportion with adopted members (fully 9 of 25, including informal arrangements, 2 cases of fictive kin, and 3 instances of fostering; there were 8 cases among the African American sample, although, again, these are small, nonrandom samples from which inferences cannot be made to the larger population). With such flexibility, the households are able to pool economic resources or carry out necessary services (e.g., shoveling snow) through mutual cooperation. They also can help someone not able to care for him- or herself, while enjoying more companionship than otherwise would have been the case. So, if this rural, "white-bread America" sample is adjusting household patterns, forming unmarried partner relationships, and engaging in informal adoption as shifting structural conditions dictate, we really can invoke Bob Dylan: "the times they are a-changin'."

CONCLUSION, COMMONALITIES, CONTRADICTIONS, AND POLICY IMPLICATIONS

By way of preface, the six ethnic groups in this ethnographic study can be divided into two categories vis-à-vis complex households: those who are committed to a nonnuclear living arrangement (the Navajo, the Iñupiat, and, to a lesser extent, the African Americans) and those who form complex households because of conditions or circumstances (the rural whites, the Hispanics, the Koreans, and, to some extent, the African Americans, who span both categories).

Turning to gender, the main chapter topic, we first review the patterns of gender stratification revealed and how these stack up in terms of my general theory. Then, we examine the mainstream U.S. trends, as well as the factors driving those trends, and compare them with observations in our six ethnic groups.

Strategic Indispensability and Discount Factors in the Six Samples: Increasingly Positive for Women?

Navajo women started with—and still have—most of the high cards in terms of my theory. Although U.S. government policies led to a drop in women's right to use land and in sheep ownership, enough remains to provide a firm foundation for the matrilineal, matrilocal kinship and inheritance system that provides women with allies, helpers, and valued resources. Considering the micro-level discount factors, (1) gender ideology remains quite egalitarian in most households, (2) women are not shy about bargaining on their own behalf, and (3) both men and women remain committed to their matrikin, especially as embodied in the grandmother and her land. Furthermore, both younger men and women (especially the "sandwich generation") are likely to share earned income with their kin. But women seem likely to remain in more frequent physical contact with their matrikin, even if this involves a never-ending series of long commutes. In short, it is hard to say that women's strategic indispensability or net balance of discount factors is becoming even greater or more favorable, but they do not appear to have eroded, either.

For the other five groups, the strategic indispensability of female labor and income, as well as the net balance of micro-level discount factors, reveal a rising trend for women. The clearest-cut example of increasing gender equality involved young women among the Iñupiat. As discussed above, they were more likely to get schooling and jobs beyond the village, and their families were increasingly beholden to them to send some of their income home so that traditional hunting and fishing activities could be maintained, despite their rising cost. With increased dependence on the young women's voluntarily contributed surplus income comes the worry about their continuing level of commitment. My theory proposes that allocating surplus income is a source of greater economic power than trying to stretch subsistence income to (barely) cover survival needs. (Indeed, this is why poor, Third World women, who generally contribute a higher proportion to family subsistence than their more affluent counterparts, get so little leverage: unlike surplus income, where the giver gains power since that person has discretion concerning how much to give to whom, there is little leeway in allocating income if it is not enough even for adequate survival. This subsistence income has to be devoted to staying alive, so it does not translate to as much of a power boost for the givers (i.e., poor Third World women). In contrast, a rich old person can make younger family members dance to his or her tune lest they be disinherited. But the young women's growing power is dampened slightly by the fact that so many have left children in the village (virtually assuring continuing contributions and commitment), as well as by the ideology that so highly values (mostly male) hunting and fishing.

Among the other purposive ethnic samples, a higher proportion of both Korean and Hispanic women earned income than is reflected in current statistics for their home countries. Given that most of their households were poor, their contribution would be strongly needed. This might not have provided as much clout as being able to allocate surplus, but it clearly earned them a plus for the low "dependence on other's income" discount factor. Also, the household's "gender ideology" discount factor probably would be less negative than in the home country due both to the women's income and to the fact that they were now living in a less patriarchal society. Factor in that both Koreans and Latinos were less likely to live with or near the husband's parents than was true among traditional, especially rural, groups in their country of origin, and the women are left with greater autonomy and economic power and fewer constraints on exercising them.

Looking at the northern rural whites and the southern urban blacks in this study, we find the same factors of more income contributed by women, more household dependence on that income, and, for the whites, a more recent de facto acceptance of women working and couples cohabiting. Both female income earning and cohabitation are linked with greater equality for women within the household (Coltrane and Collins 2001; Blumstein and Schwartz 1991). In the New York white sample, however, there was still some awkwardness in admitting nontraditional household arrangements, such as using the term *unmarried partner* for their live-in mate. For the Virginia African American sample, admitting to nontraditional household arrangements was more likely to be edged with sensitivity or pain about how their units, especially those headed by female householders, have been maligned. But these black women were not hesitant about proclaiming their roles as providers.

In recent years, African American women in general have seen their position in the labor market improve more in relative terms than many other race, ethnic, or gender groups. They have moved up the occupational ladder and have shrunk the male-female wage gap (it is now smaller than whites': $.86/$1.00 for blacks working full-time, year-round versus $.76/$1.00 for counterpart whites, per the U.S. Department of Labor 2002). Some of this is due to the fact that African American men have been disproportionately represented among those occupational groups that have fared the worst in recent decades (e.g., blue-collar workers in low-tech manufacturing) as the United States has shed such jobs to lower-wage, Third World countries. Black men also have been disproportionately represented among the incarcerated, even when con-victed of the same crime as whites. So, while African American women are doing better, they are forced to shoulder more of the burdens of the continuing legacy of racism, discrimination, and poverty. And some patterns that we used to associate (pejoratively) with black women (e.g., nonmarital childbearing, female householding) are now increasingly prevalent throughout our society, as the proportion of women earning and controlling income continues to increase.

Putting the Sample Findings into Context: The Bigger Picture

First, the movement of women into full-time careers in the labor force has been one of the most important social phenomena of the last century. While it is beyond the scope of this chapter to discuss why this has taken place (which involves tracing the evolution of the U.S. economy from agrarian to industrial to the emerging information/biotechnology age; see Blumberg 1998), we can briefly examine when and how it happened and review other trends spawned by more and more women working for pay.

The Changing U.S. Economy and Its Impact on Gender Stratification

Our analysis begins with an important fact: by 1900 (when farming still was the modal occupation for men), women had become sex-segregated into the two occupational categories destined to expand the most since then: clerical and service jobs. In 1900, 20% of women aged 18 through 64 (the prime labor force years) were considered "economically active." By 1970, it was 50% (Oppenheimer 1972). By 1998, S. Coltrane and R. Collins (2001) document, about three-fourths of married women with children were working. But the most dramatic increase was in the proportion of women with infants one year old or younger who were in the labor force, what can be considered the "last frontier" of female labor force participants (specifically, those traditionally least likely to have been employed): in 1975, the first year the Census Bureau began collecting data on working mothers, 31% of mothers of such infants worked for pay (Coltrane and Collins 2001, 359). By 1998, that proportion was 62% (U.S. Census Bureau 1999, table 107).

By 1970, too, the United States was already beginning a transition to a "postindustrial" economy.[9] More than ever, this new technoeconomic base (see note 9) has been marked by growth in job slots for clerical and service positions, many related to the information economy, and many of them still seen as "women's work" in a labor market that remains rife with gender segre-gation (Padovic and Reskin 2002).

According to Coltrane and Collins (2001, 581), the resultant "movement of women into full-time careers in the labor force" has been driving a number of trends, including (1) a high divorce rate that has stabilized (since the late 1980s) at about half of all marriages (with well-educated women with good occupations the least willing or likely to remarry), (2) a rising rate of cohabitation (per the 1999 U.S. Census Bureau *Statistical Abstract*, half of all American women 25 to 40 have cohabited), (3) a rising age of marriage, (4) lower fertility (with rising age at first birth), (5) an increasing proportion of nonmarital births, (6) rising rates of female householders, and (7) a shrinking average household size. Consequently, Coltrane and Collins (2001, 573) conclude that "women have less incentive to enter into an unequal relationship and less incentive to stay in a marriage if they are unhappy with it."

This conclusion is perfectly in line with the predictions of my gender-stratification theory. As more and more women have been earning and controlling income, there have been changes in gender stratification at both the micro level of the couple and the macro level of the society. Starting from very low levels, growth has been dramatic in recent years with respect to the proportion of women (1) in middle management, (2) in state and local political office, and (3) who own their own business (nowadays, you are more likely to be employed by a female-owned business than by a Fortune 500 firm). Overall, the level of gender inequality at the macro level has been decreasing, although at a slower pace than among U.S. couples at the micro level. Nonetheless, not only has women's average position on the "pyramids of power" (Blumberg 2004b) been rising, but a few women are scaling up toward the commanding heights.

As noted, a concomitant result is that many of the things African Americans have been criticized for vis-à-vis their family arrangements are becoming increasingly common and even normative in mainstream, white American life, whereas stay-at-home wives are now statistically in the minority.

Moreover, a new phenomenon is occurring among mainstream Americans that may further accelerate the movement toward gender equality at the micro level and, ultimately, lead to further changes at the macro level. According to P. Tyre and D. McGinn (2003), 30% of working women now earn more than their husbands, with considerable economic and emotional fallout in the household and beyond. Some of that fallout may encompass kinship and household composition patterns as such women assert greater voice in who comes to live—to help, be helped, or both—in their homes.

Side-of-House Issues in Gender Stratification and Complex Households

One of the ways in which to get ahead or fall behind in the United States is to change household or family composition. Indeed, we have known since 1974

(Morgan et al. 1974) that adding or losing extra earners or caring for more or fewer dependents, whether through marriage, divorce, death, adoption, or other means, seems to be the most important mechanism for either putting a household into poverty (or the lowest income quintile) or pulling it out. With greater economic power, women have more say in household decisions (Blumberg 1991; Blumstein and Schwartz 1991). It seems highly likely that their say extends to making decisions about adding and dropping members— and which members. In other words, as women in this country gain economic power, household composition and complexity are likely to become increasingly gendered, with women having a bigger voice and vote. One might predict that, ceteris paribus, women would prefer to incorporate their own side-of-house kin, even if these were dependents rather than earners. This opens a whole new dimension for research.

Take, for example, Kang's finding that in the Korean immigrant households, it was more likely to be the wife's mother, not the culturally normative husband's mother, whom the couple invited to join them. The wife would benefit by having her own ally and helper, rather than her mother-in-law, who is considered her superior (and legitimate and frequent critic) in the old country. The husband might approve not only for family harmony and his recognition of his wife's growing "purse power" but also because he would not lose any of his own power or autonomy. Had it been his mother (and, especially, his father), Korean norms of filial piety would have left him with less voice and fewer degrees of freedom in his own household. What about side of house and gender interactions among the other groups?

First, most of the kin in the sample of African American complex households were related to the woman of the house. Then again, the relative economic power of African American women is more pronounced and longer standing than in the case of the Koreans. Second, the skip generations among the Iñupiat tended to involve children left behind by the daughters, not the sons, thereby greatly increasing the likelihood that those absent daughters would continue contributing economically not only to their own children's welfare but also to the household's expensive, yet treasured, subsistence hunting and fishing. Third, with the Navajo, side of house and female power go hand in hand because the kinship and inheritance system favors women. Finally, in the two remaining groups, the Latinos and the rural New York whites, formally bilateral kinship currently may be a bit tilted, to differing degrees, toward the male side of house. Will that still be the case in, say, another decade, after women have consolidated the economic power that their income entails? For example, will there be less prevalence of husband's male kin in Hispanic households that have resided in the United States a decade longer, provided the wife also has a decade more experience with economic power?

Clearly, many questions remain unanswered. This chapter has barely scratched the surface of what is, for now, terra incognita for researchers: exploring the ramifications of simultaneously focusing on ethnicity, household complexity, side of house, and gender. Moreover, our study did not include the controversial, but growing, category of same-sex households (up until 2004, involving only cohabitation, not marriage). Census 2000 counted 105,480,101 households, of which 594,391 were same-sex households, 301,026 with male householders and 293,365 with female householders (Simmons and O'Connell 2003, table 1). Gender is important here, too, in affecting household composition: For example, one-third of female same-sex partners had children under age 18 in the household, compared to only one-fifth of male same-sex partner units (Simmons and O'Connell 2003, 10).

To complicate matters further, the United States is facing a huge and unprecedented demographic transformation. By 2050, the U.S. non-Hispanic white population is projected to shrink to a bare majority 50%, while the Latino population is projected to increase from an estimated 13% in 2005 to 24%; concomitantly, Asians listing one race alone are projected to rise from an estimated 4.2% in 2005 to 8% in 2050 (U.S. Census Bureau 2003). Household diversity keeps rising in step with this increasing ethnic diversity, as well as with growing alternative lifestyle diversity (e.g., same-sex couples). In short, we can expect more varied and often complex households. Still, however much they differ from the Ozzie and Harriet nuclear household in composition, all have to set their own balance of caring and coping. Now the trick is measuring, understanding, and, ideally, predicting how different groups of men, women, and children are distributed in households of dizzying and growing diversity.

Implications for the Census

Meanwhile, let us end by briefly considering how the material discussed above might affect Census Bureau policies and practices. The census has a recent history of recognizing and reflecting changes in American life: new relationship categories have been added to the census form in each census between 1970 and 2000 to reflect changing coresidence patterns. Will census categories expand again to better portray the growing array of people living in nontraditional complex households, such as those portrayed here?

The chances are that this may happen, although slowly. On the one hand, the material in this volume suggests that there should be more, and more complex, categories. On the other hand, Congressional and public pressure tends to lead to shorter and less complex census forms. As a prediction, there will be additional kin categories tested and, possibly, added to the list of household residents in some future census, but there will not (yet) be any indication of whose kin they are with respect to his side or her side. And, there may not be a solution for the Latinos' dual-last-name problem. Another prediction is that there will be more attention paid by the Census Bureau to the intersection of kinship, household composition, and gender patterns, both among the mainstream white majority and the rising numbers and proliferating groups of ethnic Americans. In the short run, this may be via special studies rather than by changing the forms.

But given present trends toward older ("grayer"), more diverse, and gender-egalitarian households among most ethnic groups, such questions as, Who benefits? Whose kin? and Who cares? will take on new resonance as we head toward the censuses of 2010, 2020, and beyond.

NOTES

1. Hypotheses 9 through 14a of my gender stratification theory (Blumberg 1984, 55–56) predict the gender division of labor in production. They posit that in relatively unstratified societies, women's work is predicted by (1) labor demand versus available supply, and (2) compatibility with simultaneous child care. In stratified societies, labor demand overshadows compatibility, with child-care arrangements adjusted to facilitate female production if those controlling the means of production find women's labor important and irreplaceable enough.

2. In repeated research among Quichua-speaking indigenous groups in the Ecuadorian Andes, I found that the strong and egalitarian gender ideology that insists all marital decisions must be joint, even when they concern income earned by one partner, had maintained women's leverage in those couples where the husband's income from off-farm seasonal work exceeded his wife's from her own activities, such as market trading (Blumberg 2001). In contrast, among *Ladinos* in Guatemala, I found a precipitous drop in women's position when they lost access to or control over income (Blumberg 1994, especially 122–28). There, the prevailing ideology is the Hispanic notion that "the woman is for the house"; so, women's income was subject to a strong and negative "micro-level discount factor" since it was considered unseemly that they earned it in the first place. Once the income vanished, the women had no leverage against the prevailing patriarchal system, and their decision-making and general household power plummeted.

3. In modern times, these matri-oriented systems have tended to be resilient not only among indigenous North American groups but in many other places also. See, for example, Schwede's 1991 study of how the Minangkabau of West Sumatra, Indonesia, the world's largest matrilineal group, who are Muslim, to boot, have managed to preserve their kinship system from pressures ranging from globalization to Islamist movements.

4. R. R. Reiter (1975) describes how rural women in bilateral, but patriarchal, villages in southern France cede control of inherited land to their husbands, the main farmers. In

rural Mexico, a young couple is more likely to reside with or near the groom's parents than the bride's (Hondagneu-Sotelo 1992; see discussion of Hispanics below).

5. Indeed, internal peace or harmony has been found to be a hallmark of matrilocal groups. If they have war, it is almost always external, whereas patrilocal groups are prone to both internal and external war.

6. Historians and those fighting to repeal the family-registry law argue that the current law was introduced by the Japanese colonizers. During the seventeenth century, prior to Japanese colonization, hoju succession was seniority based without regard to sex. In the eighteenth century, widows with grown sons were banned from becoming family heads, but any male was not yet raised over any female; that came later.

7. In addition, S. Grasmuck and P. R. Pessar (1991) studied Dominican Republic migrants in New York and the home country and found the women more satisfied than their husbands with their U.S. jobs, even though the women's jobs paid less. In part, this was because of fewer work opportunities for women in the Dominican Republic than in New York. If the couple then renegotiated a more egalitarian marriage based on the wife's earnings, she was more likely to want to remain in New York. Conversely, in all nine cases where couples that had returned to the Dominican Republic stated they wanted to go back to the United States, the woman gave as the reason that she wanted to work and be less dependent on her husband.

8. It should be reiterated, however, that in a small, purposive sample such as this, a 0 of 4 distribution on side of house cannot be generalized to any larger group of rural New York whites.

9. Elsewhere, I argue that today's emerging information/biotech economy is the fifth major "technoeconomic base" on "the mainline" in human evolutionary history. The others are (1) foraging (hunting and gathering), (2) horticultural, (3) agrarian, and (4) industrial. The emergent information/biotech/globalized society is farthest evolved in the United States (Blumberg 1998; see also Lenski 1966; Toffler 1990). (The rise and evolution of capitalism seems a key factor in the emergence of both industrial and information/biotech societies, but this is beyond the scope of the chapter.) Whenever the technoeconomic base has changed, so have most aspects of social and cultural life: religion, family/kinship systems, gender relations, and so forth (Nolan and Lenski 1999). In today's United States, the emerging information/biotech base is enhancing the strategic indispensability of women's labor, so female jobs are not likely to decrease for the foreseeable future. Rather, women seem likely to gain more relative economic power. Per my theory, in nearly every ethnic group, working women's power to shape family or household arrangements should also rise, and trends linked to women's work or economic power, such as more cohabitation and less or later fertility, will probably continue, too.

REFERENCES

Angier, N. 2002. "They're the real Bond girls: maternal grandmas are the link to family benefits." *San Diego Union–Tribune/New York Times News Service*. November 20, F1, F3.

Blumberg, R. L. 1978a. *Stratification: socioeconomic and sexual inequality.* Dubuque, IA: William C. Brown.

———. 1978b. "The political economy of the mother-child family revisited." In *Family and kinship in Middle America and the Caribbean,* ed. A. F. Marks and R. A. Romer, 526–75. Curaçao and Leiden: University of the Netherlands Antilles/Royal Institute of Linguistics and Anthropology at Leiden.

———. 1984. "A general theory of gender stratification." In *Sociological theory,* ed. R. Collins, 23–101. San Francisco: Jossey-Bass.

———. 1991. "Introduction: the 'triple overlap' of gender stratification, economy and the family." In *Gender, family, and economy: the triple overlap,* ed. R. L. Blumberg, 7–32. Newbury Park, CA: Sage.

———. 1993. "The political economy of the mother-child family: new perspectives on a theory." In *Where did all the men go? Women-headed households in cross-cultural perspective,* ed. J. Mencher and A. Okongwu, 13–52. Boulder, CO: Westview.

———. 1994. "Women's work, income and family survival strategy: Guatemala's ALCOSA Agribusiness Project in 1980 and 1985." In *Women, the family and policy: a global perspective,* ed. E. Chow and C. W. Berheide, 117–41. Albany: State University of New York Press.

———. 1998. "Gender equality as a human right: empowerment, women and human rights—past, present and future." *INSTRAW News* 28: 7–21.

———. 2001. "Adventures along the gender frontier: encounters with gender equality in Ecuador and Thailand and glimpses in Guinea-Bissau and China." In *Proceedings of the International Conference on Gender and Equity Issues: humanistic considerations for the 21st century.* Bangkok, Thailand: Srinakharinwirot University Press.

———. 2003. "Ethnicity and complex households among Latinos and Asians: an exploratory study emphasizing the foreign-born." Report submitted to the Census Bureau.

———. 2004a. "Extending Lenski's schema to hold up both halves of the sky: a new way of conceptualizing agrarian societies that illuminates a puzzle about gender stratification." *Sociological Theory* 22: 278–91.

———. 2004b. "Climbing the pyramids of power: alternative routes to women's empowerment and activism." In *Promises of empowerment: women in East Asia and Latin America,* ed. P. H. Smith, J. L. Troutner, and C. Hunefeldt, 60–87. Lanham, MD: Rowman & Littlefield.

Blumberg, R. L., and M. T. Coleman. 1989. "A theory guided look at the gender balance of power in the American couple." *Journal of Family Issues* 10: 225–49.

Blumberg, R. L., with M. P. Garcia. 1977. "The political economy of the mother-child family: a cross-societal view." In *Beyond the nuclear family model,* ed. L. Leñero-Otero, 99–163. London: Sage.

Blumberg, R. L., and P. L. Goerman. 2000. "Family complexity among Latino immigrants in Virginia: an ethnographic study of their households aimed at improving census categories." Final Report to the U.S. Census Bureau.

Blumstein, P., and P. Schwartz. 1991. "Money and ideology: their impact on power and the division of household labor." In *Gender, family, and economy: the triple overlap,* ed. R. L. Blumberg, 261–88. Newbury Park, CA: Sage.

Boserup, E. 1970. *Woman's role in economic development.* New York: St. Martin's Press.

Calley, M. 1956. "Economic life of mixed-blood communities in northern New South Wales." *Oceania* 26: 200–13.

Coltrane, S., and R. Collins. 2001. *Sociology of marriage and the family: gender, love and property.* 5th ed. Belmont, CA: Wadsworth.

Fields, J., and L. M. Casper. 2001. "America's families and living arrangements: population characteristics." Current Population Reports, P20–537. Washington, DC: U.S. Census Bureau.

Foner, N. 1978. *Jamaica farewell: Jamaican migrants in London.* Berkeley: University of California Press.

Goerman, P. 2004. "The promised land? The gendered experience of new Hispanic 'proletarian' immigrants to central Virginia." Ph.D. diss., University of Virginia.

Grasmuck, S., and P. R. Pessar. 1991. *Between two islands: Dominican international migration.* Berkeley: University of California Press.

Grieco, E. 2001. "The white population: 2000." Census 2000 brief C2KBR/01-4, issued August 2001.

Hays, S. 2003. *Flat broke with children: women in the age of welfare reform.* New York: Oxford.

Hewner, S. 2000. "Ethnic ambiguity: changing perceptions of rural Caucasians." Report submitted to the U.S. Census Bureau.

Holmes, B., and C. Amissah. 2002. "The experiences of African American households: a kinship study." Unpublished final report to the Census Bureau for the Complex Households and Relationships in the Decennial Census and in Ethnographic Studies Project.

Hondagneu-Sotelo, P. 1992. "Overcoming patriarchal constraints: the reconstruction of gender relations among Mexican immigrant women and men." *Gender and Society* 6: 393–415.

———. 2001. *Doméstica: immigrant workers cleaning and caring in the shadows of affluence.* Berkeley: University of California Press.

Jones, J. 1995. *Labor of love, labor of sorrow: black women and the family from slavery to the present.* New York: Basic Books.

Lee, R. B. 1968. "What hunters do for a living, or, how to make out on scarce resources." In *Man the Hunter,* ed. R. B. Lee and I. DeVore, 30–48. Chicago: Aldine.

———. 1969. "Kung bushman subsistence: an input-output analysis." In *Environment and cultural behavior,* ed. A. P. Vayda, 47–76. Garden City, NY: Natural History Press.

Lenski, G. 1966. *Power and privilege.* New York: McGraw-Hill.

Lombardi, J. R. 1973. "Exchange and survival." Paper read at the meetings of the American Anthropological Association, New Orleans.

Morgan, J. N., et al. 1974. *Five thousand American families—patterns of economic progress.* Ann Arbor: Institute for Social Research, University of Michigan.

Moynihan, D. P. 1965. *The Negro family: the case for national action.* Washington, DC: Department of Labor, Office of Policy Planning and Research.

Murdock, G. P. 1967. "Ethnographic atlas: a summary." *Ethnology* 6: 109–236.

Nolan, P., and G. Lenski. 1999. *Human societies: an introduction to macrosociology.* New York: McGraw-Hill.

Oppenheimer, V. K. 1972. "Demographic influence on female employment and the status of women." *American Journal of Sociology* 78: 946–61.

Padovic, I., and B. Reskin. 2002. *Women and men at work.* 2nd ed. Thousand Oaks, CA: Pine Forge/Sage.

Park, S. 2002. "What's in a name? For South Korean women, everything." *International Herald Tribune.* October 21, 6.

Perrow, C. 1967. "A framework for the comparative analysis of organizations." *American Sociological Review* 32: 194–208.

Pessar, P. R. 1988. "The constraints on and release of female labor power: Dominican migration to the United States." In *A home divided: women and income in the Third World,* ed. D. Dwyer and J. Bruce, 195–215. Palo Alto, CA: Stanford University Press.

Reiter, R. R. 1975. "Men and women in the South of France: public and private domains." In *Toward an anthropology of women,* ed. R. R. Reiter, 252–82. New York: Monthly Review Press.

Saito, K., and J. Weidemann. 1990. "Agricultural extension for women farmers in Africa." Women in Development Working Papers. Washington, DC: World Bank.

Schmeer, K. K. 2005. "Married women's resource position and household food expenditures in Cebu, Philippines." *Journal of Marriage and Family* 67: 399–409.

Schwede, L. K. 1991. "Family strategies of labor allocation and decision-making in a matrilineal, Islamic society: the Minangkabau of West Sumatra, Indonesia." Ph.D. diss., Cornell University.

Simmons, T., and M. O'Connell. 2003. "Married couple and unmarried partner households: 2000." Washington, DC: U.S. Census Bureau.

Spain, D., and S. Bianchi. 1996. *Balancing act: motherhood, marriage and employment among American women.* New York: Russell Sage.

Stack, C. 1974. *All our kin: strategies for survival in a black community.* New York: Harper & Row.

Toffler, A. 1990. *Powershift.* New York: Bantam Books.

Tyre, P., and D. McGinn. 2003. "She works, he doesn't: why 30% of working women earn more than their husbands." *Newsweek.* May 12: cover and 44–53.

United Nations. 2000. *The world's women 2000: trends and statistics.* New York: United Nations ST/ESA/STAT/SER.K/16.

U.S. Census Bureau. 1999. *Statistical abstract of the United States: 1999.* Washington, DC: U.S. Government Printing Office.

———. 2003. "Resident population by race and Hispanic origin status—projections: 2005 to 2050." In *Statistical abstract of the United States: 2003.* Section 1. Population. P18, table 15, at www.census.gov/prod/2004pubs/03statab/pop.pdf (accessed April, 2004).

U.S. Department of Labor. 2002. "Employed persons by detailed occupation, sex, race, and Hispanic origin." Current Population Survey, 2001, at www.dol.gov (accessed April 2004).

12

Who Lives Here? Complex Ethnic Households in America

Laurel Schwede

INTRODUCTION

*W*ho lives here? Who belongs here? The answers people give to such questions about their households and, more broadly, the definitions they give for the concepts of household and family are rooted in their cultures, traditions, social organizations, gender systems, settlement patterns, economic adaptations, and ways of life. In this concluding chapter, I review the ethnographic chapters to tease out links among household structures, ethnicity, kinship systems, residence patterns, economic adaptations, gender, and conceptions of household and family, as well as how they play out in each culture. For each ethnic group in this study, the ethnographers have presented fascinating background descriptions of kinship and residence patterns, compiled lists of household members and people with attachments to those households, requested information about demographic characteristics and economic adaptations, probed for respondents' conceptions of the meaning of household and family, and asked about their ideal household structure. In this chapter, I summarize the results for each of the small-scale qualitative ethnographic studies in this project and identify factors influencing the formation, maintenance, and dissolution of complex households for our ethnic groups. Then, I look at the broad brush patterns for the country as a whole, drawing on analyses of censuses and surveys by some demographers and sociologists. I examine factors mentioned in this study and in other research about how people decide who is and is not a household member. Finally, I identify implications for policy and for further research.

ETHNICITY AND HOUSEHOLD
STRUCTURE IN OUR STUDY

*The Navajo and the Iñupiat: Traditional Subsistence and Kinship
Shape Coresidence Patterns*

Navajo society has traditionally been based on the economic adaptation of
herding in the harsh, arid environment of the Southwest, which requires a low
population density, mobility, and residential fluidity. The kinship system is
matrilineal, tracing descent and inheritance primarily through the mother's
line. The residence pattern is based on a matrilocal cluster of dwellings. The
heart of this cluster is a central woman and her spouse. The cluster also includes
the dwellings of their grown daughters and sometimes sons. All of these residences are in close proximity on matrilineal land. One Navajo woman
describes the traditional, and ideal, residence pattern:

> My daughter's family someday will have their own permanent house next door.
> They will never really live more than a house away from some of their children
> because it needs to be like a tree with branches and roots nearby.

Nancy Tongue learned from both her cultural liaison, Leo Tsinnijinnie,
and her respondents that the Navajo language does not have a word conceptually equivalent to the English word "household." Asked to give a word naming
the people he lives with, Leo answered, *K'é,* which he defined as

> The people I live with who are part of my family and are my people. They are
> the ones I shake hands with, and the ones I feel good with above, in front, and
> behind. They are the ones I have peace with. K'é means family group.

Tongue suggests that k'é may be equivalent to the traditional Navajo residence
group headed by a mother that pools its sheep in a common land-use area.
This residence group does not necessarily correspond exactly to all of the relatives living in the household cluster. According to G. Witherspoon (1983), this
residence group is the fundamental unit of Navajo social organization. He suggests that the pooling of specific economic resources—sheep—is a better pre-
dictor of membership in a particular Navajo residence group than the mere
proximity of houses in a residential cluster. Nowadays, due to increasing population, past herd-reduction policies, strict land-use laws, and some forced reset-
tlement, Navajos are living closer together, more and more often in Western-
style houses, and may be coresiding with relatives they would not have lived
with in the past. Herding no longer is sufficient for subsistence, and both the
number and range of jobs on the reservation are insufficient to support the

local population. Tongue reveals that most of her households reported members, mostly males, who sporadically leave the reservation to take temporary wage-labor jobs in nearby towns or in distant states to support the traditional way of life for the family on the reservation. All of these interacting factors—matrilineal kinship system, matrilocal residence patterns, politics, land-use restrictions, growing population, and economic adaptations involving herding and temporary out-migration for work—result in a Navajo reservation household-structure pattern that appears very different in a "one-time snapshot" by a census than it does in a longitudinal study. The Census 2000 snapshot shows that Navajos on their reservation, compared to the overall U.S. population, have a much lower proportion of adults in the most productive age ranges: 18 to 64 (52.5% to 61.6%). Concomitantly, they have a much lower proportion of those aged 65 and over (5.9% to 12.1%), but a much higher proportion of those under age 18 (41.6% to 26.3%).[1] Simply put, on average, disproportionately fewer Navajo adults of working age both live with and support the young and old on the reservation than among the overall population. This affects their household structure.

However, Tongue's broader ethnographic study shows that it is important to keep in mind that many absent family members are just gone temporarily. Despite their patterns of mobility and absence,[2] they continue to contribute to the economy of reservation households and to be considered household members. As of the interview day in one Navajo household, Sandy's husband, Tom, had been away for more than half of the last year, taking a series of jobs, and he already had another one lined up upon the completion of his current temporary position. It so happened that Tom was home for a short break from his current temporary job in California. Tongue asked Tom where he lives, and he answered,

> I live here [in the reservation household] all of the time. This is my home. We don't live in California. This is our home, our land. We're just working in California because there is no work here. If there were a job here, I'd stay all the time. But they don't create jobs and so we have to leave. Lots of people have to leave like I do. . . . We come back here and stay here for a couple of weeks or maybe a month, and then we get up and go again. . . . Economics has changed everything.[3]

Taking traditional and changing patterns into account, Tongue concludes that for the Navajo

> It is the social or economic interdependence of family that defines household rather than the parameters of the physical edifice. . . . Respondents perceived a household as comprising people who are (1) linked through kinship, (2) share commodities like vehicles, gas, propane, and income (including disability or

other government support), and (3) share daily chores and household maintenance. . . . Navajos share social and economic capital.

According to this definition, family members who periodically go out to earn income to help support the reservation household would likely be considered members of that household, even though they are not physically present in the household for long stretches of time.

In one respect, the Iñupiat of cold, northern Alaska are very similar to the Navajos of the hot, arid Southwest: they, too, have basic units of social organization arising out of their traditional adaptation to a harsh (in their case, frigid) environment that appear to be based more on social networks across different housing units than coresidence within one specific physical unit. Following E. S. Burch (1975), Amy Craver distinguishes the *domestic family unit* (those family members sharing a single dwelling) from the *local family unit*. The local family unit is an interdependent social network of a few domestic family units of relatives and/or friends in several nearby dwellings. As well as pooling income, they cooperate in one or more of the following: cooperating or sharing subsistence activities, child rearing, and food, as well as pool income. Illustrating this, Craver describes interdependent networks in separate dwellings that share domestic functions, such as that of Sherry, her children, and her brother, James, in one household and their grandfather, Emil, in another. Emil hunts and shares food, which Sherry cooks for everyone and James then delivers back to Emil by snowmobile. James takes over child care for his nieces and nephews during Sherry's work-related trips away from the village. The Iñupiat differ from the Navajo, however, in two important ways. They have a bilateral kinship system, which traces descent equally through both paternal and maternal lines going back at least three generations. Craver does not mention preference for matrilocal or patrilocal residence; flexibility in postmarital residence decisions gives new couples leeway in choosing which local family unit(s) to join.

The Iñupiat also differ from the Navajo in terms of their traditional subsistence adaptation: hunting and gathering, as compared to herding. But both of these adaptations require extreme mobility and residential fluidity to and from what S. Lobo (2003) refers to as "anchor households," households with one or two central people who remain in the household and maintain it, allowing other members mobility in coming and going. Like the Navajo, the Iñupiat have an insufficient number and range of formal jobs in their villages to support the local population. Craver points out the economic paradox: Iñupiaq people must earn money to maintain the (now expensive) hunting-and-gathering way of life they cherish. As Rae Lesser Blumberg notes, the different subsistence orientations of the Navajo and Iñupiat appear to influence which adults in the productive age ranges leave to earn money or to advance their educations. Among the Navajos, it is primarily men who leave the reservation periodically for work, sometimes with their wives, while among the Iñupiat in Craver's study, young men were more likely to stay in their home villages because of the high cultural value placed on expertise in hunting. Among the Iñupiat, wealth and success are not measured only in money; the presence of a good hunter is of even greater value, according to Craver. With less cultural value placed on traditional women's tasks in the village, women in the productive age ranges may be more likely to depart Iñupiaq villages, leaving their children with their parents in grandparent-maintained households. This leads to patterns in Eskimo (the category that includes Iñupiaq) households in northern Alaska that may differ greatly from those among the total U.S. population: a much lower proportion of Eskimo adults in the most productive ages of 18 to 64 (49.2% to 61.6%), with a much lower proportion of those age 65 and above (5.9% to 12.1%), but a much higher proportion of those under 18 (43.3% to 26.3%).[4] These patterns are very similar to those on the Navajo reservation, where there are fewer working-age adults both living locally and supporting more of the young and old.

When asked about the ideal household structure, a number of the Iñupiaq respondents said they wished to live with their children and grandchildren in extended living arrangements and to preserve their traditional way of life. For many respondents, the high cost of living in an area with an insufficient number and range of income-earning opportunities seems to mean living in skip-generation families and relying on adult children to leave and send or bring back economic resources to support their way of life.

As with the Navajo, it is important to note the Iñupiaqs' strong ethos of sharing and reciprocity and the interdependence of family across housing units, including people who remain in the villages and those who leave and contribute financial resources to maintain the viability of the somewhat altered traditional way of life that they still value highly. In the words of one Iñupiaq man, "I can't live without living here. When I go to other villages, I don't get to eat my own food. I must eat my Eskimo food!"

When asked to define the word "household," half of the Iñupiat in Craver's study defined the term primarily in terms of kinship, and another sixth associated it with shared domestic functions. Just one-third defined household in terms of shared residence and structure, consistent with the census definition.

Korean and Latino Immigrants: Adapting to the Promised Land Shapes Coresidence Patterns

The interaction of kinship systems, traditional residence patterns, economic adaptations, and conceptions of household and family differ in importance for the Koreans and Latinos in this study. Both have left their natal communities for very different lives as immigrants in a new country, which requires new adaptations and new residence patterns. As Tai Kang and Patricia Goerman note, it is disproportionately adults in the most productive age ranges, especially young ones, who migrate internationally.

The distributions of household types and the age and sex distributions of Koreans and Latinos in our research areas are completely different from the demographic and household profiles of the Navajo and Inupiat in their home communities, which show low proportions of working-age adults and very high proportions of children under age 17. Comparing Census 2000 data on Koreans in Queens, New York, and Latinos in central Virginia to the overall U.S. population, we find both ethnic groups have much higher proportions of adults in the most productive ages of 18 to 64 (71.4% for Koreans, 69.3% for Latinos, and 61.6% overall) and a much lower proportion of those age 65 and above (6.9% and 3.7% to 12.1%). But for those under age 18, Koreans and Latinos in these local areas differ: Koreans had a lower proportion than the United States overall (21.6% to 26.3%), but Latinos had a higher proportion (27%).[5] The age structures of Koreans and Latinos in these local areas have a much higher proportion of working-age adults than the Native Americans in our study and than the whole population, which may affect their household structure. (See Schmidley 2001 on the prevalence of working-age adults among the Latin American and Asian foreign born.)

According to Kang, the traditional agrarian household structure in Korea was the patriarchal family, with patrilineal inheritance and descent coupled with patrilocal residence. Kang describes three levels of social structure and five fundamental social and cultural norms underpinning the traditional hierarchical system giving the father dominant authority over his wife and children. But the transformation of the agrarian Korean society during the second half of the last century led to high urbanization levels, high educational attainment, and nuclear family households. Kang tells us that the nuclear family is now the most prevalent family structure in Korea, and it remains the goal for the Korean migrants he interviewed in Queens.

Many recent Korean migrants were attracted to Queens because of its large, Korean, ethnic enclave, the availability of jobs within the Korean community, and the relative reasonableness of rents in Queens as compared with other areas of New York City. However, many found they could not afford to live in nuclear family households, so they adapted by forming complex households. Kang describes cramped complex households of nonrelated roommates, families taking in nonrelated boarders, and extended family households, 22 of which had "slice-and-split" arrangements (several people to a bedroom, two or three mattresses in the living room, or both of these). Kang also discusses how working-age adults with children in his sample are more likely to arrange for the wife's, not the husband's, mother to leave Korea and join their Queens households. There, her tasks include caring for grandchildren, keeping house, and perhaps earning money on the side to help support the family economically. These complex households with the wife's mother, rather than the husband's father, are a far cry from the patriarchal, patrilineal, patrilocal households in the home country of the past. In Kang's view, these atypical complex household structures are a result of economic factors and greater harmony that may derive from living in close quarters with an older woman without traditional authority over the young couple.

In terms of their conceptions of family and household, Korean Americans in this study defined the *kahjock* (family) as paternal and maternal kin or affines (people related through marriage) within two or three generations. Family members coresiding in a housing unit are called *eelkah*, but this term leaves out coresident nonrelatives. All three of the other Korean words that roughly translate as "household"—*Sae-dae* (household or generation), *Sik-coo* (mouths that share meals), and *Kah-coo* (mouths in a house)—were defined by Kang's Korean American respondents as meaning, or used by them to refer to, related family members. All but two of his 35 respondents espoused a family-centered definition of household that would exclude roomers, boarders, and other nonrelatives, unlike the census definition, which would include everyone sharing the same housing unit. And, in one of Kang's very interesting cases, a family-centered definition leads to a nonresident family member's being included in the household. Mrs. S lives in the home of her son-in-law, daughter, and grandchild. She also included on her mock census form her younger son, Hyunmo, who rents a bedroom in a nearby apartment in the building, saying

> He just sleeps in the rented room. He spends most of his time with the family, watches Korean TV programs, and has all of his meals with us. He is a member of our family and he is a member of our household. That is why he's included in our census report.

The Korean study provides a glimpse of the potential importance of the cultural conception of household in deciding whom to include in one's household in censuses and surveys: nonrelatives coresiding in the same housing unit may not be listed because they are not considered part of the family group, even though they may be essential to the survival of the household by contributing to the costs of maintaining it. In other households, such as the Korean one just described and an Iñupiaq one in chapter 4,[6] other relatives living outside the housing unit may be included because of their kinship ties, their close attachments to the household, and the preponderance of their time spent there.

Decisions such as these made by respondents—to exclude from a census form coresident nonrelatives or to include relatives on the census form who stay somewhere else most of the time—do not conform to the census residence rules designed to meet the census mission of counting everyone in the country in the one "correct" place. This may result in enumeration errors and possible census miscounts. It may also lead to a skewing of the distribution of household types and sizes and of household incomes in censuses and surveys.

In reading Kang's chapter, it is important to note that all but 5 of his 35 Korean respondents live, work, attend church, and socialize almost exclusively within this Korean enclave in Queens, speaking little English and restricting their contacts and involvement with overall American society. A number of others in this Korean community approached by Kang and his liaisons refused to participate in this study and in censuses and surveys in general. From Kang's description, reasons for this insularity include (1) limited ability to speak English, (2) distrust of the government and outsiders, (3) fear of being deported, (4) fear of losing leases to apartments with limits on the number of residents, (5) fear of disclosure of underground economic activities, or (6) cultural views related to social status.

Like the Koreans, the Latino immigrants carry the knowledge of traditional kinship systems, residence patterns, economic adaptations, and conceptions of family and household in their home countries, but they adapt to a different mix of conditions as recent immigrants to the United States. Residence in Mexico and some other countries has largely changed from extended to primarily nuclear families, and kinship is formally bilateral, though a number of the women in this study had lived with their husbands' parents in the home country. Most of Goerman's respondents from Mexico, El Salvador, and Honduras mentioned the nuclear, not the extended, family as their ideal and the norm in their countries.

Some of the Latinos chose to live and socialize in homogeneous ethnic clusters or small enclaves, speaking their native Spanish most of the time. Speaking little or no English and having relatively low educational attainment, many of the Latinos had low-paying jobs. Similar to the Korean immigrants, many formed complex households for economic reasons. Notably different from most of the Korean immigrant households in Kang's study, however, a sizeable proportion of the Latino respondents in the first sample appeared oriented toward a different goal: earning and saving money to support their home country households and perhaps eventually returning there to live. Many central Virginia Latinos formed large complex households in cramped trailers or apartments not only to meet the rent but also to save money to contribute to their current or dreamed-of households in their home countries or here. The *lineally extended* Korean immigrant households consisting of householder, children, and mother or mother-in-law were relatively rare among the Latinos in this study. More common among the Latinos were *laterally extended* family households consisting, for example, of a householder's spouse or cohabiting partner, adult brothers or sisters, brothers-in-law, sisters-in-law, uncles, and/or cousins, as well as their children, producing a lot of coresident nephews, nieces, cousins, and brothers- and sisters-in-law.[7] This is known as "lateral" or "horizontal" extension. Some of these laterally extended households also included one or more parents or parents-in-law, making them lineally, or vertically, extended as well, as shown in the photo on the front cover of this book.

Goerman describes some complex Latino immigrant households consisting of one or more families taking in nonrelatives. Other complex households consisted entirely of nonrelatives for economic reasons. One of these cases was particularly interesting. Eight men live in a trailer known through the grapevine to accept new people looking for a temporary place to stay. Relationships are tenuous: some of the men do not even know the names of all of their coresidents. Residents change frequently as the men respond to the availability of jobs in different parts of the state throughout the year. Sometimes, the new people are acquaintances; at other times, they are strangers from the same country. The respondent, Jorge, said, "I'll always come and go. . . . I'd like to work here and return a lot to Mexico." D. Montoya (1992) calls these "ad hoc households."

These crowded complex households are not the ideal for Latinos. Goerman makes the point that for many of her respondents, complex households are a temporary adaptation by recent immigrants to a new country. Such households lower living costs for members, which helps them achieve their goals of (1) gaining a toehold on the economic ladder to move up in the United States (where they hope to ultimately live in a nuclear family), (2) supplementing the incomes of their families in their home countries, and (3) earning enough money to go back and set up their own households in their home countries. Goerman gives evidence from other studies showing that the longer Latino immigrants stay in the United States, the more likely they are to move away from complex households toward the nuclear family-household ideal.

The cultural conceptions of family and household among Latinos are bound up with the Spanish word *hogar*. This term had strong sentimental meaning to the respondents and may be translated as either "home" or "household," according to Goerman. For most of her respondents, it implies just coresident parents and children. Some would consider extended relatives part of their hogar, but only rarely would unrelated coresident people be included. The respondents felt it would not be appropriate to use the word "hogar" to refer to a group of nonrelated people living together. *Vivienda* (dwelling) would be a better term for a group of people not necessarily related, according to one respondent. Roberto's household clearly shows this. Roberto, his partner Gema, and his brother share a two-bedroom apartment with three friends. Goerman learned that they live as two relatively separate groups of three, with Roberto, Gema, and the brother in one room and the friends in the other. In Gema's words,

> We have a small hogar in our room, my brother-in-law, my husband, and I. We eat together. I make the food for the three of us, and they make food for me. . . . [S]ometimes we go out together. Well, we're a little family now; we all depend on each other.

Gema defines her hogar, or household, in terms of emotional closeness, shared domestic function, and kinship between the brothers, as a social household, rather than in terms of coresidence within one housing unit, or as a physical household, which would include all six people living there regardless of whether they were close or shared domestic functions (the census definition). The word "hogar" is commonly used on census and survey forms in Latin American countries; it is also the word used on the Spanish-language translation of the Census 2000 census form. With strong connotations of family, especially nuclear family, in popular use by Goerman's respondents, the word "hogar" may not be functionally equivalent to the English concept of household, at least for this sample. Asking a census form question about the people in one's hogar may lead to reporting of just those who are considered family or who act as family—members of the social household rather than the physical household per se. This lack of full equivalence between the concepts of hogar and household may be a factor in undercounting Latinos in censuses.

In sum, the Korean immigrants in this study chose to live within homogeneous ethnic enclaves in Queens, where they could speak their own language and socialize primarily among themselves. The Latinos in this study chose to live and socialize within Spanish-speaking ethnic clusters in the new central Virginia migration receiving area. To adapt to life in a foreign country and to support themselves (and possibly family members in their home countries as well) economically, they formed complex households with relatives, friends, and nonrelatives within their own ethnic groups. But they hoped to get established and eventually afford to live in normative nuclear family households. The choice to stay in homogeneous ethnic enclaves or clusters, however, circumscribes the number and range of jobs available to the Koreans (and, to a lesser extent, the Latinos), perhaps paradoxically limiting the economic prospects for some of earning and saving enough money to move up to their ideal household type: the nuclear family.

Contrasts in African American and White Households

In contrast to the Latinos, the integral unit of black family structure is not the nuclear household, according to Bernadette Holmes but, rather, the extended family network of relatives and fictive kin who function as a mutual aid system. She cites E. P. Martin and J. M. Martin (1978, 1) in defining the black extended family as a

> multigenerational, interdependent kinship system which is welded together by a sense of obligation to relatives; is organized around a "family base" household; is generally guided by a dominant family figure; extends across geographical boundaries to connect family units to an extended family network; and has a built-in mutual aid system for the welfare of its members and the maintenance of the family as a whole.

In many communities, Holmes adds, the "extended family includes a network of people, both relatives and fictive kin, who make interconnected households." These networks are often dominated by women: grandmothers, aunts, sisters, and friends who provide emotional support and assistance (Holmes and Amissah 2002).

When asked to define "household" specifically, one of Holmes' respondents answered:

> A household is any group of people who have consented to live as a family. . . . Our definition of family tends to mean a close, loving relationship of people who live in the same house. . . . These relationships may or may not be biological. . . . African American families are more than willing to take on the responsibility of other members of the family. . . . It has never been within our culture to operate as nuclear families.

Holmes writes that taking on responsibility for children and other family members is an African American cultural expectation, shown by the African American proverb "It takes an entire village to raise a child." Taking on the responsibilities of a wider network of kin is also especially important for those moving up the economic ladder, as voiced in the African American adage "Lift as you climb."

A unique study on the strength of obligations felt toward close and more distant relatives, which used vignettes, corroborates Holmes' findings. A. Rossi and P. Rossi (1990) found that blacks felt much stronger obligations to more distant kin, such as nephews, nieces, cousins, aunts, and uncles, than did whites in general. And Carol Stack (1974, 58), in a pioneering ethnographic study of poor African Americans, studied larger sharing networks including fictive kin. She points out that when friends live up to expectations of sharing goods and services, they are said to be "going to sisters" (or more generically, "going to kin"), meaning that they have begun to regard and treat each other as kin. Holmes describes African American households in her study area taking on wide-ranging responsibilities for adult siblings, nieces, nephews, and grand nephews, as well as for elderly parents and nonrelatives. These responsibilities include sharing income, caring for children and keeping them out of the welfare system, and assisting other family members in need because of drugs, incarceration, unemployment, and other factors.

In one African American household, for example, Denise listed six people on her mock census form: her husband, Phillip, two adopted children, and her two grandchildren. During the interviewing, Holmes learned that the two adopted children were actually Denise's grandnephews, her sister's daughter's children. They have been living with Denise and Phillip since they were infants. At first they were brought to Denise's home temporarily in the hope that their mother (Denise's niece) would overcome her drug problem and be able to provide a home for them, but she died. The father of one of the boys died too; no other family member came forward to take them in. Denise and Phillip adopted these grandnephews and recently obtained legal custody of their own grandchildren (one was less than five years old) because their daughter could not raise them. Phillip and Denise came out of retirement to return to work so they could support the four children, but she later retired again to care for them.[8]

Holmes' African American respondents were concerned about the image portrayed in the wider society of black men as often marginal to, or absent from, black families. Holmes points to discrimination and structural factors that marginalize black men in the economy.

A. Cherlin (1996) and others, using very large quantitative databases, agree on linkages between complex household structures and the growing economic marginality of black men in a changing economy. Cherlin points out that in 1970, there were many more African American married couple households than female-householder households. This was still the case in 1980 (Bumpass and Sweet 1987), but by 1992, among black family households with children, slightly more than half were female-householder households (Cherlin 1996). As of the 1990s, black women have been less likely to marry, more likely to separate, and less likely to remarry than white women. Also, African American men have been disproportionately vulnerable to, and affected by, continuing drops in the number of unskilled, semiskilled, and skilled blue-collar jobs since the 1970s (Cherlin 1992; Wilson 1987). W. Wilson and A. Cherlin suggest that the disproportionately large decline in black married couple families may be due to concerns that marginally economically active black males will not be able to support families. The pool of marriageable men has been further reduced by incarceration for crime and drugs. At all income levels, black family households are more than twice as likely to be complex (including one or more nonnuclear relatives) (Farley and Allen 1987). Increasing numbers of African American families have responded to these economic and social dislocations by relying more on traditional social networks than on nuclear family households (Cherlin 1992).

The actual households Holmes describes show the extent of obligation and commitment African Americans feel to help close, as well as distant, kin and nonrelatives. Complex households are an adaptation to economic and social conditions for blacks, as they are for our other ethnic groups.

The rural whites in this study are adapting to economic and demographic change in a rural upstate New York area formerly based primarily on agriculture with some industry. In recent decades, agriculture and industry have both been declining, leading to a concomitant decline in local employment opportunities in this rural study area (Hewner 2000). The young have been increasingly out-migrating, leaving behind an increasing proportion of elders who are living longer and who may be in need of assistance. Under conditions like this, the traditional nuclear family formation may no longer be practical or feasible for some; alternative household structures may be gaining ground. Many older people are forming cooperative arrangements with others (e.g., cohabitors, children, grandchildren, boarders, siblings, or friends) to pool resources, care for those unable to manage alone, or simply to provide each other with companionship (Hewner 2000). Thus, scarcity of jobs and of people to help the elderly are factors affecting the formation of the rural, white complex households in this study.

The kinship system of most whites in this country is bilateral, and residence is neolocal (most form independent households upon marriage and, increasingly, upon cohabitation). In a small-scale quantitative study in Massachusetts, Rossi and Rossi (1990) found that whites in general feel strong obligations to such direct lineal relatives as children and parents, but much lower obligations to more distant lateral relatives (e.g., aunts, uncles, nieces, nephews, and cousins) than blacks.[9] There seems to be no evidence that whites have a philosophy akin to that of African Americans regarding obligations to care for distant kin (i.e., "Lift as you climb"). Blumberg (personal communication, June 2004) notes that caring and coping vary by ethnicity in our study. She suggests that blacks in this study were among the most altruistic in helping others but got the worst rap from some for their supposedly dysfunctional family structure. In this rural, white study area, with the out-migration of the young, many older whites are forming cooperative arrangements with others.

I wish to note two main patterns here. One of these is the formation of complex households for caregiving: five of the white complex households were formed to care for children and grandchildren, and six others developed to provide care for a frail, older household member.[10]

Of particular interest are the "merged households" that form as a temporary adaptation to the declining health or incapacitation of elderly relatives. Jennifer Hunter Childs describes two such "merged households": those of Nancy and Linda. The case of Nancy and her father, Jay, is especially interesting. In late 1999, Jay fell and Nancy was concerned enough about her elderly father that she sent her son, Tom, to stay at Jay's house just down the street, to watch over his grandfather. Over time, Jay's condition deteriorated to the point that Nancy and her other son packed up suitcases and stayed with Tom at Jay's house to look after him. Several times a day, Nancy or one of the boys would go back to their own house to feed their pets and take care of their house. At the time of Census 2000, Nancy had thought this arrangement would be temporary as her father was convalescing, but by the time of her interview two months later, she had decided he would not be able to live alone again. She planned to continue staying there and caring for her father, living out of her suitcases, but she also continued to maintain her own household with her children and pets. So, where should we say Nancy lives: in her own house, or in Jay's house?

In another "merged household" described by Childs, Linda is staying at her mother's house during her mother's illness and has allowed her son to move into her own house across the street. Linda feels torn between the two homes, her mother's and her own, and does not feel like she fully belongs to either one. She can only react to changes in her mother's health, and the outcome remains uncertain.

The second pattern of note in the rural white study is the surprisingly recurring pattern of fictive kinship, overgeneralizing or extending kinship-based terms, such as mother, father, grandmother, and child, to coresident people who are nonrelatives yet fulfill the requisite kin functions. Childs shows this clearly with her descriptions of two complex white households. In the first, Jack and his wife, for a time, shared their house with both his biological mother, Alice, and his adoptive mother, Dorothy, who had raised him. When conflict broke out between Alice and Dorothy, something had to give:

> [W]hen push came to shove, Alice was the outsider and Dorothy was the one we have the background with and the loyalty to. Biologically, it doesn't have anything to do with it. It's really a strange thing when it gets right down to it: Who is the mother? It's the woman who raises you.

In the second household, Grace is taking care of the child of her adopted child, Maria, technically a nonrelative to Grace. According to Grace, "mother" is defined as "someone who *has children* and *takes care of them and meets their physical and emotional needs"* (Childs's emphasis). Childs points out that Maria meets just one of these criteria (the biological mother who has children) but not the other two (the functional or social mother, who cares for them and meets their needs). Grace fulfills the functions of the mother, hence Grace, more than Maria, is this child's mother. Hunter concludes that those who raise the children are considered to be the "real" parents, even if they are nonrelatives. This is very similar to the "going to kin" pattern that Stack (1974) describes for low-income blacks: if you are a nonrelative but act like kin, you may come to be considered (fictive) kin.

Childs notes that this pattern of fictive kinship is also evident in white unmarried couple households where one partner has children. If the nonrelative partner acts like a spouse and participates in raising the children, the partner may be identified as a spouse as well as a stepparent in conversation or on a census form, even though he or she is not actually related by blood, marriage, or adoption.

Childs concludes that "people seem to be adjusting the emic meaning of kinship terms to compensate for otherwise hard-to-describe relationships," such as those between partners in cohabiting households (unmarried partner called "spouse") and between the child and his or her parent's partner (nonrelative called "stepfather" or "father"). The growing number of ambiguous living situations and relationships can lead to applications of kin terms to nonrelatives—a process of constructing kinship through choice and self-definition, as well as through biology (Stone 2004). As overgeneralization of kinship terms becomes more common, masking of household types will increase in censuses and surveys over time, perhaps skewing household types and living arrangements to an unknown extent.[11]

Among rural whites in this comparative ethnographic study, there was no clear consensus on the meaning of the word "household"; Childs discusses alternative definitions of this concept in her chapter. The closest definition, according to ethnographer S. Hewner (2000), is that "household" means something akin to a family unit, not just the physical place where you live and stay. Boarders who used the same door as household members were viewed as household members; renters using a separate entrance were not.

This section has summarized the links among household structure, kinship systems, residence patterns, economic conditions and adaptations, gender, and conceptions of household and family in each of our six ethnic studies. We now turn to the wider context.

THE "BIG PICTURE"

The results of our ethnographic studies make up a rich and complex tapestry—the six diverse groups showed some common threads, but their designs for household and family were nonetheless strikingly different. This small tapestry is part of a larger American fabric, one in which the designs and patterns of the white majority loom large in the foreground. To place our six small ethnographic studies of complex ethnic households in perspective, we must consider them against the larger whole. To do this, we turn to sociologists, demographers, and historians who study the "big picture" (e.g., Casper and Bianchi 2002, Cultrane and Collins 2000; Cherlin 1996; Coontz 1992, 2005).

In the 1950s, the most common form of the family was a nuclear family composed of a breadwinner husband, a stay-at-home wife, and their biological children, often called the "Ozzie and Harriet" family (Coontz 1992; Casper and Bianchi 2002). L. Casper and S. Bianchi argue that the increasing prevalence of this family type in the 1940s and the 1950s rested on two critical factors: (1) accepted gender distinctions where men worked outside the home and women stayed home as homemakers, and (2) a vibrant economy wherein all men could earn a sufficient income to be the sole support of the family.

These two underlying factors supporting the formation and maintenance of nuclear family households may never have existed for some of the ethnic groups in our study: The Navajo and Iñupiat used to rely on herding and hunting-and-gathering economic adaptations, respectively. Since the advent of the cash economy, however, there has never been a vibrant economy allowing all men to earn enough to live and stay permanently in their home communities and to be their families' sole support. Today, the number and range of jobs available in the areas surrounding their relatively isolated Arizona and Alaska villages are insufficient to supplement their subsistence activities. Recall Tom's vivid statement in Tongue's chapter and earlier in this chapter, "They don't create jobs and so we have to leave. . . . Economics has changed everything."

Just how insufficient these jobs in rural northern Alaska are is demonstrated by a pattern of rotating job sharing common in Iñupiaq villages, according to demographer Greg Williams of the Alaska Department of Labor and Workforce Development (personal communication 2004). He states that it is common for a person to take a clerical job with a village school or municipal agency, for example, and stay in it long enough to qualify for unemployment insurance, then to quit, turning it over to the next person, who does the same thing. Anyone staying in the job too long is considered selfish. This rotating job-sharing pattern also clearly demonstrates the strong ethos of community sharing Craver described. Williams also notes that the trends in recent years in Alaska have been to flatline or cut payments for capital projects, reducing the flow of dollars and jobs to many rural areas, and to eliminate the Longevity Bonus (about $250 a month) to people who turned 65 before 1994. These changes may stimulate even more out-migration and result in even more complex households (Williams, personal communication 2004).

Many Navajo and Iñupiaq adults of working age have to leave their communities for more economically developed areas so that they can earn money to bring or send back to the complex households they have left behind in the villages. Economic opportunities for the Koreans and Latinos are more circumscribed than for others born in this country because of the immigrants' limited English and, for some, legal status.

For the Koreans, another factor limiting their economic options is their interest in remaining within the ethnic enclave to work in Korean establishments, where the availability and range of jobs is more limited than in the economy of the whole metropolitan area of New York City. For Latino immigrants, an additional factor narrowing the range and number of available jobs is educational attainment; in Goerman's study, and in the whole country, Latino educational attainment is lower than that of many other ethnic groups (Schmidley 2001; Logan 2003). Lower educational attainment may be a factor limiting people's economic options. Census 2000 data show disparities in educational attainment between African Americans and non-Hispanic whites. Among African Americans, 27.7% had less than a high school diploma, compared to 14.6% of non-Hispanic whites. Among those in the middle range of educational attainment—having a high school diploma, associate degree, or some college—there was near equivalence between blacks and non-Hispanic whites (58.1% to 58.5%), but there were disparities for those with a college degree and above (14.3% for blacks, 27% for non-Hispanic whites) (U.S. Census Bureau 2003, calculated from tables 40 and 44). Note that these census figures include the elderly, particularly blacks, who had fewer educational opportunities open to them when growing up; among the younger generations, educational attainment is higher, and the figures are rising over time.

A second key factor narrowing the range and number of available jobs for African Americans is discrimination. Black men have been especially affected by the loss of unskilled and semiskilled manufacturing jobs to the suburbs or overseas beginning in the 1970s and 1980s (Wilson 1987). As a result, they have fallen further behind black women in job prospects. This, in turn, may have been an important factor in the more rapidly declining marriage rates for blacks as compared to whites (Wilson 1987; Casper and Bianchi 2002; Cherlin 1996; Coltrane and Collins 2000; Coontz 2005). For rural whites in upstate New York, the key factors seem to have been job shortages resulting from declines in agriculture and industry, which led to growing out-migration of the young for work, which resulted in a growing proportion of elderly people and a shortage of traditional family members to meet their rising needs.

Thus, a vibrant economy enabling virtually all men to earn a living sufficient to be the sole breadwinner for the family—Casper and Bianchi's first critical factor supporting the prevalence of nuclear family households in mainstream U.S. society in the 1950s—seems not to have been equally available to the ethnic respondents in our six study areas in 2000. And the availability of economic opportunities has declined in the intervening years. As a result of several factors—namely, the economic recession in the first years of the new millennium in this country, improved productivity, and the outsourcing of jobs, both within this country and to foreign countries—the number of manufacturing jobs declined for 47 successive months until March 2004, when it stayed level, then began rising (according to news reports). The number of jobs lost from 2001 to April 2004 was estimated to be around 2 million (according to news reports at the time), though the creation of new jobs since that time has made up for these losses.

Likewise, the second critical factor supporting the prevalence of nuclear family households in mainstream U.S. society in the 1950s—gender differences and discrimination in work—clearly does not apply equally to our six ethnic groups, as Blumberg documents in chapter 11. Navajo women have always been economically active in their herding adaptation. Iñupiaq women have traditionally been involved in important but less valued work—processing meat and fish, gathering berries and other wild plants, and making and maintaining warm clothing—rather than in hunting and whaling. As we have seen, Iñupiaq women in this study appear to have become more likely to leave their villages for schooling or jobs than their male counterparts, who are highly valued for their hunting skills.

Korean and Latino women have more economic opportunities and have greater labor force participation rates here than in their home countries and may need to be more economically active to help support their ethnic households in this country. As Blumberg points out, African American women have traditionally had a higher labor force participation rate than whites. And the rural white women in our study are becoming more economically active as small-scale agricultural production declines and is being replaced with wage labor outside the home, often in service, not manufacturing, jobs.

The increasing movement of women into the labor force is seen as a critical factor in changes in household structure and demographics over the last decades (Coltrane and Collins 2000; Casper and Bianchi 2002; Cherlin 1996; Coontz 1992; Blumberg 1991). Women's increasing movement into the labor force has contributed to a dramatic shift in the distribution of male breadwinner families by class over the last half-century, according to S. Coontz (2005). In the 1950s, in nearly all middle-class and most working-class families, wives did not have outside, paid jobs, at least until their children left home. Today, however, male breadwinner families predominate not in the middle, but at the poorest and richest ends of the economic distribution in this country, in the bottom 25% and the top 5% of households (Coontz 2005).

FACTORS INFLUENCING HOUSEHOLD STRUCTURE
AND CONCEPTIONS OF HOUSEHOLDS

All of this leads to our conclusion that household structure and the cultural conceptions of household and family are the result of the interaction of multiple factors.[12] The key factors influencing household structure and conceptions of household in this study are the interplay of economic conditions in the local area specifically available to people of each ethnic group, as well as residence patterns, kinship types, gender systems, and the choices people make in responding to the matrix of opportunities and constraints in their local areas and beyond. Thus, we suggest that the mix of factors influencing household structure and conceptions of household in the same geographical area at the same time can and do differ, depending on ethnicity and culture.

I. Wallerstein and J. Smith (1991) focus on the links between family structure and changes in the world economy, noting that households expand in size when the economy is bad and contract again when the economy is good. Interestingly, Wallerstein and Smith propose a unique definition of household that is not widely accepted: the household is the income-pooling unit, which is not necessarily confined to those within one physical structure but, rather, can include people in a network of several housing units that may or may not be in the same locality. This definition would cover the complex households of the Navajo, the Iñupiat, and the blacks, as well as the cross-national households of Latino immigrants sending money to their home country households, whether they intend to return there or not.

Our complex households research project would suggest modifications of Wallerstein and Smith's general argument as far as complex household structure and ethnicity are concerned. Changes in family and household structure appear to be much more closely linked to economic and subsistence conditions in the immediate local area than to the overall world monetary economy, as Wallerstein and Smith posit. In this study, decisions (1) to form complex households or (2) for some members to leave for other areas in order to supplement the income of the local household (resulting in de facto complex households) appear often to have been made primarily on the basis of economic conditions and opportunities in the immediate local area (including conditions for non-monetary subsistence activities) that members of each ethnic population perceive as available to them and choose to pursue. Further, we suggest that the interaction of local economic conditions with gender systems and cultural conceptions of household structure are critically linked to changes in household structure. The same conditions that Casper and Bianchi found supportive of the prevalence of nuclear family arrangements for some subpopulations—many whites in the 1950s, for example—may not support nuclear family arrangements as modal household types for other subpopulations, such as those of some ethnic minority groups, immigrants, the working class, or the poor.

THE COMPLEMENTARY ROLE OF QUALITATIVE AND QUANTITATIVE DATA IN UNDERSTANDING AND MEASURING HOUSEHOLD STRUCTURE

In this book, we have examined household structure, using both qualitative and quantitative data.

In the ethnographic chapters, our ethnographers presented rich, qualitative descriptions of household structures and living arrangements in complex households, often from the perspective, and in the words, of the ethnic respondents themselves. As we have seen in the preceding chapters, the complex households in each of our six ethnic-group study areas are adapting to differing matrices of economic opportunities and constraints by adopting household structures consistent with their own internal cultural values and history, which Cherlin in 1996 referred to as patterns in their "cultural repertoire." The outward form of these complex, ethnic household types may differ from the general normative household type for the country as a whole, but the caring and coping functions within them are similar.

These ethnographies give us insights into the reasons why our respondents live in complex households and show the dynamics of household change over time. The limitation of these ethnographic studies is that they include a small number of respondents (25 per study), who were selected in a nonrandom manner. While the results of these studies are illuminating, they cannot be generalized to any larger or different population or geographical area.

Quantitative data from large-scale surveys and censuses can provide statistics on ethnic subpopulations and specific geographical areas, if the sample size is large enough to provide reliable data for the smallest-sized population in one's analysis. For the time being, however, only one standardized data collection, the decennial census, is large enough to provide reliable household-structure statistics on such small populations as Asians, American Indians, and Alaska Natives, until 2010 when five-year aggregated American Community Survey data become available for the first time.

We have therefore used Census 2000 data publicly available on the Census Bureau's website to compile and present statistics on household structure for each of our six ethnic groups at two levels. We first compare and contrast household-structure statistics for each of the six ethnic groups individually with the overall patterns for the United States as a whole. We then compare and contrast household-structure statistics in specific, local, geographical areas surrounding the six ethnographic research sites that we custom-designed for this book. In addition, we also present a brief review of the big picture by sociologists and demographers, who analyze large statistical and survey databases.

Our aim in presenting both qualitative and quantitative data in this book is to demonstrate that both quantitative and qualitative studies are needed to help us document and understand the dynamics of changing household structures and the factors associated with these changes. Quantitative studies permit us to document the numbers and types of households in the country or a specified geographical area and to document changes in the distribution and types of these households over time. Qualitative studies allow us to tailor research to specific subpopulations of interest to us, regardless of their proportion in the population, and to interact directly with respondents to learn about their living situations and household arrangements and why they choose to live as they do. These studies can also suggest improvements for large-scale quantitative studies as well as new hypotheses for further research. Quantitative and qualitative methods complement each other and can be used iteratively to enhance our knowledge of how people live.

ARE CENSUS RELATIONSHIP CATEGORIES ETIC OR EMIC?

Many demographers, sociologists, economists, and other social scientists use relationship categories from censuses and surveys in their analyses as if they are objective, etic categories that apply equally well to all people in this country. In the introduction, Anna Chan mentions that we start our book with the assumption that the Census 2000 relationship question and its relationship categories represent an objective etic framework of our overall culture that can be applied consistently and equally to all ethnic subpopulations. We weigh this assumption by examining how well the Census 2000 relationship question and categories match the subjective, emic concepts of relationships held by the respondents themselves in our six ethnic studies.

Recall from figure 1.1 that the Census 2000 relationship question asked about relationship to the householder (Person 1) and offered nine specific, relative categories (husband/wife, natural-born son/daughter, adopted son/daughter, stepson/stepdaughter, brother/sister, father/mother, grandchild, parent-in-law, and son-/daughter-in-law) and an "other relative" category with a write-in line. It also offered four nonrelative categories (roomer/boarder, housemate/roommate, unmarried partner, and foster child) and an "other nonrelative" category without a write-in line.

In the six ethnographic chapters, the researchers demonstrate that this relationship question, with its categories, constrained the types of relationships and households that can be defined. For example, the category of "grandchild," which would seem clear to the majority of people in this country, was insufficient for the Navajo, because in their kinship system, grandchildren from the woman's side are called *tsui*, while those from the man's side are named *nali*.[13] In the Latino study, we learn that the Spanish translation of "foster child" on the census form as *hijo de crianza* may lead to confusion and overreporting of foster children for the Latinos because the two concepts are not functionally equivalent (see also Carrasco and Musquiz 2003). The English term refers to a child placed in a home by a government agency in exchange for a monthly payment to support that child. Our ethnographers tell us that this type of formal foster-child system does not exist in any of the Latino sending countries they know of. The Spanish term is understood to mean a child of a relative or friend that a person is raising informally. And, we learn in the white and black studies that terms for relatives—such as mother, father, husband, wife, grandmother, and aunt—may be generalized to people who are not related by blood, marriage, or adoption, but who fulfill the role expectations and functions of those kin roles and are known to researchers as fictive kin.

As Childs points out, this is especially the case in cohabiting households where we do not have clear terms designating relationships between nonrelatives who are functioning as a family. This becomes more of an issue as the number of self-identified unmarried partner households increases. Using Census 2000 data, Simmons and O'Connell (2003) report that 5.5 million couples were living together and marked the "unmarried partner" category for the relationship question. About one in nine of respondents in these unmarried couple households marked "unmarried partner" for a coresident of the same sex, while the remainder were composed of self-identified unmarried partners of the opposite sex.[14]

Our qualitative research thus shows that, rather than being etic categories that can be objectively and universally applied to all situations, the Census 2000 relationship categories are social categories derived from and embedded in one specific context—mainstream American culture and institutions at a specific point in time—and based on a lingering ideal household structure of a "married couple with children," even though this is no longer the modal household type in our country.[15]

We wish to make two points in this regard. First, this mainstream American cultural context can and does change over time, and it may be advisable to reexamine the relationship categories for each census. The categories used by the Census Bureau also reflect the relationships in our society deemed most important to delineate specifically, as well as our society's norms for household composition during the time leading up to each census. These categories express relationships based on kinship and marriage (e.g., natural-born child and husband or wife), cohabitation (e.g., unmarried partner), and economic (e.g., housemate or roommate) or legal ties (e.g., adopted or foster child). In the 1970 Census, just five specific relationship categories were printed: household head, wife, child, roomer/boarder/lodger, and inmate/patient; respondents could write in other relationships. Since the 1970 Census, the United States has become increasingly diverse, and every subsequent decennial census has included a greater number of relationship types deemed important to delineate specifically as their own stand-alone response categories, rather than lumping them into a miscellaneous "other" category (for a full discussion of these changes, see Schwede 2003). Most of the changes made each decade from 1970 to 2000 were made to further delineate relationships in (1) married couple families, (2) blended families (stepchildren), and (3) families including in-laws (parent-in-law, son-in-law, daughter-in-law), as well as (4) to identify grandchildren, and (5) unmarried partners. The Census Bureau has made steady progress in expanding census relationship categories over these decades in capturing more diverse lineal household types. But we have just begun to explore more diverse lateral living arrangements (such as nephews, nieces, cousins, brothers-and sisters-in-law, uncles, and aunts), which were tabulated from optional write-ins to the Census 2000 relationship question.

The second point we wish to stress regarding the degree of objectivity of census and survey relationship categorizations is that some of the relationship terms used in the United States, such as foster child and adopted child, are culture-bound terms that derive from our Western European–American system of classifying kin and apply to specific social and legal institutions in the United States. These categories either may not exist in other countries or the terms may mean something different. Categories such as these may not be understood by people from different cultures or of other nationalities and may lead to errors in the recording of relationships and to issues of cross-cultural and subpopulation validity. And, since data from the relationship question and categories are used to develop household typologies and tabulate the number of households falling into each category for each of our ethnic groups, we may not be getting the full picture of the ethnic diversity of household types in this country.

Thus, what may be taken as an objective set of relationship categories used in U.S. censuses and surveys is not objective, but a social construct arising from, and evolving in tandem with, a specific sociocultural system characteristic of mainstream society in the United States. The "objective" set of relationship categories cannot fully characterize relationships for our ethnic subpopulations in this study and may skew the distribution of household types in as yet unknown ways. Our conclusion is this: The census relationship categories should not be considered an etic system but, rather, an emic system of our overall culture that is limited in its ability to reflect the range of complex ethnic households fully.

FACTORS IN DECIDING WHO IS A HOUSEHOLD MEMBER

Throughout most of this text, we have been looking at similarities and differences in complex households through the lens of kinship and ethnicity. Might there be common conceptual themes running through these separate ethnographic studies in terms of criteria used by respondents to determine who is a coresident and who is and is not a household member?

In a small-scale qualitative study in 1990, E. Gerber identified a set of terms and concepts that low-income African Americans used to describe who lived or stayed with them. She presented respondents with nine specially constructed vignettes of ambiguous living situations to learn what factors they considered in determining where the mobile person in the vignette usually lives. For example, one of the vignettes involved a young man who spends alternate nights at the homes of his girlfriend and his mother. He can come and go from his mother's, but his girlfriend has refused to give him a key. Does he usually live with his girlfriend? From her analysis of responses to the vignettes, Gerber developed a special conceptual scheme that people may use to decide who lives with them when the situation is not clear-cut. This scheme for determining residence involves three main dimensions: (1) official living place, such as address of record, (2) control of the space and the implications of that control (generally, the "space provider" can set rules that the "space sharer" must follow), and (3) stability in terms of permanent ("live") versus temporary ("stay") residence status (Gerber 1990). While length of stay can be one measure of permanency or temporariness, it is not the only one. Also very important are cultural expectations of where people live and belong, and what is likely to happen in the future. In this conceptual system, *expectations*, *agreements*, and *intentions* are important to consider in determining where a person lives and whether he or she may be considered a household member. Expectations and agreements include such factors as whether the space sharer is given a key, enabling him or her to come and go at will; whether he or she agrees to contribute food, money toward expenses, or both; and whether he or she is expected to share child-care responsibilities. Intentions include whether the person is committed to living in the household long term or is thinking of, or planning to, move. Sometimes the intentions of a space sharer to stay put or move are not stated or obvious. In those cases, the space provider who responds to censuses and surveys for the household may have to try to divine a coresident's intentions before deciding whether to record that person as a household resident. One important way of gauging a person's intention to stay or go is by determining where most or all of the person's belongings are. Are they in one place or divided among two or more places? For example, observing changes in where a person's belongings are may help to identify the time of transition from a visiting to a cohabiting relationship. W. Manning and P. Smock (2004, 15) vividly show this with a white man's account of the gradual progression toward cohabitation with his girlfriend:

> It began by an attrition of this thing at her parents' house. In other words, she stayed at my house more and more from spending the night once to not going home to her parents' house for a week at a time. . . . [T]here was no official starting date. I did take note when the frilly "fufu" soaps showed up in my bathroom that she'd probably moved in at that point.

It is not just the intentions of the space sharer that are important; those of the space provider may also be important—and differ from those of the space sharer. For example, if a space sharer has outstayed his welcome and has not contributed anything to the household in terms of sharing expenses or helping with chores, the space provider may very much want that space sharer to leave and thus not consider that person a household member because he or she will (hopefully) soon be gone.

At the time Gerber wrote this paper, she noted that this conceptual system was identified for low-income black people only. But, without a comparison group, she could not say whether any of the set of principles she described would apply more generally in American culture. In a later small-scale study along the same lines in the Washington, D.C., area, Gerber included low-income African Americans, low-income Hispanics, and middle-class whites. This research not only confirmed that her conceptual system was applicable to low-income African Americans but also established that it was applicable for low-income Hispanics and middle-class whites as well (Gerber 1994a, 1994b). She added that when making residence decisions, actual presence in a place was less salient to respondents than stable, long-term social affiliations due to factors like kinship, ownership, and cooperation. However, she noted that findings from another study of residence, the Living Situation Survey, showed significant regional variations in the meaning of key residence terms (e.g., "live" and "stay").[16] As a result, Gerber (1994a) said that findings from these two small-scale studies could not be generalized without more research.

In developing the core protocol for our six ethnographic studies of complex households, we included some questions related to Gerber's conceptual system for residence decisions. For example, we asked the ethnographers to probe respondents when they discussed the meaning of "to live" versus "to stay." We also asked the researchers to probe deeply in identifying attachments people said they had to the household where they were living, as well as to any other households with which they might identify. We wanted the ethnographers to explore these issues so that we could see if Gerber's categories applied to the wider range of ethnic respondents in our study.

Let's now see how Gerber's categories match up with what our ethnic respondents told us, as described in the preceding ethnographic chapters. Let's start with Gerber's first criterion: official residence. Tongue's study of the Navajo demonstrates that the seemingly clear concept of official residence can be very ambiguous in certain ethnic groups or situations. As Tongue demonstrates, "official living place" is a very malleable concept in remote regions of the Navajo reservation where street names mean nothing: Navajos may live in dwellings to the left of the cottonwood tree and to the right of the sheep herd, with no street names or official addresses. For the Navajo, post office boxes come the closest to an official address, even though the boxes may not be located anywhere near where people actually live, eat, and sleep. Each Navajo person, including children, may have one or more personal or shared post office boxes in different areas. When asked for their post office box numbers, they do not always give the same number. Which box address they give often depends on who is asking and why. They may give a different box address to the Tribal Council to establish whether they are eligible for housing or grazing benefits than they give to the IRS to declare how many dependents they have.

In terms of the stability-of-residence (permanence versus temporariness) component of the conceptual system identified by Gerber, the duration of stay is not nearly as important as the sense of belongingness and the expectation that the person will return, even if he or she just stays in the reservation household for a week or so before heading out on another temporary wage-labor job and is gone most of the time. Gerber refers to this sense of belonging as "enduring ties." Aspects of this principle in determining residence, in addition to intentions and agreements, are very apparent in the Navajo study, where household members may go to another state to work for months on end, possibly leaving one or more of their young children in the reservation household, to bring back money to support the household.

Among Tongue's cases that do not fit basic census categories is the grandmother who listed just three people as living in her hogan on her mock census form. The problem is that Tongue thought 10 should be listed. This grandmother, Mary, listed two other people—her husband and her son—as living in the hogan that belongs to her. She did not include her daughter, Liz, and her daughter's four children; nor did she include two other grandchildren who clearly lived in the same hogan and shared the same outhouse. What in this grandmother's conceptual system explains why she would exclude her daughter and four of her grandchildren from a listing of who lives in her hogan?

Tongue tries to puzzle this out and learned that Liz has a separate post office box, a separate refrigerator, and a separate bank account. In Gerber's terms, Liz is not fully participating in sharing and cooperative agreements: she has few "attachments" to Mary's household. But two other criteria identified by Gerber appear to be critical here: control of space (her second criterion) and the respondents' expectation/intention that this arrangement would be temporary (her third criterion).

The hogan belongs to Mary. She expects that Liz will build her own dwelling next door and move into it with her children as soon as the building approval comes through. This case certainly illustrates that temporary residence, or "staying," is not just a matter of duration but of expectation and intention concerning future changes. Tongue points out that there is no telling when the building freeze will be lifted and this construction can start—it could be years—but this daughter is not considered a coequal by her mother in terms of residence, as evidenced by Mary not listing Liz as a resident of the household on the mock census form.

Tongue has independently identified all three of the basic principles of Gerber's conceptual system for the Navajo. Without knowing it, Tongue explicitly goes beyond Gerber's original system. She basically posits an additional component to Gerber's conceptual system of residence, namely, emotional closeness, that may supersede kinship per se. A relatively low level of emotional closeness may have been another factor in Mary's decision to exclude her daughter and grandchildren from this mock census form. Tongue sums this up: "Navajos share social and economic capital," she writes. The suggestion is that those who do not share enough may not be considered residents or members.

Craver provides further empirical support for the generalization of Gerber's conceptual system of residence, that is, determining who lives here. As revealed in chapter 4, an important criterion for determining household membership is whether or not the person maintains a physical presence in the household by leaving children or even personal belongings there. Craver describes the household of Sally, the grandmother who cares for Angela's son Daniel, while Angela lives and works in a larger community and returns periodically with her other three children. By leaving Daniel in her mother's house, coming to stay periodically, and providing some financial support, Angela expresses her intentions regarding, commitments to, and agreements with her natal household.

The Iñupiaq household of Dennis also illustrates features of the conceptual system about how to determine residence. Dennis's son, Harry, has an intermittent job—several weeks on and several weeks off—in a distant locale. When Harry is not away at his job site, he alternates between staying with Dennis and visiting his girlfriend. It appears that Harry stays less than half of the time with his father and, as a result, probably should not be counted there for census purposes. Notwithstanding the census, Dennis considers Harry a household member because Harry keeps some of his belongings there, and Dennis expects Harry to continue returning to his household.

Another example emerges from the Korean sample. The elderly woman discussed earlier in this chapter, Mrs. S, included her younger son, Hyunmo, on her mock census form, even though he rented and slept in another apartment, hence, technically should not have been included on her mock census form. Mrs. S also used some features of this conceptual system for determining residence: she took into account where her son spent most of his time during the day, where he ate all of his meals, and where he "belonged," but she discounted where he slept and where he kept his belongings.

Kang also points to other households where nonrelatives clearly coresided in the same housing unit and shared the housework, food, and expenses, yet were not listed as living there or not considered household members. In the Korean conceptual system, it appears that you need to be a relative by blood or marriage in order to be counted as a "true member" of the household. (However, being a true member of the household does not necessarily preclude listing other people on a census form, for the census form asks who lives or stays here, not who is a household member.) Gerber's other criteria did not seem to carry as much weight among the Koreans as among the other groups. In other words, the Koreans' definition of who lived here focused almost exclusively on blood and marriage; for the most part, her other dimensions did not apply.

Concerning the Latino migrants to central Virginia, there are two very interesting cases. In the first, when Lorena filled out her mock census form, she included her husband, herself, and her children but omitted her sister-in-law and brother-in-law, even though this couple had been staying in her house for the last four months, which included Census Day. When Goerman probed, she learned that Lorena omitted this couple from the census form because they were only staying temporarily. Their intention was to save money and establish their own household in their home country in the next month or so, so they were not considered permanent residents and, hence, were not listed on the mock form. This gives us added insight into Gerber's third category: stability (temporariness versus permanence).

In the second Latino example, during the May 2000 interview, Carmen listed two brothers-in-law on her mock census form in addition to her nuclear family members. These men travel back and forth on an annual cycle between their home country and Carmen's house but were living in her household at the time of the interview. Carmen was unsure about whether she should list a third brother-in-law, Pedro, another cyclic migrant who happened to be back in the home country at the time of the interview. Pedro had stayed in her household for most of the last calendar year but left around Christmas to spend the holidays in Mexico. On the May interviewing date, Pedro had not been living in this couple's household since December, but he was expected to come back again from Mexico in the next month or so and often stayed for two years at a time. Carmen was not sure if Pedro should be listed on the form or not. He had clearly been a part of this household in the past, and there was the expectation that he would return soon and stay for two years. Should Pedro be considered a household member in the interim six-month period while he was out of the country? He had spent most of the last calendar year at the house and would probably spend more than half of the current calendar year in that house, but he was not staying there on Census Day and, hence, officially, he should not be included in this household.

This case illustrates Gerber's point that complex living situations may not be easily classifiable according to census rules. Rather, respondents may be using other features in a conceptual system to decide whether a person in an ambiguous living situation is or is not a resident or a household member. In this example, the respondent was categorizing membership not only on the basis of temporariness or permanence and the person's level of attachment, intentions, and agreements, but also on the basis of whether the person was actually present in the household at the time of the interview.

Holmes notes that for all of her black respondents, the definition of household extended beyond the physical housing unit to include expectations and agreements about economic and emotional sharing:

> There is a clear expectation that individuals should contribute both in expressive and instrumental terms. Working together, pooling resources, and sharing responsibilities are central to this definition.

Holmes adds that a third African American respondent summed this up: "It doesn't matter what you contribute, but you must contribute."

All three of Gerber's categories—official living place, control of space and its implications, and stable residence status—are clearly revealed by Reginald, an African American in Holmes' study:

> The term household means a place where you stay, where you keep your belongings, where you have family-related activities, where you rest, relax, . . .

> have income, a place where you invite friends. But most importantly, I think it
> is a place . . . you . . . call your own, you are paying, you are renting, or you
> are buying to own. That is a household.

Sometimes, a living situation is very unstable, and residence status is not easily resolvable. One such situation arises in "merged households" resulting from caregiving. We recall the reaction of Linda, who is realizing that what she had expected to be a short stay at her mother's house for caregiving purposes during her mother's illness is stretching out to be long term, with no clear resolution in the immediate future; it could continue unchanged for a long time or change unexpectedly. Linda does not feel that she belongs either in her own house, where her son now lives, or in her mother's house. Her implicit agreement to stay with her mother to care for her means that she cannot resolve her own residential ambiguity until some exogenous change in her mother's health necessitates some change in their living situations. Thus, the concept of temporary residence may be stretched out to cover months or years, pending some resolution of a destabilizing living situation such as this. This situation falls under Gerber's third category for determining residence: stability (or the lack of it).

This section has shown that the principles of Gerber's conceptual system for determining residence do apply to a much wider range of ethnic respondents than the African Americans, whites, and nonwhite Latinos in her studies. We find the principles in this conceptual system very useful in trying to understand people's responses to the question Who lives here? While it was not our intention to expand Gerber's theory, it turns out that Tongue has identified what we think is a fourth component (emotional closeness) that can be added to Gerber's conceptual system for determining residence. This may or may not supersede kinship when determining where a person lives.

CHANGING HOUSEHOLD COMPOSITION AS A SURVIVAL STRATEGY

In this book, we have attempted to show that many of our ethnic respondents in complex households use shifting household composition as a survival strategy, which often complicates the issue of where these people live and how they should be counted in a census based on the notion that each person has one "correct place" where he or she lives and should be counted. We have identified five main survival strategies. The first survival strategy related to changing household composition is identified in the Navajo and Iñupiaq studies and involves sending household members who are earners out to other areas for often lengthy periods to support the household at home, while considering them household members in perpetuity, regardless of how long they might be living elsewhere. This clearly contradicts the census residence rule that one should be counted where he or she lives "most of the time," over the course of a year or so. The second survival strategy, identified in the Korean and Latino studies, entails housing nonrelative earners to help meet household expenses but not necessarily considering them household members and not necessarily including them on a mock census form because they are not "family." The third strategy in those same groups entails bringing in additional relatives from the home country—such as Latino parents to help with a business or a Korean mother-in-law—to help share expenses, domestic labor, or childcare responsibilities, but perhaps not including them as household members if the relatives continue to cycle back and forth to the home country. The fourth strategy involves adding dependents, such as related and unrelated young children (African American) or the spouse and children of an adult son trying to establish himself elsewhere (white), which may necessitate lifestyle changes for core residents. The fifth survival strategy entails leaving one's own household to reside temporarily at an elderly relative's house (or moving the older person in with you) to respond to a long-term health crisis with no clear answer as to where one now lives and what will happen in the future. These are just a few of the survival strategies identified in this book. Complex living situations like these do not fit neatly into census residence rules designed to determine the "correct" place where one lives or stays and should be listed in the census. Furthermore, complex household forms, as we have seen, are not the sole predictors of how families function (Coontz 2001).

RESEARCH AND POLICY IMPLICATIONS

In this book our contributors have suggested that a variety of complex household structures may emerge as part of survival strategies that people adopt. The forms these complex households take are a result of the interplay of local economic conditions specifically available to and chosen by people of each ethnic group and the kinship system type, preferred residence patterns, and gender systems in what Cherlin refers to as the group's "cultural repertoire." We also have seen that this interaction of factors can and does play out in different household structures in different subpopulations. As a result of our findings, we suggest that our expanded conceptual system for determining residence, building on Gerber's work, may be generalizable to an even wider range of ethnic and alternative lifestyle groups, and we call for more research in this area.

As America continues to become increasingly diverse racially and ethnically, as well as in terms of emerging patterns such as gay cohabitation and marriage, the "Ozzie and Harriet" household, even extended lineally to include elderly parents and grandchildren (which serves as the implicit template for the relationship categories used on census forms), becomes less descriptive of alternative lifestyles in the general population. As we saw in the section titled The "Big Picture," demographers have documented dramatic changes in our household structure and economy for the country as a whole since the 1950s. There is reason to think more changes are in store as minority, ethnic subpopulations increase faster than non-Hispanic whites and (if current projections hold) become the majority in the United States in the 2050s.

Given the current trends in this country—such as increasing racial and ethnic diversity, partly as a result of increasing immigration, increasing cohabitation of both heterosexual and homosexual couples, the cultural upheaval over gay marriage and the proposal to amend the constitution to prohibit gay marriages, economic restructuring with a continuing loss of manufacturing jobs, and the globalization of job outsourcing—we predict that household structure in the United States will continue to change and diversify, at perhaps even faster rates. As two distinguished sociologists, S. Coltrane and R. Collins (2000, 586), put it,

> In the face of increasing inequality between rich and poor, more ethnic diversity in the population, and expanding choices for those with sufficient resources, we expect to witness even more diversity in family forms and practices. Families of various structures and types have sustained people throughout human history and will continue to do so in the future.

We think there may be important implications for the collection in censuses and surveys of data about relationships and for the construction of household-type distributions. Asking respondents about relationships solely to Person 1 on the census form can and does mask other relationships in some households, with the primary example being cohabiting households that include the children of one of the partners, such as a woman and child with her unmarried partner. The type of this household depends on who is listed as Person 1. If the woman is listed first, this is classified as a female-householder family household, but if he is listed first, the very same household is categorized as a male-householder nonfamily household, even if they are functioning as a family (Chan, chapter 1; Schwede 2004a, 2004b). Inconsistent recording of household type, such as this, as a result of weaknesses in the method of asking the relationship question may be skewing data used by researchers, policy makers, and others (see also Brandon 2003; Coontz 2001).

According to Census 2000 data, the number of unmarried partner households has been growing rapidly. Of all households in Census 2000, 5.2% consisted of self-reported unmarried couples (Simmons and O'Connell 2003); these are more prevalent in some ethnic groups. While Asians and whites had the lowest rates of self-reported unmarried couple households compared to the total number of their households (3% and 4.9%), other ethnic subpopulations had higher rates: American Indians and Alaska Natives (9.3%), Native Hawaiians and Other Pacific Islanders (7.5%), Latinos (7.5%), and African Americans (6.4%).[17]

There were also unique patterns for children across these racial and ethnic groups. Of all children in households in Census 2000, 5.7% lived in households that included an unmarried partner of the householder. While Asian and non-Hispanic white children had the lowest rates of living in self-identified unmarried couple households (4.7% and 2.3%), children in the other groups had higher rates: American Indian and Alaska Native (10.9%), Latinos (8.3%), and African Americans (7.6%).[18]

There is also evidence (Lugaila and Overturf 2004, 7, 8) that complex, laterally extended households including nieces, nephews, and other more distant kin are more prevalent among some race and ethnic groups. For example, African American children account for 15% of all U.S. children, but they account for 29% of young relatives of the householder other than sons, daughters, and grandchildren. Similarly, Latino children account for 17% of all children but for 38% of relatives other than sons, daughters, and grandchildren in households. Lugaila and Overturf (2004) have concluded from this and other data that Latinos may more often live in extended families. Such studies are consistent with the Counting Couples Workshop (U.S. Census Bureau 2001, 9, 10) recommendations to "identify the specific relationship of children to adults in the household" and "include special populations," like ethnic/racial minorities.

These data from Census 2000 indicate that at least some types of complex households—those comprised of unmarried couples or laterally extended kin—are more prevalent among African Americans, Latinos, American Indians, Alaska Natives, and Native Hawaiians and Other Pacific Islanders than among non-Hispanic whites and Asians overall. As noted, previous studies have shown that complex households, as well as ethnic minorities, seem to be at higher risk for census miscounts.

Another issue with policy implications is the persistent differential undercount of ethnic minorities in past censuses. For decades, measuring and overcoming differential counts of racial and ethnic subpopulations has been the major focus of Census Bureau research, and it will continue to be in the future. The disproportionately greater growth rates of minority subpopulations vis-à-vis non-Hispanic whites, which are projected to result in the shrinking of the non-Hispanic white population to less than 50% of our country's population sometime in the 2050s, mean that differential undercounts may affect an increasing number of people in the future. This could happen unless we can better identify, understand, and mitigate factors that contribute to undercounts. We hope our study of complex ethnic households and the factors associated with their formation, maintenance, and dissolution, as well as the expansion we have made to Gerber's conceptual system for residence determinations, will contribute to future efforts to improve the accuracy of the census.

In the 2004 Population Association of America Annual Meeting session, "New Strategies in Demographic Measurement," organized by Census Bureau Director Louis Kincannon, an important paper relevant to this discussion was presented. Dr. John Long, then-chief of the Census Bureau's Population Division, identified "changes in residence patterns and mobility" as one of four emerging demographic trends in our country. The other emerging factors Long mentioned are changes in racial and ethnic heritage, increases in international migration, and an increasing rate of change in social and demographic factors. In his presentation, "New Approaches to Measuring Emergent U.S. Demographic Trends," Long discussed the tension between continuity and change in our censuses and surveys. On the one hand, we want to keep questions and concepts the same, providing benchmarks and enabling us to make valid comparisons with past censuses and surveys. But we also want to be able to identify and accurately reflect emerging changes in the population, which may require revisions to questions and concepts. The danger is that changes to the questions, concepts, or both of these might themselves change the data, leading to a break with the past in terms of comparability.

In this book, we have extensively documented changes in residence patterns and mobility by focusing on household structure and linking these changes to other emerging trends identified by Long—race/ethnicity, international migration, and an increasing rate of change in social and demographic factors. We have also linked these with economic conditions, kinship systems, and gender systems.

As documented earlier in this chapter, census relationship categories have expanded in the last three decades to reflect emerging diversity in our country's population and in household structures and relationships concomitant with other demographic trends that may be increasing in pace. We hope that the results of the complex households research in this volume will stimulate new research and suggest possible revisions to questions and concepts so that we can better answer the question Who lives here? in complex ethnic households in America.

NOTES

1. Calculated from SF-2, PCT 5 by sex and age for Navajos alone or in combination on the Navajo reservation and for the total U.S. population.

2. There are striking parallels between the Navajos and the Minangkabau of two upland villages in West Sumatra, Indonesia (Schwede 1991). Despite having a very different economic adaptation from herding—a combination of wet and dry rice agriculture—the Minangkabau, like the Navajo, are also matrilineal and have a preference for living in matrilocal household clusters or, more so in the past, large, matrilocally extended households. A combination of insufficient economic infrastructure (particularly jobs) in the local area and population pressure were two potent factors contributing to both temporary and more long-term out-migration, primarily of men in the past, but increasingly including women. Out-migrants had a strong obligation to send money back both to their own village households and to the community as a whole to build a new mosque or water system. These factors contributed to village demographic profiles in Indonesian censuses of 1980 and 1991 showing a preponderance of old and young people and more women than men. There was evidence that the decision to leave the area for work was not solely the migrant's individual decision but often a component of a larger family survival strategy to support families staying in the village and to preserve their unique matrilineal social organization. Thus, the lack of a sufficient number and range of jobs in the local area seems to be a critical factor affecting household structures across a wide range of subsistence adaptations.

3. Tom's wife clearly agreed that her husband was a household member and listed him on her mock census form as living or staying at their residence as of April 1, 2000, even though he'd been away for more than half of the year and likely was not there on Census Day. Situations such as this cause a problem for census enumeration based on residence in one housing unit. According to census residence rules concerning "usual residence," he should not have been included in the reservation household if he was gone most of the time; yet, he is clearly a core member of this household. Excluding the primary breadwinner would have seriously skewed the economic portrait of this household had it been administered the census long form that collects household income data.

4. Calculated from SF-2, PCT 5 by sex and age for Eskimos in five Alaska Native Region Corporation areas and for the total U.S. population.

5. Calculated from SF-2, PCT 5 by sex and age for Koreans alone and in combination in Queens and Latinos in central Virginia and for the total U.S. population.

6. Craver describes a very similar Iñupiaq household in which adult sons are living in a dwelling next to the parents' house. The sons spend most of their time with the family, eat all of their meals there, and are considered household members. In the census, however, these young men would be considered a separate household since they "live" in a separate housing unit.

7. In Census 2000, there were no stand-alone response categories in the relationship question for nieces, nephews, cousins, and brothers- or sisters-in-law; to record these specific relationships, respondents had to check off the miscellaneous "other relative" category and go to the effort of writing in the relationship on the blank line. While some respondents would go to this effort to document exact relationships of more distant relatives, others

would not choose to do so, and this would result in masking some unknown number of households with nieces, nephews, aunts, uncles, cousins, brothers- and sisters-in-law.

8. This case demonstrates a problem with the relationship categories used on the census form. In this particular case, the relationship categories were not mutually exclusive; Denise could designate the boys either as adopted children or as grandnephews. Her choice of "adopted child" to indicate their relationship to her masked the kinship tie of these two children; we might have assumed that these boys, like many adopted children, were nonrelatives. Of the eight African American children listed as adopted children in Holmes' study, all but one were also related by blood.

9. The results in the text are for the white population overall. Rossi and Rossi found marked differences in the strengths of obligations to near and distant kin among whites based on ancestry: Portuguese and Irish respondents had significantly stronger scores on obligations to distant kin compared to those of British and other Western European descent. This finding highlights the importance of ancestry, which is rarely discussed by demographers. There can be notable differences within the white population that are masked when whites are treated as a homogeneous group. Those authors note that Asians had higher obligations to more distant lateral relatives than most whites.

10. Hewner's special interest as an anthropologist/gerontologist/nurse was on caregiving for the elderly. She selected some caregiving households for inclusion in her study, as they are of special interest to her. As a result, the number of complex households in her study formed for caregiving purposes is likely to be higher than the incidence of these types of households in the general white population of the country at the time of this writing. However, as the baby boom generation moves inexorably into retirement age in the next few years, there is likely to be a major increase in caregiving households, especially merged households. This will have enormous policy implications.

11. L. Bumpass, K. Raley, and J. Sweet (1995) argue for broadening the definition of stepfamilies to include cohabiting unions with a child of just one partner, as well as those formed after nonmarital childbearing or marital disruption. According to them, one-quarter of unmarried mothers were living with the child's father at the time of birth in the late 1980s. Cohabitation is becoming a more accepted living situation (Seltzer 2000).

12. The complexity of defining household versus family is part of the reason why this is one of the oldest debates in the social sciences. Anthropologists, sociologists, and historians have been debating and proposing solutions to this household-family debate for the better part of a century. A small sampling of this literature includes S. J. Yanagisako (1979); R. Netting, R. Wilk, and E. Arnould (1984); J. Jacquette (1993); E. Gerber (1994a) on how respondents define "household"; and R. Wilk and S. Miller (1997).

13. It might be argued that the availability of the "other relative" write-in line overcomes the limitations of the official relationship categories. Any categories not specifically printed on the census form, such as nephew/niece, uncle/aunt, cousin, brother-/sister-in-law, can be written in by the respondent. Likewise, unusual variations specific to certain subpopulations—such as the Navajo distinction of *nali* and *tsui*—can be written in. However, there are two drawbacks to this. First, the numbers of relatives, such as cousin, obtained by tallying the number of times these categories are physically written in by respondents should not be interpreted as reliable or valid indicators of the numbers of such

relatives in the population. The reason is that the use of this write-in line is optional, as stated in note 7 above; not all people completing a form will be willing to go to the extra effort of writing in these relationships, so the counts are almost sure to be lower than the actual incidence of these relationships in the population. Adding nephew/niece, uncle/aunt, cousin, and brother-in-law/sister-in-law as stated, stand-alone categories to the relationship question would require less effort on the part of respondents and would likely produce more reliable and valid data on these distant relatives. Second, coding and classifying a very wide range of written-in relationship categories, some in foreign languages, is quite time-consuming and expensive. There has been discussion in the Census Bureau as to whether the value of obtaining the range of exact relationships in the write-in line outweighs the costs of processing and analyzing write-ins. Alternative versions of relationship questions with and without the "other relative" write-in line are being tested in the 2005 National Content Survey to identify possible effects of removing the write-in line on quality of data and item nonresponse. The removal of the write-in line would mean that these categories— nephew/niece, uncle/aunt, brother-in-law/sister-in-law, and cousin—which seem more common in some of the ethnic subpopulations in this study, would all be lumped into one "other relative" category in the datasets and that they could not then be disaggregated.

14. The number of self-reported unmarried partner households is likely to be an under-count of all unmarried partner households for, as Childs tells us, some cohabiting people do not mark the "unmarried partner" category. Also, only one cohabiting couple can be counted per household; any additional unmarried couples are masked because relationships are reckoned to Person 1 only. One Latino household had two coresident unmarried couples, just one of which was identified in the census relationship question.

15. One of the reasons for the decrease in "married couple with children" households from 44% in 1960 (Lugaila 1992) to 24.4% in 2000 (Fields and Casper 2001, using Current Population Survey data) is the huge growth in the number of one-person households, from 13.3% in 1960 to 25.8% in 2000 (Hobbs and Stoops 2002, using census data). This rapid growth of one-person households was made possible in part by increases in longevity, enabling people to live long beyond their child-rearing ages, coupled with the widespread availability of Social Security payments in retirement, enabling increasing numbers of people to live alone. We have adduced evidence in this book to show that "married couple with children" households are also declining or changing as a result of other trends, such as higher rates of divorce, increases in remarriages, blended families, and cohabiting unmarried partners with and without children, as well as increasing immigration, changing migration streams, and disproportionate growth rates of minority populations vis-à-vis non-Hispanic whites.

16. The Living Situation Survey (LSS) was a one-time 1993 exploratory survey to identify unusual living situations that may have coverage implications for censuses and surveys. The Research Triangle Institute conducted this survey for the Census Bureau in 999 households nationwide, oversampling minorities and renters. Gerber and Schwede developed the questionnaire and included questions to explore the factors respondents use to determine usual residence and household membership. Using LSS data, L. Schwede and Y. Ellis (1994) analyzed consistency between household respondents and others in the household as to the household membership status of household residents. They used log-linear analysis to deter-

mine which of 12 types of household attachments were associated with being considered household members.

17. Calculated using U.S. Census Bureau American FactFinder data in table PCT 22 in Summary File 2, using "by Hispanic origin" (for Latinos) and non-Hispanic origin and one race alone (for the race groups)—to avoid duplication. May 2, 2004.

18. Calculated from table 6 data in Lugaila and Overturf (2004) for those reporting just one race.

REFERENCES

Blumberg, R. L. 1991. "Introduction: the 'triple overlap' of gender stratification, economy, and the family." In *Gender, family, and economy: the triple overlap*, ed. R. L. Blumberg, 7–32. Newbury Park, CA: Sage Publications.

Blumberg, R. L., and P. L. Goerman. 2000. "Family complexity among Latino immigrants in Virginia: an ethnographic study of their households aimed at improving census categories." Complex households and relationships in the decennial census and in ethnographic studies, final report. Available from the Statistical Research Division, U.S. Census Bureau, Washington, DC.

Brandon, P. 2003. "Using 'relationship matrices' for more accurate identification of children's living arrangements and circumstances." Paper prepared for the Measurement Issues in Family Demography Conference in Bethesda, Maryland, November 14.

Bumpass, L., K. Raley, and J. Sweet. 1995. "The changing character of stepfamilies: implications of cohabiting and nonmarital childbearing." *Demography* 32 (3): 425–36.

Bumpass, L., and J. Sweet. 1987. *American families and households, for the National Committee for Research on the 1980 Census.* New York: Russell Sage Foundation.

Burch, E. S. 1975. "Eskimo kinsmen: changing family relationships in northwest Alaska." American Ethnological Monograph 59. Seattle. University of Washington Press.

Carrasco, L., and M. Musquiz. 2003. "Using focus groups to improve Spanish census forms." Unpublished Census Bureau report, presented at the meetings of the American Association of Applied Linguistics, Arlington, VA, March 2003.

Casper, L., and S. Bianchi. 2002. *Continuity and change in the American family.* Thousand Oaks, CA: Sage Publications.

Cherlin, A. 1992. *Marriage, divorce and remarriage.* 2nd ed. Cambridge, MA: Harvard University Press.

———. 1996. *Public and private families: an introduction.* New York: McGraw-Hill.

Coltrane, S., and R. Collins. 2000. *Sociology of marriage and the family: gender, love and property.* 5th ed. Belmont, CA: Wadsworth Thomson Learning.

Coontz, S. 1992. "'Leave It to Beaver' and 'Ozzie and Harriet': American families in the 1950s." In *The way we never were: American families and the nostalgia trap*, 23–41. New York: Basic Books.

———. 2001. "Not much sense in those census stories." *Washington Post*, July 15.

———. 2005. *Marriage: a history from obedience to intimacy, or how love conquered marriage.* New York: Penguin Group.

Farley, R., and W. Allen. 1987. *The color line and the quality of life in America. The population of the United States in the 1980s. A census monograph series for the National Committee for Research on the 1980 Census.* New York: Russell Sage Foundation.

Fields, J., and L. M. Casper. 2001. "America's families and living arrangements." Current population reports P20-537, issued June 2001. U.S. Census Bureau, Washington, DC.

Gerber, E. 1990. "Calculating residence: a cognitive approach to household membership judgments among low-income blacks." Unpublished Census Bureau report.

————. 1994a. "The language of residence: respondent understandings and census rules." Unpublished final report of the Cognitive Study of Living Situations. Available from the Center for Survey Methods Research, Statistical Research Division, U.S. Census Bureau, Washington, DC.

————. 1994b. "Respondents' understanding of residence terminology in cognitive research and in the Living Situation Survey." Bureau of the Census 1994 Annual Research Conference, March 20–23, 434–49.

Hewner, S. 2000. "Household complexity among white rural elders: impact of demographic change in rural America." Executive summary: ethnographic research on complex households in western New York State: impact of migration and economic change on the complexity of household composition among rural Caucasians. Complex Households and Relationships in the Decennial Census and in Ethnographic Studies Project report. U.S. Census Bureau, Washington, DC.

Hobbs, F., and N. Stoops. 2002. "Demographic trends in the 20th century." Census 2000 special reports CENSR-4, issued November 2002.

Holmes, B., and C. Amissah. 2002. "The experiences of African American households: a kinship study." Unpublished final report to the Census Bureau for the Complex Households and Relationships in the Decennial Census and in Ethnographic Studies Project.

Jacquette, J. 1993. "The family as a development issue." *Women at the center: development issues and practices for the 1990s*, ed. G. Young, V. Samarasinghe, and K. Kusterer, 45–62. West Hartford, CT: Kumarian Press.

Lobo, S. 2003. "American Indian mobility in the San Francisco Bay Area. Comparative ethnographic research on mobile populations. Census 2000 evaluation report supporting document." U.S. Census Bureau, Washington, DC.

Logan, J. 2003. *How race counts for Hispanic Americans.* Albany: Lewis Mumford Center, University of Albany.

Long, J. 2004. "New approaches to measuring emergent U.S. demographic trends." Paper presented at the Population Association of America Annual Meeting, Boston, Massachusetts, April.

Lugaila, T. 1992. "Households, families and children: a 30-year perspective." Current population reports P23-181. Washington, DC: U.S. Government Printing Office.

Lugaila, T., and J. Overturf. 2004. "Children and the households they live in: 2000." Census 2000 special reports CENSR-14, issued February 2004.

Manning, W., and P. Smock. 2003. "Measuring and modeling cohabitation: new perspectives from qualitative data." Paper presented at the Measurement Issues in Family Demography Conference: Counting Couples II, Bethesda, Maryland, November 14. In Proceedings of the Measurement Issues in Family Demography Conference (Counting Couples II), compact disc.

Martin, E. P., and J. M. Martin. 1978. *The black extended family.* Chicago: University of Chicago Press.

Montoya, D. 1992. "Ethnographic evaluation of the behavioral causes of undercount: Woodburn, Oregon." Ethnographic evaluation of the 1990 decennial census report 25. Prepared under a joint statistical agreement with the University of Oregon. Washington, DC: U.S. Census Bureau.

Netting, R. McC., R. Wilk, and E. Arnould. 1984. *Households: comparative and historical studies of the domestic group.* Berkeley: University of California Press.

Rossi, A., and P. Rossi. 1990. *Of human bonding: parent-child relations across the life course.* New York: Aldine de Gruyter.

Schmidley, A. D. 2001. "Profile of the foreign-born population in the United States: 2000." Current population reports, Special Studies P23-206. Washington, DC: U.S. Government Printing Office, issued December 2001.

Schwede, L. 1991. "Family strategies of labor allocation and decision making in a matrilineal, Islamic society: the Minangkabau of West Sumatra, Indonesia." Unpublished PhD diss., Cornell University.

———. 2003. "Complex households and relationships in the decennial census and in ethnographic studies of six race/ethnic groups: final report." Census 2000 Testing and Experimentation Program Ethnographic Study. Available at www.census.gov/srd/www/byname.html (accessed December 24, 2005).

———. 2004a. "Household types and relationships in six race/ethnic groups: conceptual and methodological issues." In *Proceedings of the American Statistical Association Section on Survey Research Methods,* 4991–98. Alexandria, VA: American Statistical Association.

———. 2004b. "Households and families in six race/ethnic groups: issues for surveys identified in qualitative studies." Population Association of America Annual Meeting poster, April 2.

Schwede, L., and Y. Ellis. 1994. "Exploring associations between subjective and objective assessments of household membership." In *Proceedings of the American Statistical Association Section on Survey Research Methods,* 325–30. Alexandria, VA: American Statistical Association.

Seltzer, J. 2000. "Families formed outside of marriage." *Journal of Marriage and the Family* 62: 1247–68.

Simmons, T., and M. O'Connell. 2003. "Married couple and unmarried partner households: 2000." Census 2000 special reports CENSR-5. Washington, DC: U.S. Census Bureau.

Stack, C. 1974. *All our kin: strategies for survival in a black community.* New York: Harper & Row.

Stone, L. S. 2004. "Contemporary directions in kinship." In *Kinship and family: an anthropological reader,* ed. R. Parkin and L. Stone. Williston, VT: Blackwell Publishing.

Wallerstein, I., and J. Smith. 1991. "Households as an institution of the world-economy." In *Gender, family, and economy: the triple overlap,* ed. R. L. Blumberg, 225–44. Newbury Park: Sage Publications.

Wilk, R., and S. Miller. 1997. "Some methodological issues in counting communities and households." *Human Organization* 56 (1): 64–69.

Wilson, W. 1987. *The truly disadvantaged: the inner city, the underclass, and public policy.* Chicago: University of Chicago Press.

Witherspoon, G. 1983. "Navajo social organization." In *Handbook of North American Indians: Southwest,* ed. W. C. Sturtevant and A. Ortiz, Vol. 10. Washington, DC: Smithsonian Institution, 524–35.

U.S. Census Bureau. 2002. "Counting couples: improving marriage, divorce, remarriage, and cohabitation data in the federal statistical system: highlights from a national workshop." The Counting Couples Workshop, sponsored by the Data Collection Committee of the Federal Interagency Forum on Child and Family Statistics in Washington, DC. National Institutes of Health in Bethesda, Maryland, December 13–14, 2001. Suitland, MD: U.S. Census Bureau.

———. 2003. "2003 statistical abstract of the United States, table 40: selected characteristics of the white and black populations: 2000." Available at www.census.gov/prod/2004 pubs/03statab/pop.pdf (accessed March 2004).

Yanagisako, S. J. 1979. "Family and household: the analysis of domestic groups." *Annual Review of Anthropology* 8: 161–205.

About the Contributors

Rae Lesser Blumberg is the William R. Kenan Jr. Professor of Sociology at the University of Virginia in Charlottesville, Virginia, and professor emerita of sociology at the University of California, San Diego. Her work revolves around her general theory of gender stratification and a still-evolving theory of gender and Third World economic development. She has gathered data for her theories in almost all of the 40 countries (on every continent except Antarctica) where she has worked in development under the auspices of the World Bank, USAID, United Nations agencies, and international nongovernmental organizations. She received her degrees from Northwestern University and has authored over 90 publications.

Anna Y. Chan received her Ph.D. in human development and family studies from Cornell University, in Ithaca, New York, in 1997. She is currently a research social scientist in the Statistical Research Division at the U.S. Census Bureau. Chan is a subject-matter expert on research and development of methods for collecting basic demographic information and repairing nonsampling errors in Census Bureau surveys and censuses. She has published book chapters and journal articles on interracial minority families and survey measurement design issues. Her current research includes the development of roster procedures in government demographic surveys, coverage issues, and complex households in ethnic minority populations.

Jennifer Hunter Childs is a social science researcher with the U.S. Census Bureau's Center for Survey Methods Research/Statistical Research Division. She has an M.S. in psychology from the University of Maryland, College Park. As Jennifer Hunter, she contributed to decennial census efforts by evaluating the relationship categories and distinctions between group quarters and housing units relating to seniors' housing and group homes for developmentally disabled and mentally ill individuals. She has been involved in cognitive and field research on cohabitation and has written an article entitled "Measuring Cohabitation" in *Polling America: An Encyclopedia of Public Opinion* (2005).

Amy Craver works as an anthropologist for the Fish and Wildlife Service, Office of Subsistence, Fisheries Information Service. She is also affiliated with University of Alaska, Anchorage, as a research associate and adjunct instructor. Craver's research is based on folklore and cultural anthropology with an emphasis on community-based research, oral history, and household rural economies. Craver earned a B.A. in humanities from Evergreen State College in Olympia, Washington, and an M.A. in folklore from Indiana University's Folklore Institute in Bloomington. Currently, she is completing her Ph.D. dissertation on extended kinship networks in northern Alaska.

Patricia L. Goerman received her Ph.D. in sociology from the University of Virginia in 2004. Her dissertation is a study of Latino immigrants settling in nontraditional southeastern states. Through her work on projects with the Census Bureau and her dissertation research, she has conducted in-depth interviews with large numbers of Hispanic immigrants in central Virginia. She holds an M.A. in sociology from the University of Virginia and a B.A. in Spanish, English, and Latin American and Iberian Studies from the University of Wisconsin, Madison. She is currently working as a postdoctoral research fellow at the Census Bureau.

Bernadette J. Holmes is a professor of sociology and criminal justice at Norfolk State University in Norfolk, Virginia. She earned her Ph.D. in sociology from Ohio State University in Columbus. Her areas of specialization are gender, criminology, and community development. Her research has focused on black families and on the determinants of satisfaction and subjective well-being. She teaches courses on black families, violence against women, and the criminal justice system. She is the recipient of a Fulbright/Hayes Fellowship to Morocco, the Hampton University Linback Distinguished Teaching Award, and the Dean's Award for Excellence for her contributions to the School of Liberal Arts and Education at Hampton University.

Tai S. Kang received his Ph.D. in sociology from the University of Minnesota and teaches at the University of Buffalo, State University of New York. His research interests include social psychology, social gerontology, medical sociology, and quantitative methods. Representative publications include "Mental Health Status of Asian American Elderly" in *The Encyclopedia of Cross-Cultural Anthropology* (1994); "A Multivariate Comparison of Elderly African

American and Caucasians' Voting Behaviors," in *International Journal of Aging and Human Development* (1991); "Adjustment Patterns of the Korean American Elderly: Ideal Type," in *Journal of Minority Aging* (1983); and "Linking Forms of Hypothesis to Types of Statistics," in *American Sociological Review.* He also edited *Nationalism and the Crisis of Ethnic Minorities in Asia* (1979).

Laurel Schwede is a research social scientist in the U.S. Census Bureau Center for Survey Methods Research/Statistical Research Division. She first explored households and families in her 1991 Cornell University Ph.D. dissertation in anthropology, "Family Strategies of Labor Allocation and Decision Making in a Matrilineal, Islamic Society: The Minangkabau of West Sumatra, Indonesia." She proposed and comanaged the Complex Households Projects. She also designed and conducted research to improve census coverage of the homeless, minorities, and juvenile facilities and to improve census questions on relationships, race, and ethnicity. She has coauthored, with Hanna Papanek, "Women are Good with Money: Earning and Managing in an Indonesian City," in *A Home Divided: Women and Income in the Third World*, edited by D. Dwyer and J. Bruce (1988). She works on Census 2010 interdivisional residence rule and coverage and group quarters teams.

Nancy E. Tongue has worked as an applied anthropologist in the American Southwest, Pacific Northwest, New York City, and Chile. Affiliations include Johns Hopkins University, New School University, the National Park Service, and the Smithsonian. Her work examines the role that cultural traditions play in health care and family dynamics. She has conducted extensive fieldwork in Arizona with the Navajo, where she has concomitantly incorporated her ethnographic films into community educational programs. She currently "lives" in New York City, where she works as a consultant, but she episodically "stays" in Arizona. Nancy is also an abstract sculptor, photographer, and outdoor adventurer.